W9-BHF-443

Administrative Law
PRINCIPLES AND ADVOCACY

JOHN SWAIGEN

2005
Emond Montgomery Publications Limited
Toronto, Canada

Emond Montgomery Publications Limited
60 Shaftesbury Avenue
Toronto ON M4T 1A3
http://www.emp.ca/college

Printed in Canada.

Edited, designed, and typeset by WordsWorth Communications, Toronto.
Cover design by John Vegter, CBC Art Department.

We acknowledge the financial support of the Government of Canada through the Book Publishing Industry Development Program (BPIDP) for our publishing activities.

The events and characters depicted in this book are fictitious. Any similarity to actual persons, living or dead, is purely accidental.

Library and Archives Canada Cataloguing in Publication

Swaigen, John, 1944-
    Administrative law : principles and advocacy / John Swaigen.

Includes bibliographical references and index.
ISBN 978-1-55239-073-3

    1. Administrative law—Canada—Textbooks.   I. Title.

KE5015.S93 2004   342.71'06   C2004-907216-1
KF5402.S93 2004

To Arel, Julia and Sarah Lynn

Contents

PART I PRINCIPLES AND THEORY

CHAPTER 1
Introduction to the Legal System

CHAPTER 2
Administrative Agencies and Tribunals

CHAPTER 3
The Foundations of Administrative Law

CHAPTER 4
Fairness: The Right To Be Heard

CHAPTER 5
Fairness: Bias

PART II ADVOCACY

CHAPTER 6
Advocacy Before Administrative Agencies and Tribunals

CHAPTER 7
Tribunal Procedures Before Hearings

CHAPTER 8
Tribunal Procedures During Hearings

CHAPTER 9
Presenting Evidence at a Hearing

CHAPTER 10
Management and Control of the Hearing Process

CHAPTER 11
Conduct Outside the Hearing

CHAPTER 12
Tribunal Decision-Making Procedures

APPENDIXES

Preface

In 1951, when Robert Reid, later Justice Reid of Ontario's Divisional Court, was asked to teach administrative law at Osgoode Hall Law School, he discovered that there were no Canadian textbooks on the subject to assist him. Administrative law did not even exist as a heading in Canadian legal encyclopedias. In his foreword to a text on Canadian administrative tribunals, Justice Reid tells how he tried with limited success to scrounge advice and notes that would help him put together a course on administrative law.

Today, over 50 years later, there are numerous texts on administrative law. There are practical guides for lawyers, for tribunal members, and even for expert witnesses. There are scholarly treatises. There are texts on specific issues such as bias and delegated legislation. But, to my knowledge, there is still not one text designed specifically for students in institutions of higher learning (other than law faculties). University and college teachers generally use texts written for other purposes, supplemented by photocopies of materials they have collected. There is very little that addresses both theory and practice and that does so in plain language.

This book attempts to fill this gap. It is designed primarily for students who are studying to be paralegals, community legal workers, or law clerks, and for students who will work for government departments, regulatory agencies, or tribunals. It describes the underlying principles of administrative law and the variety of applications of those principles in a way that facilitates learning. It also contains practical advice on dealing effectively with departments, agencies, or tribunals.

The book deals with both theory and practice. It addresses issues ranging from the very concrete and specific—for example, how to conduct research or lead evidence—to more abstract questions of ethics and courtesy. It makes suggestions about how to carry out these responsibilities fairly, effectively, and efficiently. It also explains the responsibilities of representatives to their clients and to the agencies and tribunals they are trying to persuade on their clients' behalf, as well as the obligations of these agencies.

No two government agencies are alike, and the fact that each agency has been designed to meet a particular need makes it a challenge to determine in any specific case how the principles of administrative law apply to it. Tribunals, for example, come in all shapes and sizes. They range from those that resolve relatively simple issues to others that deal with complex issues involving specialized knowledge. Some tribunals have only one party before them. Others hear numerous parties and intervenors. Tribunals can have procedures that are relaxed and informal, or procedures that are similar to those of a court. Tribunals may make recommendations to a minister, or they may make binding decisions. The decisions made by some tribunals can be appealed to a court, or to another tribunal, or to a government official, or there may be no right of appeal at all.

Similarly, other government departments and agencies also carry out a wide variety of functions and have many different structures. That's why it is important to learn how each agency operates before attempting to persuade its staff of the righteousness of a client's cause—whether this means persuading a social service agency that the client is eligible for financial assistance, attempting to obtain a building permit, showing eligibility for transportation services for the elderly or disabled, or getting faster service from a slow bureaucracy.

Given this variety in tribunals and tribunal procedures, a "one size fits all" approach to describing and prescribing appropriate behaviour for advocates and government agents will fit no one perfectly. I hope, however, that the book's double approach to the practice and theory of administrative law will fit well enough.

I would like to thank Bernie Aron, Judith Goldstein, David Lampert, and Gary Yee for their assistance. Gary, an experienced tribunal chair and counsel, provided an outline and notes for a community college course he taught in administrative law as well as papers he has written, which were very useful to me in developing this book. Judith, Bernie, and David, who collectively have a wealth of experience working with tribunals and regulatory agencies and teaching administrative law, provided helpful advice and comments on drafts of this book.

I would also like to thank the superb editors at Emond Montgomery and WordsWorth Communications. Peggy Buchan developed the project, Christine Purden copy-edited the manuscript, Jim Lyons coordinated production, and Paula Pike indexed the final work. I am very grateful for their efforts.

Finally, I would be pleased to receive suggestions for improvement from both students and teachers. Comments can be sent to my attention at info@emp.ca.

PART I

Principles and Theory

CHAPTER 1

Introduction to the Legal System

LEARNING OBJECTIVES

After reading this chapter, you will understand

- what is meant by the term "law";
- why we need laws, as well as other, less formal rules, to govern our conduct;
- what kinds of behaviour are regulated by laws;
- how laws are made;
- who has the authority to make laws;
- what distinguishes various categories of laws; and
- how different kinds of laws are administered and enforced.

This introduction is mainly for readers who have had limited exposure to law or political science.

The law is the last result of human wisdom acting upon human experience for the benefit of the public.

Samuel Johnson

WHAT IS A LAW?

There are various ways of defining the concept of a **law**. For the purposes of this book, a law is described as a rule made by a body of elected representatives or their delegates or by a court, using procedures that are also prescribed by law. All the steps set out in the procedural rules must be followed. For example, in the case of laws made by Canada's federal Parliament, a provincial legislature, or the council of one of the territories, the proposed law must be

- read three times in the open assembly,
- debated,
- passed at the second and third reading by a majority of the elected representatives present, and
- assented to by the Queen's representative (the governor general for federal laws and the lieutenant governor for provincial laws).

If any of those steps are missed, the law will not be valid.

WHY DO WE NEED LAWS?

People often think of laws as rules that prohibit them from doing something and punish them if they break the rule. Although that is the nature and effect of many laws, laws do not just impose duties; they also create rights. In addition, laws create a framework to ensure that the many complex activities of contemporary society are carried out in an honest, fair, efficient, and effective manner. Laws are, in effect, a blueprint or a set of "rules of the road" for carrying on business, protecting consumers, regulating the use and development of land, conferring government benefits, protecting human dignity and preventing discrimination, and distributing and redistributing wealth. Imagine driving a car in a crowded city if there were no rules requiring motor vehicle safety, driver training, when to stop and go, when to make turns, how fast to go, and which side of the road to drive on. Imagine the chaos if half the drivers chose to drive on the right-hand side of the road and the other half decided to drive on the left!

HOW DO LAWS DIFFER FROM OTHER RULES?

In a democratic society, people have considerable freedom to do what they want in any way they want. However, certain behaviour is restricted either by formal laws imposed by governments and the courts, or by other kinds of rules that are followed by most people but are less strictly enforced. These other rules may be imposed through social pressure or by mutual agreement (social norms), or may be accepted as a condition of belonging to some group or organization, such as a school, business, church, or club. Compliance with these rules is, in a sense, a matter of choice for the individual, although breaking a rule may lead to penalties, such as loss of membership in a group. In contrast, compliance with laws is required.

While governments and the courts can restrain the activities of ordinary people, they can do so only by passing, enforcing, or applying a law. As discussed above, in order to be valid as a law, any rule made by a government in the form of a law must be passed by a majority of the elected representatives, using the prescribed procedures. Similarly, any restraints imposed by tribunals or courts must be authorized by laws passed by governments or made by judges.

Law will never be strong or respected unless it has the sentiment of the people behind it.

James Bryce, *The American Commonwealth*, vol. 2 (1888)

Governments and courts must also follow laws that set out the procedures for applying or enforcing laws, and they must limit their activities to those that are **delegated** to them by a valid law. In other words, governments, tribunals, and courts are not entitled to do whatever they want, but only what validly made laws authorize them to do. This limit on the right of governments, tribunals, and courts to control the conduct of citizens is known as the **rule of law**.

According to the rule of law, all law making is governed by a supreme law called the **constitution**. The constitution establishes the basic institutions of government, reflects some of the fundamental values of society, and determines the values or goals that all other laws must reflect. In this way, the constitution governs the validity of all other laws. This relationship between the constitution and the creation of other laws is discussed in more detail below.

The purpose of the rule of law is to prevent arbitrariness and, at worst, tyranny. By restricting the powers of government, and by setting out strict rules for the passing, application, and enforcement of laws, the democratic system deters those who are granted these powers from acting impulsively or capriciously, making up the rules as they go along. It also deters individuals or groups from assuming or exercising powers that they do not legitimately possess.

Using the rule of law as a method of curbing the powers of government prevents many abuses. To avoid arbitrariness, the rule of law requires that like situations be treated alike and different situations be appropriately distinguished from each other. In addition, new rules are subjected to a predetermined process of scrutiny by elected representatives. They are not imposed in a dictatorial fashion with no accountability.

A Hollywood take on the meaning and importance of law:

Let me tell you what justice is. Justice is the law. And the law is man's feeble attempt to lay down the principles of decency. And decency isn't a deal, it's not a contract or a hustle or an angle! Decency—decency is what your grandmother taught you. It's in your bones.

Morgan Freeman as Judge Leonard White in *The Bonfire of the Vanities*

THE CANADIAN CONSTITUTION AND ITS LIMITS ON LAW MAKING

The constitution of Canada is the supreme law of the land. All other laws must conform to it. The constitution consists of a combination of principles of democracy inherited from Britain as traditions and a statute passed by the Parliament of Canada called the *Constitution Act*. A court can declare any law that conflicts with the constitution to be invalid, or the effect of such a law may be restricted by a court or, in some circumstances, by a tribunal. An invalid law is called "unconstitutional." No one is required to follow an unconstitutional law.

There are two parts of the constitution that determine the validity of laws passed by the federal and provincial governments and of municipal bylaws. The first is the division of powers. The second is the *Canadian Charter of Rights and Freedoms*.

Division of Powers

The constitution allocates law-making powers between the federal government and the provinces according to subject matter.[1] If one level of government passes a law that regulates a subject granted to the other level by the constitution, the law is

---

1 The division of powers is found primarily in the *Constitution Act, 1867*, 30 & 31 Vict., c. 3 (formerly known as the *British North America Act*). Some clarification of the division of powers is also found in the *Constitution Act, 1982*, RSC 1985, app. II, no. 44.

considered invalid. For example, if a provincial government passes a criminal law, an area of jurisdiction that the constitution grants exclusively to the federal government, that law cannot be enforced.

The Charter

The second part of the constitution to which laws must conform is the *Canadian Charter of Rights and Freedoms*.[2] The Charter sets out a list of fundamental freedoms, democratic or political rights, legal rights, mobility rights, and equality rights belonging to persons. Any law or government action that infringes these rights to a greater extent than can be justified in a free and democratic society is either invalid or has no effect to the extent that it infringes these rights. That is, the rights set out in the Charter are not absolute.

The Charter allows a court (and in some cases, tribunals) to balance the civil liberties of individuals and corporations against the collective rights of the public as a whole. If the constitutional rights of a person are infringed by a law or by the way the law is implemented, the government is required to demonstrate that the infringement is important for the benefit of the community and that the intrusion is no greater than is necessary to achieve this social benefit.

If the government can justify the extent to which the law infringes a right or freedom guaranteed by the Charter, the courts will consider the law to be valid. If the government cannot justify the infringement, the law will not be binding on the person whose right or freedom it infringes.

WHO MAKES THE LAWS?

Our system of government has three basic branches—legislative, executive, and judicial. In general, the legislative branch (such as the federal Parliament or provincial legislatures) makes laws; the executive branch (such as government departments or police forces) enforces laws; and the judicial branch (the courts) interprets laws.

Our system also has three levels of government—federal, provincial (or territorial), and municipal. As discussed above, and in more detail below, the division of powers between the federal and provincial governments is set out in the constitution. For example, criminal law is under federal jurisdiction, and employment law is under the jurisdiction of each of the provinces. Some subject areas, such as family law, are shared. The provinces also have the power to delegate authority over local issues to municipal governments. For example, municipalities generally have the authority to pass and enforce bylaws governing land development and public transit.

As indicated in the chart below, the federal and provincial governments have all three branches of government, and the municipal governments have only legislative and executive branches. The territories have judicial branches, but their judges are appointed by the federal government, not the territorial governments.

---

2   The *Canadian Charter of Rights and Freedoms* is contained in part I of the *Constitution Act, 1982*, supra note 1. Before 1982, the civil liberties of Canadians were not part of the constitution. There were some federal and provincial statutes, such as the federal *Canadian Bill of Rights*, Quebec's *Charter of Human Rights and Freedoms* (RSQ, c. C-12), and the human rights codes of other provinces, that guaranteed civil liberties, but they did not have constitutional status; that is, they did not override conflicting statutes.

Level of government	Branch of government		
	Legislative	*Executive*	*Judicial*
Federal	✓	✓	✓
Provincial	✓	✓	✓
Territorial (Nunavut, Yukon, and the Northwest Territories)	✓	✓	✓ (Judges are appointed by the federal government.)
Municipal	✓	✓	

Each of these levels and branches of government must stay within the authority granted to it by the constitution or by another statute. This concept of "separation of powers" follows from the principle of the rule of law. It is intended to be a safeguard against any of the three levels or branches becoming too powerful and abusing its authority. A challenge of administrative law is to ensure that this safeguard continues to operate while society benefits from the flexibility and efficiencies that can result from delegating powers. The authority, structure, and levels of government are described more fully below.

The Three Branches of Government

LAW-MAKING POWERS OF THE LEGISLATIVE BRANCH

The legislative branch consists of individuals elected by citizens (the general public) to represent them in the federal Parliament, the provincial legislatures, councils of the territories, and municipal councils. It is called the legislative branch because under Canada's constitution, its members have a monopoly on the power to **legislate** (pass laws). More specifically, these elected representatives as a group pass statutes (or **acts**) or, at the municipal level, bylaws. The federal and provincial legislatures can also make other kinds of laws called **regulations**, or they can pass a statute in which this authority is delegated to a body that is part of the executive branch. Regulations are detailed rules that "flesh out" the meaning and requirements of a statute. They are discussed in more detail below, under the heading "Statute Law."

Delegation of Law-Making Powers to Ministries, Agencies, Boards, and Commissions

A body of elected representatives such as a provincial Legislative Assembly will occasionally pass a law that delegates the power to make binding rules or regulations to an agency created by that assembly. Only in these circumstances does an unelected agency have the authority to make binding rules. Sometimes the rules are procedural; in other cases, they are more substantive. (See "Delegation of Legislative Functions.")

Delegation of Law-Making Powers to Territories

The three northern territories are a hybrid. Like municipalities, they have no powers of their own, but only those delegated to them by statute. However, in practice,

Delegation of Legislative Functions

- **Substantive rules** Ontario's *Conservation Authorities Act* establishes conservation authorities to protect watersheds from flooding and erosion, and permits them to make binding regulations that govern development of land along riverbanks. Other commissions established by the Ontario government have the right to amalgamate municipalities or close hospitals.

- **Procedural rules** Ontario's *Statutory Powers Procedure Act*, which sets out various procedural requirements to be met by administrative tribunals, also permits tribunals to make their own rules for the conduct of certain aspects of their proceedings, such as postponement of a hearing, preliminary motions, and pre-hearing conferences.

each territory has almost the same law-making powers as a province. The federal government has passed statutes giving each of the three territories powers to pass **ordinances**, which are similar in content to provincial and federal statutes.

LAW-MAKING POWERS OF THE EXECUTIVE BRANCH

The second branch of government is the executive, which consists of the federal or provincial Cabinet, or the executive committees of municipal councils, and their staff—the many civil servants who report to the ministers of Cabinet and to the municipal councils and their committees. This branch administers and enforces the laws that the legislative branch passes. However, in the case of the federal and provincial governments, the Cabinet, and sometimes individual Cabinet ministers, also make the regulations that implement the statutes. This is actually a legislative function, but it has been delegated by the legislators to the executive. (For this reason, regulations are sometimes called "delegated legislation.")

These cabinets and committees of municipal councils consist of a group of elected representatives chosen by the other elected representatives. In theory, this system preserves the accountability of the people who carry out the laws as well as the people who make them. However, these elected groups are just the tip of the iceberg. They preside over an extensive network of hired civil servants, as well as members of agencies, boards, and commissions (ABCs, collectively known as **agencies**) appointed by the executive, who are not directly accountable to the electorate. In the federal and provincial governments, each Cabinet minister is responsible for the work of a **department** (called a **ministry** in some provinces). A department consists of hundreds or thousands of civil servants who carry out the laws and administer government programs. In many cases, the minister will also be responsible for several agencies established by the government.

LAW-MAKING POWERS OF THE JUDICIAL BRANCH

The third branch of government is the judiciary. The judiciary consists of the courts and judges who decide disputes between citizens (individuals or organizations) and between the government and citizens as to the interpretation or application of the law. They decide whether someone has broken the law, and, if so, what punishment will be imposed, what compensation must be paid, or what other action the violator must take.

Judges are appointed by the executive branch of the federal or provincial government. Once appointed, they are independent and have the right to decide disputes, including disputes between the government and citizens, without fear of losing their job, having their salary reduced, or being subject to any other form of government interference or pressure. The judiciary therefore provides an important protection for the citizen against violations of the law either by the government or by other citizens. The duties of the judiciary include interpreting laws and striking down laws that are passed without proper authority. Moreover, since the passage of the *Canadian Charter of Rights and Freedoms*, the courts can strike down any law that violates fundamental rights and freedoms set out in the Charter.

Judges also have a legislative function within certain areas of law. The body of law that is made by judges is called "common law." It is discussed later in this chapter under the heading "Types of Law."

The Three Levels of Government

As discussed earlier, in Canada we have three levels of government—the federal government, the provincial governments (and territorial councils), and municipal governments. Each is presided over by an assembly of elected representatives, which exercises the government's law-making powers.

The federal and provincial governments are permanently established under our constitution. Municipal and territorial governments have no constitutional status or permanence. The existence of municipalities depends upon the will of the provincial government, and their powers are limited to those specifically granted by provincial statute. For this reason, municipalities are often referred to as "creatures of the province." Similarly, territorial councils owe their existence and their law-making powers entirely to the federal government.

Laws that apply throughout the whole country are passed by the federal **Parliament**, which consists of the House of Commons, whose members are elected, and the Senate, whose members are appointed by the government of the day. These laws are called federal laws.

Provincial laws apply throughout a province. They are passed by the provincial **legislature** or **Legislative Assembly**[3] (in Quebec, known as the "National Assembly").

Municipal bylaws apply only within the boundaries of a municipality. They are passed by the municipal council, consisting of elected councillors (sometimes called "aldermen"). Similarly, territorial ordinances are passed by the elected councils of the territories and apply only within the territory.

Each level of government has the constitutional or statutory authority to pass laws in certain subject areas. In some areas, there may be overlap or duplication between the law-making powers of these levels of government. Where there is such overlap, if a higher level of government has the authority to pass a law and has done so, any conflicting laws or bylaws passed by a lower level of government cannot be enforced.

---

3 Provincial legislatures are also known as "provincial parliaments." To avoid confusion, this book will use the term "Parliament" to refer only to the federal legislature.

FEDERAL LAW-MAKING POWERS

The federal government has authority under s. 91 of the constitution to make laws in a variety of fields that were considered at the time of Confederation (1867) to require uniform standards throughout the entire country. Generally, federal laws deal with matters of national concern, such as criminal activity, monetary policy, foreign relations, interprovincial and international trade and commerce, and interprovincial and international transportation.

PROVINCIAL LAW-MAKING POWERS

The provincial government may make laws under s. 92 of the constitution governing matters that were considered in 1867 to be primarily regional or local in nature. These include the regulation of business activities that take place within the province; the regulation of professions; the creation of local infrastructure such as roads, water treatment plants, and sewer systems; the creation of the structure of municipal government; the establishment of municipal boundaries; and land use planning.

MUNICIPAL LAW-MAKING POWERS

Municipal councils may make bylaws governing conduct within the municipal boundaries, such as licensing local businesses, zoning, policing, and operating schools and libraries. However, as discussed earlier, the powers of municipal governments are limited to those specifically granted by laws passed by the provincial legislature.

OVERLAPPING OR UNCLEAR LAW-MAKING AUTHORITY

For many areas of conduct, the constitution is silent or ambiguous with respect to the level of government that has authority to pass laws. In some cases, the particular subject area did not exist in 1867; examples are atomic energy, aeronautics, telecommunications, and the Internet. In other cases, matters that were primarily of local or regional interest in 1867 have since taken on national dimensions.

Confusion often arises because a law has aspects that fall within both federal and provincial powers. For example, the provinces have authority to regulate labour relations, but the federal government regulates telecommunications. Therefore, if a law regulates union activities at a telephone company, it will be unclear which level of government has the authority to pass the law. A court will have to decide whether the dominant purpose of the law is the regulation of labour relations or the regulation of telecommunications.

TYPES OF LAW

Laws can be divided into categories in several ways. These categories overlap, so that an individual law may fall into more than one of the categories. A body of law, such as administrative law, may be a combination of laws in two or more categories.

It is important to understand how categories of laws are distinguished from each other. Some of the categories to be distinguished are

- common law and statute law;
- public law and private law;
- statutes and subordinate legislation; and
- substantive law and procedural law.

The distinctions between these categories are briefly explained below.

Common Law and Statute Law

In Canada, we have laws developed by the courts as well as laws passed by governments. The laws made by courts are called "common law." "Statute law" is the body of law (**legislation**) made by elected representatives, consisting of statutes, regulations, territorial ordinances, and municipal bylaws.

A harmful activity may become the subject of both common law and statute law. Under common law, a person who is harmed by a particular activity (a **tort**, or wrong) is given the right to sue the wrongdoer for compensation (**damages**) or for an order to stop carrying on the activity (an injunction). Under a statute, the government may designate the same activity as an "offence" and impose a punishment for it. (See "Interaction of Common Law and Statute Law.")

Interaction of Common Law and Statute Law

A car driver carelessly injures a pedestrian, who sues for compensation under the common law tort of negligence. If the court upholds the claim, the driver will be required to compensate the victim for the harm she has suffered. However, careless driving is also an offence under the provincial highway traffic statutes, and the police may lay a charge against the driver. If the driver is found guilty, he may be required to pay a fine or may be sentenced to prison or have his driver's licence or vehicle permit suspended.

The differences between common law and statute law are described in more detail below.

COMMON LAW

Common law is the body of rules established by judges over the centuries in the course of making decisions in disputes between citizens and between citizens and their government. The common law embodies certain rights and principles on which the courts base their decisions. Among the most important of these are principles of fairness or reasonableness.

There is a hierarchy of courts, and cases that are heard by a lower court may sometimes be appealed to one or more higher courts. Once a court has established the principles that should apply to a particular type of situation, in all future cases similar to the one in which the principle was established, all other courts that are lower in the judicial hierarchy must apply that principle in deciding the case. This is called the requirement to follow **precedent**. (In Latin, it is known as the doctrine of *stare decisis*.) It is this requirement to follow precedent that gives the principles the force of law.

Other courts will usually apply the principle previously established by a court at the same level in the judicial hierarchy. However, two courts at the same level may reach conflicting decisions about what is the proper principle to apply to a particular situation. Where such conflict arises, a higher court, ultimately the Supreme Court of Canada, will settle the matter.

> The judges developing the common law proceed from case to case,
> like the ancient Mediterranean mariners, hugging the coast from point
> to point and avoiding the danger of the open sea of system or science.
>
> Lord Wright, "The Study of Law" (1938) vol. 54 *Law Quarterly Review* 185, at 186

An example of a common law principle and how it developed following the doctrine of *stare decisis* is the doctrine of "negligence." Until 1932, the courts had ruled that a person injured by the use of a product could not sue the manufacturer unless he or she had purchased the product directly from the manufacturer. In other words, the manufacturer could be sued under the common law principles governing contracts (explained below) if there was a breach of the contractual obligation to provide a safe product, but not otherwise.

In 1932, however, in the case of *Donoghue v. Stevenson*,[4] Britain's highest court established a new principle: if it is foreseeable that a person's actions might cause someone harm, the person carrying on the activity has a duty to take reasonable steps to prevent the harm whether or not there is a contract between the parties. This means, among other things, that if a manufacturer makes a defective product, it can be held responsible for injuring anyone who might foreseeably use the product, whether the person purchased the product from the manufacturer, bought it from a store that purchased it from the manufacturer, found it on the street, or was given it as a gift. Because of the requirement that all lower courts follow precedent, this principle of legal liability has been adopted by the courts in jurisdictions, such as Canada and the United States, that inherited the common law system from Britain, and it forms the basis for the common law doctrine of negligence.

If Canada's highest court, the Supreme Court of Canada, declares that a right exists or a principle applies, all courts must follow this rule unless and until the Supreme Court modifies or changes its ruling—something that occurs infrequently. These principles are gathered together and published in legal texts, and important decisions of the courts are published and also made available on computer databases. By referring to these sources, lawyers and others undertaking legal research or legal action can keep abreast of how the courts are applying these principles in their interpretation of the law.

STATUTE LAW

From time to time, the government enacts **statutes** that incorporate or supersede many of these common law rights and obligations.

Common law principles may be incorporated into statutes either in the form in which they were developed by the courts or with changes that reflect current needs. When the common law rules are included in statutes with little or no change, the process is referred to as **codification**. Examples are Ontario's *Statutory Powers Procedure Act*[5] (SPPA), Alberta's *Administrative Procedures Act*[6] (APA), and

---

4 *Donoghue v. Stevenson*, [1932] AC 562; 101 LJPC 119; 147 LT 281.

5 RSO 1990, c. S.22.

6 RSA 2000, c. A-3.

Quebec's *Administrative Justice Act*[7] (AJA), which set out basic rules of procedural fairness for tribunals that formerly were part of the common law.

On other occasions, a statute is passed to replace a common law doctrine that the legislature considers to have outlived its usefulness. (For example, at common law, jilted lovers could sue their fiancé(e) for breaking a promise to marry them—a tort that has now been abolished by statute in some provinces.)

A statute may be passed to make it an offence to do something that is considered wrong and requires compensation at common law, so that a person who commits the offence will also be subject to punishment such as a fine or jail. A statute may also be passed to establish a new procedure or set up a bureaucracy to enforce certain common law rights, so that people are not required to use the more cumbersome procedures of the courts to address infringement of those rights. Sometimes the purpose of affirming common law rights in a statute is to clarify ambiguities or remove contradictions created when courts are inconsistent in interpreting or applying a principle.

As discussed earlier, **statute law** consists of statutes, regulations, and bylaws. Both the federal and the provincial governments have the authority to pass statutes. These laws usually do not set out all the rules that the public must obey. Instead, they set out a framework for creating the more detailed rules contained in accompanying regulations. Usually, the statute permits the Cabinet of the governing party (referred to in statutes by its formal name—provincially, the lieutenant governor in council, and federally, the governor in council) to make regulations, but occasionally a statute delegates the power to make regulations to an individual Cabinet minister or a regulatory agency or board. There is no constitutional requirement that regulations be scrutinized by the federal or provincial legislature, although in practice there are often parliamentary committees that review some aspects of these rules before they take effect.

To be valid, the contents of regulations must be explicitly or implicitly authorized by the wording of the statute under which they are made. If regulations set out requirements that go beyond the matters that the statute permits them to address, the regulations are not valid.

As stated earlier, statute law also includes **bylaws**, which are passed by elected municipal councils. These bylaws are often voluminous and very detailed, because municipal councils do not have the power either to make regulations or to delegate such power to committees or boards. As a result, compliance requirements must be included in the bylaw itself. Bylaws are valid only if the provincial statutes granting municipalities the power to pass laws state that the municipality may pass bylaws of that nature.

Public Law and Private Law

PUBLIC LAW

Different authors have suggested different definitions of **public law**. In general, public law deals with the structure and operation of government. It regulates how the three branches at each level of government carry out their responsibilities.

---

7 RSQ, c. J-3.

Public laws govern the relationship between an individual or private organization and the government, the relationship between one government and another (for example, between the government of Canada and the government of Ontario or of India), and relationships between departments and agencies of the same government. Criminal law, constitutional law, administrative law, and treaties made under international law are all considered part of the public law.

Public laws dictate how government bodies may raise money (for example, by imposing taxes or levying fees or fines), how they may spend money (for example, building roads or airports, operating schools, providing medicare, giving subsidies to businesses, or hiring police), and what procedures they must follow to account for money spent (financial administration). (See "How Public Laws Regulate Provincial Elections.")

How Public Laws Regulate Provincial Elections

In Ontario, for example, the provincial *Representation Act* determines the size and boundaries of electoral districts, which in turn dictate how many seats there will be in the Legislative Assembly. The *Elections Act* authorizes the lieutenant governor to decide the length of the election campaign. The *Election Finances Act* determines how much money candidates may spend on their campaigns and what activities they may spend money on; it also requires disclosure to the public of amounts raised and the identity of donors. The *Public Service Act* sets out rules governing which public servants are permitted to engage in partisan campaigning and what limits are imposed on their activities. Under the *Broadcasting Act*, radio and television stations and networks must make advertising time available to all political parties on an equitable basis during elections. If the political parties cannot agree on how to divide the time among them, a broadcasting arbitrator appointed under the *Canada Elections Act* may allocate the amount of air time for each party.

Administrative Law

As indicated above, public law regulates the structure and activities of all three branches of government—legislative, executive, and judiciary. **Administrative law** is a branch of public law that regulates the executive branch.

Until the 20th century, the executive branch at the federal and provincial levels consisted largely of a set of departments headed by ministers and staffed by civil servants. However, as government became involved in a broader range of activities requiring more expertise, flexibility, and independent advice, a variety of **administrative agencies** developed to supplement, or in some cases replace, the role of the departments in meeting these needs. Administrative law developed as a way of ensuring that these departments and agencies do not exceed their authority, abuse their power, or follow unfair procedures when making decisions.

Procedural fairness is a fundamental principle of administrative law. The two pillars of procedural fairness are

1. the duty to give persons notice of decisions that may affect them and an opportunity to be heard before such decisions are put into effect, and

2. the duty to provide an impartial decision maker.

Other principles of administrative law include the requirement that agencies act only within their jurisdiction (the powers granted to them by statute), rules governing how agencies exercise their discretion, and the rule against subdelegation of decision-making powers. These terms and rules are explained in more depth in later chapters.

PRIVATE LAW

Private law is the body of laws that regulate how individuals or corporations are required to treat each other. Private law includes torts, contract law, property law, and family law.

Both private and public laws can be statutory or can consist of common law rights and remedies. Moreover, a single law may have both public and private aspects or components. For example, Ontario's *Trespass to Property Act*[8] (TPA) prohibits trespassing on both public and private property. Although financial compensation for harm is usually a matter of private law and fines are normally imposed only under public law, the TPA permits a court that convicts someone of trespassing both to impose a fine and to award compensation.

Statutes and Subordinate Legislation

As discussed earlier, although only elected legislatures can pass statutes, these statutes may grant the Cabinet, individual Cabinet ministers, and special interest bodies the authority to make more detailed regulations that flesh out the meaning and requirements of the statute. These regulations are sometimes called **subordinate legislation** or **delegated legislation**. They are valid only if they conform to the statute under which they are passed.

Substantive Law and Procedural Law

Laws may also be characterized as substantive or procedural. **Substantive law** is concerned with the substance of a problem or the legal issue that the law is designed to solve or address. **Procedural law** sets out procedures for implementing substantive law; a simple example is the combination of substantive and procedural provisions of the *Criminal Code*[9] dealing with theft.

The *substantive* provisions of the Code make it an offence to take someone else's property without the owner's consent. Its *procedural* provisions specify how the police and courts will treat someone once he or she is believed to have committed theft. These procedures deal with the steps taken by the police (such as fingerprinting) in arresting someone and laying charges; the procedures that the courts will follow before trial, such as granting bail and holding preliminary inquiries; the procedures during the trial, such as reading the charge, entering a plea, and calling evidence; and the procedure for deciding what sentence to impose if the person is convicted of the crime.

---

8 RSO 1990, c. T.21.

9 RSC 1985, c. C-46, as amended.

The difference between substantive law and procedural law is important be-cause the characterization of a law as substantive or procedural affects whether it can apply to conduct that took place before the law was passed (that is, "retroac-tively") and how far authorities can stray from following the strict letter of the law and still have their actions upheld by the court. Generally, officials have more flexibility and leeway in applying procedural laws than in applying substantive laws. Also, procedural laws may apply retroactively, but substantive laws do not.

HOW VARIOUS TYPES OF LAW ARE ADMINISTERED AND ENFORCED

Enforcement by Government Agencies

Different laws are administered and enforced in different ways.

Violations of criminal laws, for example, are usually investigated by federal, provincial, or municipal police forces. Charges for such violations are laid by the police and prosecuted by federal and provincial Crown prosecutors in the criminal courts.

Breaches of federal and provincial regulatory statutes are sometimes investi-gated by inspectors in government departments and sometimes by police. Charges for violating municipal bylaws are sometimes laid by police and sometimes by bylaw enforcement officers employed by the municipality. The prosecutors are usually lawyers or prosecution officers hired by the government department or agency responsible for administering the law in question.

Enforcement by the Person Affected

As discussed above, common law rights and remedies are considered private law rather than public law. That is, although the government or the courts have estab-lished the rights and obligations governing certain private relationships, and the gov-ernment provides the court system in which the rights may be enforced, the government does not consider that there is a sufficient public interest in the outcome of such disputes to justify the government's also providing a staff of investigators, inspectors, and prosecutors. The person aggrieved must pursue a remedy at his or her own expense, usually hiring a lawyer to advise and represent him or her in court.

Some statutory rights also must be pursued privately by the person entitled to redress. For example, certain remedies available to consumers under consumer protection statutes must be pursued by the consumer against the seller. The gov-ernment does not enforce these rights.

Many laws do not create duties whose breach leads to punishment or payment of compensation. Some laws create a set of procedures that must be followed or standards that must be met in undertaking certain activities. For example, where a developer requires the approval of government authorities before proceeding with a project, the developer generally must submit an application, plans, and other specified information to the government agency, which then assesses the proposal against legislated standards and decides whether or not to grant approval.

Other laws confer privileges or benefits (such as social assistance or compensa-tion for injuries suffered in the workplace or losses to the victim of a crime) on classes of people who qualify for these benefits. In some cases, the government hires staff or provides resources or funding to assist the person in making a case for receiving the benefits. In other cases, the person must apply for the benefits on his or her own, or with the assistance of an advisor hired at the person's own expense.

In most provinces, for example, the government has staff who represent employees who are challenging decisions to deny workers' compensation benefits. A few provinces also provide this assistance to small employers. Individuals challenging immigration decisions are often represented by lawyers or legal workers employed by independent community legal clinics that receive funding from the government. In contrast, most governments provide no legal assistance to individuals challenging government decisions to refuse access to records under freedom-of-information laws.

In some cases, government officials make the initial decision whether to issue a licence, approve an activity, enforce a right, or confer a benefit under a statute. In other cases, the government creates an arm's-length agency (that is, an agency with some independence or separation from the government) to make the initial decision on how to apply or implement the law. In either case, the person or persons affected may be entitled to appeal the decision to an arm's-length agency, such as a tribunal or a court.

Often, the arm's-length agencies that are established for these purposes are administrative tribunals. Administrative tribunals are an important part of our system of government, and they play a significant role in administering our statute laws.

Tribunals, as well as other government decision makers, are regulated by the branch of public law known as administrative law. Administrative law evolved out of the legal system described above, and the fundamental principles on which it is based are rooted in that broader legal system. The next chapter provides a detailed discussion of these relationships and principles.

CHAPTER SUMMARY

Laws are binding rules made by governments. They regulate almost every aspect of human life, from birth to death; a vast range of social and economic activities; and formal relationships among citizens (both individuals and organizations) and between citizens and government.

There are three levels of government that make laws—the federal, provincial, and municipal or territorial governments. There are also three branches of government that, respectively, pass, apply, and interpret laws—the legislature, the executive, and the judiciary.

Laws take a variety of forms and regulate particular spheres of conduct. They can be categorized in a number of ways—as common law or statute law, as public law or private law, as statutes or subordinate legislation, and as substantive law or procedural law. How a law is administered and enforced, and by whom, depends on the nature of the law and the category into which it falls.

KEY TERMS

act *see* statute

administrative agency *see* agency

administrative law law that governs the organization, duties, and quasi-judicial and judicial powers of the executive branch of government, including both central departments and agencies; a branch of public law

agency   any body such as a board, commission, or tribunal established by government and subject to government control to carry out a specialized function that is not an integral part of a government ministry or department

bylaw   law enacted by a subordinate legislative body, such as a municipality, under the authority of a statute

codification   the collection of the principles of a system or subject of law into a single statute or set of statutes

common law   a body of law set out in court decisions; derives its authority from the recognition given by the courts to principles, standards, customs, and rules of conduct (generally reflecting those accepted in society) in deciding disputes; distinguished from statute law

constitution   the body of binding fundamental rules that govern the exercise of power by government; to be valid, all other laws must conform to this set of fundamental rules

damages   a sum of money awarded by a court as compensation for harm or loss caused by a violation of the law

delegate   entrust a person or body to act in another's place

delegated legislation   *see* subordinate legislation

department   a unit of the executive branch of government over which a minister presides; usually established to administer a specific set of laws and programs relating to a particular subject area, such as health, protection of the environment, government finance, or stimulation of business activity

law   a rule made by a body of elected representatives or their delegates or by a court, using procedures that are also prescribed by law

legislate   pass statutes and bylaws, and make regulations

legislation   the creation of law; the statutes, regulations, and bylaws passed by bodies of elected representatives or their delegates

Legislative Assembly   the body of elected representatives constituting the legislative branch of a provincial government; in Quebec, known as the "National Assembly"; also called the "legislature" or "provincial parliament"

legislature   in Canada, the body of elected representatives constituting the legislative branch of the federal or a provincial government; *see also* Legislative Assembly; Parliament

ministry   *see* department

ordinances   laws enacted by the northern territories, similar in content to provincial and federal statutes

Parliament   the body of elected representatives constituting the legislative branch of Canada's federal government; also called the "legislature"

precedent   a decision or judgment of a court of law that is cited as the authority for deciding a similar situation in the same manner, on the same principle, or by analogy; *see also stare decisis*

private law   law that governs the conduct of persons other than government; distinguished from public law

procedural law   law that prescribes methods of administration, application, or enforcement of a law; for example, the provisions of the *Criminal Code* that specify the procedures followed when a person is believed to have committed an offence such as theft; distinguished from substantive law

public law law that deals with the structure and operation of government; governs the relationship between individuals or private organizations and the government, between governments, and between departments and agencies of the same government; includes administrative law; distinguished from private law

regulations detailed rules that flesh out the meaning and requirements of a statute; made under the authority of a statute, either by Cabinet or by a body to which this power is delegated; also called "subordinate legislation" or "delegated legislation"

rule of law the principle that governments, as well as individuals and corporations, must follow the law; in particular, governments may take actions that limit the activities of citizens or their access to rights or benefits only in accordance with substantive and procedural requirements prescribed by law

stare decisis Latin term referring to the principle that courts should decide similar cases in the same way unless there is good reason for them to do otherwise; the rule that courts must follow previous decisions made by higher courts; *see also* precedent

statute law passed by Parliament or a provincial legislature; also called an "act"; often specifically provides for the authority to make regulations or to delegate this power; distinguished from subordinate legislation; *see also* statute law

statute law in Canada, the body of laws passed by Parliament or a provincial legislature; generally, the body of laws passed by an assembly of elected representatives of the public; distinguished from common law

subordinate legislation legislation made by a body other than Parliament or a provincial legislature (such as Cabinet, a Cabinet minister, an agency, or a municipal council), as authorized by statute; generally includes regulations, proclamations, rules, orders, bylaws, or other instruments; also called "delegated legislation"; distinguished from a statute

substantive law law that is concerned with the substance of a problem or the legal issue that the law is designed to address; for example, the provisions of the *Criminal Code* setting out the elements of the offence of theft; distinguished from procedural law

tort a wrongful act or omission causing an injury, other than a breach of contract, for which recovery of damages is permitted by law

REVIEW QUESTIONS

1. What is a "law"? How does a law differ from other rules or customs that people follow?

2. What is the "rule of law" and what is its purpose? To whom does it apply?

3. What are the three branches of government in Canada, and what are the functions of each?

4. What are the three levels of government in Canada? Describe briefly the law-making power of each level of government.

5. What is a "constitution"? How does the constitution of Canada restrict the power of governments to pass or implement laws?

6. Name four different ways in which laws can be categorized? Give an example of a law that falls into each category and explain why that law fits within that particular category.

7. What are the consequences of breaking a law? Are the consequences the same for all categories of law? Explain.

8. Who administers and enforces laws? Is the answer the same for all laws? Explain.

EXERCISES

1. Using any of the research tools described in appendix B, find and briefly describe the contents of
    * two examples of a statute that regulates government elections;
    * two examples of a statute that protects consumers;
    * two examples of a statute that establishes a government agency;
    * two examples of a statute that prohibits certain conduct and imposes penalties for violating the prohibition;
    * two examples of a statute that regulates a trade, profession, or business;
    * two examples of a statute that provides a right of compensation for harm done by individuals or corporations; and
    * two examples of a statute that provides a right of compensation for a loss resulting from government action.

2. Categorize each of the above laws as public or private, or substantive or procedural. If the law fits into both of these categories, list them both. (For example, a statute may be public and substantive, or private and procedural.)

3. Explain why you have chosen the category or categories in each case.

4. Explain briefly some of the rights and obligations imposed by these laws.

5. Explain who administers or enforces each of these laws.

6. Discuss briefly some of the procedures that are followed in enforcing or administering these statutes.

FURTHER READING

Lisa Braverman, *Administrative Tribunals: A Legal Handbook* (Aurora, ON: Canada Law Book, 2001), chapter 1.

Nora Rock and Dayna E. Simon, *Foundations of Criminal and Civil Law in Canada* (Toronto: Emond Montgomery, 2000).

Linda Silver Dranoff, *Everyone's Guide to the Law: A Handbook for Canadians*, revised ed. (Toronto: HarperCollins, 2001).

Philip Sworden, *An Introduction to Canadian Law* (Toronto: Emond Montgomery, 2002).

CHAPTER 2

Administrative Agencies and Tribunals

LEARNING OBJECTIVES

After reading this chapter, you will understand

- where administrative agencies fit into the executive, legislative, and judicial branches of government;
- the kinds of agencies that governments establish and why they establish them;
- how this system of agencies developed and how they have modified the traditional approach to administering and enforcing laws;
- the issues that these agencies raise for government accountability and independence;
- what administrative justice tribunals are and how they compare with other agencies;
- the kinds of decisions that are likely to be referred to tribunals rather than government officials; and
- how tribunals are similar to courts and how they are different.

Since it deals with the exercise of governmental power, administrative law is itself part of constitutional law. Nor is there any other department of constitutional law which displays such an active conflict of forces. We are here on the most lively sector of the front in the constant warfare between government and governed. Whole new empires of executive power have been created. For the citizen it is vital that all power should be used in a way conformable to his ideas of liberty, fair dealing, and good administration.

H.W.R. Wade, *Administrative Law* (Oxford: Oxford University Press, 1961), 3

INTRODUCTION

As discussed in chapter 1, there are three branches of government in Canada: the legislative branch, the executive branch, and the judicial branch. The structure of the legislative and judicial branches of government has remained largely the same over the past century. However, the structure of the executive branch has changed dramatically. A complex network of administrative agencies, boards, and commissions (ABCs; also referred to collectively as agencies) gradually evolved in response to the growing complexity of Canadian society. There are now so many departmental offshoots or freestanding agencies that they have become recognized as a separate "sector" within the executive branch. Some commentators go so far as to call them the "fourth branch" of government.

This chapter discusses how and why agencies are established, how they function, how they affect the traditional division of powers among the three branches of government, and what issues these "hybrid" entities raise for government accountability and independence. The chapter also takes a closer look at administrative tribunals and compares and contrasts their roles and functions with those of courts.

THE TRADITIONAL ROLE AND STRUCTURE OF THE EXECUTIVE BRANCH

In its traditional form, the executive branch of the federal and provincial governments consisted of centralized departments or ministries, each headed by a Cabinet minister who was a member of Parliament or the provincial legislature. This minister was responsible to the legislature both for making policy and for implementing it, including the way in which civil servants in the department (numbering in the hundreds or even thousands) carried out their functions. This system was called "responsible government" because the minister was responsible to the executive branch (the prime minister or premier and his or her Cabinet colleagues), as well as to the Canadian public for the work of the department.

Unlike the minister who headed the department, the civil servants who carried out the work of a department were largely insulated from political pressure by a number of mechanisms. First, they reported not to the minister but to another civil servant, the deputy minister of the department, who was appointed by the prime minister or premier. Second, the rules for hiring and firing civil servants were established and carried out by independent commissions, not politicians. Third, the hiring, remuneration, promotion, and dismissal practices and operation of the civil service were governed by legislation. This system promoted hiring on the basis of ability and expertise rather than political connections, and the security of tenure of civil servants enabled them to "speak truth to power."

The traditional departmental structure thus rested on two cornerstones: accountability of the minister to the public as a member of the legislature, and insulation of the civil service from political influence through an independent system of hiring, remuneration, promotion, and dismissal.

Over the years, though, this relatively simple structure became more complex as governments responded to changes in society and as the corresponding demands on governments grew more diverse. Special-purpose agencies were established outside the traditional structure of the executive branch to carry out civil service functions with greater flexibility, efficiency, and expertise.

THE DEVELOPMENT OF ADMINISTRATIVE AGENCIES

The first administrative agency in Canada was established in 1851, 16 years before Confederation. The Board of Railway Commissioners was set up under the *Rail-*

way Act, primarily to approve rail rates. In 1912, the British Columbia government set up its first administrative agency, the Workmen's Compensation Board. World War I, the Great Depression, and World War II all stimulated the federal and provincial governments to become more involved in regulating the economy and in influencing social and cultural issues. As Canadian society expanded and became more complex, so did the structures that governments created to meet its needs and address its problems.

The simple government structure of a few departments, each reporting to a Cabinet minister, was not flexible enough to respond to these changes in society and to accommodate these expanding and changing roles of government. Instead, governments tried to tailor their responses to the needs of each situation. The result was a proliferation of special-purpose bodies. For example, between 1945 and 1984, the number of agencies more than doubled in Saskatchewan and almost doubled in Ontario, with significant growth in other provinces as well. When Robert Macaulay conducted his review of Ontario's ABCs in 1989,[1] he found that there were about 1,500 across Canada, and 580 in Ontario alone. By 1990, there were at least 120 federal administrative commissions, boards, and councils.

CATEGORIZING AGENCIES, BOARDS, AND COMMISSIONS

Agencies, boards, and commissions perform a wide variety of functions: they give advice, set standards, regulate businesses and professions, coordinate the activities of government departments, and provide goods and services. Ontario's Management Board Secretariat divides the province's agencies into seven categories:[2]

- *Advisory agencies*   These agencies provide advice to a ministry and assist in the development of policy or the delivery of programs, but they do not make decisions or carry out programs. The Livestock Medicines Advisory Committee and the Commodity Futures Advisory Board are two such agencies.

- *Operational service agencies*   These agencies deliver goods or services to the public, often at a low fee or no fee. The Ontario Tourism Marketing Partnership Corporation is an example of such an agency.

- *Operational enterprises*   These agencies sell goods or services to the public in a commercial manner. They may compete with the private sector, or they may be monopolies. Examples are the Niagara Parks Commission, the Liquor Control Board of Ontario, and the Ontario Lottery Corporation.

- *Regulatory agencies*   These agencies make independent decisions (including inspections, investigations, prosecutions, certifications, licensing, and rate setting) that limit or promote the conduct, practice, obligations, rights, and responsibilities of individuals, businesses, and corporate bodies. Examples include the Ontario Film Review Board and the Workplace Safety and Insurance Board.

- *Adjudicative agencies* (often referred to as "tribunals"; discussed in more detail below)   These agencies make independent decisions, similar to

---

1   Robert W. Macaulay, *Directions: Review of Ontario's Regulatory Agencies Report* (Toronto: Queen's Printer for Ontario, 1989).

2   *A Guide to Agencies, Boards and Commissions* (Toronto: Queen's Printer for Ontario, 1995).

those of courts, that resolve disputes over the obligations, rights, and responsibilities of individuals, businesses, corporate bodies, and government decision makers under existing policies and laws. They may also hear appeals from previous government decisions. Two such agencies are the Ontario Labour Relations Board and the Ontario Municipal Board.

- *Crown foundations*   These agencies solicit, manage, and distribute donations of money or other assets to support public organizations such as art galleries, museums, amateur sports associations, theatre groups, and universities. Examples are the Art Gallery of Ontario Crown Foundation and the University of Toronto Foundation.
- *Trust agencies*   These agencies administer funds or other assets for beneficiaries named under a statute. Examples include the Workplace Safety and Insurance Board and the Ontario Public Service Pension Board.

The Ontario government also recognizes a category of agencies called "nonscheduled agencies," which do not fit into any of the categories above. Examples include university and hospital governing boards.

To this list may be added at least two further kinds of agencies. The first is "watchdog" bodies, such as the ombudsman and other ombudsman-like agencies. They are established to monitor whether government departments and agencies are carrying out their duties fairly, effectively, and efficiently and to address individual complaints of unfair treatment. These officials often are appointed by and report to the legislative assembly as a whole, rather than to the government. Their independence from the government may be enhanced by security of tenure and salaries that are the same as those of senior officials such as judges or deputy ministers, rather than negotiated with the government. In most provinces these watchdog agencies include the ombudsman, the provincial auditor, the information and privacy commissioner, and the chief electoral officer. Some provinces also have an integrity commissioner, who investigates whether members of the legislature have conflicts of interest. Ontario and the federal government also have an environment commissioner. The federal government has no ombudsman, but there is an auditor general, a chief electoral officer, an integrity commissioner, a privacy commissioner, an information commissioner, and a commissioner of official languages.

The second kind of agency is royal commissions and other commissions set up to carry out public inquiries. These bodies are usually established by governments to investigate and to make findings and recommendations about a specific problem. Once they have reported their findings they dissolve, and the government that appointed them may or may not implement their recommendations. Usually, prominent judges or academics are appointed to conduct the inquiries, but the government sometimes supplies their staff. Examples include inquiries into the future of medicare, the causes of the outbreak of severe acute respiratory syndrome (SARS) in 2003, the cause of the Westray mine disaster in Nova Scotia, and racism in various provincial justice systems.

In his 1989 review of Ontario's ABCs, Robert Macaulay divided ABCs into eight categories:[3]

---

3 Ibid.

- agencies that investigate and advise, and that may hold hearings in doing so;
- agencies that deal with appeals from decisions of government or other regulators;
- agencies that resolve problems between individuals or between individuals and the government;
- agencies that monitor and regulate substantial segments of the economy;
- agencies that deal with land use planning, assessment, and values;
- agencies that deal with employment, wages, pensions, and social assistance;
- agencies that set standards and quotas, including marketing boards; and
- agencies that deal primarily in natural resources, preservation, and conservation.

It is important to understand that some of these agencies carry out more than one function. An agency may have any combination of advisory, regulatory, investigative, policy-making, adjudicative, and other functions. It may have to follow one set of rules when carrying out one function and another set when carrying out another. Sometimes, the functions of an agency overlap in such a way that the official responsible for carrying out the different functions cannot do so without a conflict of interest or appearance of bias. In these cases, the conflict of functions or interests is resolved using principles of administrative law (discussed in more detail below).

WHY GOVERNMENTS CREATE ADMINISTRATIVE AGENCIES

There are numerous reasons why a government may choose to set up an administrative agency rather than delegate a task to a department:

- *To demonstrate independence*   The government may want to ensure that decisions on certain issues are not seen to be "political." An agency that is independent, and that is perceived to be independent, can demonstrate that its function and decisions are free of political influence.

- *To reduce the size, workload, or budget of a department*   The government may establish an outside agency to carry out some of the functions of a department in order to save space, achieve more efficiency in the delivery of services, or reduce costs.

- *To reduce conflicts of interest*   Where one government department carries out two or more functions that may come into conflict, the conflict may be resolved by "hiving off" some of the department's functions to independent bodies. For example, until the 1990s, the Ontario Ministry of the Environment was responsible for regulating municipal water treatment and sewage treatment plants, but it also designed, built, owned, or operated many of these plants. Therefore, if one of these water or sewage treatment plants violated environmental laws, the ministry might be reluctant to impose stringent operating conditions on its own facilities or prosecute its own staff. To prevent this conflict, the government created a separate agency, the Ontario Clean Water Agency, in 1993.

- *To provide flexibility in human resources*   The government may want to avoid some of the hiring practices, employment standards, salary and benefits rules, tenure requirements, and reporting requirements that must be followed when employing civil servants. For example, in Ontario, the Civil Service Commission regulates salaries, job classifications, recruitment, benefits, and hours of work for civil servants. Ministries are required to follow these rules when hiring, promoting, setting wage levels, or firing. However, the government is not bound by these rules when appointing members of many agencies, boards, and commissions. It can pay less, appoint members who have no prior experience or qualifications for the job, and limit the length of the appointments or the opportunities for reappointment.

- *To provide expertise and specialization*   The government may want to obtain expertise in a particular subject matter that is not readily available within the civil service. The use of outside bodies to bring expertise to a problem is common in the setting of technical standards, the provision of advice, and the regulation of specialized businesses, trades, and professions.

- *To ensure representativeness*   The government may want to involve members of the general public or particular interest groups in making some decisions.

- *To avoid permanence*   The government may want the flexibility to create a body to deal with a current problem or issue, and then disband it or restructure it as needs change.

- *To reduce labour costs*   Appointment to an agency is usually considered an honour; as a result, highly skilled and dedicated people are often willing to work for fees much lower than they can command in the marketplace. Moreover, many agencies are composed wholly or largely of part-time members. Talented individuals who might not be willing or able to work full-time for low wages are often willing to give a few days or weeks a year at reduced levels of compensation.

- *To signal a new or different approach*   The government may create an outside agency where existing agencies have been found wanting in their approach to a problem, or where a new approach to an existing problem is desired. Similarly, the government may create a new agency to regulate an activity or matter that was previously unregulated. Examples of areas that were once unregulated are human rights, the environment, and rent review. More recent examples include access to government information, the protection of privacy, and genetic engineering.

- *To achieve coordination or uniformity*   Where similar or related functions are carried out by several departments or ministries, the government may create a new agency to carry out those functions, or it may set up an advisory agency to help coordinate the activities of all the departments. The result may be a more consistent approach, greater effectiveness or efficiency, or a pooling of resources. The Canadian Food Inspection Agency is an example of a coordinating agency. It was created in 1997 to bring together food-inspection activities previously carried out by four federal government departments—Agriculture Canada, Fisheries and Oceans Canada, Health Canada, and Industry Canada.

ADMINISTRATIVE AGENCIES, ACCOUNTABILITY, AND ADMINISTRATIVE LAW

As discussed above, the traditional departmental structure of the executive branch balanced accountability and independence and maintained the separation of powers between the branches of government. However, the development of ABCs challenged the traditional methods of balancing accountability and independence in the civil service and potentially undermined the separation of powers.

The heads and members of ABCs were appointed by ministers, not by the legislative assembly. Also, they were often not civil servants and therefore were not subject to the same methods of accountability or mechanisms to avoid political pressure. They were not accountable to the legislature the way ministers were, nor were they protected from political pressure by civil service staffing rules. They often lacked the expertise and permanence that contributed to the independence of the civil service.

The development of ABCs also threatened to undermine the separation of powers between the different branches of government. Some of these agencies not only carried out the traditional functions of the executive branch—implementing laws and developing administrative policies and practices—but also performed legislative and judicial functions. This led to a blurring of roles that potentially undermined the separation of powers that prevents abuse of authority.

Thus, the need for an appropriate balance between accountability and independence required the development of a body of "administrative law" to regulate how government in general, but more particularly the executive branch, carries out its functions.

MULTIPURPOSE AGENCIES

Many administrative agencies are multipurpose bodies; that is, they have several functions. Administrative law often requires multipurpose agencies to separate their functions and follow different rules when carrying them out, in order to ensure fairness.

For example, the Law Society of each province is authorized by statute to regulate the practice of law in the province. The statutes require all lawyers to be members of the Law Society and to comply with the standards it sets. The laws regulating the legal profession require law societies to

- provide professional education;
- set standards for professional conduct;
- randomly audit the records of lawyers to determine whether they are following the rules, even without a complaint of misconduct;
- investigate complaints of misconduct or incompetence; and
- determine whether these complaints are valid, and take appropriate disciplinary action or action to improve competence.

In cases of alleged professional misconduct by a lawyer, the Law Society is investigator, prosecutor, and adjudicator. If an audit or investigation turns up evidence of a lawyer's misconduct, lawyers on the staff of the Law Society will prepare a case against the alleged offender and they will present this case before a panel of members of the governing body. The panel will then decide whether the charges of misconduct are justified and, if they are, what discipline to impose.

Each of these functions may require different procedures to ensure that they are carried out in a manner that is fair to members. For example, the setting of standards for the conduct of lawyers is a "legislative" function, and there is no requirement to give all Law Society members notice of the process, or to allow members to make submissions regarding the process. There may or may not be a requirement to show members all the information and studies that the governing body relied on in formulating the standards.

Similarly, if a member is being investigated for misconduct or incompetence, there may be no requirement to notify the member of the investigation, or to give the member an opportunity to review the evidence or tell his or her side of the story. The reason for this is that investigation can result only in a recommendation whether to take further action; it cannot result in a binding decision that will prevent the lawyer from practising law.

However, if the prosecuting staff decide to launch a disciplinary proceeding, they must give the member notice of the charges and the opportunity to see and answer the evidence on which the decision was based.

The Key Requirement: Separation of Functions

A key concern when an agency has multiple functions is to structure the agency to avoid unfairness in carrying out the functions. The reason for this is that it is often inappropriate for the same person to carry out two or more functions that may be incompatible.

Particularly when an agency is investigator and prosecutor as well as adjudicator, it is important to keep these functions separate from each other. This may be achieved by ensuring that the investigators, prosecutors, and adjudicators are different people and by isolating the activities of investigators, prosecutors, and decision makers to prevent each of them from unduly influencing the others or usurping the functions of the others. Failure to ensure separation may invalidate the process.

In many cases, a multifunction agency is structured to create a "tribunal" that is separate from the investigators and prosecutors in the agency. The functions of tribunals are explained in more detail below.

A key principle is, "No man shall be a judge in his own cause." This means that the prosecutor and the decision maker may not be the same person, because a person who is responsible for proving a case against someone cannot be expected to be impartial in deciding whether it is proven.

Therefore, the functions of prosecuting and evaluating the evidence of the prosecutor are often incompatible. In some situations, however, the legislature permits the same person to be both investigator and adjudicator. This "inquisitorial" process is discussed below.

A Further Requirement: No Delegation of Authority

A further requirement that ensures the separation of functions is that an adjudicator may not delegate his or her decision-making authority. (This "subdelegation" doctrine is described in chapter 3, The Foundations of Administrative Law.) If the decision maker is not sufficiently independent of the prosecutor, there is a risk that the decision maker will inadvertently defer to the wishes of the prosecutor in making his or her decision.

Similarly, it is important to ensure that the prosecutor has a reasonable level of independence from the investigator. The prosecutor should be in a position to objectively and independently assess the accuracy and comprehensiveness of the evidence uncovered by the investigator, and to make an informed recommendation or decision whether the evidence is sufficient to warrant laying a charge. If the evidence, in the prosecutor's view, is suspect or even false, he or she must be able to refuse to support it.

Many agencies that have multiple and potentially conflicting functions create internal structures and barriers intended to prevent such problems, or at least to reduce the chances of occurrence and, when they do occur, to moderate their impact. For example, the Ontario Human Rights Commission investigates complaints of human rights violations and makes findings whether the complaints are valid. If the commission finds that there is insufficient evidence to warrant a hearing, it dismisses the complaint after the investigation. If, however, the commission finds evidence of discrimination, it does not itself decide whether to uphold the complaint, but rather presents the case to a separate tribunal.

In summary, the function of the preliminary inquiry committee [of the College of Physicians and Surgeons of Saskatchewan] is to investigate; the function of the discipline committee is to hear and adjudicate; and the function of council is to deal with reports of the discipline committee and to impose penalties for misconduct. ...

It must be added that the division of functions as outlined above is necessary to preserve fairness in a situation where the college, through its agents, committees and governing bodies, in disciplinary matters which can have grave consequences to its members, acts in various stages as investigator, prosecutor, and adjudicator—in more common terms, it acts as policeman, prosecutor, judge, jury and executioner. The separation of functions ensures that at least two or three different bodies must review the case. It guards against the possibility that knowledge acquired or biases induced by one stage of the proceedings will not [sic] improperly influence a later stage of the proceedings. Furthermore, investigation and adjudication often require quite different approaches. Finally, there are procedural safeguards built into each step of the disciplinary process, and action outside of that process would deprive the doctor under investigation of those safeguards.

Wagner v. College of Physicians and Surgeons of Saskatchewan (1984), 33 Sask. R 127 (QB)

ADMINISTRATIVE TRIBUNALS IN THE ABC SCHEME

Introduction

Some agencies are required by statute or by common law to follow procedures similar to those of courts in making decisions. These agencies are called administrative justice tribunals, or more simply **administrative tribunals** or **tribunals**. Tribunals may also be called boards, commissions, or some other name. They are created by special statutes passed by Parliament or a provincial legislature for the purpose of adjudicating disputes over statute-based rights, entitlements, and duties.

Tribunals resolve disputes between individuals or businesses or between individuals and the state. They generally use a more formal, court-like process than that followed by government staff when deciding whether to grant approvals or bestow benefits. There is no fixed boundary between tribunals and other government decision makers. All government decision-making processes that affect people's rights and entitlements fall somewhere on a continuum, from very informal procedures carried out primarily behind closed doors, to procedures similar to those of a court, involving adversarial techniques and usually conducted in public.

The government creates different kinds of decision-making processes for different kinds of decisions, guided by principles of efficiency, effectiveness, and fairness.

For straightforward administrative decisions, the government usually delegates the decision-making function to an internal decision maker, using informal procedures. However, where there is a dispute between a person and a government official who has made a decision that adversely affects that person, or where there is a dispute between two or more parties, the government often establishes a **quasi-judicial** tribunal to resolve the dispute. Tribunal decisions often uphold, grant, or take away rights or privileges, so to ensure that the decision-making process is a

Examples of Quasi-Judicial Tribunals

- Federal and provincial parole boards such as the Ontario Parole Board and Earned Release Board decide whether inmates of jails and prisons may be released before they have served their full sentence.

- Property tax assessment review boards such as the Alberta Assessment Appeal Board hear appeals by property owners of their property tax assessments.

- Tribunals such as Ontario's Social Benefits Tribunal determine applicants' eligibility for social assistance payments.

- The federal and provincial human rights commissions determine whether persons have suffered discrimination based on prohibited grounds such as sex, age, race, or religion, and, where appropriate, order remedial action and compensation.

- Ontario's Criminal Injuries Compensation Board determines whether an applicant's injuries were caused by criminal conduct and, if they were, how the provincial government should compensate the injured person.

- Land use planning tribunals such as the Alberta Planning Board and the Ontario Municipal Board hear cases relating to municipal planning and financing, including appeals from municipal government decisions about zoning and official plans.

- The Ontario Child and Family Services Review Board hears applications from children to be released from secure treatment facilities (where they have been placed because of concern that they may harm themselves or others), as well as appeals from refusals of government officials to approve the adoption of a child.

- Federal and provincial energy boards such as the National Energy Board, the Alberta Energy and Utilities Board, and the Ontario Energy Board set the rates that hydroelectric utilities and gas distributors may charge their customers.

- Licensing bodies such as the Alcohol and Gaming Commission of Ontario decide whether it is in the public interest to issue liquor licences to restaurants and other facilities that wish to serve alcohol, and may suspend or revoke a licence if it is abused.

fair one, tribunals are required to follow certain rules. (See "Examples of Quasi-Judicial Tribunals.")

Administrative law is sometimes treated as being synonymous with these rules of procedural fairness (or natural justice, as they are sometimes called); however, this book treats administrative law as including other legal principles as well. Many texts on administrative law focus on tribunals and the law that governs them. Much of this book will also focus on administrative tribunals. But an introduction to administrative law must recognize that tribunals are not the only kind of government body regulated by administrative law. Administrative law also applies to government departments and other kinds of government agencies.

The Place of Tribunals in the Government Structure

Administrative tribunals are often viewed as part of the executive branch, but they also perform functions similar to those of the judicial branch. Accordingly, they are sometimes described as "hybrid" bodies, because they do not fit neatly into either the executive or the judicial branch. In fact, administrative tribunals were initially viewed by some political scientists as illegitimate for just this reason. Concerns were expressed particularly about their lack of accountability to the public.

In recent years, however, tribunals have become so integral to our system of government that they are now accepted as legitimate, although some concerns remain. Politicians and civil servants may doubt whether tribunals are sensitive enough to government policy or understand the limited resources available to carry out government functions. Parties appearing before tribunals may fear that an agency whose members have been appointed by the Cabinet or the legislature will not be sufficiently independent of politicians and bureaucrats to ensure that everyone gets a fair and impartial hearing. In other words, politicians and civil servants often view tribunals as being too independent, while others regard them as not being independent enough.

The Source and Scope of Tribunal Powers and Duties

Every administrative tribunal is governed by its **enabling legislation**, the statute that creates the tribunal for a specific purpose and other statutes that set out its powers and duties. The powers and duties of a tribunal are often supplemented by common law requirements for fair procedures where the statute is silent on the rights of the parties, and by any additional powers that are reasonably necessary to carry out the statutory powers. The powers and duties of tribunals may include holding hearings, requiring witnesses to attend and give evidence, receiving evidence, and deciding a dispute between parties in favour of one or the other.

In some cases an agency may have a mandate not only to decide a dispute but also to perform related tasks, such as investigating, regulating, prosecuting, advising, or setting policy. In these cases, to ensure fairness and impartiality, the agency is usually divided into separate bodies with different members or staff to perform different functions. The tribunal that carries out the dispute resolution function may operate as a separate body within the agency, with safeguards to ensure that it operates independently from the other bodies of the agency. In some cases, such as human rights agencies, the tribunal may be a completely separate agency with different personnel, a separate budget, and separate statutory powers and duties.

Why Governments Delegate Decisions to Tribunals

A government often establishes a tribunal in the following circumstances:

- The government wants to create a mechanism to review the decision of a government decision maker. In many cases an initial decision may be made in an informal manner, so a statutory right to appeal the decision to a tribunal ensures that the decision can be judged objectively and fairly.

- The decision maker must resolve a dispute between two or more individuals or companies rather than deciding an issue strictly between the government and an individual.

- The decision has serious consequences for a person. Some decisions can affect an individual's livelihood or the public's health or safety. An informal decision-making process for such decisions is inappropriate. The higher the stakes that are involved, the more likely it is the agency making the initial decision will be a tribunal.

Advantages of Tribunals Over Government Administrators or Politicians

In some ways, the decision-making function of a tribunal is similar to that of an administrator in a government department who decides whether to issue an order, grant a licence, or confer a benefit. In other ways, this function is similar to that of a court that applies relevant laws in a structured forum.

If the decision is essentially political or administrative, then why not have an administrator in a government department or a politician make the decision?

Governments create administrative tribunals for many of the same purposes that they delegate functions to agencies. For example, the government may create a specialized tribunal

- to demonstrate the impartiality of a decision-making process and avoid any perception that the decision maker is biased (that is particularly important where the decision of a government official or minister is being reviewed, since an appeal to someone within the same department may not appear to be impartial);

- to ensure fairness of procedure and outcome through the use of a procedure similar to that of a court;

- to send a message to the community that the issue is important to the government;

- to distance the government from potentially unpopular or controversial decisions;

- to allow for citizen participation (to give the public affected by a government decision the opportunity to participate in the decision-making process);

- to involve experts in the decision; or

- to handle cases more efficiently or cost-effectively by creating a new agency than by expanding or modifying the structure of an existing ministry.

Advantages of Tribunals Over Courts

If the purpose of having decisions made outside the government bureaucracy is to ensure that the decision is made at arm's length from the government and follows procedures similar to those of a court, then why not delegate the function to the courts? Some of the answers are apparent from the discussion above.

- Where it is desirable to have the decisions made by a person's peers or by experts, judges may not be any more appropriate than civil servants or politicians. A panel with some community membership may bring a different sensitivity and personal experience to its tasks from that brought by a court.

- Over time, the members of a specialized tribunal can develop expertise in administering a particular set of laws. This expertise can ensure that an area of law is interpreted in a consistent fashion and that the interpretation reflects certain social values, professional standards, or government policies.

- Tribunals can include representatives of interest groups affected by the tribunal's mandate, or individuals with professional backgrounds relevant to the subject matter covered by the tribunal. In a dispute between competing interest groups, a tribunal that includes representatives of each group as well as one or more neutral members may ensure that the interests of each group, and of the general community, are all represented. For example, labour relations boards and workers' compensation tribunals often consist of one member selected by a union, one member selected by company management, and one neutral party chosen by the other two members or specified by the enabling legislation.

- Tribunals may have certain structural advantages over courts. Tribunals can be less formal and more accessible than courts. It may be possible to ensure fairness with fewer procedural safeguards than those in courts. The public may be more comfortable appearing before tribunals than before courts: individuals do not always need a lawyer to participate effectively (though representation by legal counsel is not uncommon).

- Tribunals can often hear cases quickly and without delay. The rules and practices of each tribunal can be tailored to meet the specific needs of the parties and to avoid unnecessary "red tape."

The traditional rationale for the establishment of administrative tribunals is cheapness, expedition, and expertise. The objectives are freedom from what is popularly seen as the undue delay and cost of court proceedings and the inexperience of judges trained in the law but not in matters of social improvement.

Re Roosma and Ford Motor Co. (1888), 66 OR (2d) 18, at 24 (Div. Ct.)

Similarities Between Tribunals and Courts

Common law and statutes that govern tribunals often grant tribunals the freedom to be more informal than courts, but there are limits to this informality. These limits have been imposed by the common law doctrine of procedural fairness, by the particular statutes that create particular tribunals, and by statutes such as Ontario's *Statutory Powers Procedure Act*[4] (SPPA) and Quebec's *Administrative Justice Act*,[5] which set out minimum rules of procedure for some tribunals in those provinces.

Like courts, tribunals generally must follow a fair process, which means that affected persons must have the right to be heard, and to be heard by an impartial decision maker. These principles of natural justice or fairness, which will be discussed in more detail in chapter 3, The Foundations of Administrative Law, include rules governing notice, disclosure, the presentation of evidence, the questioning of witnesses, adjournments, submissions, and representation by counsel or other agents.

Like courts, tribunals generally must

- ensure that all parties have been given reasonable notice of the proceedings before the hearing begins; *SUFFICIENT NOTICE*

- ensure that all parties have an opportunity to present their case; *OPPORTUNITY TO APPEAR*

- ensure that all parties have been informed of the case they have to meet; *INFORMED*

- allow all parties to present evidence and to cross-examine witnesses or test the accuracy of the evidence against them in other ways; *ADVOCATE & PRESENT EVIDENCE*

- grant adjournments if a party would otherwise be deprived of a reasonable opportunity to present its case fully; *ADJOURNMENT OPPORTUN*

- give all parties a chance to make final submissions; *FULL & FINAL SUBMIS*

- allow all parties to be represented by a lawyer or agent; *REPRESENTATION*

- avoid any statements or actions that would suggest that the tribunal has prejudged issues or displays a bias for or against a party; and *ENSURE NO BIAS FOR OR AGAINST*

- apply the law that governs the proceedings and take into account considerations that are relevant under that law. *LAWS TO GOVERN PROCEEDIN RULES*

IN PERSON, PHONE IN WRITING.

Differences Between Tribunals and Courts

Tribunal procedures are generally less formal and more flexible than those of courts. The more relaxed rules and procedures of tribunals can be an advantage or a disadvantage to the parties. The differences between tribunals and courts in matters of substance and style are summarized in tables 2.1 and 2.2.

Similarities and Differences Between Tribunal Members and Judges

For the most part, the responsibilities of tribunal members, their requirements for impartiality, and the scope of their decision-making power are similar to those of judges. There are differences, however, and the extent of the similarity or difference is open to debate and may vary from tribunal to tribunal.

Like judges, tribunal members are expected to render impartial decisions that are not influenced by political pressure or by connections to any of the parties that appear before them. Unlike courts, however, tribunals are expected to apply government policies. And, unlike judges, tribunal members have no security of tenure and their appointments may be terminated by the government. That is, some of

---

4 RSO 1990, c. S.22.

5 RSQ, c. J-3.

TABLE 2.1 Substantive Differences Between Tribunals and Courts

Tribunals	Courts
Tribunal members are not required to follow previous tribunal decisions. Two decisions of the same tribunal can interpret the same provision of a law in different ways.	Lower courts are bound by the decisions of higher courts. All judges of a court must interpret the law the way a higher court interprets it.
Tribunals can accept any evidence that is reliable, including some evidence that courts would disallow. Tribunals vary greatly in what they will accept as evidence. Some tribunals will accept virtually any evidence.	Courts require parties to follow complicated rules of evidence that are designed to prevent misleading information from coming before the court. These rules of evidence are difficult, even for lawyers, to understand and apply correctly.
Tribunals generally require little or no advance disclosure of evidence. This results in an earlier hearing and lower initial costs, but can also result in "trial by ambush" and costly requests for adjournment to make up for surprises during the hearing. It can also result in excessive arguments and objections that new information has "prejudiced" a party (unduly harmed its ability to prepare or present its case).	Courts generally require parties in civil cases to disclose their evidence before the hearing. (In criminal cases, only the prosecutor must disclose evidence in advance.) This results in lengthy delays and substantial cost before the hearing begins, but it reduces surprises and improves the efficiency of the hearing. Disclosure also facilitates settlements and may shorten or eliminate the need for a hearing.
Some tribunals have staff who investigate, prepare a case, present evidence, and argue for a particular outcome, along with the other parties.	Courts rely entirely on the parties to present the evidence and the arguments on which the court will base its decision.
Some tribunals are permitted to follow less formal or less adversarial procedures.	Courts usually follow a formal and adversarial process.

TABLE 2.2 Style Differences Between Tribunals and Courts

Tribunals	Courts
Tribunal members often identify themselves at the start of a hearing. Sometimes they have nameplates in front of them.	Judges are often anonymous. Sometimes they do not identify themselves, nor do court clerks identify them.
Seating arrangements may vary from tribunal to tribunal. At some tribunals, all participants, including the adjudicator, sit around the same table.	Seating arrangements in courts are standardized. Often the judge sits on a dais at the front of the courtroom, elevated above the participants.
The practice regarding sitting or standing varies from tribunal to tribunal, but bowing is uncommon and robes or gowns are never worn.	Courts have more ceremonial trappings. Everyone stands when the judge enters. The lawyers and agents always stand when they are addressing the judge and examining or cross-examining witnesses. The lawyers and the judge bow to each other when the judge enters the court, and the lawyers bow to the judge when they leave. In certain courts, lawyers and judges wear robes or gowns.
The practice of oath swearing varies from tribunal to tribunal. Under Ontario's SPPA, for example, the oath is optional, and tribunals may require it or dispense with it.	Witnesses must swear an oath or solemnly affirm that they will tell the truth.

the safeguards afforded to judges to assist them in withstanding political pressures are not afforded to many tribunal members.

Like judges, tribunal members are expected to avoid interests and associations that may suggest that their decisions are not impartial. However, many tribunal members serve in a part-time capacity, and may be involved in business, professional, volunteer, and social activities that might be unacceptable for judges.

Like judges, tribunal members are required to apply and interpret the law, and may not substitute their own view of what the law should be for the decisions of the legislators. Unlike judges, however, tribunal members may have considerable discretion (power to choose a course of action from among a variety of options) in applying the law, or they may be expected to interpret or follow government policies.

Like judges, tribunal members are expected to decide cases on the basis of the evidence put before them. But while judges are required to decide cases using only the evidence put before them by the parties, tribunal members with specialized knowledge and expertise may have some latitude in applying their knowledge or understanding of professional standards and norms in making a decision. (The limits of this flexibility are discussed below.)

ADJUDICATION

Adjudication is the process of receiving and considering the evidence and arguments presented by both sides in a dispute and making a binding decision by applying relevant law to the issues in the case. In our tribunal system, the adjudicator is often relatively passive, for the most part weighing and evaluating the evidence and arguments submitted by opposing parties, and generally taking only a limited role in deciding what evidence will be sought out and brought before the tribunal. The adjudicator's role is to watch and judge. He or she is like a referee who makes sure the parties follow the "rules of the game," but is not permitted to favour one party or the other.

In some tribunals, however, adjudicators may have the right to take a more active role in investigating and collecting evidence and information. (See the description of inquisitorial systems, below.)

Adjudication may be contrasted with other methods of resolving disputes, such as negotiation, mediation, and conciliation, in which the facilitator or decision maker interacts with the parties in ways that may be quite different from the techniques used by an adjudicator. In these methods of dispute resolution, often called **alternative dispute resolution**, the person facilitating conflict resolution may use a variety of techniques and tools to help the parties reach an agreement without the need for a formal hearing by someone who issues a binding order.

Adjudication and these other forms of dispute resolution each have their strengths and weaknesses. Chapter 7, Tribunal Procedures Before Hearings, includes a brief discussion of which approach works best in which circumstances. There is considerable literature that discusses in more detail the relative merits of different types of dispute resolution.

The Adversarial and Inquisitorial Systems of Adjudication

There are two different approaches to the conduct of hearings: the adversarial and the inquisitorial.

Many tribunals have taken a passive role because Canada's common law principles of natural justice were developed within the **adversarial system** of dispute resolution. In this system, the parties themselves determine what evidence is brought before the tribunal, and the tribunal is not permitted to actively seek out evidence beyond that presented by the parties. It is required, though, to give the parties extensive opportunities to put forward their case and to challenge the case put forward by others. In Ontario, this approach is driven by the requirements of the *Statutory Powers Procedure Act*, which sets out numerous rules of procedure for most tribunals, many of which are based on the adversarial approach.

The adversarial system is based on a number of related assumptions: that the parties are in the best position to decide what evidence is useful; that both parties have adequate financial resources and access to information to participate effectively in the process; and that there is no substantial power imbalance between the parties. In disputes between government officials, who have access to substantial expertise and resources, and individuals, who frequently have limited financial resources and limited expertise, a purely adversarial process may not be the best way to bring out the truth and clearly articulate the individuals' goals and interests.

In contrast to the adversarial system, the **inquisitorial system**, which is often found in Europe, requires the tribunal to conduct the investigation and collect the evidence. Adjudicators may have much greater latitude to examine and cross-examine the parties and witnesses, and may even call witnesses on their own initiative. An inquisitorial system can help re-establish the balance between "weak" citizens and "strong" government, particularly if the adjudicator's authority to obtain information does not prevent the parties from playing a substantial role in bringing forward evidence and making representations.

In an adversarial system, one of the parties usually has the burden of proof. In an inquisitorial system, the tribunal itself may have the burden of finding enough evidence to determine whether a party is entitled to a remedy. In other words, in an inquisitorial system, a party could win even if he or she doesn't show up for the hearing!

Adversarial or Inquisitorial?

Some tribunals are permitted by their governing legislation to be more inquisitorial than adversarial. If the enabling legislation contains one or more of the following provisions, it is likely that a tribunal has some leeway to follow an inquisitorial process:

- the statute refers to the decision-making process as an "inquiry" rather than a "hearing";
- the statute says the tribunal "may" hold a hearing or inquiry rather than "shall" hold one;
- the statute gives the tribunal power to collect evidence independently of the parties;
- the statute requires the tribunal to determine what constitutes the public interest or is necessary to protect public health or ensure public safety, rather than to resolve a dispute between individuals about property or money; or
- the statute requires that the adjudicators have special expertise in the subject matter.

In Ontario, the *Statutory Powers Procedure Act* establishes the minimum procedural safeguards that most tribunals must follow. The procedures prescribed by the SPPA reflect the adversarial approach. Therefore, if an enabling statute in Ontario limits or excludes the application of the SPPA to the decision-making process, this may be a sign that the statute expects (or does not prohibit) a more inquisitorial process.

Examples of Inquisitorial Tribunals

Federal and provincial parole boards and information and privacy commissioners often follow an inquisitorial approach. In Ontario, the Information and Privacy Commissioner is an example of a tribunal that is authorized to follow an inquisitorial procedure. The commissioner decides whether to require the government to disclose documents to individuals and companies as requested under the *Freedom of Information and Protection of Privacy Act*.[6]

If the government refuses to disclose a document and an individual has appealed this refusal, a traditional adversarial hearing—where everything is done in public and the parties have the right to see all the relevant information that the other party has—would defeat the purpose of the process. Through the hearing, the requesting party would learn what is in the document that the government is refusing to disclose. He or she would win by default, and the process would be unfair to the government.

Therefore, instead of giving the parties full access to each other's information in a hearing open to the public, the commissioner conducts hearings in writing. If the government provides any information to the commissioner that would reveal the contents of the document, the commissioner does not share this information with the requester, despite the usual requirements of fairness that all evidence be available to all parties.

Since the requester does not know what is in the document being withheld, his or her ability to ask probing questions or to argue that the document should be disclosed is limited. To reduce the potential unfairness of this barrier to the requester, the commissioner plays an active role in ensuring fairness by setting out for the parties what he or she considers to be the relevant legal and factual issues to be resolved, by questioning both parties, and by actively seeking additional information not provided by parties where such information would be helpful in reaching a decision.

Combining Adversarial and Inquisitorial Techniques

Not all tribunals follow a purely adversarial or purely inquisitorial approach. Some combine elements of both processes. In tribunal proceedings, the extent to which adjudicators are permitted to conduct an investigation, intervene in the parties' presentation of evidence and argument, or withhold information provided by one party from another depends on the tribunal's mandate, the wording of the enabling legislation, and what is fair in the circumstances.

---

6   RSO 1990, c. F.31.

[T]he traditional advocacy skills of the lawyer are generally inapplicable to appearances before the National Parole Board. Parole hearings are inquisitorial rather than adversarial, which indicates that Parliament intended that there be many differences between this and other tribunals. For example, there are no parties in the sense of adversaries between whom a *lis inter partes* (a dispute between two or more parties) may be said to exist. Similarly, although those institutional and parole personnel most familiar with the prisoner's case do attend parole hearings, they are not usually present as witnesses, and questions may only be put to them through and with the permission of the attending Board members. Again, counsel does not lead the client through his version of events; rather the Board members closely question the prisoner as to what, in their opinion, is important.

David P. Cole, "The Bridge of Sighs: Appearing Before the National Parole Board," in Franklin R. Moskoff, ed., *Administrative Tribunals—A Practice Handbook for Legal Counsel* (Aurora, ON: Canada Law Book, 1989), 69

CHAPTER SUMMARY

Traditionally, three separate branches of government in Canada regulated citizens' conduct: the legislative branch, which passed laws; the executive branch, which implemented and enforced them; and the judicial branch, which resolved disputes by interpreting and applying the laws. As society became more complex and government regulation became more pervasive, governments began to establish a new kind of organization, the administrative agency, to carry out some of the functions traditionally carried out by the three branches.

These agencies typically carry out the work of the executive branch, but sometimes they combine the functions of two or more of the branches of government. One kind of agency, the tribunal, is similar to a court, although it often conducts its work in a less formal manner than a court.

Different tribunals differ in their practices, and their procedures range from the purely adversarial, in which the tribunal is passive and the parties control the presentation of evidence, to the inquisitorial, in which the tribunal plays a larger role in collecting information and presenting evidence.

Tribunals are required to follow many of the same procedures that courts follow to ensure that all parties receive a fair hearing. Both tribunals and courts apply the law, but tribunals also apply government policy and often base their decisions on their interpretation of the public interest as well as on the rights or interests of the parties.

Although tribunals are technically part of the executive branch of government, their adjudicative function resembles that of the judicial branch. Like courts, tribunals must be independent from the executive branch in order to remain impartial. They are not as independent as courts, however, and tribunal members lack the security of tenure that secures the independence of judges.

KEY TERMS

adjudication   the process of receiving and considering the evidence and arguments presented by both sides in a dispute and making a binding decision by applying relevant law to the issues in the case

administrative agency   *see* agency

administrative tribunal   *see* tribunal

adversarial process   a type of hearing in which the judge or adjudicator does not actively seek out the truth or investigate but relies on opposing parties or their representatives to present evidence and challenge each other's evidence; the adjudicator's decision is based on the evidence presented, regardless of how complete the evidence may be

enabling legislation   a statute that sets out the powers of an agency; it is often, but not always, the statute that establishes the agency; some agencies are established by one statute, but carry out functions under several statutes, each of which may give it powers for the purpose of the functions governed by that statute

inquisitorial process   a type of hearing in which the judge or adjudicator plays an active role in investigating, collecting facts, putting forward evidence, and questioning witnesses

quasi-judicial   similar to that of a judge; often used to describe the functions of a tribunal when it must make a decision regarding the substantive rights of a person

tribunal   a type of agency that is not a court but operates like a court in deciding disputes between individuals and companies or between individuals or companies and the government

REVIEW QUESTIONS

1. How do agencies, boards, and commissions differ from the traditional departmental structure of the executive branch of government?

2. What historical developments led to the creation of a separate area of "administrative law" within the broader category of public law?

3. Describe seven functions that are often carried out by agencies.

4. Give seven reasons why a government might set up a separate agency instead of having a department carry out a function.

5. What is a tribunal?

6. Under what kinds of circumstances does the legislature delegate the job of making a decision to a tribunal rather than to a body such as a ministry or a court?

7. What are the two main systems of adjudication used by tribunals? How do they differ from each other? What are the advantages and disadvantages of each system?

8. When you read a statute that governs the operation of a tribunal, what "clues" would you look for in determining which model of adjudication the tribunal follows?

9. List eight areas of dispute that are typically delegated to tribunals for resolution.

10. List as many similarities between courts and tribunals as you can.

11. List as many differences between courts and tribunals as you can.

EXERCISES

1. a. Using the tools described in appendix B, find an example of each of the following anywhere in Canada (not including any examples specifically mentioned in this book):

    - a government department or ministry that reports to a Cabinet minister;

    - an advisory agency;

    - an agency that regulates the sale or distribution of a product or commodity;

    - an agency that gives grants to individuals or to businesses, charities, or other bodies;

    - an agency that operates a business or provides a service to consumers; and

    - a tribunal.

    b. For each organization, briefly describe (where applicable)

    - how its members are appointed and by whom;

    - its main functions;

    - whether its members and staff are members of the public service;

    - what statutory steps, if any, the agency must take before making decisions that affect the public; and

    - what procedures the legislature has put in place to ensure that the agency is accountable for its activities (for example, the requirement to produce an annual report, undergo audit by a government auditor, submit its budget to the government for approval, or have its individual expenditures approved by the government before or after they are made).

2. Ontario's *Freedom of Information and Protection of Privacy Act* gives individuals the right to obtain copies of all records in the custody or under the control of ministries and other agencies of the Ontario government, subject to certain exceptions listed in the Act.

    To obtain access to a record, an individual must apply to the ministry or agency that has possession or control over the record. Within 30 days, the institution must issue a decision whether or not to release the record.

    If the institution refuses access to the record, the requester may appeal the refusal to the Information and Privacy Commissioner.

    The *Freedom of Information and Protection of Privacy Act* sets out the method by which the commissioner must process this appeal. On the basis of the Act's description of the commissioner's powers and procedures, do you think the Act establishes an adversarial or an inquisitorial process?

Which of these processes is better suited to the function that the commissioner must carry out? Explain?

Compare the process used to challenge an institution's decision to refuse access to documents under Ontario's *Freedom of Information and Protection of Privacy Act* with the process under the federal *Access to Information Act*. How do the two systems differ? Which system is preferable, and why?

FURTHER READING

Robert Macaulay and James Sprague, *Practice and Procedure Before Administrative Tribunals* (Toronto: Carswell) (looseleaf), chapters 1 to 4.

Robert W. Macaulay, *Directions: Review of Ontario's Regulatory Agencies Report* (Toronto: Queen's Printer for Ontario, 1989).

Murray Rankin, "Cabinets and Courts: Political Tribunals and Judicial Tribunals" (1990) vol. 3 *Canadian Journal of Administrative Law and Policy* 301.

CHAPTER 3

The Foundations of Administrative Law

LEARNING OBJECTIVES

After reading this chapter, you will understand

- the role of administrative agencies;
- the need for a special set of laws to regulate these agencies;
- the meaning of "jurisdiction" and why agencies must act within jurisdiction;
- the meaning of "discretion" and how discretion must be exercised;
- the rule against subdelegation;
- the requirement that tribunals follow fair procedures when deciding disputes;
- the relationship between "procedural fairness" and "natural justice";
- the components of procedural fairness;
- the main statutes setting out the rules of fair procedure; and
- the application of rules of fair procedure in different contexts.

The effect of agencies on the lives of Canadians is pervasive. They impact almost every aspect of our daily lives morning through night. Behind the waking sounds of the clock radio is the CRTC, the licensor of the radio station. The electricity powering the radio is provided by Ontario Hydro. The furnace, hot water heater and the stove may all run on natural gas which is provided under federal and provincial regulation. The eggs and the milk in the morning omelette are subject to grading and production quotas set by provincial egg and milk marketing boards.

... This plethora of governmental agencies is a reflection of the increase in government services and responsibilities since the second world war. There are now about 1,500 agencies in Canada of which 580 are in Ontario. They range widely in size and nature from the Wolf Damage Assessment Board to the Ontario Labour Relations Board. They also vary in the way they function and in their relations with the government and the public.

...

Administrative agencies have evolved in the years since the second world war into a significant and important manifestation of government. Because each agency has been created individually and on an *ad hoc* basis, there is extraordinary variety and inconsistency in their powers, methods of operation, relations with their ministries, etc.

Robert W. Macauley, *Directions* (Toronto: Queen's Printer for Ontario, 1989), 1-1 and 1-2

WHAT IS ADMINISTRATIVE LAW?

Administrative law applies primarily to the executive branch of government, rather than the legislative or judicial branches. It is the body of rules and principles that regulate how the government departments and agencies that administer and enforce our laws, and other bodies created or given powers by statute, must behave when carrying out their functions. Administrative law also encompasses the authority of the superior courts to supervise how these departments and agencies carry out their powers, the procedures that these courts follow, and the remedies that the courts can provide when departments or agencies act outside their authority or exercise their powers in an unreasonable or unfair manner.

Fundamental Principles of Administrative Law

Administrative law is founded on three central principles:

1. Decision makers who exercise powers granted by statute ("administrators") must stay within their legal authority or "jurisdiction."

2. Administrators must exercise their judgment in a reasonable manner when they have "discretion" in making decisions.

3. Administrators must follow fair procedures when making decisions that affect a person's rights or interests. This principle is known as "procedural fairness" or "natural justice." It protects the rights and interests of persons affected by a decision by providing for

   a. the right to notice of an intended decision and the right to be heard; and

   b. the right to an impartial decision maker.

There is also a fourth principle, known as "the rule against subdelegation," which is important but less central to administrative law.

These fundamental principles are discussed in detail throughout this chapter.

Why Did Administrative Law Develop?

Chapter 2, Administrative Agencies and Tribunals, described the evolution of the executive branch of government to include, in addition to government departments, a whole new sector of administrative agencies. The main reason for the creation of these agencies was that governments were taking on a much larger role in regulating social and economic activities. As well as moving into new areas of regulation, governments were applying stricter or more detailed requirements or standards. To support this expanded role, the powers of central departments were increased, and the new agencies were given wide-ranging responsibilities intended to complement, or in some cases replace, various functions otherwise performed by departments. Their responsibilities included legislation, enforcement, administration, and adjudication.

The more government intervened in the daily lives of citizens, and the broader the powers granted to its departments and agencies, the more important it became to put in place a system of rules for scrutinizing and regulating these activities. In particular, it was essential to maintain the separation of powers among the three branches of government, by preventing departments and agencies that were part of the executive branch from encroaching on the functions of the legislative and judicial branches. It was also necessary to promote the accountability of departments and agencies; to ensure that they acted fairly; and, at the same time, to protect their independence.

One way of accomplishing these objectives was to develop a body of law that constrained the actions of government departments and agencies. Initially (as discussed below), the courts took the lead by developing a set of fairness principles. Later, these and other principles and rules were codified in statutes. This body of principles and rules is what we now know as "administrative law."

Who Is Subject to Administrative Law?

Administrative law governs the exercise of powers granted by statute. Thus, any individual or body exercising a power granted by statute or regulation is subject to the principles of administrative law. This means that in addition to government entities, organizations such as universities, hospitals, and self-regulating professions that are established or given powers by statute must follow the principles of administrative. In other words, "it is not the nature of the body but the source of the power it is exercising that determines whether it is subject to those principles."[1]

Although administrative law applies primarily to bodies created by statute when they make decisions authorized or required by statute, this general description is incomplete. For example, the courts will intervene from time to time to ensure that statutory bodies act properly even when they are carrying out functions that do not involve statutory decision making, such as investigation or the making of non-binding recommendations.

In addition, the same principles of law apply to ensure that non-government, non-statutory voluntary organizations, such as trade associations, clubs, and churches, abide by their own rules and apply those rules fairly when they are taking action that affects the interests or rights of their members. That is, the organization must stay within its "jurisdiction" as set out in its own rules (rather than in a statute), and it must follow a fair procedure when, for example, it wishes to revoke a membership or fire a staff member.

There is some disagreement among writers on administrative law as to whether the application of similar principles means that administrative law itself applies to voluntary organizations. While many maintain that it does apply, a few writers treat this as a similar but separate, unnamed area of law, or as a part of employment law.

---

1 The Law Society of Upper Canada, *Public Law—Reference Materials*, 45th Bar Admission Course Materials (Toronto: Law Society of Upper Canada, 2002), chapter 1, at 1-1.

Evolution of Administrative Law

FAIRNESS PRINCIPLES

As mentioned above, in response to concerns about the expansion of powers of government bodies, the courts began to develop rules of fairness in decision making. Initially, these rules applied to agencies that had duties similar to those of a court in settling (adjudicating) disputes over rights. Later, the rules were expanded to other agencies whose decisions affect a person's rights. In recent years, the courts have begun to extend the application of fairness principles even to decisions that affect reasonable expectations rather than rights.

Natural Justice

Historically, the courts drew a rigid line between "quasi-judicial" functions—that is, the kinds of functions that tribunals typically carry out—and other functions characterized as legislative, policy-making, investigative, or administrative. They took an "all-or-nothing" approach to rights to challenge the fairness of procedures used by government bodies.

In *Minister of National Revenue v. Coopers and Lybrand*,[2] the Supreme Court of Canada applied the traditional approach reflected in s. 28 of the *Federal Court Act*.[3] The court ruled that if a body is making a decision that is "required by law to be made on a judicial or quasi-judicial basis," it must follow the rules of **natural justice** and apply procedures similar to those of a court. Otherwise, the body was largely free to make the decision without consulting people who would be affected by it, since the courts would not consider the fairness of the process.

The court said that in deciding whether a process was quasi-judicial, the following factors should be considered:[4]

- whether anything in the language of the statute suggests that a hearing is contemplated before a decision is reached;
- whether the decision directly or indirectly affects the rights and obligations of a person affected by the decision;
- whether an adversarial process is used in making the decision; and
- whether there is an obligation to apply substantive rules to many individual cases, rather than an obligation to implement social and economic policy in a broad sense.

The court said that if the answer to all these questions was "yes," the person affected by the decision was entitled to be given notice of the decision and had a right to be heard. In addition, the decision maker was required to follow procedures similar to those applied by a court, although the actual procedures might vary from case to case.

---

2 *Minister of National Revenue v. Coopers and Lybrand*, [1979] 1 SCR 495.

3 Section 28 of the *Federal Court Act*, RSC 1985, c. C-7, states that "the Court of Appeal has jurisdiction to hear and determine an application to set aside a decision or order, other than a decision or order of an administrative nature not required by law to be made on a judicial or quasi-judicial basis."

4 Supra note 2, at 504.

On the other hand, if a decision could not be considered quasi-judicial, few, if any, procedural safeguards would apply. On this basis, a wide variety of executive or administrative decisions were not subject to the rules of natural justice.

Procedural Fairness

In another case decided in the same year, however, the Supreme Court of Canada changed its position. In *Nicholson v. Haldimand-Norfolk Regional Board of Commissioners of Police*,[5] the court decided that the requirement to follow fair procedures did not depend on whether a function could be described as "quasi-judicial" or fell into some other category. Instead, certain basic procedural rights applied to any government decision that would affect a particular individual or group more than it would affect the general public. In such cases, affected persons must be given notice of the decision and the reasons for it, and an opportunity to respond. This principle or doctrine was called **procedural fairness**.

The courts have described the right bestowed by the doctrine of procedural fairness as a *right to be heard*. This is not the same as a *right to a hearing*, the kind of formal proceeding held by a court or tribunal. Thus, one way to describe the difference between natural justice and procedural fairness is that natural justice requires that a person affected be given a right to a formal hearing, while procedural fairness requires that a person affected be consulted before a final decision is made.

Gradually, the requirement of procedural fairness has been extended from the person most directly affected by a decision to others who may be less directly affected. (See the example "Entitlement to Procedural Fairness.") In addition, principles of procedural fairness are increasingly being applied to legislative, investigatory, and advisory functions, although the development of rules of fairness in these contexts is still in its infancy.

Entitlement to Procedural Fairness

The owner of a restaurant applies for a licence to sell liquor under provincial liquor control legislation. If her application is refused, under the rules of procedural fairness (as well as the rules of natural justice), the applicant is entitled to an opportunity to challenge the decision. However, if the neighbours of the restaurant owner oppose the application, they also have a right to bring their concerns, and the evidence supporting those concerns, to the attention of the decision maker.

According to the rules of procedural fairness, the decision maker is required to notify the neighbours of the application and to give them an opportunity to present their objections before the final decision is made. If the decision maker refuses the licence and the applicant challenges the decision, the neighbours are also entitled to notice of this challenge and an opportunity to participate in the appeal proceedings.

Legitimate Expectations

Finally, the courts have begun to rule that natural justice also requires government agencies to consult affected individuals in cases that do not involve their rights.

---

5 *Nicholson v. Haldimand-Norfolk Regional Board of Commissioners of Police*, [1979] 1 SCR 311.

Where a person has no right to continue receiving the benefit of a government practice, but has come to rely on it, he or she will sometimes be entitled to an opportunity to comment before this practice is changed. Even if a person claiming some benefit or privilege has no legal right to it, he or she may still have **legitimate expectations** of receiving the benefit or privilege, and the courts will require some consultation before removing it. A person may have legitimate expectations based on reassuring statements that the government has made about the continuance or availability of the benefit or privilege, or based on a pattern of conduct that implies that the benefit or privilege will continue.

OTHER CENTRAL PRINCIPLES

The principles most frequently dealt with in texts on administrative law are those of natural justice or procedural fairness. These principles apply to any official exercising a power to give something to or take something from members of the public, as well as to one particular type of agency—the administrative tribunal. However, as discussed at the beginning of this chapter, there are several other fundamental principles of administrative law that apply to government generally, including departments and administrative agencies. These principles relate to jurisdiction, discretion, and subdelegation, and they are discussed in the sections that follow. The final section of the chapter provides a more detailed explanation of the rules of procedural fairness or natural justice.

JURISDICTION

What Is Jurisdiction?

Jurisdiction is a central concept of administrative law. Simply defined, "jurisdiction" refers to the scope of the authority or powers conferred on a government body or official by legislation or by common law. This concept is expressed in the principle that government bodies and officials must always act within their legal authority or powers.

Requirement To Act Within Jurisdiction

As discussed in chapter 1, when making any decision, government bodies and officials are bound by the rule of law. This has two important consequences related to jurisdiction:

1. The powers and duties of any government department, agency, or official are limited to those established by a law.

2. Any agency that has powers and duties under legislation must follow the procedures set out in the legislation when exercising those powers and duties.

Agencies and their officials do not have the right or the authority to ignore provisions of the law even if they believe that they are justified in doing so. Their task is not to determine what the law *should* be. That function belongs to the elected members of the legislature or the municipal council. The role of agencies and officials is to interpret and apply the law as it is written, in every case that comes before them.

Jurisdiction and Procedural Fairness

According to the simple definition set out above, in administrative law, the requirement to stay within jurisdiction means not doing anything outside the statutory authority granted to the agency or official. It also means doing everything a statute requires an agency or official to do. For example, if a statute requires an agency to make a decision and the agency fails to do so within a reasonable time, the agency is said to be **declining jurisdiction**.

"Jurisdiction" may also have a broader meaning in certain contexts. For decision makers who determine the rights and obligations of others, and tribunals that resolve disputes, there is also the duty to exercise those powers in accordance with the rules of procedural fairness. Consequently, some courts and writers on administrative law also describe failure to follow a fair procedure as "exceeding jurisdiction," "acting outside jurisdiction," or "making a jurisdictional error." However, courts differ as to whether failure to follow procedural fairness should be treated as a question of jurisdiction.

Fairness also comes into play in interpreting an agency's powers. An agency must interpret the powers given to it by legislation in the context of these rules of fairness. That is, even though the wording of a statute appears to authorize a tribunal to do something, if taking that action would involve a breach of fairness rules and if the statute is open to interpretation, the proper interpretation of the statutory power is the one that does not violate fairness requirements.

DISCRETION

What Is Discretion?

The role of an administrator becomes most interesting when the law does not provide the answer. In many cases, the law grants **discretion** to an official. Discretion is the right to choose from a variety of options.

Many administrative decisions involve an element of discretion. Legislators cannot contemplate all of the circumstances and conduct to be regulated within a specific field of activity, whether it be product marketing or maintaining professional standards. Someone must be given the responsibility of applying the legislation to each situation as it arises. Also, legislation is ineffective if no one is appointed to ensure compliance. Such a person is granted discretion to determine whether a specific situation is covered by the legislation and whether some sort of compliance order or other remedy is warranted. Also discretion is often conferred so that considerations of policy and the public interest can be taken into account.

Sara Blake, *Administrative Law in Canada*, 2d ed. (Toronto: Butterworths, 1997), 81

Requirement To Exercise Discretion in a Fair or Reasonable Manner

When an official is granted discretion, just applying the law to the facts often will not provide the "right" answer. It may also be necessary to determine which of several possible applications of the law is the most fair or reasonable in the circumstances. However, this does not mean that officials are free to do whatever they think is fair or reasonable. The rule of law requires that decisions be based on the intent and purpose of the statute granting the discretion, not on an official's personal beliefs and values. Otherwise, the exercise of discretion in decision making would lead to perpetual inconsistency and uncertainty—a situation contrary to the purpose of laws.

The courts have therefore developed a rule that discretion must be exercised reasonably (although the word "fairly" would be equally appropriate). There are several principles that govern whether the exercise of discretion is reasonable or unreasonable. Among these are principles requiring decision makers to avoid looking at options either too broadly on the one hand or too narrowly on the other.

Limits on the Right To Choose Between Options

There are four limits on a decision maker's right to choose among options:

1. Discretion must be exercised within the "four corners" or boundaries of the statute (in other words, within the decision-maker's jurisdiction). The fundamental rule in the exercise of discretion is that the choices made must be both consistent with the purpose of the statute and within its wording.

2. The second rule is closely related to the first: in making choices, officials must consider only relevant factors—those that are consistent with the purpose and wording of the statute. They must not take into account extraneous or irrelevant factors—those that are outside the scope of the statute.

3. Similar cases should be treated in a similar way. There must be no discrimination between persons on the basis of irrelevant considerations.

4. Discretion must be exercised in good faith. Officials act in bad faith when they deliberately ignore the limits set out above for an improper purpose. For example, if the exercise of discretion is influenced by outside pressure or by the official's personal feelings toward a party, the choice is made not only on the basis of an irrelevant factor, but also in bad faith.

Limits on the Authority To Rule Out Options: The Rule Against Fettering Discretion

While the principles set out above require officials to rule out irrelevant or inappropriate options, there are also principles that require them *not* to rule out other options. When officials rule out options that the law requires them to consider, they are said to be **fettering their discretion.**

In certain situations, officials may have statutory authority to refuse to deal with matters over which they have jurisdiction. For example, a statute may give an official authority not to process a request where it is obvious that the request has no possibility of success. Similarly, a tribunal may have statutory authority not to hear a case where the documents submitted indicate that the case has absolutely no merit. Generally, however, the authority to rule out options is subject to two limitations:

1. An official with a power to exercise discretion cannot refuse to exercise that discretion. If an official has discretion, he or she must use it to make a decision on a matter within his or her jurisdiction when called upon to do

so by a member of the public entitled to a ruling. The official cannot say, "I don't like any of the options, so I refuse to make a decision." The official is required to select one of the available options. These options often include granting the request, refusing the request, or granting the request subject to appropriate terms and conditions. The official cannot say, "I am not going to consider whether I should exercise my discretion favourably or not."

2. An official with a power to exercise discretion cannot refuse to consider any factor that is relevant in deciding which option to choose. For example, some environmental protection laws permit government officials to order the current owner and all past owners of a property to pay for cleaning up pollution, regardless of whether they contributed in any way to causing the pollution. For example, the official has discretion to order a person who owned the property in 1990 to clean up pollution caused by the current owner, more than 10 years after he or she sold the property. However, this does not mean that the official can disregard the fact that the previous owner had nothing to do with the pollution. This is still a relevant factor that must be considered in deciding whether to order that person to pay for the pollution cleanup.

Officials have no authority to refuse to exercise their discretion in the ways described above. As long as the law allows them choices, they are required to give genuine consideration to each of those choices.

In practice, the rule against fettering discretion means that tribunals, for example, cannot make any binding rules that would require different panels to make consistent decisions in similar cases or would prevent panel members (adjudicators) from considering all options. Consequently, tribunals can never ensure that their decisions are entirely consistent. Nevertheless, adjudicators, as well as other government administrators, should attempt to minimize the degree of inconsistency in their own decisions and between their decisions and those of other panel members or officials. The next section suggests several ways in which decision-making bodies can reduce inconsistency without fettering the discretion of their officials.

[D]iscretion must still be exercised within a reasonable interpretation of the margin of manoeuvre contemplated by the legislature, in accordance with the principles of administrative law governing the exercise of discretion, and consistent with the *Canadian Charter of Rights and Freedoms*.

L'Heureux-Dubé J in *Baker v. Canada (Minister of Citizenship and Immigration)*, [1999] 2 SCR 817, at 853-54

Ways To Minimize Uncertainty and Inconsistency Without Fettering Discretion

POLICIES AND GUIDELINES

Where inconsistency in the exercise of discretion is a potential problem, it is advisable for the government department or agency to develop policies or guidelines to promote both consistency and fairness in decision making. However, these policies or guidelines must never be treated as binding rules or be used to justify the exclusion of choices provided by the law. A requirement to follow such directives slavishly also is a fettering of discretion.

Sometimes, a government department will establish policies for its administrators to apply in carrying out their functions, including the exercise of discretion. If a tribunal is called upon to review how those administrators did their job and it has the power to substitute its own views as to how the regulatory regime should apply, it is usually also appropriate for the tribunal to consider those government policies. However, the tribunal may not treat the policies as strict requirements, or this too will constitute a fettering of discretion.

The original decision maker or the tribunal reviewing the decision must follow ministerial directives only when required to do so by statute. If there is no statutory requirement, the directives should be considered, but both the original decision maker and the reviewing tribunal can refuse to follow the directives provided that the facts of a particular case justify their choice.

CONSULTATION

When an official is considering a decision that would be inconsistent with an earlier decision of the department or agency, consultation with others may be helpful. Government officials are generally free to consult other staff members when making decisions, and generally they are not required to disclose those consultations. Tribunal members, on the other hand, are more constrained in their ability to consult outside the hearing.

Except where a statute governing a tribunal excludes or places stricter limits on the right to consult, it is acceptable for an adjudicator to seek advice from other tribunal members, staff, counsel, or the chair as long as

- the adjudicator makes the final decision,
- the consultation is voluntary on the adjudicator's part,
- no one who is consulted puts pressure on the adjudicator to make a particular decision, and
- no new issues or facts are introduced without the parties being notified and permitted to comment.

CAUTION IN OVERTURNING DISCRETIONARY DECISIONS

In some cases, a tribunal reviewing discretionary decisions of a government official has statutory authority to overturn a particular decision only if the official was clearly "wrong," in the sense of acting outside his or her mandate, ignoring relevant evidence, or deciding on the basis of irrelevant factors. In other cases, however, the tribunal is given broad discretion to substitute its own decision for that of the official.

This kind of broad discretion should be exercised with caution. In the civil courts, higher courts will usually refuse to overturn a lower court's discretionary decision where the only basis for doing so is that the higher court prefers its own discretionary decision. The reason for this is obvious: when a tribunal superimposes its discretion on the discretion of another administrator, the certainty and predictability that a legal system should provide are eroded. Therefore, even if there are no explicit limits on a tribunal's exercise of discretion, discretionary decisions by other administrators are usually overturned only if they are unreasonable or unfair, or if the administrator followed an improper procedure in reaching the decision. In either case, the tribunal's reasons for overturning the decision should be clear. (See "Reviewing Discretionary Decisions.")

Reviewing Discretionary Decisions

Government departments and agencies do not always provide their administrators with policies or principles to assist them in discretionary decision making. When a tribunal reviews a decision made in these circumstances, it is helpful if the tribunal has established its own guidelines for deciding whether to overturn the decision or not.

Sometimes guidelines may emerge from the decisions of individual tribunal members.

Sometimes they may be developed by the tribunal as a whole. Both approaches are appropriate as long as the guidelines are not used to fetter discretion.

If guidelines are developed by the tribunal as a whole, they should generally be published. Parties to cases brought before the tribunal are entitled to know in advance what criteria the tribunal will apply in exercising its discretion.

SUBDELEGATION

The fourth important principle of administrative law is that *generally*, an official to whom the legislature has delegated decision-making power may not in turn delegate that power to someone else. This rule is expressed in the Latin phrase *delegatus non potest delegare*, which means "a delegate cannot delegate."

The purpose of the rule against **subdelegation** is to preserve the quality and ensure the fairness of decisions. The presumption behind the rule is that the legislature has chosen the delegate carefully, and another person may not have the same knowledge, skills, or qualifications. Equally important, when decision making takes place outside the established structure for the exercise of statutory powers, accountability for decisions may be compromised.

Subdelegation may be permitted in certain circumstances. Sometimes it is specifically authorized by a statute. Where there is no statutory authorization, whether subdelegation is allowed may depend on whether the power being delegated can be described as purely administrative (often requiring little or no exercise of discretion) or as quasi-judicial. Courts are more willing to subdelegate purely administrative functions than the authority to make decisions involving the exercise of discretion or determination of substantive rights. In practice, delegation of decision-making authority occurs across a wide spectrum of activities, and it is difficult to determine in any given case whether a delegation not explicitly authorized by a statute is valid or not.

PROCEDURAL FAIRNESS OR NATURAL JUSTICE

Distinction Between Procedural Fairness and Natural Justice

As discussed earlier in this chapter, traditionally the courts drew a distinction between decisions categorized as administrative and those characterized as quasi-judicial.

If a decision was considered administrative, there were no minimum procedures that had to be followed to ensure a fair outcome unless these procedures were explicitly or implicitly set out in the statute that authorized the decision-making process. For example, a decision as to whether an individual qualified for the services of a homecare provider would probably have been considered an administrative decision. If the official considering the application ignored the criteria that he was required to apply in making the decision and decided to deny access to the services, the individual might be able to successfully challenge the decision in the courts on the grounds that the official was acting outside his jurisdiction. However, there was no requirement for the official to give the applicant notice of his intention to make a negative decision, reasons for the decision, or an opportunity to challenge the decision. As a result, the applicant would likely never know whether the official had acted outside his jurisdiction or not, because in many cases the applicant would have no way of finding out what criteria the official had used in making the decision.

On the other hand, if the decision was considered quasi-judicial, the official was required to give the individual a hearing before making the decision. Refusal of a business licence or approval to carry out some regulated activity (such as the construction of a building) usually fell into this category.

Generally, if a government administrator denied a right or entitlement, the decision was considered quasi-judicial and the rules of natural justice had to be followed. If, on the other hand, an administrator denied a privilege or benefit, the decision was merely administrative and not subject to any common law rights of natural justice. Similarly, if a tribunal made a binding ruling, the ruling was considered quasi-judicial; but if a tribunal made a recommendation to government, the decision was generally considered administrative.

In practice, the line between administrative and quasi-judicial decisions was "sometimes dim and the consequences of drawing it [were] sometimes uncertain."[6] After decades of criticism of this often arbitrary distinction, as discussed earlier, in 1979 the Supreme Court of Canada ruled that certain minimal rules of fair procedure apply to the exercise of any statutory power that may result in the deprivation of a right or the denial of a benefit. At a minimum, anyone adversely affected by such a decision must be told the reason for it and given an opportunity to respond, or at least to "be heard" if not to have a full "hearing."[7] This rule applies whether the decision in question is characterized as administrative or as quasi-judicial.

Now, the standard of treatment required of all agencies, including tribunals, is referred to as "procedural fairness." "Natural justice" is still sometimes used to describe the particular kind of procedural fairness that applies to tribunals.

What Is the Duty To Act Fairly?

The duty to act fairly, also known as the "fairness doctrine" or the principle of procedural fairness, is simple to state: Whenever a public body (or, in some cases, a private one) makes a decision that affects a person's interests more directly or substantially than it affects the general public, that body has two obligations:

---

6   Robert F. Reid and Hillel David, *Administrative Law and Practice*, 2d ed. (Toronto: Butterworths, 1978), 119.

7   *Nicholson v. Haldimand-Norfolk Regional Board of Commissioners of Police*, supra note 5, at 328.

1. a duty to notify the person of the intended decision and to provide an opportunity to challenge that decision if it is unfavourable; and
2. an obligation to provide an impartial decision maker.

The fairness principle, while easily stated, is not so easy to apply. It is a procedural rule rather than a substantive rule. That is, it does not provide a right to a fair decision, but a right to a decision reached through a fair process. What constitutes a fair process will vary from case to case. It will depend on the character of the body making the decision, the kinds of functions that the body carries out, the nature of the decision, and the importance of the decision to persons who are affected by it. These aspects of the rule are discussed further below.

Which Bodies Must Act Fairly?

The duty to act fairly can apply to all kinds of regulatory bodies as well as to many kinds of decisions. However, the procedural safeguards to be applied may be more rigorous for some agencies than for others. In particular, tribunals are required to follow formal procedures similar to those of the courts. In addition, the second component of the duty to act fairly—the obligation of impartiality—applies more strictly to tribunals than to other government decision makers.

Decisions Subject to the Requirement To Act Fairly

The Supreme Court has said that procedural fairness obligations arise when an agency makes "any administrative decision which is not of a legislative nature and which affects the rights, privileges or interests of an individual."[8] Statutes that have codified this fairness right describe in various ways the types of decisions to which the requirement applies. (See "Decisions Requiring Procedural Fairness.")

Decisions Requiring Procedural Fairness

Alberta's *Administrative Procedures Act* applies when a person's "rights" are affected (s. 1(b)). More particularly, the Act refers to decisions that grant or revoke permission to do something; affect a status provided for under a statute; approve an act that would otherwise be illegal; prohibit someone from doing something that would otherwise be legal; or impose a duty on someone (s. 1(c)).

Ontario's *Statutory Powers Procedure Act* applies to decisions that affect a person's legal rights, powers, privileges, immunities, duties, or liabilities, including eligibility to receive a benefit or a licence (s. 1(1)).

Quebec's *Administrative Justice Act* applies generally to "decisions made in respect of a citizen," but specifically mentions indemnities and benefits (s. 1).

The kinds of decisions that typically attract a duty to act fairly include the following:

- *Licensing* Licensing is the approval of some ongoing activity, usually professional or commercial in nature, such as permission to practise law or medicine, sell real estate or cars, own or drive a taxi, operate a waste disposal site, or run a trucking firm. All of these are regulated activities, subject to specific criteria for qualification and to standards or rules of conduct.

---

8 *Cardinal v. Kent Institution*, [1985] 2 SCR 643, at 653.

- *Issuing permits*   The issuing of permits usually involves approval of individual projects. For example, building a house, constructing a septic system, installing a dock at the cottage, or damming a stream are all activities requiring an application to government for permission to proceed with the project.

- *Granting or denying a benefit*   Government administrators decide whether individuals qualify for financial allowances such as social assistance, insurance benefits, pension payments, or tax relief.

- *Determining eligibility to receive a service*   Government officials also decide whether individuals qualify to receive certain publicly funded services. For example, some individuals who are disabled may be entitled to a specialized transportation service provided by the local public transit authority. An official in a government office or agency may be responsible for determining whether an applicant has the extent or type of handicap that qualifies him or her for this service. Similarly, a community care access centre may assess the circumstances of an elderly person living at home to determine whether he or she qualifies for the assistance of a nurse, cook, or cleaner in order to remain in the home and avoid institutional care.

Decisions Not Subject to the Requirement To Act Fairly

Generally, government bodies and officials are not required to engage in public consultation before they make legislative or policy decisions, or decisions that address minor administrative matters. (However, see "Legitimate Expectations: The Exception to the Rule.")

Legislative or policy decisions establish rules or guidelines that apply to a particular group of persons. Often the group is very large. Although the decision

Legitimate Expectations: The Exception to the Rule

Although there is generally no duty to consult for policy or minor administrative decisions, there is an exception under the rule of legitimate expectations. Where a department or agency raises expectations of a certain result or that a certain procedure will be followed, either by promises or by a course of action on which people have relied, the department or agency may not change its practice or procedure where the change will have an adverse effect, without first notifying the persons who will be affected and giving them an opportunity to comment on the proposed change.

may have a substantial impact on any particular person, because everyone in the group is affected by the decision, no one has a right to be consulted. For example, when statutes are passed by elected assemblies, the proposed legislation is scrutinized by the entire body of elected representatives, and any representative may vote against the measure. However, the legislators have no additional duty to inform the persons who will be affected or to seek public input before the proposed statute becomes law.

In practice, such consultation often does take place, through discussion papers and invitations to make submissions to committees of the legislature or municipal council. Similarly, when Cabinet or a minister makes a regulation, although there is no common law duty to consult those affected or the general public, sometimes discussion does take place, and a few statutes now require it.

Components of Procedural Fairness

DUTY TO GIVE NOTICE AND AN OPPORTUNITY TO BE HEARD

The kind of notice that must be given and the nature of the opportunity to be heard vary according to the authority responsible for making the decision and the impact of the decision on the person affected.

The responsible authority is determined by the legislature. A particular type of decision may be delegated to an individual official or to a more formal tribunal.

Where the decision is delegated to an official, the duty of fairness is relatively simple. Often the official need only give notice of the intended decision; explain in writing the rationale for it and the facts on which it is based; and provide affected persons with an opportunity to respond. Usually an opportunity for a written response is sufficient. Sometimes a chance to respond orally is considered adequate. Rarely is it necessary to provide the kind of hearing held by a court.

Where the decision is delegated to a tribunal, much more stringent requirements apply. They often include the opportunity to be heard in person, to be represented by an advocate or lawyer, to summon witnesses to appear and testify, and to cross-examine the witnesses of the government. In addition, there is often an opportunity for others who may be affected by the decision, such as business competitors or neighbours, to participate in the proceedings.

The categories of administrative bodies involved range from administrative tribunals whose adjudicative functions are very similar to those of the courts, such as grievance arbitrators in labour law, to bodies that perform multiple tasks and whose adjudicative functions are merely one aspect of broad duties and powers that sometimes include regulation-making power. The notion of administrative decision-maker also includes administrative managers such as ministers or officials who perform policy-making discretionary functions within the apparatus of government. The extent of the duties imposed on the administrative decision-maker will then depend on the nature of the functions to be performed and on the legislature's intention. In each case, the entire body of legislation that defines the functions of an administrative decision-maker, and the framework within which his or her activities are carried on, will have to be carefully examined. The determination of the actual content of the duties of procedural fairness that apply requires such an analysis.

Imperial Oil Ltd. v. Quebec (Minister of the Environment)
(2003), 231 DLR (4th) 577, at 598-99 (SCC)

OBLIGATION OF IMPARTIALITY

The duty of impartiality applies to all who carry out decision-making functions within the structure of government. However, it applies in different ways to different administrative authorities. Impartiality has a very different application in decision making by government officials than it has in relation to tribunals. In addition, the Supreme Court of Canada has recently stated that impartiality does not apply to ministers in the same way that it does to tribunals.[9]

The right to an impartial decision maker has two components:

1. the decision maker must approach the decision with an open mind; and

2. the decision maker must be independent.

Only the first requirement applies to government administrators. These officials are not expected to act independently; indeed, their very purpose is to carry out government policy. However, they are still expected to be unbiased, to act in good faith, and to avoid conflicts of interest. For example, a person who is responsible for purchasing equipment for a government department and is closely related to the owner of a company competing for a contract should not take part in the decision-making process because there is an appearance of partiality.

Tribunals, on the other hand, often hear cases in which the government is one of the parties. To be able to provide a fair hearing, they must have sufficient structural separation and independence from government that they can make decisions without fear of reprisals and without even an appearance of bias.

A tribunal may appear to have a built-in bias where one of the parties that appears before it is a government department that approves its budget, appoints its members, provides its staff, or exercises control in other ways that may suggest that the department has influence over the tribunal's decisions. This kind of built-in bias is called **institutional bias**. If an agency's independence is restricted by the statutory framework that governs it, the appearance of bias does not prevent the tribunal from hearing the case, since the legislature has the right, subject to any violation of the constitution, to impose such restrictions. However, if institutional bias results from administrative arrangements that are not required by law, the entire tribunal could be disqualified from hearing a case. (See "Importance of Separation of Functions.")

Importance of Separation of Functions

Some government agencies are multipurpose bodies with responsibility for a variety of functions. Where individuals or groups within a multipurpose agency carry out conflicting functions, there is a risk of bias in decision making.

Agencies should be guided by the maxim "No man shall be judge in his own cause." A person who examines the basis for a dispute and forms an opinion on the correct outcome should not also act as the prosecutor and make the final decision. If the person has already reached a conclusion and is arguing that it be accepted, that person cannot be impartial in deciding whether the decision is correct and fair.

For this reason, Crown prosecutors in criminal cases are independent of the police who conduct the investigation, and they have the power to drop charges even if the police believe that the case should proceed to trial. Similarly, it is improper for a prosecutor to have any discussion with a judge outside the courtroom about a case that he or she is arguing.

The same kinds of restrictions apply to agencies. When an agency undertakes an investigation, carries out a prosecution, holds a hearing, and renders a decision, it is important to avoid conflicts of interest between the individuals or groups carrying out these different functions.

---

9 *Imperial Oil Ltd. v. Quebec (Minister of the Environment)* (2003), 231 DLR (4th) 577, at 599 and 601 (SCC).

The duty of impartiality ranks among the fundamental obligations of the courts. The *Canadian Charter of Rights and Freedoms* recognizes the right of any person charged with an offence to be tried by an independent and impartial tribunal (s. 11(d)). In the matters which fall within the legislative jurisdiction of Quebec, s. 23 of the *Charter of Human Rights and Freedoms*, RSQ, c. C-12, recognizes the right to a fair hearing by an independent and impartial tribunal as a fundamental human right. The concept of impartiality refers to the decision-maker's state of mind. The decision-maker must approach the issue submitted to him or her with an open mind, not influenced by personal interests or outside pressure. It is not sufficient that the decision-maker be impartial in his or her own mind, internally, to the satisfaction of his or her own conscience. It is also necessary that the decision-maker appear impartial in the objective view of a reasonable and well-informed observer. The duty of impartiality, which originated with the judiciary, has now become part of the principles of administrative justice.

Imperial Oil Ltd. v. Quebec (Minister of the Environment) (2003), 231 DLR (4th) 577, at 595-96 (SCC)

Where Fairness Obligations Are Found

In addition to any policies, rules, or guidelines that an agency might voluntarily impose on itself, there are four main sources of fairness obligations that bind agencies:

1. common law,
2. individual enabling statutes,
3. statutes of general application to agencies or tribunals, and
4. the *Canadian Charter of Rights and Freedoms.*[10]

For the most part, the rules of fair procedure have been developed by judges as part of the common law. A number of these rules have been incorporated into provincial statutes establishing tribunals. These statutory requirements are discussed below. Other fairness principles originating in the common law are reflected in provisions of the Charter, also discussed below.

In practice, procedural fairness requirements for an agency usually consist of the following:

- a few statutory rules;
- rules of procedure, guidelines, and practice directions developed by the agency; and
- supplementary requirements imposed by court decisions that have "read into" the statute any additional requirements needed, in the court's opinion, to ensure fairness.

---

10 Part I of the *Constitution Act, 1982*, RSC 1985, app. II, no. 44.

ENABLING STATUTES FOR INDIVIDUAL TRIBUNALS

Quebec's *Environmental Quality Act*[11] (EQA) is a typical example of an enabling statute that codifies fairness procedures. It permits the minister of the environment to issue pollution-prevention and pollution-cleanup orders. It sets out the procedures that the minister must follow to ensure fairness and also provides for an appeal of the order to the Administrative Tribunal of Quebec (ATQ). The fairness procedures that the tribunal must follow are set out in a separate statute, the *Administrative Justice Act*[12] (AJA). These procedures are discussed in the next section, dealing with statutes of general application.

The EQA permits the minister to order a person who has caused contamination to do studies, to prepare a remediation plan, and ultimately to decontaminate the polluted soil or water. At least 15 days before the order is to take effect, notice and a copy of the order must be sent to the person who will be required to carry it out. The order must include a statement of the minister's reasons for issuing it. The notice must tell the recipient when the order will take effect and offer that person an opportunity to make "observations." The notice must also be accompanied by a copy of every analysis, study, or other technical report considered by the minister in deciding to make the order (s. 31.44).

Notice must also be given to the owner of the property, if this is someone other than the person ordered to carry out the work, and to the clerk of the municipality where the contamination is located (s. 31.44). The municipality, the owner of the property, and any other person affected by the order have the right to appeal it to the ATQ (s. 96).

STATUTES OF GENERAL APPLICATION:
ONTARIO, ALBERTA, QUEBEC, AND BRITISH COLUMBIA

As discussed earlier, the concept of procedural fairness is based on common law principles developed and applied by the courts. Once common law principles are well established, governments often codify them by setting them out in a statute.

At various times, the federal government and several provinces have considered proposals to set out in a statute some minimum rules of fair procedure based on the common law principles, which all agencies, or at least all tribunals, would be required to follow unless specifically exempted. This approach has the benefit of promoting consistency in the application of fairness procedures among tribunals and of making the rules available in one place. Despite these obvious advantages, only Ontario, Alberta, Quebec, and British Columbia have passed statutes incorporating such general codes of procedure.

Ontario's *Statutory Powers Procedure Act*[13] (SPPA) and British Columbia's *Administrative Tribunals Act*[14] (ATA) apply only to tribunals, and not to government officials. The SPPA sets out procedures that all tribunals must follow (unless exempted by another statute) when they are required by law to hold a hearing or to give parties an opportunity for a hearing before the tribunal exercises "a statutory

---

11 RSQ, c. Q-2.

12 RSQ, c. J-3.

13 RSO 1990, c. S.22.

14 SBC 2004, c. 45.

power of decision" (s. 3(1)). British Columbia's ATA applies to tribunals, but only to the extent that the tribunal's enabling statute explicitly provides for this. Thus, a statute that establishes or governs a tribunal may not state that the ATA applies, or it may provide that some of the provisions of the ATA apply to the tribunal, but not others. When the ATA was passed in June 2004, it amended 25 enabling statutes to make the ATA apply, at least in part, to a number of tribunals dealing with matters such as health, transportation, housing, labour relations, employment standards, property assessment, and preservation of farmland.

Alberta's *Administrative Procedures Act*[15] (APA) also applies to persons authorized to exercise a "statutory power" (s. 2 and s. 1(a)); but in contrast to the Ontario Act, it applies only to seven agencies designated by a regulation under the APA and to a few others designated under other statutes.

Unlike the SPPA and the ATA, the APA does not apply only when the law requires a hearing before a tribunal. Its provisions apply before any statutory decision affecting rights or interests is made. However, the APA requirements are less stringent and formal than those imposed by the SPPA. They reflect the limited and flexible requirements of procedural fairness that the courts have imposed on internal government decision makers, rather than the stricter rules of natural justice that tribunals are required to follow. Thus, although the APA covers both formal, adversarial hearings and more informal internal decision-making processes, its requirements are geared toward the latter and may not always be adequate to cover the former.

The SPPA and the APA use different words to describe the kinds of decisions to which the specified hearing procedures do and do not apply. However, the results are similar. Both statutes apply to decisions authorized by a statute or regulation under a statute that affect the legal rights, powers, privileges, immunities, duties, or liabilities of a person, or a person's eligibility to receive some benefit, licence, or approval. The required procedures do not apply to hearings held by a court, legislative activities, or investigations or inquiries that result in a non-binding recommendation. The ATA, on the other hand, applies to all decisions of the tribunals to which it applies.

Because the SPPA and the APA apply to persons who have been authorized under a statute to make decisions that affect the rights of individuals, and not more restrictively to government or public authorities, their procedural requirements must also be followed by non-governmental organizations whenever they are making a decision that they have been empowered to make by a statute. Therefore, entities such as hospitals, universities, self-governing professions, and even private clubs and churches may sometimes have to follow the procedures set out in the SPPA or the APA.

Both the SPPA and the APA require the decision-making body to give notice to anyone whose rights will be affected by its decision. Under s. 3 of the APA, this is notice of the intention to make a decision, since the statute does not apply only to bodies that hold hearings. Under s. 6 of the SPPA, the tribunal must give notice of its hearings. Both statutes leave it up to the decision maker to decide the timing of the notice, although s. 10 of the APA gives the provincial Cabinet authority to establish deadlines. With respect to the content of the notice, other than stating

---

15 RSA 2000, c. A-3.

that notice must be "adequate," the APA leaves this matter to be determined by the decision maker; however, s. 10 of the APA gives the Cabinet authority to make regulations specifying the information to be provided in a notice. Section 6 of the SPPA requires that the notice must include

- the statutory authority for the hearing;
- the time and purpose of the hearing;
- whether the hearing will be held orally, electronically, or in writing; and
- other requirements specific to each type of hearing.

The APA also requires that notice must be given of the intention to hold a hearing and specifies information that must be included in all notices, as well as appropriate methods of delivering the notices. However, it does not specify who are parties to hearings or otherwise sufficiently affected by the proceedings that they are entitled to notice. That is left to the enabling statute for each tribunal.

The APA, SPPA, and ATA all require the decision maker to give parties an opportunity to provide relevant evidence. However, under s. 10.1 of the SPPA and under the ATA, the tribunal must permit reasonable cross-examination at an oral or electronic hearing, while s. 5 of the APA requires the decision maker to provide an opportunity for cross-examination only if information adverse to the interests of the party cannot be adequately contradicted or explained by other means.

The ATA and SPPA give parties the right to be represented by a lawyer or other agent, but s. 6 of the APA states that the right to make representations to the decision maker does not include the right to be represented by a lawyer.

Under the SPPA, the "default" position is a requirement for an oral hearing. Any departure from this format to a written or electronic hearing must be justified (ss. 6(4)(b) and 6(5)(c)). In contrast, s. 6 of the APA states that the right to make representations does not include the right to make them orally unless written representations are not adequate.

The APA, ATA, and SPPA all make it optional for the tribunal to require an oath before a witness or other party provides evidence, and permit the decision maker to receive evidence that would be inadmissible in court.

Although the APA is less specific than the SPPA and ATA about the information that must be given in a notice of intention to make a decision, it does impose a duty on the decision maker to inform the party whose rights will be affected by its decision of any facts in its possession or allegations contrary to the interests of the party in sufficient detail to permit the party to understand those facts or allegations, and to explain or contradict them (s. 4 of the APA). The SPPA does not contain a similar provision.

Finally, the APA and ATA require the decision maker to give all parties a written decision, including the reasons on which a decision is based. The APA goes even further, and also requires that the decision include the decision maker's findings of fact (APA, s. 7; ATA, ss. 51 and 52). In contrast, the SPPA requires a written decision with reasons only on the request by a party, and no statement of facts is required (s. 17(1)).

The SPPA and ATA deal with many issues that are not addressed in the APA, primarily issues that arise in the context of a formal hearing of the type required for tribunals and not in the context of the kinds of informal decision-making processes covered by the APA. Other matters covered by the SPPA and ATA include the authority of the tribunal to make rules of procedure, the summonsing of witnesses and their presentation of evidence, penalties for the failure of a witness to obey a summons, disclosure of evidence by parties (rather than by the tribunal as contemplated by the APA), pre-hearing conferences, correction of errors in tribunal decisions, enforcement of decisions, effect of appeals on the operation of decisions, and powers of the tribunal to control its process.

Quebec's *Charter of Human Rights and Freedoms*[16] states that every person has a right to a full and fair public hearing by an independent and impartial tribunal when that person's rights are to be determined. What is full and fair is left to be decided by the courts in their interpretation of this provision, and to be fleshed out in other statutes, such as the AJA.

Quebec's AJA sets out minimum rules for all administrative decisions, followed by more stringent rules for the ATQ and other bodies set up to resolve disputes. The ATQ (which, as noted above, was established by the AJA) replaces numerous individual tribunals with one large tribunal that has several divisions and makes decisions in various areas of regulation. The tribunal has a social affairs division, a territory and environment division, an immovable property division, and an economic affairs division.

Under the AJA, all administrative decision makers are required to act in a manner that is consistent with a duty to act fairly (s. 2). This includes giving citizens an opportunity to provide the decision maker with any information useful in making the decision, making the decision expeditiously, communicating the decision clearly, and providing the person affected with any information needed to permit the person to communicate with the decision-making authority (s. 4).

When an authority intends to order someone to do something, it must first inform the person of its intention and the reasons for the proposed order, advise the person of the substance of any complaints against him or her, and give the person the opportunity to present observations and produce documents (s. 5.5).

Adjudicative agencies are required to act not only fairly, but also impartially. Procedures specified under ss. 10-13 of the AJA include

- holding hearings in public (except where a hearing behind closed doors is necessary to maintain public order);
- rejecting evidence that is obtained improperly or is privileged;
- giving the parties the opportunity to prove facts and present arguments;
- providing assistance to parties where necessary and fair;
- allowing parties to be represented by lawyers or agents; and
- providing parties with a final decision in writing, including the reasons on which it is based.

THE CANADIAN CHARTER OF RIGHTS AND FREEDOMS

As discussed in chapter 1, the Charter is the part of the constitution that guarantees Canadians certain basic rights and freedoms. The Charter can provide those who deal with government agencies with a higher level of procedural protection than is traditionally required by common law and statutes. The rights and freedoms found in the Charter can impose fairness requirements on agencies in two ways:

---

16 RSQ, c. C-12.

1. If a statutory provision weakens fairness protections provided by the common law in a way that violates rights under the Charter, the courts can strike down that provision.

2. If a statute does not require a procedure that gives effect to a right or freedom set out in the Charter, the courts can read into the statute a requirement to follow such a procedure.   *FAIRNESS, PROTECTION*

The Charter provides for two classes of rights and freedoms:

1. In the first class are rights addressed by ss. 9, 11, 13, and 20, which are available primarily or only with respect to penal matters—usually decided by courts rather than tribunals or agencies. Generally, these provisions cannot be used to enhance common law or statutory fairness requirements for agencies, although ss. 11 and 13 may apply in some circumstances.

2. In the second class are rights addressed by ss. 7, 8, 12, and 14, which do not refer to the penal context. These are the principal provisions that may apply where government conduct affects a person's right to fair treatment, whether a punishment is involved or not.

The accompanying chart lists these applicable Charter provisions with a brief description of the right addressed by each section.

Protection of Procedural Fairness Under the Charter

Principal provisions	*Protected right*
Section 7	Life, liberty, and security of the person
Section 8	Security against unreasonable search or seizure
Section 12	Protection against cruel and unusual punishment
Section 14	Assistance of an interpreter in a proceeding

Other applicable provisions	
Section 11	Procedural safeguards where a person is charged with an offence
Section 13	Protection against self-incrimination by a witness who testifies in a proceeding

Section 7 provides protection against government interference with the right to life, liberty, and security of the person except in accordance with principles of fundamental justice. In Canada, since the abolition of capital punishment, no government body has the power to take a person's life. However, tribunals (as well as courts) do have the power to deprive a person of liberty—for example, by ordering that a person be confined to a mental hospital, requiring a person to accept medical treatment against his or her will, or refusing parole to a convict. Security of the person is affected when government action results in serious psychological stress.

The result is that s. 7 is potentially available whenever a government authority deprives a person of liberty or threatens the security of the person. The Supreme Court of Canada has confirmed that s. 7 can apply to tribunals and other government decision makers, but to date it has not extended the degree of fairness required by "fundamental justice" beyond what would likely be required by the common law doctrine of procedural fairness. Any statutory or common law procedure that does not entail a level of fairness appropriate to the process involved may not comply with s. 7.[17] However, it is generally not necessary to apply s. 7 in the context of decisions of tribunals, because application of the common law principles of procedural fairness will usually accomplish the same end.

I am of the view that section 7 is implicated when the state, by resorting to the justice system, restricts individuals' physical liberty in *any circumstances*. Section 7 is also implicated when the state restricts individuals' security of the person by interfering with, or removing from them, control over their physical or mental integrity. Finally, section 7 is implicated when the state, either directly or through its agents, restricts certain privileges or liberties by using the threat of punishment in cases of non-compliance.

Lamer J in *Reference re the Criminal Code (Man.)*, [1990] 1 SCR 1123, at 1177-78

Section 8 of the Charter prohibits unreasonable search or seizure. It applies to prevent government authorities from searching premises, seizing property, or demanding that a person produce documents or property or provide information unless those authorities have grounds to believe that an offence has been committed. Even then, a search or seizure is considered "reasonable" only after authorization has been obtained from a court. These restrictions do not apply to routine inspections or audits of regulated businesses and industries.

The reason the courts have given for requiring a warrant where government officials are investigating an offence, but not requiring one for a routine inspection or other administrative action, is that the right to be free from these kinds of scrutiny arises only where there is a reasonable expectation of privacy. The courts have decided that it is not reasonable for people carrying on businesses to expect to be free from routine inspections and inquiries.[18]

This does not mean that regulatory agencies have unrestricted powers to demand information or enter premises and take property. The courts have decided that once a regulatory agency has found evidence of an offence that may lead to the laying of charges, the agency must cease asking questions and making searches, and must obtain a search warrant for further searches or demands.[19]

---

17 *Blencoe v. British Columbia (Human Rights Commission)*, [2000] 2 SCR 307; and *New Brunswick (Minister of Health and Community Services) v. G. (J.)*, [1999] 3 SCR 46.

18 *Thomson Newspapers Ltd. v. Canada (Director of Investigation and Research, Restrictive Trade Practices Commission)*, [1990] 1 SCR 425; and *R v. McKinlay Transport Ltd.*, [1990] 1 SCR 627.

19 *R v. Inco Ltd.* (2001), 146 OAC 66; leave to appeal denied by the Supreme Court of Canada, March 7, 2002. See also *R v. Jarvis*, [2002] 3 SCR 757; and *R v. Ling*, [2002] 3 SCR 814.

> In a modern industrial society, it is generally accepted that many activities in which individuals can engage must nevertheless to a greater or lesser extent be regulated by the state to ensure that the individual's pursuit of his or her self-interest is compatible with the community's interest in the realization of collective goals and aspirations. ... It follows that there can only be a relatively low expectation of privacy in respect of premises or documents that are used or produced in the course of activities which, though lawful, are subject to state regulation as a matter of course.
>
> La Forest J in *Thomson Newspapers Ltd. v. Canada (Director of Investigation and Research, Restrictive Trade Practices Commission)*, [1990] 1 SCR 425, at 506-7

As stated above, s. 11 of the Charter generally applies in the context of penal matters. It provides certain procedural safeguards, such as the right not to be punished more than once for the same offence. However, a precondition for the application of s. 11 is that a person must be "charged with an offence." Generally, it is courts rather than tribunals that deal with offences.

Certain kinds of conduct brought before tribunals are referred to as "offences"—for example, serious violations of professional standards by lawyers, police officers, doctors, and other regulated professionals. However, the Supreme Court of Canada has ruled that s. 11 applies to administrative action when a finding of guilt can lead to a "true penal consequence"—namely, imprisonment or a fine that, by its magnitude, appears to have been imposed for the purpose of remedying a wrong done to society at large, rather than just disciplining an individual.[20] There are few circumstances in which an agency has the power to impose such punishments.

Section 12 of the Charter provides for the right of an individual not to be subjected to cruel and unusual treatment or punishment. In the context of administrative agencies, a decision to deport an immigrant, to require students to undergo random tests for drugs, or even to ban smoking in prisons might be argued to be cruel and unusual treatment.

Section 13 protects the right of a witness who testifies in a proceeding not to incriminate himself or herself. In contrast to the United States, where a person can refuse to testify before courts and tribunals if the testimony would reveal that he or she has committed an offence, a witness called before a Canadian court or tribunal must testify, even if this means providing evidence that he or she has committed a criminal or regulatory offence. However, this evidence, or any further evidence obtained as a result of this testimony, may not be used against the witness in any future prosecution of that person.

Section 14 of the Charter provides for the right to an interpreter in any proceedings where a party or witness does not understand or speak the language used, or is deaf. This section applies to proceedings before either a court or a tribunal.

Section 14 may not apply at the first level of decision making—for example, when a government official is making a decision that may be appealed to a tribunal. However, if the consequences of the action are significant, as in the case of a

---

20 *R v. Wigglesworth*, [1987] 2 SCR 541, at 559.

deportation hearing or a hearing before the Immigration and Refugee Board to determine whether a person is eligible for refugee status, the affected individual would probably be entitled to an interpreter if he or she did not have a good grasp of the English or French language.

So far, the courts have rarely found that Charter rights and freedoms apply to administrative actions by tribunals and other agencies. As discussed above, many of the guarantees of fair process provided by the Charter apply only to courts, and the application of the rules of procedural fairness in proceedings before tribunals and other agencies will often achieve the same result. The Supreme Court has ruled, for example, that the constitutional guarantee of independence for courts does not generally apply to tribunals.[21] However, the court has recognized that there may be circumstances in which the Charter could require a tribunal to be independent.[22] As the court said in the *Ocean Port Hotel* case, "The Constitution is an organic instrument, and must be interpreted flexibly to reflect changing circumstances."[23]

CHAPTER SUMMARY

Traditionally, the regulation of social and economic activities in Canada was a responsibility shared by three separate branches of government: the legislative branch, which passed laws; the executive branch, which implemented and enforced them; and the judiciary, which interpreted laws and resolved disputes by applying them to the facts of the particular case. As society became more complex and government regulation became more pervasive, governments began to establish a new kind of organization, the administrative agency, to carry out some of the functions formerly performed by the three branches.

For the most part, these agencies (also called boards, commissions, tribunals, and other names) were responsible for certain functions of the executive branch. However, they sometimes combined the functions of one or both of the other branches as well. In particular, tribunals had duties very similar to those of a court, although they were usually carried out in a less formal manner.

Because the functions of government were increasingly affecting the lives of Canadians, and in particular, because the new administrative agencies were not directly accountable to the public, it became apparent that a legal structure was needed to prevent government departments and agencies from exceeding their authority or acting in an arbitrary manner.

Initially, the courts developed several principles of administrative law to guide and restrict the exercise of statutory powers. The powers granted to a government body by statute constitute its jurisdiction, and administrative law prohibits an agency from straying beyond those powers in carrying out its functions. Similarly, a person to whom the legislature has delegated a function cannot delegate it to someone else unless the legislation authorizes such subdelegation.

---

21 *Ocean Port Hotel Ltd. v. British Columbia (General Manager, Liquor Control and Licensing Branch)*, [2001] 2 SCR 781.

22 Ibid., at paragraph 24.

23 Ibid., at paragraph 33.

Where government agencies have discretion, they must exercise it within their jurisdiction and in a reasonable manner. They must not fetter their discretion, but they may promote consistency in the exercise of discretion by, for example, developing policies and guidelines, consulting staff and other members of the tribunal, and applying caution in overturning discretionary decisions made by other administrators.

Most important, all government decision makers must follow a fair procedure when making decisions that affect a person's rights or interests. At a minimum, decision makers must consult affected parties and provide them with an opportunity to present their views before a final decision is made. In the case of tribunals, there are more rigid rules of procedural fairness called the rules of natural justice, which require a full hearing before the tribunal makes its decision. In addition, procedural fairness requires that tribunals must be impartial. Members of the tribunal must not be biased for or against a party to their proceedings, must keep an open mind, and must not have a conflict of interest. In addition, the tribunal itself must be structured in a way that ensures the independence of its members, particularly from other government bodies or officials.

KEY TERMS

declining jurisdiction   failure of an official or agency to carry out a statutory function that it has a duty to perform

discretion   the power of a government official or agency to choose a course of action from among a variety of options available under the law

fettering discretion   in relation to the actions of a statutory decision maker, refusing to consider an option that is available under the law, or refusing to consider any factor that is relevant to the choice of an option, when making a decision that affects a person's rights or interests

institutional bias   bias or the appearance of bias on the part of a group of decision makers in an agency, or of the agency as a whole, arising from aspects of the agency's structure or functions that suggest a lack of independence from a government official or body affected by a decision of the agency

jurisdiction   the scope of the authority or powers conferred on a government body or official by legislation or by common law

legitimate expectations   the principle that public officials who create the expectation of a certain result, or that a certain practice or procedure will be followed, should not be able to change that result, practice, or procedure where the change will have an adverse effect, without first notifying affected persons and giving them an opportunity to comment on the proposed change

natural justice   a body of rules or set of principles of fair procedure that tribunals must follow; *see* procedural fairness

procedural fairness   the requirement that a decision maker acting under a statutory power of decision must give any person whose rights or interests may be affected by the decision reasonable notice of the intended decision and an opportunity to respond, even if the function of the decision maker is not quasi-judicial in nature; *see* natural justice

subdelegation   in relation to a power or authority that a statute has delegated to a
particular person, the act of delegating that power or authority to another person

KEY CASES

Compelling Testimony: The Right To Remain Silent

*Thomson Newspapers Limited v. Canada (Director of Investigation and
Research, Restrictive Trade Practices Commission)*, [1990] 1 SCR 425

FACTS: Thomson Newspapers and some of its representatives were ordered to
appear before the Restrictive Trade Practices Commission to testify and produce
documents. The orders were issued in connection with an inquiry to determine
whether the company had engaged in predatory pricing. If the corporation refused
to comply with the orders, it could be punished. The corporation applied to the
court for a declaration that s. 17 of the *Combines Investigation Act*, under which the
orders were issued, violated the right to remain silent.

ISSUE: Did a corporation or its representatives have a right to remain silent when
under investigation for a trade violation?

DECISION: Section 17 of the *Combines Investigation Act* did not breach the Charter.
Unlike the United States, Canada does not have a blanket right to remain silent. The
Charter protects individuals from self-incrimination in certain circumstances. However, where a corporation is under investigation for a regulatory offence, a blanket
right to remain silent would thwart the aims of the Act since investigation would be
next to impossible. The power to compel testimony is important to the overall
effectiveness of an investigation under the Act. An absolute right to refuse to answer
questions would represent a dangerous and unnecessary imbalance between the
rights of the individual and the public's legitimate interest in discovering the truth
about trade practices. Section 17 strikes an appropriate balance. Since the investigation would not ultimately result in a criminal conviction for either the corporation or its representatives, there was no risk of self-incrimination. Also, corporations
have no right against self-incrimination since they cannot testify against themselves.

Impact of the Charter on Procedural Fairness

Blencoe v. British Columbia (Human Rights Commission),
[2000] 2 SCR 307; 2000 SCC 44

FACTS: Blencoe was serving as a minister in the government of British Columbia. In
1995 he was accused of sexual harassment. The premier removed him from Cabinet and dismissed him from caucus. After an investigation by the British Columbia
Council of Human Rights (now the British Columbia Human Rights Commission), hearings were scheduled before the British Columbia Human Rights Tribunal in 1998, over 30 months after the initial complaints were filed.

Following the allegations, media attention was intense and Blencoe suffered
from severe depression. He considered himself "unemployable" in British Columbia due to the outstanding human rights complaints against him. He commenced
judicial review proceedings in 1997 to have the complaints stayed, claiming that
the commission had lost jurisdiction due to an unreasonable delay in processing
the complaints. Blencoe alleged that the unreasonable delay caused serious preju-

dice to him and his family, and deprived him of his right under s. 7 of the *Canadian Charter of Rights and Freedoms* to liberty and security of the person contrary to the principles of fundamental justice.

ISSUE: Were Blencoe's constitutional rights to liberty and security of the person under s. 7 of the *Canadian Charter of Rights and Freedoms* violated by the lengthy delay?

DECISION: The Supreme Court of Canada held that the Charter applied to actions of the British Columbia Human Rights Commission, and s. 7 could theoretically be applicable. However, there is no constitutional right outside the criminal context to be "tried" within a reasonable time. Section 7 was not triggered in this case. The state had not violated Blencoe's liberty, because it had not prevented him from making "fundamental personal choices." Nor had the state violated his right to security of the person, because the direct cause of the harm to Blencoe was not the state-caused delay in the human rights process, but the allegations. It was the allegations against him that caused him to lose his position and suffer from negative press. At best, he was deprived of a speedy opportunity to clear his name.

Impact of the Charter on Procedural Fairness

New Brunswick (Minister of Health and Community Services) v. G. (J.),
[1999] 3 SCR 46

FACTS: The New Brunswick minister of health and community services had temporary custody of three children and sought to extend the custody order. The children's mother was indigent and receiving social assistance. Her application for legal aid was denied because custody applications were not covered under the legal aid guidelines. She then sought an order directing the minister to pay for counsel to represent her in the custody proceedings, and she sought a declaration that the legal aid guidelines violated s. 7 of the *Canadian Charter of Rights and Freedoms*.

ISSUE: Do indigent parents have a constitutional right to state-funded counsel when a government seeks to suspend custody rights?

DECISION: There was a constitutional obligation, under s. 7 of the Charter, to provide state-funded counsel in this case. The minister's application to extend the custody order threatened to restrict the mother's right to security of the person guaranteed by s. 7. When an indigent parent wants a lawyer to defend custody against the government, the judge must first ask whether the parent applied for legal aid or other state-funded legal assistance. The parent must first exhaust all possible avenues for obtaining state-funded legal assistance. The judge must then ask whether the parent can receive a fair hearing if unrepresented, giving consideration to the seriousness of the interests at stake, the complexity of the proceedings, and the capacities of the parent. If the judge is not satisfied that the parent can receive a fair hearing unrepresented, the government must provide state-funded counsel.

Procedural Fairness

Nicholson v. Haldimand-Norfolk Regional Board of Commissioners of Police, [1979] 1 SCR 311

FACTS: Nicholson was hired as a constable under an employment contract that included a 12-month probationary period. After 11 months, Nicholson was promoted. A few months later, the municipality terminated Nicholson's employment. A provision of a regulation under the *Police Act* provided that no police officer was subject to any penalty except after a hearing on appeal, subject to exceptions including the authority of the board "to dispense with the services of any constable within 18 months of his appointment to the force."

ISSUE: Was Nicholson entitled to procedural fairness?

DECISION: Nicholson could not claim the procedural protections of a constable who had worked for longer than 18 months. However, he had the right to be treated fairly. He should have been told why his employment was being terminated and allowed the chance to respond. If this had been done, and the board's decision was not arbitrary and was made in good faith, his termination would not have been reviewable.

Procedural Fairness and the Appearance of Impartiality

Imperial Oil Ltd. v. Quebec (Minister of the Environment),
[2003] 2 SCR 624; 2003 SCC 58; (2003), 231 DLR (4th) 577

FACTS: There was environmental contamination at a site once operated by Imperial Oil, and the minister of the environment ordered Imperial to pay for and submit a site-characterization study. Imperial refused to do the study, and asked the Administrative Tribunal of Quebec to quash the minister's order. One of Imperial Oil's arguments was that the rules of procedural fairness were violated because the minister was in a conflict of interest. The minister had been involved in earlier decontamination work and was being sued concerning contamination of the site by the present owners of the land. This case was heard by the tribunal, then by the Superior Court, then by the Quebec Court of Appeal, and eventually by the Supreme Court of Canada.

ISSUE: Did the minister have the appearance of impartiality required by the rules of procedural fairness?

DECISION: The minister had the authority to issue this kind of order under the *Environment Quality Act*, which allows for broad ministerial discretion. The minister's decision under the statute was mainly political, involving his duty to serve the public interest. He was not performing an adjudicative function. While the minister did have to comply with procedural fairness rules, such as providing notice to interested persons and providing reasons for the decision, the concept of impartiality did not apply to this decision. The minister was representing the public interest, not his own personal interests. The minister's decision was upheld.

Rule Against Subdelegation

Can-Du Air Ltd. v. Canada (Minister of Transport)
(1994), 25 Admin. LR (2d) 231 (FCTD)

FACTS: Can-Du Air Ltd. applied to the minister of transport for a certificate allowing it to operate a heliport. Can-Du passed all safety, operational, and environmental inspections. However, the minister of transport refused to approve the certificate based in part on the opposition of the city council and the deputy minister of municipal affairs, who claimed that the heliport was against the public interest.

ISSUE: Did the minister of transport make an unauthorized delegation of her decision-making power by relying on the opinions of the city council and the deputy minister of a different ministry?

DECISION: The minister of transport did not improperly subdelegate her power. Neither the city council nor the deputy minister of municipal affairs made the final decision. Rather, the minister of transport considered their opinions and agreed with them that the heliport would not be in the public interest.

REVIEW QUESTIONS

1. How do administrative agencies differ from the traditional departmental structure of the executive branch of government?

2. To what kinds of bodies does administrative law apply?

3. Explain two historical developments that led to the creation of a separate area of administrative law within the broader category of public law.

4. What are three goals that administrative law achieves?

5. What are the three main components or principles of administrative law?

6. What are the two components of procedural fairness?

7. What is an agency's "jurisdiction," and why is it important that an agency not act outside its jurisdiction?

8. What is "discretion," and what considerations must a decision maker bear in mind when exercising discretion?

9. What kinds of action or inaction constitute an abuse of a decision maker's discretion?

10. What is subdelegation? Why is it often not permitted? In what circumstances is it allowed?

11. What is the difference between "procedural fairness" and "natural justice"?

12. What kinds of agencies are required to apply the rules of natural justice?

13. What kinds of decisions must be made using procedures recognized by the courts as fair?

14. What kinds of decisions, if any, are exempt from the requirement to act fairly?

15. What are the components of impartiality, and how do they apply to tribunals and other agencies?

16. Where would you look to find the principles of procedural fairness that apply to

    a. agencies in general, and

    b. a particular agency?

EXERCISES

1. In chapter 1, you learned that laws can be divided into several categories: common law and statute law, public law and private law, statute law and subordinate legislation, and substantive law and procedural law. Into which of these categories does administrative law fit, and why?

2. Using the tools described in appendix B, find an example of each of the following anywhere in Canada (not including examples specifically mentioned in this book):

   • a government department or ministry that reports to a Cabinet minister;

   • an advisory agency;

   • an agency that regulates the sale or distribution of a product or commodity;

   • an agency that gives grants to businesses, charities, or other bodies, or to individuals;

   • an agency that operates a business or provides a service to consumers; and

   • a tribunal.

3. For each organization, briefly describe (where applicable)

   • how its members are appointed and by whom;

   • its main functions;

   • whether its members and staff, if any, are members of the public service;

   • what statutory steps, if any, the agency must take before making decisions that affect the public; and

   • what procedures the legislature has put in place to ensure that the agency is accountable for its activities (for example, the requirement to produce an annual report, whether the agency is subject to audit by a government auditor, or whether the agency must submit its budget to the government for approval or have its individual expenditures approved by the government before or after they are made).

FACT SCENARIO

A law society is an association established by a statute of the Legislative Assembly of a province (the *Law Society Act*). A law society is not a government agency. Rather, its membership consists of every lawyer in the province. Its board of directors consists of 40 lawyers (called "benchers") elected by the members from among their ranks, as well as four "lay benchers" appointed by the provincial government. Elections are held every four years.

The statute gives the law society authority to regulate the legal profession in the province. The purpose of the law society is to ensure that anyone who practises law in the province is knowledgeable and competent, and to protect the public against incompetent and dishonest lawyers.

The law society administers a course that all law students must pass before they can practise law. If a professor fails a student, the student has a right to appeal his or her mark to a committee of the law society. If a law student passes the course, the law society issues a "licence" authorizing that person to practise law.

The law society specifies standards of conduct that all lawyers must meet and practices that must be followed in maintaining a law office, such as keeping certain books and records, particularly financial records. It sets these standards through regulations under the *Law Society Act* and through binding rules that it can make under that Act, as well as policies and guidelines that are not binding. The benchers make these regulations, rules, policies, and guidelines.

Through its benchers, the law society also makes recommendations to the provincial government about changes to the *Law Society Act*; new regulations that the government, rather than the benchers, may enact; and other changes to practices and legislation that are favourable to its members—for example, increases in the rate of payment for legal aid cases and regulation of paralegals and others who are not lawyers but do certain kinds of legal work.

The law society also provides continuing education programs that lawyers are encouraged to attend.

All practising lawyers in the province are required to carry malpractice insurance provided by a branch of the law society. The *Law Society Act* prohibits the practice of law without payment of the insurance premiums.

The law society carries out random audits of law firm financial records to ensure that they are being kept properly. It also carries out random reviews of lawyers' files to ensure that a lawyer is providing satisfactory service to his or her clients.

In addition, the staff of the law society investigate complaints of malpractice brought by clients and by other lawyers. If the staff find that there has been a breach of any regulation or rule of the *Law Society Act* and a lawyer has fallen below an appropriate standard of conduct, a hearing is conducted before a panel of benchers to determine whether the lawyer is to be disciplined.

Lawyers on the staff of the law society act as prosecutors, bringing forward the evidence collected by other staff during the investigation. At the end of the hearing, the panel may find the lawyer guilty or not guilty of professional misconduct. If the lawyer is found guilty, possible disciplinary measures include a reprimand, mandatory re-education, a suspension of the licence to practise, or a permanent revocation of the licence.

1. Which of the functions described above are subject to the rules of procedural fairness, and which are not?

2. Of the functions that are subject to the rules of procedural fairness, which ones are subject to the more stringent requirements of natural justice?

Explain your answers.

FURTHER READING

Sara Blake, *Administrative Law in Canada*, 2d ed. (Toronto: Butterworths, 1997), chapters 2, 3, and 5.

Robert Macauley and James Sprague, *Practice and Procedure Before Administrative Tribunals* (Toronto: Carswell) (looseleaf), chapters 2, 3, and 5B.

David J. Mullan, *Administrative Law*, 3d ed. (Scarborough, ON: Carswell, 1996), chapter 3.

CHAPTER 4

Fairness: The Right To Be Heard

LEARNING OBJECTIVES

After reading this chapter, you will understand

- the relationship between natural justice and procedural fairness;
- the two main components of the rules of procedural fairness;
- the components of a hearing process that determine whether the process is a fair one;
- the common law rules of procedural fairness; and
- what departures from common law procedural fairness rules are permissible.

The Islands Protection Society is an environmental body that is comprised of approximately 1200 members. It concerns itself with matters of environmental interest in the Queen Charlottes. The society has filed a notice of appeal with respect to [two permits to spray pesticides on 300 hectares of timber on the Queen Charlotte Islands]. The society has requested that the appeals be conducted by way of oral public hearings. The [Environmental Appeal] Board denied this request and concluded that the appeals would be determined solely on the basis of written submissions. ... It is agreed that generally, in the absence of legislation, there is no absolute obligation upon an administrative tribunal to hold oral hearings in order to comply with the rules of natural justice. However, in this case the clear implication from the legislation is that an oral hearing is required. The legislation in this case contemplates the holding of open public hearings with full participation by interested parties. The Lieutenant Governor in Council has deemed the spraying of pesticides to be of such significance that it has given concerned members of the community who are not parties to the action the right to appeal or intervene. The issue of whether the board ought to either set aside or uphold the granting of the permits is of obvious public importance. It would be fundamentally wrong and against the rules of natural justice to hear and determine matters of such public importance without holding public hearings in which oral evidence and representations can be heard.

Islands Protection Society v. Environmental Appeal Board (1986), 8 CCLR (2d) 30

Over the centuries, the common law has developed principles to ensure that government decision makers, when making decisions that significantly affect people's rights, follow procedures that treat everyone fairly. In the past, these requirements applied only to decision makers making quasi-judicial decisions and were called the rules of natural justice. Today, they are called the rules of procedural fairness, and they apply whenever agencies make any decision, whether administrative or quasi-judicial, that affects people's rights, privileges, and interests.

The terms procedural fairness and natural justice are often used interchangeably. The distinction between administrative decisions and quasi-judicial decisions no longer governs whether procedural fairness is required. However, the actual procedures that are required still depend to some extent on the nature of the decision to be made, including where it falls on the decision-making spectrum, from purely administrative to quasi-judicial.

The term natural justice is sometimes still used to refer to the more stringent fairness rules that apply to tribunals. Procedural fairness is a broader term that encompasses fairness rules for all types of decision makers, whether they are bureaucrats or tribunals.

All government decision makers must follow fair procedures when making decisions that affect people's rights, privileges, and interests. For officials who follow an informal decision-making process, the duty to be fair often only entails giving notice of the intended decision and an opportunity to respond. For tribunals that hold a formal hearing, however, fairness often requires more elaborate procedures. These procedural restrictions apply to tribunal staff as well as tribunal members, and they apply both inside and outside the hearing room.

WHERE PROCEDURAL FAIRNESS RULES ARE FOUND

The procedures that tribunals must follow are usually set out in statutes. However, the statutes are often silent about the procedures that internal government decision makers must follow. These procedures may be set out in departmental guidelines or policies. For the minimum requirements that a bureaucrat *must* follow in a particular case, it is frequently necessary to look to common law fairness principles and try to apply them to the particular situation.

The Supreme Court in *Baker*[1] said that in determining the appropriate level of fairness and the specific procedures that must be followed, one should look at

- the nature of the decision (where it falls on the spectrum from administrative to quasi-judicial decision-making processes);
- the nature of the statutory scheme;
- the importance of the decision to the affected person;
- the extent to which the person affected has legitimate expectations of a particular process; and
- the extent to which the legislature intended the decision maker to have discretion to choose its own procedure.

---

1   *Baker v. Canada (Minister of Citizenship and Immigration)*, [1999] 2 SCR 817.

PERMISSIBLE DEPARTURES FROM COMMON LAW PROCEDURAL FAIRNESS REQUIREMENTS

If a statute or regulation sets out a more specific requirement than the common law fairness requirement, the statutory requirement takes precedence, regardless of whether it is more onerous or less onerous than the common law requirement.

For example, in Ontario, a person is entitled to refuse medical treatment unless a doctor convinces the Consent and Capacity Board that the patient lacks the mental capacity to make an informed decision. The *Health Care Consent Act, 1996*[2] requires that the hearing take place within seven days. This short time-frame takes precedence over the general rule that each side must be given adequate notice of the hearing. In other circumstances, under other statutes, "adequate" notice might be a month; in these circumstances, adequacy is determined by the fact that the hearing itself must be held quickly.

Similarly, although the evidence and arguments presented by one party must usually be shared with other parties, some statutes permit the adjudicator to scrutinize the information provided by one party without sharing it with the other parties, where allowing others to see it would result in some serious harm or loss to the party who provided the information. Statutes that give the public a right of access to government records while protecting personal privacy generally fall into this category. If the government refuses access to a document, this decision can be appealed to a tribunal. The tribunal will scrutinize the document to determine whether to order the government to release it, but the person seeking access to the document will not be permitted to see it, even though this would help him or her to argue his or her case effectively. If the applicant could see the document, he or she would win by default, the government would lose by default, and the proceedings would, effectively, be unnecessary.

THE COMMON LAW PRINCIPLES OF PROCEDURAL FAIRNESS

The basic principles of procedural fairness may be reduced to just two: the right to be heard and the right to an unbiased decision maker. Each of these pillars of procedural fairness has a number of components. This chapter discusses the components of the right to be heard. The components of the right to an unbiased decision maker are discussed in chapter 5, Fairness: Bias.

The Requirement To Provide a Form of Hearing

Whenever a government decision maker intends to make a decision that will substantially affect a person's individual rights, privileges, or interests, that person must be given an opportunity to be heard. However, that does not always mean holding a hearing, in the sense of a formal procedure like that of a court, where witnesses are sworn in, asked questions, and cross-examined. Rather, it means that all the information necessary to make a fair decision is received and considered.

There is no single formula for a hearing. In some cases, the presentation of the necessary information in writing will be considered a hearing; in other cases, the

---

2 SO 1996, c. 2, sched. A.

presentation of oral evidence and cross-examination of witnesses will be considered a hearing. In general, the higher the stakes are, the more procedural safeguards are necessary for a procedure to be considered a hearing.

The complexity and comprehensiveness of the procedures required for a hearing will depend on the nature and complexity of the issues involved and the seriousness of the consequences to the parties and the public of the tribunal's decision. For example, suppose that two parties oppose each other and the credibility of witnesses is in issue. A process that does not allow parties to know what witnesses have said about them and does not provide an opportunity for cross-examination will not be considered a hearing—or it will be considered an unfair hearing. Where there is only one party, a less formal process will sometimes meet the procedural fairness requirements of a hearing.

If a court is not satisfied that the decision-making process was fair, it may say that the decision maker failed to hold a hearing, or it may characterize the process as an unfair hearing. "Hearing" and "fair hearing" are sometimes used interchangeably.

The administrative statutes that govern provincial tribunals specify the minimum procedures that will be considered a "hearing" or a "fair hearing": in Ontario, the *Statutory Powers Procedure Act*[3] (SPPA); in Alberta, the *Administrative Procedures Act*;[4] in Quebec, the *Administrative Justice Act*;[5] and in British Columbia, the *Administrative Tribunals Act*.[6]

In Ontario, the requirements for a fair hearing before tribunals subject to the SPPA are generally more stringent than the requirements for hearings before tribunals that are not subject to the SPPA. Historically, one of the most significant differences between tribunals subject to the SPPA and other tribunals was that tribunals under the SPPA were generally required to hold an oral hearing in which the parties, witnesses, and tribunal members were all physically present and to permit cross-examination of all witnesses. Amendments to the SPPA in the 1990s changed this, allowing tribunals to hold written and electronic hearings without consent as long as such hearings do not prejudice any of the parties. In electronic hearings, some form of cross-examination of witnesses may still be required. In written hearings, the exchange of written questions and answers may be substituted for oral cross-examination.

Some tribunals that are not subject to the SPPA are specifically authorized by legislation to hold their inquiries in writing—for example, hearings by a board of review under ss. 14(3) and (5) of Ontario's *Family Benefits Act*.[7] Others can do this without legislation because the courts accept that the issues they deal with can be addressed in writing without creating unfairness, or because any potential unfairness in holding a written hearing is outweighed by the negative effects of holding a hearing where all parties are present. For example, a victim of crime may apply to the Criminal Injuries Compensation Board for compensation for injuries resulting from a crime. The board must be satisfied that the crime really occurred and that

---

3 RSO 1990, c. S.22.

4 RSA 2000, c. A-3.

5 RSQ, c. J-3.

6 SBC 2004, c. 45.

7 RSO 1990, c. F.2.

the damage was real, but the potential trauma to the applicant from allowing the perpetrator of the crime to be present and cross-examine the victim could outweigh the value of permitting the evidence to be tested in this manner.

The Requirement To Give All Parties an Opportunity To Be Heard

The tribunal's duty of fairness is owed not only to the person who initiated the process or from whom rights or privileges may be taken away. It also has a duty to ensure that all other parties and persons who may be substantially affected by the decision are given an adequate opportunity to present their cases. This principle is expressed in the Latin phrase *audi alteram partem* ("hear the other side").

One man's word is no man's word; we should quietly hear both sides.

Johann Wolfgang von Goethe

An adequate right to be heard usually implies a measure of equality, although precise equality is not always necessary. For all parties to be heard, it is not always necessary for all parties to present oral evidence in the presence of the tribunal and for witnesses to be cross-examined. In some cases, as long as each party has had an opportunity to submit written material and to respond to the other parties' written material, the hearing will be considered a fair one. In other cases, nothing less than a right to be present, give testimony orally, and cross-examine opposing witnesses will conform to the *audi alteram partem* principle.

COMPONENTS OF THE RIGHT TO BE HEARD

The Right to Notice

All parties and other persons whose rights, privileges, or interests may be substantially affected by the tribunal's decision are entitled to notice of the proceeding. This includes an explanation of the reason for the hearing, which usually involves setting out the decision that is being reviewed, the reasons for it, and the legal and/ or policy basis for the decision. The notice must also state the location of the hearing, the date the hearing will be held, and the time it will start.

The purpose of notice is to give the parties sufficient information about the subject matter of the hearing to allow them to prepare their case, and to give them enough time to do so. The notice should also give the parties a reasonable opportunity to arrange to attend the hearing themselves and to arrange for their representatives and witnesses, if any, to be present at the hearing. If persons other than the parties may be affected by the tribunal's decision, they must also be given notice; the notice should provide these other persons with information about their right to apply for party status or to participate in the proceeding in other ways.

Thus, the adequacy of the notice has two components:

1. sufficient explanation of what the hearing is about so that participants can prepare to address the issues; and

2. sufficient time to prepare.

Adequate notice also involves scheduling the hearing at a time when affected persons can be available.

The first element of notice is particularly important, but is not always followed. Decision makers whose decisions are being reviewed by a tribunal do not always explain their decisions in a form that allows the person challenging their decision to know exactly what they decided or why. This leads to confusion at hearings and unnecessary complexity, cost, and delay. For example, an adjournment may be necessary to provide further details of what was decided and why.

Sometimes the tribunal is responsible for drafting the notice explaining what the hearing is about and giving notice to interested people, and sometimes the notice is drafted by the decision maker whose decision the tribunal will review. For example, when a person appeals a municipality's land use planning decision to the Ontario Municipal Board, the board sets the date for the hearing but the municipality is responsible for sending out the notices.

LIMITS ON THE RIGHT TO NOTICE

In the absence of a statutory requirement, the right to notice does not include a right to disclosure of evidence. Disclosure of evidence means providing parties with all relevant information in the other side's possession that may be useful as evidence at the hearing. The purpose of disclosure is to give all parties, before the hearing begins, a reasonable opportunity to know the evidence that will be produced against the party, as well as evidence in the possession of other parties that may help them. Disclosure gives a party an opportunity to produce at the hearing evidence supporting its position that is in the possession of an opposing party when the other party may not put it before the tribunal because it would not help that party's case. Disclosure thus prevents "trial by ambush."

At common law, traditionally there was no right to advance disclosure of evidence in proceedings before tribunals, other than a right to know the basic substance of the proceeding. Instead, the common law required that, on the presentation of surprise evidence by one party, a request by the other party for an adjournment must be granted to allow the other party to prepare an adequate response.

The courts have been unwilling to recognize advance disclosure of evidence as a component of procedural fairness. However, the Ontario Court of Appeal has held that a tribunal cannot compel parties to disclose evidence in advance unless it is empowered by statute to do so or procedural fairness requires this.[8] In Ontario, the SPPA gives tribunals the power to require disclosure of evidence as well as particulars. Particulars are details and clarifications of allegations made by one party against another, or, where the tribunal staff presents the case, allegations made by the tribunal staff against a party.

The Right To Be Present

Parties have the right to be present at the hearing throughout the entire hearing process. This right allows parties to participate effectively in the process leading up to the decision in their case and to respond to all evidence and arguments brought by another party (or the tribunal, in cases where tribunal staff are the "prosecutors"

---

8   *Ontario (Human Rights Commission) v. Dofasco Inc.* (2001), 57 OR (3d) 693 (CA).

or accusers). No part of the hearing should be conducted without all parties being present, unless a party has voluntarily given up his or her right to attend, or has engaged in conduct that justifies depriving him or her of this right. (Barring a party from being present is limited to extreme circumstances—for example, where a party's conduct is so disruptive that it is impossible for the tribunal to conduct a hearing in the party's presence.)

One implication of the right to be present is that tribunal members may not discuss the matter with any party in the absence of any of the other parties.

The right to be present includes the right to attend any site visit that the tribunal might hold. (Site visits, or "taking a view" as they are sometimes called, are discussed in chapter 9, Presenting Evidence at a Hearing.)

In a written hearing, the right to be present takes the form of a right to receive all relevant information presented to the tribunal and a reasonable opportunity to respond to it.

In an electronic hearing, the right to be present is satisfied if all parties are able to hear each other and the adjudicator in a teleconference, or to see and hear everyone else in a video conference.

LIMITS ON THE RIGHT TO BE PRESENT

There are several circumstances in which a tribunal may proceed in the absence of a party:

- If a party has been served with notice of a hearing and does not attend, a tribunal may proceed in the party's absence. If a party does not attend, the adjudicator must be satisfied that the party was properly served with notice of the hearing. If there is satisfactory evidence that the party was served, the hearing may then proceed in the party's absence. (However, it is usually reasonable to expect a tribunal to wait at least 30 minutes and to ask one of the other parties or tribunal staff to contact the party and find out the reason for the absence before proceeding.)

- Where a party persists in disrupting proceedings, the tribunal may exclude the party to maintain order.

- If a party "walks out" of a hearing as a form of protest, the party has waived his or her right to be present.

- There may be rare occasions where the sensitivity of evidence justifies allowing a party's representative to have access to it, but not the party—for example, where the tribunal rules that the evidence must be kept confidential and there is compelling reason to believe that the party will not maintain confidentiality.

The Right To Be Represented

Parties have the right to present their own case or to have their case put forward by a lawyer or other representative. Moreover, parties have a right to choose who will represent them, and the tribunal must make reasonable efforts to accommodate the schedules of such representatives. This right of representation generally includes the right to have the representative question the client's own witnesses and cross-examine the witnesses called by other parties, to raise objections to procedures or the admissibility of evidence, and to make submissions.

LIMITS ON THE RIGHT TO BE REPRESENTED

The right to be represented is not absolute. For example, under s. 23(3) of Ontario's SPPA, tribunals may refuse to allow a representative (other than a lawyer) to take part in the proceedings if the conduct of the representative demonstrates that he or she is incompetent to perform the task, or if he or she does not comply at the hearing with the duties and responsibilities of an advocate or adviser. Tribunals that are not subject to the SPPA could probably do the same because of their inherent right to control their process. If the tribunal does bar a representative from participating, under some circumstances fairness may require the tribunal to adjourn the proceedings to permit the party an opportunity to find another representative. In other circumstances, however, it may be reasonable to require the party to continue without a representative. Parties do sometimes have to accept responsibility for their choice of representatives.

The right to be represented also does not give a party an absolute right to an adjournment to obtain representation. A party is entitled to a reasonable opportunity to find a lawyer or other suitable representative. However, if the tribunal finds that the party has not taken advantage of the opportunity and a delay will cause serious inconvenience to other parties and raise the cost of the hearing, the tribunal may be justified in refusing an adjournment to find a lawyer or agent.

It is good practice for the tribunal or its members to advise parties as early as possible of their rights to be represented, to inquire whether parties intend to be represented, and to ask how much time will be needed to find representation and what efforts will be made. If the tribunal has taken these steps, a tribunal member is in a much better position to establish whether reasonable steps have been taken to obtain representation and to refuse an adjournment that he or she believes is being requested for the purposes of delay.

Parties are not always entitled to their first choice of representative. If a hearing date has been set, lawyers and agents have a responsibility to the tribunal and to their clients not to accept retainers if they know that they will not be available on that date. There may be exceptional cases where a representative is justified in accepting a case even though he or she is not available on the date set for the hearing (for example, where efforts to find other counsel have been unsuccessful, or where the lawyer or agent has an intimate knowledge of the case that other representatives would not have). In some circumstances, however, the tribunal may be justified in refusing to adjourn a hearing when a party chooses a representative who is not available at the date scheduled for the hearing, even if this will result in the party losing the opportunity to be represented. Obviously, any step that will deprive a party of his or her right to be represented should be taken only if the party is first given a reasonable opportunity to find a representative who will be available on the date of the hearing, and only after considering all the implications for the parties and the public purse.

The Right To Present Evidence

Parties have the right to present evidence in order to establish the facts in the case. Only after the facts are clear is it possible to determine how the law should apply to them.

Parties must have a reasonable opportunity to produce relevant information in an attempt to prove the facts they want the tribunal to accept, and to disprove unfavourable allegations by other parties. Usually, the main witnesses are the parties themselves. However, the parties often call other people as witnesses and may also present documents, pictures, and physical objects as evidence.

A corollary of the right of a party to present evidence is that there must be an appropriate mechanism to require other persons who have relevant information to provide it to the party or to the tribunal. Usually, this mechanism is a summons (sometimes called a "subpoena") issued by the tribunal to a witness that requires the witness to attend the hearing, bring relevant documents, and present evidence. Failure to comply with a summons issued under Ontario's SPPA is an offence. For Ontario tribunals that are not subject to the SPPA, their governing statute may make it an offence to ignore a summons.

In addition, rules that require the disclosure of evidence in advance of a hearing are meant to ensure that parties obtain the evidence necessary to exercise their right to present evidence, so that the tribunal does not have to first serve summonses compelling witnesses to attend the hearing.

LIMITS ON THE RIGHT TO PRESENT EVIDENCE

The right to present evidence does not always mean that a party has the right to present evidence orally in the presence of tribunal members. In some circumstances, an electronic or written hearing may be sufficient. Moreover, a tribunal may refuse certain kinds of information for several reasons—for example, because the information was not disclosed in advance of the hearing in compliance with the tribunal's rules of procedure, or because the information is irrelevant or unreliable (see chapter 10, Management and Control of the Hearing Process).

The Right To Cross-Examine

Parties have the right to know the evidence being brought against them and to respond to it. They must have a fair opportunity to learn of any information that is unfavourable to them and to correct or contradict it.

In an oral hearing, this right generally requires the tribunal to provide each party with an opportunity to cross-examine the other party's witnesses, unless there is some other equally effective method of testing a witness's evidence. In fact, the right to cross-examine witnesses in adversarial proceedings has been described as "fundamental" and "a vital element" of the system.[9] The purpose of cross-examination is to give parties an opportunity to challenge the evidence given by the other side's witnesses. Cross-examination may show that the evidence is untrue, bring out additional significant facts, or shed a different light on what the witness has said.

Where a tribunal is permitted to hold a written hearing or inquiry, or is not subject to the SPPA or some other statutory duty to allow cross-examination, the tribunal may meet the requirements of procedural fairness by giving a party access to all the written evidence and submissions on which the tribunal may rely, as well as the opportunity to respond in writing to the evidence and submissions.

---

9 *Howe v. Institute of Chartered Accountants (Ontario)* (1994), 27 Admin. LR (2d) 118, at 137 (CA), per Laskin JA (dissenting); *Innisfil (Township) v. Vespra (Township)* (1981), 123 DLR (3d) 530, at 545 (SCC).

LIMITS ON THE RIGHT TO CROSS-EXAMINE

The right to cross-examine does not mean that a party or a party's representative is allowed to ask irrelevant, inflammatory, abusive, or repetitive questions. Ontario's SPPA and British Columbia's ATA give tribunal members the right to place reasonable limits on cross-examination, and it is likely that other tribunals' inherent right to control their process gives them the same authority.

Whether a tribunal has the right to disallow cross-examination in order to ensure an inexpensive and expeditious hearing may vary from case to case. The Workplace Safety and Insurance Appeals Tribunal allows a limited form of cross-examination in some circumstances, which it calls "cross-questioning." (See chapter 9, Presenting Evidence at a Hearing, for a discussion of limits on "friendly" cross-examination.) Ontario's Information and Privacy Commissioner requires parties at oral hearings to direct questions to the witness through the adjudicator.

The Requirement That the Person Who Hears Must Decide

The person who hears a case is the only person who may decide the case. This has two implications. First, it is generally improper for an adjudicator who was absent for any part of a hearing to take part in making the decision. (There may, however, be exceptions, such as when all parties consent and there is an effective way of informing a new or substitute tribunal member of the evidence heard in his or her absence.) Second, it is improper for anyone associated with a tribunal, such as the chair, other tribunal members, or tribunal staff, to put pressure on a hearing panel to make the decision in favour of one party or another or to change an intended decision.

EXCEPTIONS AND LIMITS TO THIS REQUIREMENT

Subject to certain statutory restrictions,[10] if a member of a tribunal or panel cannot complete the hearing for some reason (for example, prolonged illness or death), the remaining members may complete the hearing and render a decision. Generally, a departing member's place cannot be taken by a new member or adjudicator partway through the hearing, unless all parties consent to the replacement. It would be improper for the tribunal to put any pressure on the parties to accept such an arrangement. In some cases, however, the parties may agree that, rather than continuing with few members, it is better to have a new member join the panel and permit that member to rely in part on a transcript or agreed statement of the evidence given earlier in the hearing. If the panel consisted of a single member, his or her departure would mean that the hearing has to start over. To avoid that result, the parties might prefer to have the member's replacement read transcripts or agreed statements of the evidence and complete the hearing using this information.

The rule that only a member who hears a case can decide it does not prohibit that member from seeking the advice of other tribunal members, tribunal counsel, or tribunal staff (a practice sometimes known as "collegial decision making").

---

10 For example, the remaining members may not be permitted to render a decision where a statute requires that the panel include representatives of groups opposed in interest, such as management and a labour union, and the remaining members do not include a representative of each interest group; or where the statute specifies that a panel must consist of a certain number of members.

However, there are limits on the scope of such consultation. First, consultation must be voluntary unless required by statute. It is improper for the tribunal chair or other members to put pressure on the adjudicator to consider their views. Second, the consultation should be limited to questions of law and policy. If new issues or legal arguments are raised as a result of consultation, the parties should be given an opportunity to address them. Finally, the tribunal member must not rely on evidence or facts provided by his or her colleagues without taking precautionary steps. The member must notify all parties that he or she is considering relying on other evidence, and must give the parties an opportunity to challenge not only the accuracy of the evidence but also his or her right to consider it. (The right to consultation is discussed in more detail below.)

The Requirement To Base the Decision Solely on the Evidence

Parties have the right to expect that the tribunal's decision will be based on the facts established at the hearing, and not on other information. An adjudicator who relies on facts within his or her own knowledge or on facts learned outside the hearing compromises the integrity of the hearing process. Not only is there a possibility that such information is incorrect, but parties would not have an opportunity to respond to it or to influence how the adjudicator uses it.

EXCEPTION TO THIS REQUIREMENT

There is an exception to this rule known as "judicial notice" or "administrative notice." Adjudicators are entitled to "take notice" of facts that would be known to a well-informed member of the community (for example, that Ontario is a province of Canada) or that would be known by a well-informed member of a professional group, particularly when the tribunal consists of members of that profession. (This exception is described in more detail in chapter 12, Tribunal Decision-Making Procedures.)

The Requirement To Give Reasons for the Decision

It is now established that procedural fairness requires tribunals and other decision makers to provide reasons for their decisions, at least in situations where the decisions may affect an individual's rights, privileges, or interests, or where reasons are necessary for the exercise of a right of appeal. This duty is also reflected in Alberta's *Administrative Procedures Act* (s. 7), Quebec's *Administrative Justice Act* (ss. 5 and 13), British Columbia's *Administrative Tribunals Act* (s. 51), and Ontario's *Statutory Powers Procedure Act* (s. 17(1)) (but only where a party requests reasons).

However, the courts have yet to require that reasons be detailed or well thought out. In *Baker*,[11] the case in which the Supreme Court first ruled that reasoned decisions are a component of procedural fairness, the court accepted the notes of an administrator as the Immigration Department's "reasons" for a decision to deport a woman under the *Immigration Act*. In another case, a court accepted that checking a box on a prescribed form was enough to fulfill the requirement to provide reasons.[12]

---

11 Supra note 1.

12 *Liang v. Canada (Minister of Citizenship and Immigration)*, [1999] FCJ no. 1301 (TD).

CHAPTER SUMMARY

All government decision makers must follow fair procedures when making decisions that affect people's rights, privileges, and interests. However, what is "fair" depends on the nature and function of the decision-making body. Traditionally, agencies were required to follow fair procedures, known as principles of natural justice, only when exercising their powers in a quasi-judicial manner. Today, all agencies must, at a minimum, give affected people an opportunity to comment before making decisions. Procedures similar to those of courts are followed primarily by tribunals, and tribunals must apply the rules of procedural fairness more rigorously than other agencies.

The requirements of natural justice for tribunals were dictated originally by the courts. Today, however, many of the rules of procedural fairness are prescribed by statute, either a statute that establishes a tribunal or sets out its powers or, in some cases, a statute that has general application to a variety of tribunals.

One of the basic components of natural justice is the right to a hearing. The right to a hearing includes the right to reasonable notice; the right to be present throughout the proceedings; the right to be represented by a lawyer or agent; the right to present and to challenge evidence; the right to have the decision made only by the person who heard the case, without interference by others; the right to have the decision based solely on the evidence; and the right to be given reasons for the decision.

KEY CASES

Disclosure and Fairness

Howe v. Institute of Chartered Accountants (Ontario)
(1994), 19 OR (3d) 483; 27 Admin. LR (2d) 118 (CA)

FACTS: Howe was a chartered accountant charged with breaching the *Rules of Professional Conduct* by the Professional Misconduct Committee of the Institute of Chartered Accountants of Ontario. An investigation report was written by J., who was advised by the committee that the report would be kept confidential. The committee therefore refused to disclose the report to Howe, who applied to the Divisional Court for an order compelling disclosure. The Divisional Court refused the application, ruling that the application for judicial review was premature because there was an appeal remedy still available.

ISSUE: Was judicial review of a preliminary ruling appropriate?

DECISION: The court should interfere with a preliminary ruling, such as the tribunal's refusal to order disclosure of the report, only where the tribunal did not have jurisdiction. There was no denial of natural justice. There was a complete remedy by way of appeal, and the panel would have full authority to consider the request for disclosure when it was convened.

Procedural Fairness and Legitimate Expectations

Baker v. Canada (Minister of Citizenship and Immigration), [1999] 2 SCR 817

FACTS: A woman with Canadian-born children was ordered deported and told to make her application for permanent-resident status from outside Canada, as is normally required. She then applied for an exemption from this requirement, based on humanitarian and compassionate considerations. A senior immigration officer refused her request by letter, without providing reasons for the decision. However, she received the notes of the investigating officer, which were used by the senior officer in making his decision. The woman's application for judicial review was first heard by the Federal Court Trial Division, then by the Federal Court of Appeal, and finally by the Supreme Court of Canada.

ISSUE: What was the appropriate duty of procedural fairness in this case?

DECISION: The duty of procedural fairness depends on the particular statute and the rights affected. Factors that will affect the content of the duty of fairness include the following: the nature of the decision and the process used to make it; the provisions of the relevant statute; the importance of the decision to the people affected; the legitimate expectations of the person challenging the decision; and the agency's choices of procedure.

There was no legitimate expectation affecting the content of the duty of procedural fairness in this case. Important interests were affected, but a lack of an oral hearing did not constitute a violation of the requirement of procedural fairness, because the opportunity to produce full and complete written documentation was sufficient.

Nevertheless, the immigration officer's notes gave the impression that the decision might have been swayed by the fact that the woman was a single mother with several children and had been diagnosed with a psychiatric illness. This raised a reasonable apprehension of bias. Also, the notes did not indicate that the decision was made in a manner that properly considered the interests of the children. The immigration officer's decision was quashed.

REVIEW QUESTIONS

1. What are the elements of a fair hearing before a tribunal?

2. If you are appearing before a tribunal, what are three sources of law you would review to determine the procedures that the tribunal is required to follow to ensure a fair hearing?

3. Explain the phrase *audi alteram partem*.

4. What are the characteristics of an adequate notice of a hearing?

5. Under what circumstances, if any, can a tribunal receive evidence or hear submissions in the absence of a party?

6. Does a party always have the right to be represented by a lawyer? If so, is the party always entitled to his or her first choice of lawyer? Does a party have a right to be represented by someone who is not a lawyer?

7. Does a party always have a right to cross-examine other witnesses? What methods other than cross-examination may a party use to challenge the evidence of an opposing party?

8. If a tribunal member is absent during the presentation of some of the evidence, under what circumstances may he or she participate in making the decision in the case?

9. When is the term "natural justice" rather than "procedural fairness" used to describe the duty of a government organization to hear a person's views before making a decision that affects him or her?

10. What are the components of a fair hearing?

11. Tribunal procedures are usually considered fair only if they do the following things: give potential parties notice of a hearing, allow parties to be present throughout the whole hearing, allow parties to be represented by counsel or agents, and allow parties to cross-examine the witnesses of other parties. What are the limits or exceptions to the duty to follow these procedures?

EXERCISES

1. The provincial government proposes to establish a fund to compensate travellers who did not get what they paid for after they arranged a vacation through a travel agency. For example, if the hotel is half finished and infested with cockroaches and the chartered flight doesn't arrive to take them home, travellers would apply to the fund to be reimbursed for their losses.

   The fund would be established by amending the *Travel Agents Act*, which regulates this industry. The amendment would permit the government to make regulations determining who must pay into the fund, how much they must pay, how and under what circumstances travellers may make claims, and what criteria will be used in determining whether to compensate them and the amount of compensation.

Is the government required by principles of procedural fairness to provide any individuals or groups with an opportunity to be heard before amending the statute? If so, who is entitled to procedural fairness and what kind of consultation or hearing would satisfy the requirements of procedural fairness?

2. The legislature passes the amendments to the *Travel Agents Act*, and the minister of tourism proceeds to draft regulations to establish the compensation fund. The regulations provide that all licensed travel agents must pay a specified amount into the fund each year. Every travel agency must pay the same amount, regardless of size and income. However, the amount may be increased or decreased based on the number of past claims against the agency. The minister announces the amount that each travel agency will be required to pay into the fund each year.

The Consumers Association of Canada complains that the amount of the payment is too low and that the criteria for payment are too narrow to provide fair compensation. The travel agents, on the other hand, claim that it is unfair to increase the amount of contribution based on claims against travel agencies, because problems that travellers encounter are often beyond the agency's control. In addition, small agencies claim that the proposed contribution is too high and will put them out of business. They feel that it would be fairer to base the contribution on the annual income of the travel agency.

   a. Is the government required by principles of procedural fairness to provide any individuals or groups with an opportunity to be heard before making the regulation? If so, who is entitled to procedural fairness and what kind of consultation or hearing would satisfy the requirements of procedural fairness under these circumstances?

   b. Would your answer be any different if, in a letter to the Travel Agents Association, the minister of tourism had stated two years earlier that he understood the need to take into account the size of travel agencies in setting fees and would consult with the association before making a regulation?

3. The regulation establishing the compensation fund has been made. It provides for aggrieved travellers to make claims to the fund. It states that a customer is entitled to be reimbursed for travel services paid for but not provided. The registrar of travel agencies, an official of the ministry, is designated to decide whether to approve claims.

The registrar develops criteria for determining who is eligible, such as the kind of information that a customer must provide to support her claim, and guidelines and procedures governing the application process.

Does procedural fairness require that the registrar provide an opportunity for consultation or a hearing before finalizing these criteria, guidelines, and procedures? If so, who is entitled to procedural fairness and what kind of consultation or hearing would satisfy the requirements of procedural fairness under these circumstances?

4. Amelia X applies for compensation from the fund. She alleges that she paid the Wings of a Dove Travel Agency for a vacation in a four-star hotel, but the hotel turned out to be a two-star hotel. The registrar is concerned about whether the information she has provided supports her claim and is considering refusing the claim.

    Does procedural fairness require that the registrar provide an opportunity for consultation or a hearing before finalizing these criteria, guidelines, and procedures? If so, who is entitled to procedural fairness and what kind of consultation or hearing would satisfy the requirements of procedural fairness under these circumstances?

5. If the registrar refuses Amelia's claim, does procedural fairness require that she have a right to appeal the decision? If so, what appeal procedures would satisfy the requirement for procedural fairness under these circumstances?

6. Suppose the *Travel Agents Act* does provide Amelia with a right to appeal the registrar's decision to a tribunal, the Travel Compensation Fund Appeal Board. Do the principles of procedural fairness apply to this tribunal? If so, what appeal procedures would satisfy the requirement for procedural fairness under these circumstances? Would the principles of procedural fairness require that anyone other than Amelia have an opportunity to participate in the appeal?

FURTHER READING

Sara Blake, *Administrative Law in Canada*, 2d ed. (Toronto: Butterworths, 1997), chapter 2.

Julie Maciura and Richard Steinecke, *The Annotated Statutory Powers Procedure Act* (Aurora, ON: Canada Law Book, 1998).

CHAPTER 5

Fairness: Bias

LEARNING OBJECTIVES

After reading this chapter, you will understand

- the meaning of impartiality and bias in the context of administrative agencies;
- why impartiality is an essential component of procedural fairness;
- the relationship between conflict of interest and bias;
- the difference between individual bias and institutional bias;
- the kinds of interests and conduct that may lead parties to believe that an adjudicator is biased;
- the relationship between an agency's independence and its impartiality; and
- factors that may be taken into account in determining whether an agency has an institutional bias.

[I]n considering whether there was a real likelihood of bias, the court does not look at the mind of the justice himself or at the mind of the chairman of the tribunal, or whoever it may be, who sits in a judicial capacity. It does not look to see if there was a real likelihood that he would, or did, in fact favour one side at the expense of the other. The court looks at the impression which would be given to other people. Even if he was as impartial as could be, nevertheless if right-minded persons would think that, in the circumstances, there was a real likelihood of bias on his part, then he should not sit. And if he does sit his decision cannot stand. Nevertheless, there must be a real likelihood of bias. Surmise or conjecture is not enough. There must be circumstances from which a reasonable man would think it likely or probable that the justice, or chairman, as the case may be, would, or did, favour one side unfairly at the expense of the other. The court will not inquire into whether he did, in fact, favour one side unfairly. Suffice it that reasonable people might think he did. The reason is plain enough. Justice must be rooted in confidence: and confidence is destroyed when right-minded people go away thinking: "The judge was biased."

Lord Denning in *Metropolitan Properties Co. (F.G.C.) Ltd. v. Lannon*, [1969] 1 QB 577, at 599

IMPARTIALITY: THE SECOND PILLAR OF PROCEDURAL FAIRNESS

As discussed in chapter 4, Fairness: The Right To Be Heard, the first pillar of procedural fairness is the right to be heard. The second pillar of procedural fairness is impartiality. Parties have a right to have their case heard by an adjudicator who is impartial. An impartial decision maker is one who is not biased for or against any of the parties and who would not be perceived as biased by a reasonable and well-informed observer.

THE TWO ELEMENTS OF IMPARTIALITY: INDIVIDUAL IMPARTIALITY AND INSTITUTIONAL IMPARTIALITY

Impartiality has two elements. First, the decision maker must be free from individual **bias**. Second, the tribunal or other agency to which the decision-maker belongs must not be structured in a way that suggests that its decisions will be biased in favour of one party or another. The impartial, unbiased adjudicator will not have prejudged the issues or have a predisposition in favour of one side or the other.

In the case of tribunals, the impartiality requirement has two components. First, the decision maker must start the hearing with an open mind and must reserve judgment until all evidence and arguments have been presented. If he or she is inclined to support one party's position over the other's, and if this bias is not institutional (see below), the decision maker is said to be influenced by personal bias.

Second, to be perceived as impartial, the tribunal itself must be reasonably independent of any government agency that is a party to its hearings. If the tribunal is structured in a way that does not permit its members to decide freely between the parties in accordance with the applicable law, the decision makers are said to be influenced by **institutional bias**.

ACTUAL BIAS AND REASONABLE APPREHENSION OF BIAS

A decision maker is biased when he or she does not approach a decision with an open mind. A decision maker may not have an open mind for various reasons. For example, the decision maker may stand to benefit financially from the outcome of a decision, or may be in love with or may strongly dislike a person who will be affected by the decision.

Where a decision maker has a predisposition to decide one way or the other because of some personal interest, it is improper for the decision maker to participate in making the decision. However, even if a decision maker does not believe that a relationship or interest causes him or her to have an actual bias, the decision maker should not participate in a decision if there is a significant appearance that he or she is biased. A tribunal member should not hear a case where a reasonable and well-informed observer of the situation would assume that the member would probably be biased. This appearance of bias is called a **reasonable apprehension of bias**.

The apprehension of bias must be a reasonable one held by reasonable and right-minded persons, applying themselves to the question and obtaining thereon the required information. ... What would an informed person, viewing the matter realistically and practically—and having thought the matter through—conclude. Would he think that it is more likely than not that [the judicial officer], whether consciously or unconsciously, would not decide fairly.

de Grandpré J in *Committee for Justice and Liberty v. Canada (National Energy Board)*, [1978] 1 SCR 369, at 394-95

It is clear from the authorities that the reasonable person is very well informed, right-minded, practical and realistic. The person must be knowledgeable of all of the relevant circumstances, including "the traditions of integrity and impartiality that form a part of the background and apprised also that impartiality is one of the duties that judges do swear to uphold."

If the words or conduct, no matter how inappropriate or troubling, do not amount to reasonable apprehension of bias, then the findings of the judge will not be affected.

In summary, there is a strong presumption of judicial integrity that may only be displaced by cogent evidence establishing a real likelihood of bias. It is trite to note that this burden is higher than a simple balance of probabilities, but lower than proof beyond a reasonable doubt. The burden lies with the person alleging a reasonable apprehension of bias. A reasonable apprehension of bias is determined by the well informed, right minded individual who is aware of all of the circumstances, including the nature of the case, its surrounding circumstances, and the presumption of judicial integrity.

R v. Pilarinos, [2001] BCJ no. 2540, at paragraph 143 (SC)

Apart from individual bias, the entire agency may appear to be biased when it is structured in such a way that a well-informed person would have a reasonable belief that the agency is likely to favour a particular party or class of parties in a substantial number of cases. The extent to which the tribunal is independent of the parties is not conclusive evidence of whether there is institutional bias. However, independence or lack of it is one of the most important factors in determining whether there is institutional bias or a reasonable apprehension of institutional bias.

ELEMENTS OF INDIVIDUAL BIAS

The Relationship Between Bias and Conflict of Interest

Bias and **conflict of interest** are often used interchangeably. However, conflict of interest is only one source of bias or perceived bias; other sources include a dislike of one of the parties or prior knowledge of facts that are prejudicial to one of the parties. Conflict of interest is a specific kind of bias—a financial interest in the outcome of a particular case, or, more generally, any interest that is incompatible with his or her function as a member of a tribunal.

Indicators of Possible Bias

As stated earlier, an adjudicator is to approach each case with an open mind. Certain kinds of behaviour toward the parties during a hearing may suggest that an adjudicator does not have an open mind. Other circumstances, apart from the adjudicator's behaviour in the hearing room, may also cast doubt on his or her impartiality and raise a reasonable concern about possible bias.

The kinds of activities, conduct, interests, relationships, and associations of a decision maker that may give rise to an appearance of bias include:

- meets with one party in the absence of other parties;
- has a close friendship with a person whose interests may be affected by the outcome of the case;

- has a close relative whose interests may be affected by the outcome of the case;
- has a financial interest in the outcome of the case;
- belongs to an association that has taken positions on issues that must be decided by the tribunal;
- expresses opinions about the issues in the case before all the evidence and arguments have been heard;
- intervenes in the hearing process in a way that persistently favours one party over another;
- expresses a strong like or dislike for a party or its witnesses;
- is in or has been in litigation against a party or witness in a proceeding;
- has or has had in the recent past a significant business or professional relationship with a party or witness; or
- takes gifts or favours from a party or witness.

ELEMENTS OF INSTITUTIONAL BIAS

Impartiality Versus Independence

As stated above, there is a difference between institutional impartiality and institutional independence. The Supreme Court of Canada has stated that the impartiality of a decision maker is determined by examining his or her state of mind; but the independence of a tribunal is a matter of its status:

> The status of a tribunal must guarantee not only its freedom from interference by the executive and legislative branches of government but also by any other external force, such as business or corporate interests or other pressure groups.[1]

The duty of a tribunal to be impartial is not the same as a duty to be independent. The Supreme Court of Canada has made it clear that while the Canadian constitution requires that courts be independent of the other branches of government, there is generally no similar requirement for tribunals, although it is possible that independence could be found to be a constitutional requirement in limited circumstances.[2] Tribunals are generally required to be independent only where a statute provides for this. For example, s. 23 of Quebec's *Charter of Human Rights and Freedoms*[3] explicitly provides that Quebec tribunals must be independent.

However, in deciding whether a tribunal is impartial, the courts will consider the degree of independence as one indication of impartiality or institutional bias.

What Constitutes Independence?

To meet the constitutional requirement of judicial independence, judges must have security of tenure, financial security, and control of the operations of their courts. In considering whether a tribunal is impartial, the courts will look at the same factors they look at when deciding whether judges are independent.

---

1   *R v. Genereux*, [1992] 1 SCR 259; (1992), 88 DLR (4th) 110, at 128; 70 CCC (3d) 1.

2   *Ocean Port Hotel Ltd. v. British Columbia (General Manager, Liquor Control and Licensing Branch)*, [2001] 2 SCR 781.

3   RSQ, c. C-12.

However, as agencies of the executive branch of government, tribunals are not expected to have the same degree of independence as courts. Whether the lack of independence of a tribunal will be enough to create an appearance of institutional bias will depend on the types of decisions it is required to make, and to what degree the tribunal is expected to implement government policy.

Factors To Consider in Determining Whether There Is Institutional Bias

The most important considerations in determining whether there is institutional bias are:

- the closeness of the relationship between an agency or tribunal and a government department that is affected by its decisions; and
- where an agency has multiple functions, the extent to which these functions overlap in a manner that suggests that some employees have inappropriate influence over others.

FACTORS IN DETERMINING WHETHER THE AGENCY–GOVERNMENT RELATIONSHIP CONTRIBUTES TO INSTITUTIONAL BIAS

In deciding whether the relationship between an agency or tribunal is so close to the government that there is an appearance of institutional bias, the courts may look at a number of factors. Usually, no single factor is conclusive; it is the overall impact on independence or the appearance of independence that matters. Factors that the courts may consider include:

- Are agency or tribunal members appointed for a fixed term, or do they hold their offices "at pleasure"? (The term "at pleasure" means that an appointment may be terminated whenever the government pleases.)
- If the appointment is for a fixed term, how long is the term? (The longer the term is, the greater will be the appearance of independence.)
- Are members' salaries fixed, or can the government raise or lower them at will? (Fixed salaries will contribute to the appearance of independence.)
- Are the appointments part-time or full-time? (A part-time appointment raises a greater concern that an agency or tribunal member might be denied work if he or she makes a decision that is unsatisfactory in the eyes of the government or the chair of the agency.)
- To what extent does an agency chair have discretion over which members to appoint to hearing panels? (If the selection process is not random, this increases the ability of the chair to influence the outcome of hearings by appointing members who he or she feels, from experience, are likely to be sympathetic to one side or the other.)
- Are the staff of an agency selected or employed by the agency or by the government? (Where the government is sometimes a party to proceedings, the fact that tribunal staff owe their livelihood to the government rather than the agency can create an appearance of bias.)
- To what extent is an agency required by government rules to follow government policy? (The more an agency must follow policy, the lesser will be the appearance of independence.)

- Does the minister to whom an agency chair reports conduct the performance evaluation of the chair, and what criteria are used in evaluating the chair's performance? (If the agency makes decisions that can adversely affect the government, the possibility of an unfavourable performance appraisal can be perceived as interfering with the ability of the agency to be impartial, particularly if the criteria used involve an assessment of the wisdom of the very decisions that affect the government.)

- Does the government department to which an agency reports determine the agency's annual budget? (If the department controls the budget, there may be an appearance that it is able to reduce the budget to punish unfavourable decisions and increase it to reward favourable ones.)

FACTORS TO CONSIDER IN DETERMINING WHETHER OVERLAPPING FUNCTIONS CONTRIBUTE TO INSTITUTIONAL BIAS

As discussed in chapter 2, Administrative Agencies and Tribunals, many regulatory agencies carry out multiple functions. The concentration of a number of functions within a single agency is not necessarily a problem. However, a multifunctional structure creates an appearance of bias when those who are responsible for recommending or prosecuting proceedings against a person are also involved in deciding whether to take away the person's rights, privileges, or benefits. The tribunal that makes the final decision will not be considered impartial if those who recommended or pursued charges can influence the decision—for example, by providing additional information that is not known to all parties, or by providing private legal advice.

To avoid an appearance of institutional bias, there should be a clear separation of roles between those who investigate and recommend administrative action, those who argue the case before the tribunal, and those who make the decision. There will be a perception of institutional bias when, for example, an agency lawyer who is responsible for approving proceedings against a person, or for arguing a case before a tribunal, privately advises the tribunal as to how it should decide the case. A perception of institutional bias will also arise where an official recommends action against an individual, and then appoints or serves as a member of the panel that will decide whether to take the action.

Statutory Exceptions to the Requirement of Institutional Impartiality

Despite a tribunal's general duty to be impartial, a lack of independence or impartiality will not disqualify a tribunal from deciding a case if its partiality is clearly mandated by statute. The only exception to this exception is where the statutory provisions that curtail independence or impartiality are unconstitutional.

If the built-in bias is "necessary" in the sense of being required by statute, the bias will be acceptable. For example, a statute may provide that

- a tribunal must follow government policy;
- the chair must report to the minister of a department that appears as a party before the tribunal;
- the minister has the right to approve the tribunal's rules of procedure;

- the chair must provide any information about the tribunal's operations that the minister requests; and

- the minister approves the agency's budget.

Together, these requirements might raise doubts about the tribunal's impartiality. However, any bias resulting from these requirements is immune from attack in the courts because it is clearly authorized by statute.

RAISING AN ALLEGATION OF BIAS

Alleging that a tribunal member or other decision maker is biased, or appears to be biased, is a serious matter. Bias allegations should not be made lightly. Apart from any other reason to exercise caution, the first rule of good advocacy is to not alienate the decision maker. Moreover, the courts have made it clear that restraint must be exercised when making such allegations.

However, if it is necessary to raise the question of whether there is an appearance of bias, it is important to do it as early as possible. The courts will consider a party that does not raise an allegation of bias during a hearing to have waived the right to argue it in court. In addition, if a party knows of facts that may give rise to an appearance of bias before a hearing begins, it may be possible to raise the matter discreetly with the tribunal chair or tribunal member and resolve it without the need to raise it during the hearing in a public forum and risk embarrassing the tribunal and its member. Moreover, it is more convenient and less expensive for everyone if a tribunal assigns a different member before a hearing begins than if a member is forced to withdraw from a hearing in mid-stream.

If an advocate becomes aware of facts that may create an appearance of bias after a hearing has begun, and on sober reflection continues to believe it is necessary to raise the issue, how this is best done will depend on the circumstances of each case.

In many cases, it will still be appropriate to raise this issue privately with the tribunal member or the tribunal chair and give the member an opportunity to stand aside without a public spectacle. However, any such discussion should take place in the presence of all other parties.

If the member does not step down after a private discussion and the advocate still believes the member should not continue, it will then be necessary to raise the question in the open hearing and ask for a formal ruling by the tribunal member. If the member does not agree that his or her participation will result in a reasonable apprehension of bias, it is probably not necessary to immediately seek judicial review of the decision. Continuing to participate in the hearing will not then be considered a waiver of the right to raise the issue in later court proceedings.

TRIBUNAL RESPONSE TO AN ALLEGATION OF BIAS

How to respond to a bias allegation is a difficult and sensitive question. The tribunal member may become aware of facts that he or she is concerned may give rise to an appearance of bias. If the hearing has not yet begun, the simplest solution is to ask the chair of the tribunal to assign a different adjudicator. Alternatively, if the adjudicator thinks that there may be an appearance of bias but feels that he or she is not, in fact, biased, he or she may disclose the facts to the parties and volunteer to step aside. If the parties do not accept this offer, the adjudicator may then proceed without fear of his or her decision on the hearing being challenged.

If some parties argue that there is no bias, but others argue that the adjudicator should stand aside, the adjudicator faces a difficult decision. If it will not cause substantial cost or inconvenience to the parties, it is best for the adjudicator to stand aside under these conditions regardless of his or her own views as to whether there is any reasonable apprehension of bias. However, if standing aside after a hearing has begun will lead to substantial delay or expense for the parties, and the adjudicator feels that he or she has no bias or conflict of interest and any appearance of bias is insufficient, he or she may decide to continue in the public interest.

If the adjudicator raises the issue of bias, he or she may bring forward not only the facts that suggest a bias, but any facts that he or she feels will show that there is no bias. However, if any of the parties dispute or demand proof of the mitigating facts, the adjudicator is in a difficult position, as he or she may not become a witness in the proceeding over which he or she is presiding. If a party raises the issue of bias and brings out facts that support it, it is unclear whether the adjudicator can state facts that rebut the inference of bias.

Even though the adjudicator has a personal interest in the outcome of a bias application, he or she is still the appropriate person to rule on whether there is a reasonable apprehension of bias. Normally, this would not be decided by someone else—for example, the tribunal chair.

CHAPTER SUMMARY

The impartiality of the decision maker is an essential element of procedural fairness. Not only must the decision maker actually be unbiased; he or she must also appear to be unbiased. There are two kinds of bias: individual and institutional. A biased individual is one who does not approach a decision with an open mind because he or she has a personal interest in the outcome of the case. Institutional bias arises, or appears to arise, when the structure or functioning of an agency or tribunal leads it to favour, or appears to lead it to favour, one party or class of parties over another in a substantial number of cases.

Institutional bias is likely to be perceived when an agency is too close to a government department that is a party to its proceedings, or where the overlapping functions of agency staff result in an appearance that those who investigate or prosecute are also involved in making the final decision on someone's rights, privileges, or interests.

Although the rules of procedural fairness require impartiality, these rules can be, and often are, overruled by statutory requirements to do exactly what is perceived as unfair. Common law fairness requirements overrule statutory requirements only where the latter violate a person's rights or freedoms under the Charter.

KEY TERMS

bias   an interest, attitude, relationship, or action that leads a decision maker to favour one party over another

conflict of interest   a situation in which a decision maker has a personal or financial interest in the outcome of the proceeding that can affect his or her ability to make a fair decision

institutional bias   bias that arises, or appears to arise, when the structure or functioning of an agency or tribunal leads it to favour, or appears to lead it to favour, one party or class of parties over another in a substantial number of cases

reasonable apprehension of bias   the appearance of bias to a reasonable and well-informed observer

KEY CASES

Individual Bias

Committee for Justice and Liberty v. National Energy Board, [1978] 1 SCR 369

FACTS: The National Energy Board was considering competing applications for a pipeline in the Mackenzie Valley. The person assigned to be chair of the three-member panel had previously had involvement with one of the companies competing for the application.

ISSUE: Should the chair be rejected from the panel based on a reasonable apprehension of bias?

DECISION: There was no actual bias, because the chair did not have anything to personally gain or lose. However, his involvement in the decisions leading to the pipeline company's application for a certificate gave rise to a reasonable apprehension of a bias. There must be no lack of public confidence in the impartiality of adjudicative agencies. This was particularly true in a case where the board was to have regard for the public interest.

Institutional Bias

2747-3174 Quebec Inc. v. Quebec (Régie des permis d'alcool), [1996] 3 SCR 369

FACTS: After a hearing, the directors of the Régie des permis d'alcool revoked a company's liquor permits on the ground of disturbance of public tranquility. The company sought to have the decision quashed because the Régie did not comply with the guarantees of independence and impartiality set out in the Quebec *Charter of Human Rights and Freedoms*, RSQ, c. C-12.

ISSUE: Was there a reasonable apprehension of bias where the same people might be involved in prosecuting and adjudicating?

DECISION: Flexibility must be shown toward administrative tribunals with respect to impartiality; however, the Régie's structure and multiple functions raised a reasonable apprehension of institutional bias. The fact that the Régie, as an institution, participated in the process of investigation and adjudication was not a problem; however, a separation among the directors involved in the various stages was necessary to eliminate the apprehension of bias. The same people might be called upon to review files in order to advise the Régie on the action to be taken, and present arguments to the director and draft opinions. Prosecuting counsel must never be in a position to participate in the adjudication process. The Régie's decision was quashed.

Institutional Bias

Dulmage v. Ontario (Police Complaints Commissioner)
(1994), 30 Admin. LR (2d) 203 (Ont. Div. Ct.)

FACTS: A board of inquiry panel was established under the *Police Services Act*, RSO 1990, c. P.15 to investigate allegations that a woman had been strip-searched in public by a police officer. One of the appointed members of the three-person panel was president of the Mississauga chapter of the Congress of Black Women of Canada, both at the time of the alleged event and at the time of the hearing. An application was made to disqualify this member on the basis of reasonable apprehension of bias, because inflammatory public statements concerning the events had been made by another official of the same organization in Toronto.

ISSUE: Was the test for reasonable apprehension of bias met?

DECISION: There was a "reasonable apprehension of bias on the part of the reasonable person," because the alleged incident received significant attention in the media, and the officer of the Congress of Black Women of Canada who made the public statements had demanded the suspension of the officers involved. The panel member was from Mississauga and the public statements were made in the neighbouring city of Toronto. This was enough to create a reasonable apprehension of bias, and an order was granted directing that the hearing take place before a different panel.

Institutional Bias

Ocean Port Hotel Ltd. v. British Columbia (General Manager, Liquor Control and Licensing Branch), [2001] 2 SCR 781; 2001 SCC 52

FACTS: Investigations of a hotel and pub led to allegations that it had committed five infractions of the *Liquor Control and Licensing Act*, RSBC 1996, c. 267 and regulations under the Act. Following a hearing, the Liquor Control and Licensing Branch imposed a penalty that included a two-day suspension of the hotel's liquor licence. The hotel appealed to the Liquor Appeal Board by way of a hearing *de novo*. Four of the five allegations were upheld, and the penalty was confirmed.

The hotel applied to the courts to overturn the board's decision on the grounds that the structure of the board did not leave it independent enough to be impartial.

Pursuant to s. 30(2)(a) of the *Liquor Control and Licensing Act*, the chair and members of the Liquor Appeal Board "serve at the pleasure of the Lieutenant Governor in Council." Members are appointed for a one-year term and serve on a part-time basis. All members but the chair were paid on a per diem basis. The chair established panels of one or three members to hear matters before the board "as the chair considers advisable." The BC Court of Appeal held that the members of the board lacked the necessary independence and set aside the board's decision.

ISSUE: Were the members of the Liquor Appeal Board sufficiently independent to make fair decisions on violations of the Act and to impose penalties?

DECISION: The Supreme Court of Canada allowed the appeal. Generally, the degree of independence required of a particular government decision maker or tribunal is determined by the tribunal's enabling statute. The legislature's intention that board members should serve at pleasure was unequivocal. The statute was not ambiguous.

There is a fundamental distinction between administrative tribunals and courts. Unlike courts, administrative tribunals are not constitutionally required to be independent. They are created precisely for the purpose of implementing government policy. Although tribunals may sometimes attract Charter requirements of independence, as a general rule they do not. The board is not a court, it is a licensing body. The suspension of the hotel and pub's liquor licence was an incident of the board's licensing function. Licences were granted on condition of compliance with the Act, and could be suspended for non-compliance. The exercise of power fell squarely within the executive power of the provincial government.

REVIEW QUESTIONS

1. What is the relationship between bias and conflict of interest?
2. What is the difference between an actual bias and a reasonable apprehension of bias?
3. Explain the difference between individual bias and institutional bias.
4. What is the difference between impartiality and independence? What is the relationship between them in relation to whether an agency is following a fair procedure?
5. What factors will a court consider in determining whether an agency is independent?
6. What factors will a court consider in determining whether a lack of independence makes an agency institutionally biased?
7. What are some circumstances that might lead a reasonable and well-informed observer to assume that a decision maker is biased?
8. When is the appropriate time to raise an issue of bias and what procedure should be followed?
9. What steps should an adjudicator take if a question of bias or conflict of interest arises?

EXERCISE

The Department of Consumer Relations, headed by the minister, is responsible for regulating used car dealers. The registrar, an employee of the department, has the right to recommend that a tribunal, the Licence Appeal Board, revoke the business licence of a dishonest car dealer.

A customer of Active Auto Sales, managed by James M., complained to the ministry that the company had turned back the odometer on a vehicle that it had sold to him. After investigating this complaint, the ministry determined that turning back odometers was standard practice of this dealership. The company was charged and convicted of fraud, but no charges were laid against James. Despite this, the registrar recommended to the board that it revoke James's licence to sell cars, as well as the licence of his employer, on the grounds that given his position in the company, James had to be involved in the fraudulent activity.

The board held a hearing to decide whether to accept the registrar's recommendation to revoke the two licences. In addition to arguing that he was unaware of the illegal activities, James argues that the board is disqualified from deciding whether to revoke his licence because it is not independent of the ministry, and therefore it has an institutional bias.

The *Consumer Protection Act* establishes the board. It states that the board will report to the minister of consumer relations; that the chair and members of the board will not be civil servants; that the premier will appoint the chair and members of the board; and that the chair will decide which members and how many members will be assigned to each appeal. The board is required by the statute to follow rules of natural justice such as giving notice of hearings, hearing evidence, allowing parties to be represented by counsel or agents, permitting cross-examination, and giving written reasons for its decisions. The statute also provides for the board to summon witnesses, hold pre-hearing conferences, and conduct mediation. The statute allows the board to make rules of procedure that are approved by the ministry. The board may make practice directions and issue guidelines for hearings without the ministry's approval. The statute also states that the board must have regard to any relevant ministry policies when making its decisions.

Each year the board chair proposes a budget for the following year. Because the board reports to the minister, the minister is responsible for approving the board's budget. The chair hires the board staff, but the practice is that a human resources officer from the ministry is involved in the interviews and takes part in making the decisions. The ministry establishes the salary range for each board staff member, but within that range, the chair decides what salary to offer and whether employees get a raise each year. The chair cannot terminate the employment of a board staff member without ministry approval.

It is the government's policy that each minister enter into a memorandum of understanding (MOU) with the chair of the board, governing the relationship between the board and the ministry. Each time the minister or the chair changes, a new MOU is to be signed by both parties. The current chair was appointed one year ago, but the minister has not signed a new MOU.

Although the Act says that the premier appoints the members, in practice this is done on the recommendation of the minister. The MOU between the minister and the previous board chair provides that the minister will consult with the chair before deciding which members to recommend for appointment.

The members are appointed "at pleasure" for a fixed term of two years. Traditionally, appointment at pleasure means that an employee may be terminated without any notice. The MOU provides that the minister will seek the advice of the chair when deciding whether to reappoint members at the end of their term. However, there is a government policy that members may not be reappointed for more than one two-year term, regardless of the quality of their performance. About 60 percent of the members are appointed on a part-time basis. One of them is a former investigator at the ministry.

The salary levels for the chair and members are established by the government.

The current chair was once the director of the legal department of the ministry. He left the ministry three years ago. Before being appointed chair, he was in private practice as a lawyer for one year, then was the director of the Policy Branch of the Ministry of Finance in the provincial government.

Is there an institutional bias that would prevent the board from hearing this case? Play the role of James's lawyer and argue that the board has no jurisdiction to hear this case. Then play the role of counsel for the registrar and argue that the board has no institutional bias.

FURTHER READING

Sara Blake, *Administrative Law in Canada*, 2d ed. (Toronto: Butterworths, 1997), chapter 3.

Robert D. Kligman, *Bias* (Toronto: Butterworths, 1998).

PART II

Advocacy

CHAPTER 6

Advocacy Before Administrative Agencies and Tribunals

LEARNING OBJECTIVES

After reading this chapter, you will understand

- what steps you should follow in preparing to represent a party before an agency that is not a tribunal;
- how to represent your client effectively in this administrative process;
- how to obtain the information you need where processes are not transparent;
- what steps you should follow in preparing to represent a party before a tribunal; and
- how to be an effective advocate before a tribunal.

It is not easy or particularly useful to write a general section on how to prepare a case to be presented to an agency mainly because each agency is a world unto itself.

Robert Macaulay and James Sprague, *Practice and Procedure Before Administrative Tribunals* (Toronto: Carswell) (looseleaf), chapter 19, paragraph 19.1

INTRODUCTION

Part I provided the foundation for understanding administrative law, carrying out legal research, and interpreting laws that may apply in a particular case. Part II focuses on the application of this knowledge

1. in **advocacy**, or representations on behalf of a client, before tribunals and other administrative agencies; and

2. in the conduct of hearings and decision-making processes by tribunals.

This chapter describes the fundamentals of effective advocacy. It outlines the basic steps that should be followed in most situations. Subsequent chapters provide a more detailed discussion of the procedures involved in preparing for and participating in a hearing before a tribunal.

ADVOCACY BEFORE AN ADMINISTRATIVE AGENCY

Understanding the Decision-Making Structure

As discussed in part I, different procedures apply to decision making by tribunals and other administrative agencies. Tribunals are required to hold public hearings and follow quasi-judicial procedures. Other agencies make their decisions behind closed doors. They often do not describe in detail the procedures that they will follow. They may obtain information from many sources and do not always reveal what information they have relied on, or what policies, guidelines, or criteria they have applied. Officials at several levels in the organization's hierarchy, and even in several different departments, may play a role in reaching the final decision, and officials from other agencies also may be consulted. (See "Bureaucratic Decision Making.") Often there is no blueprint that sets out the responsibilities or functions of these various participants.

This decision-making structure can make the job of the **advocate**, or **representative**, a difficult one. A great deal of detective work, along with some guesswork, may be needed to find out who is involved in making decisions, and when and how

Bureaucratic Decision Making

A developer wants to tear down several houses that he owns and build a complex of apartment buildings and a shopping mall. Before he can proceed, he must apply to the municipality's planning department for rezoning of the property from "single family residential" use to a combination of "multi-unit residential" and "commercial" use.

Several departments and agencies will likely provide input before a decision will be made on the application. The roads department will advise whether the existing network of roads can handle the additional traffic that the new development will generate. The school board will consider whether the local schools can accommodate the children who may live in the apartment complex. The environment department may require proof that the soil is not contaminated. The parks department may want land set aside for recreation. Other considerations will include the impact of the development on the sewage and water supply systems, noise levels, and aesthetic considerations such as the visual impact of the buildings and whether their design is con-

sistent with that of surrounding buildings.

The developer will be required to submit studies and plans to address these concerns. The objective of the developer, and the representative who acts on his behalf, is to persuade all the authorities involved that this development will be beneficial to the community. At the same time, neighbours as well as competing businesses may try to persuade the same authorities that the negative effects of the project should cause them to reject it.

The side that provides the most effective advocacy will be the one that wins the day. Ultimately, the planning department, taking into account input from other departments, consultants, lobbyists, and other interested parties, will make a recommendation to the municipal council, and the municipal council will make a binding decision. The losing party may be able to appeal the council's decision to a tribunal. However, different approaches are required in presenting an application to municipal departments and councillors and presenting a case before a tribunal.

decisions are made. Since much of the information that the advocate needs may not be written down anywhere, or, if written, may not be public, the process of shepherding an application through the bureaucracy consists mainly of asking questions and finding out the points in the process at which recommendations and decisions will be made, who will make them, and what internal policies and criteria those officials will apply in arriving at their decisions.

To me, a lawyer is basically the person who knows the rules of the country. We're all throwing the dice, playing the game, moving the pieces around the board, but if there is a problem, the lawyer is the only person who has read the inside top of the box.

Jerry Seinfeld, *Seinfeld*, "The Visa," episode 56, broadcast January 27, 1993

Steps in the Advocacy Process

Advocacy before an agency that is not a tribunal involves some or all of the steps outlined below.

DETERMINE WHAT LAWS AND POLICIES APPLY

As discussed in part I, government decision makers exercise powers granted by statute. The statute or regulation that delegates those powers generally sets out broad rules for decision making, including the nature and scope of the decision, the persons responsible for making the decision, the general procedures to be followed, and the criteria to be applied. The details of the process are often left to be determined by the decision-making body. They are found in written policies or guidelines, or in informal administrative practices.

DETERMINE STAGES IN THE PROCESS AND DEADLINES

There are often stages in the decision-making process at which recommendations and interim or tentative decisions are made. At some or all of these stages, there may be an opportunity for the advocate to provide input. Therefore, it is important to identify those stages and to find out the deadlines for making comments and suggestions or providing information.

DETERMINE WHO MAKES THE DECISION AT EACH STAGE

As mentioned earlier, often several departments or branches will be consulted during the decision-making process. Each will bring to bear its own perspective and will want to ensure that its particular areas of concern are addressed. Consequently, the advocate will need to find out who is involved at each stage and make contact with the various participants.

DETERMINE CONCERNS OF THE AGENCY AND OTHER STAKEHOLDERS

As well as determining who is involved, it is important to understand the particular concerns of each participant. For example, certain issues related to an application may be raised internally by agency staff. Other stakeholders may raise additional concerns with politicians and agency officials. For example, if a client is applying for a licence to open a casino and neighbours wish to block the application, the advocate should try to find out the details of their concerns both from the neighbours themselves and from agency officials.

TAILOR SUBMISSIONS

Submissions on the client's behalf should focus directly on the issues identified by the decision makers and by external opponents to the application. The arguments should be presented within the framework that the agency will use in making the decision. For example, they should refer to any policies, guidelines, and criteria that support the application and explain why those that do not support it should not be given weight in the circumstances of the case.

OBTAIN REASONS FOR THE DECISION

Once the final decision has been made, it is part of the advocate's job to ensure that the client is informed of the reasons for the decision. Generally, the agency will have either a statutory or a common law duty to give reasons.

Under s. 7 of Alberta's *Administrative Procedures Act*[1] (APA), administrators must provide written reasons for their decisions. In contrast, under s. 13 of Quebec's *Administrative Justice Act*[2] (AJA), there is no requirement for agencies other than tribunals to provide their reasons in writing. These agencies are, however, required to communicate their decisions "in clear and concise terms" and if they are making an unfavourable decision on an application for a licence or permit, they must give reasons. Ontario's *Statutory Powers Procedure Act*[3] (SPPA) and British Columbia's *Administrative Tribunals Act*[4] (ATA) do not require agencies other than tribunals to provide reasons.

Obtaining Access to Information

In arriving at a decision, an agency other than a tribunal is not required to disclose the information on which the decision is based. Consequently, it is often necessary for the applicant's representative, and other outside parties, to take steps to obtain this information.

The decision makers and support staff involved in the process will usually maintain a file containing the application, internal and external comments on it, analysis of issues, expressions of concern, studies, and other related facts. It is important for the advocate to collect as much of this information as possible, beginning at an early stage in the decision-making process, in order to be able to anticipate and respond to decision makers' concerns. (See "Tips for an Effective Advocacy Strategy.")

FORMAL AND INFORMAL ACCESS ROUTES

The first task is finding out what is in the file. There are two routes to obtaining this information. The formal route involves an application under freedom-of-information laws. The informal route involves direct contact with the agency itself—for example, keeping in touch with officials by telephone, arranging face-to-face meetings, writing letters, and attending any public meetings. (See "A Useful Starting Point.")

---

1 RSA 2000, c. A-3.

2 RSQ, c. J-3.

3 RSO 1990, c. S.22.

4 SBC 2004, c. 45.

Tips for an Effective Advocacy Strategy

- Participate early and often in the agency's decision-making process.

- Start at a low level in the decision-making chain.

- Ask staff at all stages for information about issues identified by the agency, policy concerns, and options under consideration.

- Propose solutions to issues and concerns, which agency staff can build into the documentation that will be considered by the ultimate decision makers.

- Avoid being hostile or overly aggressive.

- Be diplomatic but firm.

- Insist on your client's rights, including the right to access to information and the right to procedural fairness.

A Useful Starting Point

Some governments maintain lists of the kinds of information available from various departments. For example, the Ontario government maintains an electronic index of records maintained by ministry branches and by other agencies that are subject to the *Freedom of Information and Protection of Privacy Act*. This index of records is found on the Web site of the Information and Privacy Office in the Management Board Secretariat at http://www.gov.on.ca/MBS/english/fip.

The federal government and each of the provinces and territories have legislation that requires government agencies, municipalities, and, in some cases, universities and hospitals to provide access to many government records on request. The federal statute is called the *Access to Information Act*.[5] Ontario has one statute that requires disclosure of provincial government information, the *Freedom of Information and Protection of Privacy Act*,[6] and a second statute that covers municipalities and their agencies, the *Municipal Freedom of Information and Protection of Privacy Act*.[7] Under these statutes, a person can make a formal request for documents. If access is denied, the applicant has a right to appeal the decision to the federal or provincial information commissioner or to the courts.

Obtaining records through formal access-to-information procedures can be costly and time-consuming. The better way to obtain information from an agency is usually the informal route. It is often faster and cheaper, and it is particularly useful in identifying what documents are available and which officials are likely to have custody of them. Having this information will make it easier to use the formal

---

5 RSC 1985, c. A-1.

6 RSO 1990, c. F.31.

7 RSO 1990, c. M.56.

Information Requests Can Be Expensive

In addition to an application fee, a freedom-of-information agency may charge fees in amounts set out in a regulation for time spent

- searching for documents and looking through them to decide whether any part of them must be kept confidential,

- preparing a document for release by blacking out confidential portions that are exempt from disclosure, and

- other functions such as photocopying.

These fees may be substantial or even prohibitive.

In some jurisdictions, the agency is required to provide the applicant with an estimate of fees before starting to retrieve the records, and it may require payment of up to half of the estimated cost before conducting the search or preparing the documents for release. The applicant can request that the fee be waived in some circumstances or that it be reduced if it appears excessive.

procedures under freedom-of-information laws if the informal route does not produce the information that the advocate seeks.

REQUESTS UNDER FREEDOM-OF-INFORMATION STATUTES

As described above, if documents cannot be obtained through informal channels, a formal request can be made under freedom-of-information legislation. The request must be made in writing, and in some jurisdictions, a fee must accompany the application. (See "Information Requests Can Be Expensive.") There is often a standard request form, which is usually available from the agency holding the documents. In Ontario, the form can also be obtained through the Web site of the information and privacy commissioner. However, in Ontario and most other jurisdictions, it is not necessary to use the form; instead, the request can simply be sent to the agency's freedom-of-information (FOI) coordinator.

The FOI coordinator is usually well informed about the records held by the agency, their location, and their availability. Under Ontario's freedom-of-information laws, the coordinator is required to assist applicants in clarifying their request if it is unclear. The agency must respond to a request within 30 days by advising that it will or will not provide the information requested. However, the agency is entitled to a 30-day extension if a large number of records are requested, if it is necessary to search through many records to find the documents requested, or if it is necessary to consult someone outside the agency before fulfilling the request.

In Ontario, a refusal to provide documents, failure to decide whether or not to disclose them within the specified time limit, failure to conduct a thorough search for records, and the fee charged for searching for and retrieving records can all be appealed to the information and privacy commissioner (who is independent of the government) or, in some cases, to the courts. The commissioner has the authority to order the government to provide information that is not specifically exempt from disclosure.[8]

---

8 *Freedom of Information and Protection of Privacy Act*, s. 54.

In the case of documents in the possession of federal government departments and agencies, under the *Access to Information Act*, a person refused information may complain to the federal information commissioner. The commissioner cannot order the government to disclose information, but rather may recommend that it do so. If the government refuses to follow the recommendation, either the commissioner or the applicant may appeal to the Federal Court.[9]

ADVOCACY BEFORE A TRIBUNAL

There are three mistakes you should never make when appearing before a tribunal:

1. *To assume that because a tribunal performs quasi-judicial functions, it will follow the same rules or procedures as a court*   The fact that a court will not allow the presentation of hearsay evidence, for example, does not necessarily mean that such evidence will also be inadmissible before a tribunal.

2. *To assume that because a tribunal is less formal than a court, a different standard of behaviour and preparation applies*   A tribunal should be treated with the same respect as a court, and the preparation should be as thorough and the analysis as rigorous as they would be in a case before a court.

3. *To assume that all tribunals are alike*   Although tribunals are similar in some respects, there are often important differences in procedures, policies, and functions that will affect the advocate's preparation and presentation in appearing before a particular tribunal. For example, some tribunals may have adopted an informal approach to the admission of evidence; for other tribunals the prior disclosure of evidence may be mandatory.

There are three ways to avoid these errors: prepare, prepare, and prepare. An advocate should learn as much as she can about the particular tribunal before which she will appear. If she is familiar with other tribunals, how is this tribunal similar to or different from them? In what ways is the tribunal like a court and in what ways does it differ?

Every tribunal is both similar to and different from a court. However, since no two tribunals are alike, the nature of these similarities and differences varies from one agency to another. The advocate needs to clearly understand the expectations and procedures of the particular tribunal involved, rather than make assumptions that may result, for example, in her presenting irrelevant evidence or failing to submit relevant evidence.

As those who have appeared before administrative tribunals know only too well, familiarity with court practice provides only limited comfort when one is confronted with the vagaries of the practice and procedure developed by specialized tribunals in an attempt to carry out their particular mandates in a fair and efficient manner.

Michael I. Jeffery, review of Andrew J. Roman, *Effective Advocacy of Administrative Tribunals* (Toronto: Carswell, 1989), in (1989-90) vol. 3 *Canadian Journal of Administrative Law and Practice* 376

---

9 *Access to Information Act*, ss. 41 and 42.

Steps in the Advocacy Process

Advocacy before a tribunal involves the steps set out below.

FIND OUT ABOUT THE TRIBUNAL

Before appearing before a tribunal for the first time, the advocate needs to become familiar with

- the legislation under which the tribunal operates;
- the tribunal's rules of procedure and practice guidelines; and
- decisions that the tribunal has made in similar cases.

This basic information is essential as the starting point for preparation of the case. (See "Be Clear About Jurisdiction.")

Be Clear About Jurisdiction

Representatives (including lawyers, who should know better) often make incorrect assumptions about the tribunal's authority and powers. You wouldn't ask a criminal court to award damages or a civil court to impose a fine, but many representatives do not take the time to find out what remedies a tribunal can and cannot give. For example, it is surprising how often tribunals are asked to award costs, even though most of them do not have this authority.

Additional information about the tribunal may be found in its most recent annual reports, and sometimes in papers in conference proceedings written by members of the tribunal or by lawyers familiar with its practices.

Often it is helpful for an advocate to attend one or two hearings as an observer, and to talk to other representatives who have appeared before the tribunal, in order to get a sense of how the tribunal operates.

It is particularly important to find out the time limits for applying to the tribunal. Tribunals often have shorter limitation periods than courts. Sometimes an application to appeal a decision of a government official must be made within a period as short as 15 to 30 days. In many cases, a tribunal has the right to extend this time limit, but some tribunals do not. If the advocate misses the deadline, his client may lose the right of access to the tribunal, and the advocate may be open to a lawsuit for negligence.

IDENTIFY ISSUES

The **issues** are the questions that the tribunal must answer in order to arrive at a decision. They are the matters that are in dispute. They may be

- questions of fact;
- questions of what law applies, or of how to apply or interpret the law in the circumstances of the case; or
- questions of what is the correct policy to apply, or of how to interpret or apply the policy.

The issues should become apparent through the notice issued by the tribunal; through preliminary procedures such as pre-hearing conferences, motions, and disclosure; and through legal research. Discussion with other parties and representatives is also helpful. (See "Issues: Real and Apparent.")

Issues: Real and Apparent

Sometimes the real issues in a case are not what they appear to be on paper. Through discussions, you may find out that while the proceedings appear to raise many legal and factual questions, only a few of these are important. For example, a building owner may raise several legal objections to compliance with an order to make repairs, based on allegations that the building inspector exceeded his jurisdiction or followed an unfair procedure. The "real" issues may be that the owner needs more time to look into less expensive repairs and that the building inspector is convinced that the owner is flouting the law.

DETERMINE BURDEN OF PROOF AND STANDARD OF PROOF

Textbooks and reported decisions of courts elaborate on which party has the onus or **burden of proof** and what is the **standard of proof**. The burden of proof is the obligation to provide sufficient evidence to prove a point in dispute. The standard of proof refers to the quantity and kind of evidence that will be considered sufficient to prove the point.

In a particular case, is it the government authority that made the decision that must prove that the decision was correct? Or is it the client who is appealing the decision who must prove that the decision was wrong or unfair? Is expert evidence or documentation necessary to resolve the issue? Or will the tribunal accept the observations and opinions of ordinary people? Answers to these questions can often be found in past decisions of the tribunal or other authorities. Sometimes tribunal staff can provide assistance in this area.

COLLECT EVIDENCE AND IDENTIFY WITNESSES

Once the issues have been identified, it is necessary to determine what evidence is needed to resolve them and which documents or witnesses can prove the points in issue.

SECURE ATTENDANCE OF WITNESSES

The advocate should ensure that her witnesses will attend, or that she can successfully argue for an adjournment if they fail to attend, by serving each witness with a subpoena. This should be done as early as possible to avoid potential conflicts in scheduling.

The advocate should also find out the tribunal's procedure for issuing a summons to a witness. Under s. 12(2) of Ontario's SPPA, all summonses must be signed by the chair of the hearing panel unless the legislation establishing the tribunal provides for someone else's signature. Some tribunals will issue a blank signed summons for advocates to fill in, while others will demand evidence that the witness has relevant testimony to give.

RESEARCH THE LAW

It is surprising how many representatives, including lawyers, will propose an interpretation of the law on disputed points without doing the research and citing cases that support their statements. When a point of law is in issue, it is essential that the representative carry out the necessary research and document the relevant case law.

ORGANIZE MATERIALS

Tribunals appreciate representatives who make their job easier. There are several ways to do this:

1. Ensure that witnesses have been served with subpoenas, in order to avoid having to ask for an adjournment because of their failure to appear, and be prepared to show the court proof of service.

2. Prepare a binder of documents to be tendered and distributed to all participants at the start of the hearing. In preparing the binder,

   a. arrange documents in the order in which they will be introduced;

   b. number all pages in the binder consecutively, or use tabs to make it easy to locate a particular document;

   c. provide a table of contents listing every document included in the binder, with page or tab references;

   d. make sure that all documents listed are included, with all their pages in the right order; and

   e. prepare enough copies for all tribunal members and other participants in the hearing.

3. Provide all participants with copies of tribunal and court decisions that will be relied on in arguing the client's case. If there are many decisions, it is helpful to organize them in a **book of authorities** with a table of contents and tabs.

These suggestions may sound trivial, but they can make the difference between a case that proceeds quickly and smoothly and one filled with countless interruptions and delays. The client's case is not helped if witnesses, representatives, and panel members have to fumble through a poorly organized binder searching for a particular document, or sit around waiting while someone looks for a photocopier to replace documents included in one participant's binder but missing from others.

PLAN AN EFFECTIVE PRESENTATION

Build Confidence and Trust

Representatives have three things to offer a tribunal: their intelligence, their preparation and presentation skills, and their integrity.

Trustworthiness is a matter of integrity. When a representative appears before a tribunal, he soon gains a reputation as an advocate who can be trusted or one who cannot. The following are some of the ways in which an advocate can build trust:

- *Never mislead the tribunal*   While the advocate will want to emphasize the strengths of his case, he should also acknowledge the weaknesses. Pretending that they do not exist does not build trust or respect.

- *Do not take extreme positions or positions that clearly are not supported by the evidence or by the law* If there are cases against the advocate's position, he should make the tribunal aware of them and explain why they should not be followed in this case.

- *Focus on the most important issues and the most persuasive arguments* When an advocate raises many issues, whether peripheral or not, or presents an overwhelming array of arguments, there is a risk that the tribunal will lose sight of the merits of the client's case.

Chief Justice Taft used to tell of the lawyer from behind the cactus plants of Texas who explained his presence before the Supreme Court of the United States as follows: "May it please the court, I know that this case should never have come here, but I was afraid it was the only chance I would ever have, and as the jurisdictional grounds were present, I thought I would like to come up and argue one case before you, so that I could tell the boys back home about the time I appeared before the Supreme Court of the United States. I don't know exactly how an argument should be made before you, but I have endeavoured to divide mine in three very common-sense divisions. First, I shall argue to the court the law of the case. I shall then argue the law as applicable to the facts, and in conclusion, I will make one wild pass at the passions of the court."

May, *The Lighter Side of the Law* (1956), 163

Apply a Light Touch

A hearing is not a battleground. Although some tribunal proceedings are more adversarial than others, tribunal members appreciate representatives who treat witnesses, parties, and opposing representatives with respect, who do not raise unnecessary objections, and who do not get into time-wasting arguments with other representatives.

There are times when it is necessary to be forceful and occasionally even a little abrasive, but for the most part tribunals find honey easier to digest than vinegar.

Show Respect

An advocate should show the tribunal the same respect that she would show a court.

Tribunals are generally supposed to be less formal and less legalistic than courts. As a result, advocates may be tempted to behave as they never would in a courtroom. They may think that they are entitled

- to arrive late;

- to ask for last-minute adjournments;

- to rely on evidence that may be inflammatory, prejudicial, or unreliable;

- to make submissions on the interpretation of the law without doing legal research or producing authorities; or

- to provide documents to the tribunal but not bring any copies for the other parties.

On all these points, they are wrong.

An advocate should never argue with the tribunal members after they have made a ruling. The time for arguing a point is before the tribunal reaches its decision. Once the ruling has been made, it is disrespectful to tell the tribunal members that they are wrong or to demand that they change it.

An advocate should also not carry on an argument or debate with opposing representatives. She should address her arguments to the tribunal. Similarly, an advocate should not interrupt other representatives or witnesses, or distract the tribunal members. Whispering to the client, making faces, drumming fingers, or tapping feet is not behaviour that will endear a representative to the tribunal.

A convicted con man was found to be impersonating a lawyer. Upon learning this, the judge remarked, "I should have known he wasn't a lawyer. He was always so punctual and polite."

Anonymous

OBTAIN REASONS FOR THE DECISION

The Supreme Court of Canada made it clear in *Baker v. Canada*[10] that tribunals must give reasons for their decisions, at least when important issues are at stake.

Under s. 17(1) of Ontario's SPPA, a tribunal must provide written reasons for its decision only if it is requested to do so. Under s. 7 of Alberta's APA, as discussed earlier, all administrators and tribunals must provide written decisions with reasons, whether requested or not. Section 52 of British Columbia's ATA requires certain tribunals to provide written reasons. Under s. 13 of Quebec's AJA, all administrators are required to communicate their decisions clearly and concisely, but only tribunals are explicitly required to give written reasons.

Written reasons are more important to the loser than to the winner. They are often needed to determine whether there are grounds for a successful appeal or an application for judicial review, such as errors that the tribunal made in reaching its decision. If the tribunal does not provide reasons for its decision, the advocate should ask it to do so.

CHAPTER SUMMARY

The key to effective advocacy before tribunals and other agencies is thorough preparation. Government agencies are less transparent than tribunals. The criteria they will apply, the information they will use, and the bureaucrats or other parties who will provide advice and input to decisions are matters that are not always set out in writing or available to the public. Much of the deliberation and decision making goes on behind the scenes. Effective advocacy requires, first, learning as much as possible about the rules and procedures of agencies, and the policies, criteria, and guidelines they will apply in reaching a decision; and second, applying this knowledge at every point in the process where there is an opportunity for the advocate to affect the outcome.

---

10   *Baker v. Canada (Minister of Citizenship and Immigration)*, [1999] 2 SCR 817, at 844-48.

Thorough preparation is also the key to successful advocacy before tribunals. It is important to understand that tribunals are similar to courts in some respects but different in other ways, and that no two tribunals are alike. In addition to solid research and a clear understanding of the rules and practices of a tribunal, building trust, making reasonable compromises and accommodations, and treating the tribunal and other participants with respect are also essential components of effective advocacy.

KEY TERMS

advocacy   the act of pleading for or supporting a position or viewpoint

advocate   a person who pleads for or represents the position or viewpoint of another; also called a "representative"

book of authorities   a binder containing the cases, statutory provisions, and excerpts from legal texts that a representative will rely on in support of his or her position before a court or tribunal

burden of proof   the obligation to provide sufficient evidence to prove a point in dispute; *see also* standard of proof

issues   matters that are in dispute in a hearing; the questions that a court or tribunal must answer in order to make a decision; may be questions of fact, questions of what law applies, or of how to apply or interpret the law in the circumstances of the case, or questions of what is the correct policy to apply, or of how to interpret or apply the policy

onus of proof   *see* burden of proof

representative   *see* advocate

standard of proof   the quantity and kind of evidence that will be considered sufficient to prove a point that is in dispute; *see also* burden of proof

REVIEW QUESTIONS

1. How would your approach to preparing and presenting a case to an administrator differ from your approach to preparing and presenting a case before a tribunal? In what ways would the approaches be similar?

2. What are "issues," and how do you identify them?

3. How do you ensure that your witnesses show up for a hearing before a tribunal?

4. When would you make use of freedom-of-information statutes in representing your client?

5. In advocating a position before an administrator or a tribunal, "the best defence is a good offence." True or false? Why?

6. You should prepare and present a case before a tribunal in the same way as if you were appearing before a court. True or false? Why?

EXERCISE

Using the website of the Ontario government's Information and Privacy Office in the Management Board Secretariat, find out from the index of records whether the Ministry of Community and Social Services maintains statistics on its Ontario Disability Support Program. If so, what branch of the ministry keeps these records and what kinds of statistics are kept?

FACT SCENARIO

You are representing a client at a hearing before a tribunal that will last several weeks. Before the hearing, you prepare a book of authorities containing court decisions that support your interpretation of the law. At the beginning of the hearing, you provide copies of the book to the tribunal members and the other parties, with the intention of using the cases to support your argument at the end of the hearing.

Three days into the hearing, you discover that one of the decisions in your book of authorities has been overturned on appeal to a higher court.

1. Do you do anything, and if so, what and when?

2. What if the decision has not been overturned by a higher court, but you discover that a court in a different province has come to the opposite conclusion about the interpretation of a law that is almost identical?

3. What if the conflicting decision is in relation to a similar law, but made by a court in a different country?

4. What if you discover that although the decision that you intend to rely on has not been overturned by a higher court, a different judge of the same court has come to the opposite conclusion in a later and similar case?

FURTHER READING

Robert Macaulay and James Sprague, *Practice and Procedure Before Administrative Tribunals* (Toronto: Carswell) (looseleaf), chapter 19.

Ronald D. Manes and Valerie A. Edwards, *Manes Organized Advocacy: A Manual for the Litigation Practitioner*, 2d ed. (Toronto: Thompson Canada) (looseleaf).

Andrew J. Roman, *Effective Advocacy Before Administrative Tribunals* (Toronto: Carswell, 1989).

Alvin B. Rosenberg and Marvin J. Huberman, *Appellate Advocacy* (Scarborough, ON: Thompson Canada, 1996).

CHAPTER 7

Tribunal Procedures Before Hearings

LEARNING OBJECTIVES

After reading this chapter, you will understand

- what is required in a tribunal's notice of a hearing;
- what procedures a tribunal may use before the hearing to identify participants and issues;
- how a tribunal may help the parties to settle the dispute voluntarily before the hearing;
- how a tribunal determines the form of the hearing; and
- how a tribunal may resolve procedural and other issues before the hearing.

The legislature has left it to the arbitrator charged with deciding a collective agreement dispute to judge whether and to what extent there should be any compelled pre-hearing exchange of information. In my view, one of the considerations to be taken into account in making that judgment is the possibility that an order intended to expedite the hearing and disposition of the matter may have the opposite effect. Once there is an order compelling a party to do something it has not agreed to do, there is then the possibility of disputes about what the order means, how it applies to unanticipated circumstances, whether it has been complied with and what the consequences of non-compliance should be. The resolution of such disputes may consume the very hearing time and expense which the order was intended to save, and more, without advancing the resolution of the underlying dispute even as much as it would have been had no order been made. That will not always be so, but it is a risk which must be weighed against the possible benefits of a more structured and onerous pre-hearing disclosure process.

O.V. Gray, arbitrator, in *Re Thermal Ceramics and USWA* (1993),
32 LAC (4th) 375, at 380

BALANCING INFORMALITY AGAINST EFFICIENCY AND FAIRNESS

Tribunals differ greatly in their use of pre-hearing procedures. Some tribunals go directly from issuing a notice of hearing to holding the hearing itself, while others engage in a variety of pre-hearing processes designed to identify participants in the proceeding, to focus and narrow the issues, and to establish the procedures to be followed at the hearing. For tribunals whose hearings range from short and simple ones, with few parties and issues, to long and complex proceedings, the pre-hearing processes will vary according to the type of hearing.

As the decision of O.V. Gray, above, suggests, there are many different views as to how formal or informal tribunal procedures should be. In the past, one of the main differences between courts and tribunals was that courts used lengthy pre-hearing procedures and tribunals did not. As a result, in simple cases, a tribunal offered a cheaper and easier way for people to settle disputes. However, the lack of pre-hearing disclosure and of processes for clarifying and resolving issues before a hearing could also lead to unfairness, adjournments once the hearing began, and unnecessarily long and complex proceedings.

In order to improve efficiency and fairness, many tribunals have built into their decision-making process a variety of pre-hearing procedures. Some of these procedures may be initiated by representatives of parties. Some may be initiated by the tribunal, and representatives may be invited or required to participate.

These pre-hearing procedures are described below. They include techniques that may be used by parties or by the tribunal

- to clarify or resolve issues,

- to promote settlement, and

- to ensure that all participants have the information necessary to prepare their case for presentation at the hearing.

Notice of Hearing

Procedural fairness requires that a person who will be affected by a proposed decision must be given **notice** of the decision and an opportunity to challenge it. Therefore, once someone has initiated a proceeding, one of the first actions of the tribunal is to give notice to anyone who might have a right to participate. This will always include the person who will be most directly affected by the decision, such as the applicant for a licence, privilege, or benefit, but it may also include others with an interest in the outcome of the proceeding. For example, if a prisoner applies for parole, the parole board may notify the victims of the crime to give them an opportunity to present their views.

The notice should include, at a minimum,

- the date, time, and location of the hearing, or of a preliminary procedure such as a pre-hearing conference;

- the purpose of the hearing;

- information about the hearing or pre-hearing procedure; and

- any steps that the interested person must take in order to participate.

In Ontario, s. 6 of the *Statutory Powers Procedure Act*[1] (SPPA) also requires the inclusion of a warning that if a person receiving the notice does not attend the hearing, the tribunal may proceed in the person's absence and need not give the person any further notice. There is a similar requirement in s. 127 of Quebec's AJA.

Party Status

RIGHTS COMMONLY ATTACHED TO PARTY STATUS

Some tribunals have the power to grant rights to certain participants that are not available to others. For example, the tribunal may allow some persons to give oral evidence but restrict others to the submission of evidence in writing. However, **party status** usually gives a person and his or her representatives the right to participate fully in the proceeding.

Full participation rights typically include

- the right to give evidence,

- the right to call witnesses,

- the right to cross-examine,

- the right to make submissions and participate in final argument, and

- the right to appeal the tribunal's decision under an applicable statute or to apply for reconsideration or judicial review of the decision.

IDENTIFICATION OF PARTIES

Entitlement to be a **party** to a hearing depends on the nature of the issue to be addressed. In some situations, only the decision maker and individuals directly affected by the decision are parties. For example, in professional discipline cases, normally only the body seeking to impose discipline and the professional who may be subject to discipline are parties. However, when land is being rezoned, in addition to the owner and the decision maker, individual neighbours and ratepayer groups may be given party status.

In some cases, legislation specifies the parties to a proceeding. In other cases, particularly where the tribunal has a mandate to protect a broad public interest (for example, in land use planning, human rights, and environmental cases), the tribunal may have discretion to recognize additional parties. In addition, the common law principle of procedural fairness may require the tribunal to grant party status to an affected person.

For parties other than those identified in a statute, the tribunal may have a procedure for determining well in advance of the hearing whether there are persons with a sufficient interest to be included as parties to the proceeding. If there are, these persons will then be notified of the proceeding and offered the opportunity to bring a **motion** (an oral or written application) requesting party status before the hearing date.

From the viewpoint of the person who wishes to participate, it is important to request party status at the earliest opportunity, since preparation for the hearing

---

1 RSO 1990, c. S.22.

will take time. It is also important to the tribunal to identify the parties as early as possible, because some steps in the tribunal's process may be appropriate only after all parties have been identified. The determination of party status may be made at a pre-hearing conference (discussed below) or on approval of an applicant's formal request submitted before the hearing date.

Where a statute permits a tribunal to add parties but does not specify the criteria for granting party status, it is appropriate for the tribunal to develop such criteria, whether through individual decisions or in the form of written guidelines. Generally, in order to be a party to a proceeding, the person must demonstrate that his or her interests will be directly and substantially affected by the outcome of the hearing. If the impact on the person's interests is less immediate, he or she may still be allowed to participate as an **intervenor** (discussed below). Often, similar criteria are used in determining party status and intervenor status. These criteria are described briefly in the next section.

Intervenor Status

In some cases, a tribunal may want the option of allowing certain persons to participate, but not with the full range of rights to which a party is entitled. For example, the tribunal may want to grant someone permission to participate only in relation to certain issues; or the tribunal may want the person's input on all issues, but prefer to limit the extent of that person's participation on each issue (for example, permitting only written submissions). In such cases, the person may be granted **intervenor status**.

Some statutes may provide explicitly for "participant" or "intervenor" status as an alternative to party status. Ontario's SPPA does not. In such a case, and if the tribunal's enabling statute also is silent on this point, the tribunal may have to consider whether it has the authority to make rules of procedure governing the granting of intervenor status. If it has, the tribunal must then decide whether to set out in those rules some factors that it will consider in granting intervenor status or whether to provide guidelines listing the criteria for obtaining this status.

If the tribunal decides that it can recognize intervenors, one of the functions that members may carry out in advance of a hearing is to determine who shall be given this status and what limits, if any, will be placed on their participation. Like party status, intervenor status may be determined at a pre-hearing conference or through a motion brought by an interested party.

In the absence of any rules, guidelines, or previous tribunal decisions relating to the granting of intervenor status, a tribunal may have to balance the need for public participation against the costs associated with additional participants. Factors to consider include

- the nature of the case,
- the nature of the person's interest in the proceeding,
- the extent to which the person is likely to be affected by the outcome of the proceeding, and
- the likelihood that the person can make a useful contribution to the resolution of issues raised by the proceeding without causing injustice to the immediate parties (for example, undue expense or delay).

Pre-Hearing Conference

Pre-hearing conferences (PHCs) can be very useful to both tribunals and participants for making procedural orders and obtaining agreements from parties and other participants that will help to resolve issues, promote settlement, and allow the hearing to run more smoothly. Ontario's SPPA, British Columbia's ATA, and Quebec's AJA all provide for PHCs.

In Ontario, the matters that can be addressed at a PHC are spelled out in s. 5.3(1) of the SPPA. PHCs can be used for

- considering the possibility of settlement of issues;

- simplifying issues;

- ascertaining facts or evidence that can be agreed upon;

- setting dates for required procedures;

- estimating the duration of the hearing; and

- any other purpose that the tribunal considers appropriate (such as the identification of parties: s. 5.3(3)).

The purpose and format of PHCs may vary among tribunals, and the focus or emphasis may differ among members. In some tribunals, the panel that will hear the case conducts the PHC. In others, a different panel or member conducts the PHC. Under the SPPA, the tribunal may assign a non-member such as a staff member or mediator to conduct a PHC (s. 5.3(2)); however, a non-member may not issue any binding directions or orders (s. 5.3(3)).

It is important to use the PHC effectively. What a party can realistically expect to accomplish at a PHC depends on the nature of the tribunal's process and the circumstances of each case, including the timing of the conference. For example, if the PHC is held very soon after the proceeding is initiated, the participants may be able to set dates for disclosure of evidence, but may not be in a position to disclose their evidence or to address substantive issues.

Some tribunals require that the parties be represented at the PHC by a person who has authority to make binding decisions. If the representatives attending cannot make commitments to basic procedural decisions, such as dates for disclosure of evidence or for the hearing itself, the PHC will not be useful. Tribunal members have the right to expect that parties or their representatives will come prepared to set hearing and disclosure dates, articulate the issues, and provide a list of witnesses. However, it may not be reasonable to expect that the representatives will have the authority to make or accept settlement offers without further discussion with their clients, particularly if the PHC is held before disclosure of evidence.

If, at the time of the PHC, parties or their representatives are not prepared to deal with all the matters necessary to promote an efficient hearing process, or if there are many issues to be addressed, the tribunal may extend the conference until more progress has been made, or it may set aside portions of the agenda to be dealt with at a later date.

While PHCs are very useful for dealing with procedural issues, caution must be exercised in attempting to use them to resolve substantive issues or achieve settlement. Under s. 5.3(4) of the SPPA, if the PHC is used for settlement discussions, the presiding member may participate in the hearing only if all parties consent. If the member expresses any views on the merits of the case, there may be an appearance of bias that may disqualify the member from participating in the hearing. In addition, the member at the PHC may hear evidence that will not be put before the hearing panel. If the member participates in the hearing, the parties may be concerned that he or she may consciously or unconsciously rely on evidence that the other members of the panel have not heard.

Disclosure of Evidence

Before a hearing begins, tribunals usually require the parties to disclose the **evidence** that they will present in support of their respective positions in the case. Evidence is information that a party seeks to use in a legal proceeding to prove or disprove a contention or allegation. A tribunal's authority to order the **disclosure** of evidence may be set out in a statute of general application or in the tribunal's enabling statute. (See "Disclosure Orders.") Disclosure of evidence may take the following forms:

Disclosure Orders

Section 5.4 of Ontario's *Statutory Powers Procedure Act* gives tribunals the authority to order

- the exchange of documents,
- the oral or written examination of a party,
- the exchange of witness statements and expert witness reports,
- the provision of particulars, and
- any other form of disclosure,

provided that the tribunal has made rules governing the procedure for disclosure. This power is subject to any other statute that applies to the tribunal's proceedings. In addition, tribunals cannot require the disclosure of privileged information.

Examination for Discovery

In an examination for discovery, the persons named in the disclosure order must attend at a specified time and place and answer questions put to them by the representatives of opposing parties. Those questions and answers are recorded and transcribed.

Although Ontario's *Statutory Powers Procedure Act* does not specifically provide for examinations for discovery, the provision for oral examination of a party at any stage of the proceeding (s. 5.4(1)(b)) appears to contemplate this technique for obtaining evidence. Therefore, a tribunal may require examination for discovery through its rules of procedure, either in all cases or by permitting a party to apply to the tribunal to require this procedure in a specific case.

- *Exchange of documents* The parties are often required to exchange documents that each intends to rely on in support of his or her position. Examples are contracts or written agreements and correspondence relating to the matter in dispute.

- *Oral or written questions and answers* Some tribunals permit disclosure through oral questioning of a party (**examination for discovery**) or through the submission of written questions (**interrogatories**). (See "Examination for Discovery.")

- *Witness statements* These are written statements (sometimes called "will says") setting out the testimony that a witness is expected to give at the hearing. Often tribunals require that the witness statement be accompanied by a list of any documents to which the witness may refer during testimony.

- *Expert witness reports* Some witnesses present expert evidence on scientific or technical matters. An expert witness report sets out the witness's opinions and the facts on which they are based. The witness may also be required to disclose in the report all studies, texts, or tests upon which he or she will rely in testifying at the hearing.

- *A list of other documents* The parties may also be required to identify other documents in their possession or under their control that are relevant, but on which the parties do not intend to rely.

- *Access to other evidence* It is not always possible to bring relevant evidence to the hearing room (for example, a building or site at the centre of a dispute). In such cases, the parties may be required to provide access as part of the disclosure procedure.

TIMING OF DISCLOSURE

Many tribunals require disclosure of evidence well in advance of a hearing.[2] The time at which disclosure is required may be determined in several ways:

- through statutory or procedural rules that set predetermined disclosure dates applicable to all hearings;
- by the requirements set out in the notice of hearing;
- through discussion at a PHC;
- by a request for disclosure in the form of a motion brought by a party to the proceeding; or
- by a combination of these methods.

When timing and other disclosure requirements are decided on a case-by-case basis, all parties should be given an opportunity to make submissions as to what conditions are reasonable before the tribunal issues the disclosure order.

USE OF DISCLOSED EVIDENCE AT THE HEARING

A question that often arises is whether the information obtained through disclosure may be used as evidence at the hearing or whether parties are only allowed to use

---

2 However, tribunals may have no power to require pre-hearing disclosure unless a statute specifically provides this authority or procedural fairness requires it. See *Ontario (Human Rights Commission) v. Dofasco Inc.* (2001), 57 OR (3d) 693, at 708 (CA).

the information to help them prepare for the hearing. Some tribunals leave it to the member presiding at the hearing to determine which disclosed material can be used as evidence. Others have rules of procedure providing that all disclosed information is automatically part of the hearing record. Some tribunals treat witness statements, expert witness reports, or answers to written or oral questions as evidence that is admissible at the hearing. Others permit the use of this information at the hearing only if it contradicts evidence given orally at the hearing. In the latter case, a tribunal member may be required to rule, either before or during the hearing, on the admissibility of information obtained through the disclosure process.

If the tribunal's procedural rules do not state whether the information disclosed automatically becomes evidence at the hearing, a representative should consider asking the tribunal to clarify its position, either at a PHC or through a motion.

Both approaches—making disclosed material automatically part of the hearing record and leaving the question to be decided by the hearing panel—have advantages and disadvantages. For example, the treatment of disclosed information as evidence can shorten the hearing since written statements can be substituted for oral testimony. However, if participants know that their statements at disclosure will be used as evidence at the hearing, they may be less forthcoming; they may make preliminary motions objecting to the disclosure of some information; or they may object to the admission of information disclosed by the other party as evidence. As a result, the length and complexity of the proceeding may be increased.

Disclosure of Particulars

Ontario's SPPA allows a tribunal to order parties to disclose **particulars**, provided that this requirement is set out in the tribunal's procedural rules (s. 5.4(1)(d)). Particulars are details that explain or clarify such matters as the grounds for a party's case, the remedy or decision that the party is seeking, and the evidence or facts on which a party relies. If the legal theory or argument presented by a party is not sufficiently clear to permit other parties to prepare their response, clarifying this also could fall within the definition of particulars.

Tribunal members may be required to rule on motions demanding particulars, or they may decide on their own initiative that particulars are needed to ensure an efficient hearing process (after inviting submissions on whether such an order should be made).

Issues that a member may be required to decide in dealing with particulars include

- whether the particulars are to be provided only to the other parties in order to assist them in preparing their case;
- whether the particulars are also to be provided to the tribunal and to become part of the hearing record; and
- whether the particulars should be considered binding on the party that provided them.

The last question is especially important. If particulars are treated as binding, they may narrow the party's grounds or the issues before the tribunal.

Settlement Before the Hearing

One of the advantages of pre-hearing procedures such as PHCs, motions, and disclosure is that they give the parties an opportunity to learn the strengths and weaknesses of their own case and the positions taken by other parties. They provide not only a sense of the likelihood of success, but also an indication of the probable duration and cost of the hearing if it proceeds.

Representatives should use this information to help their clients to assess whether it is in their interests to settle, and, if so, on what terms. The main advantages of settling are that

- it allows the parties to resolve the dispute on their own terms instead of leaving the outcome in the hands of a third party; and
- it saves the parties and the tribunal the cost of proceeding with a hearing.

Parties who have reached a settlement should notify the witnesses and the tribunal as soon as possible, especially when a hearing has been scheduled and will have to be cancelled. The tribunal members and staff in particular will appreciate this consideration, and it will serve the interests of the representatives in the event of future appearances before the tribunal.

POWER OF THE TRIBUNAL TO PROCEED DESPITE A SETTLEMENT

In some cases, the tribunal may have the power to overrule a settlement between the parties and proceed with the hearing. A tribunal's authority to proceed despite a settlement may be provided by a statute. Where it is not, the case law may support the tribunal's decision to proceed in some circumstances. Generally, the tribunal will have no power to proceed where a settlement has been reached by all the parties. However, there are exceptions, usually in cases where the tribunal's role is to protect the public interest rather than the interests of the parties alone.

In addition, if some of the parties settle and others do not, the settlement may not bind the other parties or participants, and the tribunal may order that the hearing proceed. The courts have suggested that in these cases, the following considerations are relevant in determining the tribunal's authority:[3]

- whether the proceedings are intended solely to resolve a dispute between the parties to the hearing or are part of a regulatory regime designed to protect a broader public interest; and
- whether a withdrawal or settlement by some parties may be contrary to the interests of other parties or potential parties to the proceeding.

ASSISTANCE TO PARTIES IN SETTLING ISSUES

Tribunal members or staff may use a number of mechanisms to encourage parties to settle some or all of the issues before the hearing. The following techniques are ways of motivating parties to settle:

- Disclosure is often a prerequisite to settlement negotiations.
- The setting of a firm hearing date provides a deadline for settlement. Parties and their representatives often leave settlement negotiations to the eleventh hour. In many cases, without a looming hearing date, the parties do not make a serious effort to settle.
- Where the parties request an adjournment of the hearing because they are close to settlement, the adjournment should be for a short and specified

---

3 *NSP Investments Ltd. v. Ontario (Joint Board)* (1990), 72 OR (2d) 379 (Div. Ct.); *Cloverdale Shopping Centre Ltd. v. Etobicoke (Township)*, [1966] 2 OR 450.

settlement period. Otherwise, the pressure on the parties to settle will be relieved, and the settlement may evaporate. ***Sine die* adjournments** (adjournments for an indefinite period) are the enemy of settlement.

Two other mechanisms are important aids to a pre-hearing settlement: PHCs and mediation. These are discussed in the sections that follow.

Pre-Hearing Conferences

PHCs can be used as settlement conferences. While a PHC dealing with procedural matters should usually be public, serious settlement negotiations are often impossible in a public setting.

To facilitate settlement at a PHC, the tribunal may separate or "sever" the settlement portions of the conference from the procedural portions and hold the settlement conference behind closed doors. In addition, the tribunal may require the participants to agree to keep the discussions at the settlement conference confidential. If the tribunal does not automatically take these steps, a representative should consider asking it to do so.

Mediation

In addition, the members or staff of a tribunal may attempt to facilitate resolution of issues through a variety of **alternative dispute resolution** (ADR) mechanisms, such as **mediation**, conciliation, and arbitration. Mediation is the primary method used in assisting settlement before the hearing.

Mediation is the intervention in a dispute of an impartial person (a "mediator") who has no decision-making power, in order to assist the parties in reaching a settlement. The role of the mediator usually includes the following:

- structuring the negotiation process;
- helping the parties to clarify their needs and interests;
- assisting in identifying and clarifying issues; and
- advising on constructive discussion between the parties.

In addition, the mediator may offer an opinion on the likely outcome of a formal hearing or make recommendations on settlement terms or other concerns.

Typically, the parties themselves participate directly in the mediation process. Their representatives may or may not be present.

In some circumstances, mediation can have advantages over formal adjudication by the tribunal:

- It can be less time consuming and less costly than a hearing.
- It can preserve or strengthen relationships between the parties.
- It can lead to a settlement that is tailored by the parties themselves, rather than by an outsider, and is therefore more acceptable to both parties.
- It may offer a broader range of solutions than the tribunal has power to impose.

On the other hand, mediation may not be suitable in many situations—for example,

- where there is a large power imbalance between the parties;
- where the law is clearly on one party's side; or
- where it is in a party's interest to maximize delay.

In such cases, mediation may simply lead to more cost and delay before the inevitable hearing. An effective tribunal will not impose mediation in all cases, but will analyze the particular facts and circumstances of a dispute in order to determine whether mediation is likely to be useful in that case.

A different way of resolving a dispute:

In Paraguay, duelling is legal as long as both parties are registered blood donors.

If agreement is reached through mediation, the parties set it out in writing, sometimes with the assistance of the mediator. The parties may make the agreement binding by signing a contract. In some cases, the tribunal has the power to put the agreement in the form of a binding order.

The use of mediation and other ADR techniques raises a number of issues, including the following:

- whether a tribunal has the power to use ADR techniques where this authority is not explicitly provided by a statute;
- if so, whether the tribunal may make the participation of parties mandatory;
- what is the effect of agreements made by parties;
- whether, and to what extent, information revealed during ADR is privileged; and
- whether a tribunal member who conducts an ADR session may later participate in a hearing.

Some of these issues may be addressed in a statute, as is the case for tribunals governed by Ontario's SPPA (ss. 4.8 and 4.9) and British Columbia's ATA (ss. 28 and 29). For matters related to the use of ADR that are not covered by statutory provisions, the tribunal should establish a set of procedural rules. This is one of the prerequisites under the SPPA for the use of ADR mechanisms. A second prerequisite is that all parties consent to participation in the ADR process (s. 4.8(1)).

THE TRIBUNAL'S AUTHORITY TO REJECT AN ASSISTED SETTLEMENT

Another issue that arises is whether the tribunal is bound by an ADR settlement or whether, instead, it has the authority to reject the settlement and hold the hearing. This question is particularly important when the tribunal's mandate goes beyond the interests of the parties and permits a decision based on the public interest.

Unless the question is addressed by a statute governing the tribunal, the tribunal itself will determine the scope of its authority, according to its interpretation of its mandate. The tribunal's position may be found in a decision in a particular case, which other members of the tribunal follow as a matter of course, or it may be expressed in procedural rules or practice directions.

In general, if the involvement of tribunal members or staff in facilitating settlement does not imply acceptance or approval of the settlement by the tribunal, the tribunal should make this clear to the parties. Even if a tribunal does have the authority to approve or reject a settlement, it should not approve any settlement that is outside its jurisdiction.

Choice of Hearing Format: Oral, Electronic, or Written

A hearing may take one of three forms:

1. an oral hearing (the traditional form), in which the tribunal and all other participants are present in the same location and at the same time;

2. an electronic hearing, held through a teleconference or a video conference; or

3. A written hearing, in which all the evidence and arguments are distributed to the tribunal and to the other parties in written form.

The tribunal may propose the form of the hearing to the parties to the dispute, or the parties may ask the tribunal to consider their preference before making its decision.

Ontario's SPPA sets out specific rules relating to the choice between the three alternatives (s. 6). In all cases, the parties must be given notice of the form of the hearing. If the tribunal is considering holding a written or an electronic hearing, the parties must be provided with an opportunity to object and request an oral hearing instead.

Before a tribunal proposes a hearing in any form other than the traditional oral hearing, it should first consider whether the alternative is a fair and efficient method of conducting the hearing. A written hearing may be most appropriate where the facts are largely undisputed and credibility does not appear to be in issue. Where facts and credibility are in dispute, an oral or electronic hearing will usually be needed. A written hearing may also be inappropriate where any of the parties is illiterate or poorly educated, or has limited fluency in the English or French language.

An oral hearing may be more appropriate than a written hearing or a teleconference

- where it is desirable to visit an outside location, such as the site of a building;

- where witnesses must refer to maps, charts, and other visual aids; or

- where observing witnesses is important in assessing their credibility.

An oral hearing may also be preferable to a video conference hearing if the video conferencing facilities and technology are not of sufficient quality to permit such observations.

Other factors that parties and the tribunal may consider in determining the most appropriate hearing format include the following:

- convenience to the parties;

- the cost, efficiency, and timeliness of the proceeding;

- the fairness and transparency of the process; and

- the desirability or necessity of public participation in or public access to the conduct of the hearing.

Conduct of the Hearing: Preliminary Motions

There are certain issues related to the conduct of the hearing that are usefully resolved before the hearing begins. These may range from matters of procedure to more fundamental questions of jurisdiction. While the responsibility for resolving such issues rests with tribunal members and staff, it is important that when any question affects the parties involved, all parties should have an opportunity to present their views before a final decision is made.

If a tribunal holds PHCs or settlement conferences, or has an ADR process, many of these issues may be resolved through these procedures. However, there is an additional method of permitting all parties to be heard on preliminary issues: the motion. A motion is a request by one party for a ruling by the tribunal. The party making the request is often called the **moving party**.

Notice of the moving party's request (a "notice of motion") must be served on all other parties. The notice of motion sets out the date, time, and place at which the motion will be heard, the remedy that is requested, and the grounds for the request. Sometimes the moving party provides the tribunal with all the information needed for a motion, and the tribunal serves all the other parties with notice. However, in many tribunals, the tribunal staff give the moving party the information about the hearing of the motion, and that person is then responsible for serving notice on the other parties.

The evidence to be used in support of a pre-hearing motion is usually restricted to written statements, often in the form of an **affidavit**. An affidavit is a sworn statement setting out facts supporting the request. The moving party files this written evidence with the tribunal. Many tribunals require that this evidence also accompany the notice of motion.

The moving party must provide the tribunal with evidence that notice has been served on all the other parties. This evidence is called **proof of service**. Proof of service may take one of two forms:

1. a written statement by the moving party (sometimes in the form of an affidavit), affirming that the notice of motion was served on each of the other parties, and indicating how and when it was served; or

2. a statement acknowledging service written on a copy of the notice and signed by the receiving party.

The tribunal will generally provide an opportunity for other parties to serve and file responses, also consisting of written evidence supporting their position. In addition, the parties may be entitled to cross-examine each other's witnesses as to the accuracy of their written statements. The transcripts of any cross-examinations are provided by the parties to each other and to the tribunal.

The reliance on written evidence in deciding pre-hearing motions is an important difference from the procedure followed at many main hearings. At an oral or electronic hearing, most of the evidence is typically provided orally by witnesses.

If any party fails to attend the hearing of the motion, the presiding member of the tribunal must check whether that party was properly notified of the motion. If the party seeking a remedy cannot provide proof of service of the notice, the hearing should not proceed.

Examples of motions that may be presented before a hearing are discussed briefly below.

MOTION FOR DIRECTIONS

A motion for directions requests clarification of a procedural matter, usually one that is not addressed in the tribunal's rules of procedure.

MOTION FOR SUMMARY DETERMINATION (DISMISSAL)

The courts have the power to dismiss a case without a hearing where there is clearly no possibility that the case will succeed. The reason may be either that

An Example of a Motion for Directions

The Wild Peonies Protection Tribunal was established to allow the public to challenge a government land-use planning decision that would permit destruction of wild peony habitat. The tribunal's rules of procedure state:

> On the request of a party at any time before a hearing, another party must provide written answers to written questions that are relevant to the proceedings where this would simplify or shorten the hearing.

The applicant, a naturalist group, claims that the respondent, a developer, should not be permitted to build a condominium because it will harm a rare species of peony. Under this rule, the developer asks the naturalist group for details of how it determined that the flowers growing on his property are the rare peonies, rather than a more common variety that is almost identical in appearance. The naturalist group answers the question, but adds that this information is only for the developer's use in briefing his expert witness, a botanist, and the written response is not to be used as evidence at the hearing.

The developer responds that he has every intention of submitting the written response at the hearing, because there is nothing in the tribunal's rules to prevent this.

Rather than wait to have the tribunal make a ruling during the hearing, the naturalists make a motion asking the tribunal to specify whether its rule permits the admission of the written response as evidence at the hearing, or whether he can use the information only to prepare his expert witness.

Motion for Summary Determination: British Columbia

Under s. 31 of British Columbia's *Administrative Tribunals Act*, a tribunal may dismiss all or part of an application if

- the tribunal has no jurisdiction over the application;
- the applicant missed the time limit for filing;
- the application is frivolous, vexatious, trivial, or an abuse of process;
- the application was made in bad faith or for an improper purpose;
- there is excessive delay in pursuing the application;
- the applicant did not comply with an order of the tribunal;
- there is no reasonable prospect of success; or
- the application has been appropriately dealt with in another proceeding.

However, the tribunal must abide by the following two conditions:

- before dismissing an application for any of these reasons, the tribunal must give the applicant an opportunity to make submissions; and
- after dismissing all or part of an application, the tribunal must notify all the parties and give reasons in writing.

there is no remedy available under the law or that there is no evidence on which a remedy can be granted. Some tribunals also permit a party to request dismissal of a case on this basis.

For a tribunal, permitting parties to bring such motions is a two-edged sword. On the one hand, if a case clearly cannot succeed, it is difficult to justify the time and cost involved in proceeding with a hearing. On the other hand, parties will frequently bring a motion for dismissal even when they cannot provide sufficient evidence to support the request. In these cases, the availability of this kind of motion often increases the length, cost, and complexity of the proceeding, and makes it less efficient.

An additional concern is that the hearing of a motion for dismissal may turn into a hearing of the main issue in the case on its merits.

MOTION TO DECIDE A JURISDICTIONAL ISSUE

A party may bring a preliminary motion that the tribunal has no jurisdiction to hear the case or to rule on a particular issue in the case. An example of a jurisdictional issue, discussed in the next section, is whether the tribunal has the authority to decide constitutional questions. Tribunals may prefer to address and resolve such issues before proceeding with a full hearing.

MOTION TO DECIDE A CONSTITUTIONAL QUESTION

Constitutional questions fall into two broad categories:

1. challenges to the constitutional validity of a federal or provincial statute, a municipal bylaw, or a rule of common law; and

2. questions as to whether the constitution affects how such laws or rules apply in a particular case.

For example, a law that bars access to certain services on the basis of a person's sexual orientation may be challenged as invalid; or it may be considered valid, but not applicable in certain circumstances.

Constitutional questions are generally decided with reference to the division of powers between the federal government and the provincial governments, or to the effect of the *Canadian Charter of Rights and Freedoms*[4] on the tribunal's process or decisions. Such questions are often raised in the form of a preliminary motion, before the date set for the hearing. However, they may also be raised at the beginning of the hearing or at any time during the hearing.

Authority of the Tribunal To Decide Constitutional Questions

Not all tribunals have authority to decide constitutional questions or to grant the remedies requested. In some cases, only a court has the jurisdiction to hear a constitutional question.

The authority of a particular tribunal to decide constitutional questions may be set out in a statute governing the tribunal. If there is no statutory reference, it can be difficult to determine whether the tribunal has this power.

In the 1990s, the Supreme Court of Canada established tests for determining whether tribunals can decide constitutional questions; however, these tests were

---

4 Part I of the *Constitution Act, 1982*, RSC 1985, app. II, no. 44.

complex and created much uncertainty. In 2003, the Supreme Court reduced the confusion by ruling that if a tribunal has authority to interpret laws generally, this authority will be presumed to include the ability to decide constitutional issues unless the context requires the opposite conclusion.[5] The tests are still evolving.

Authority of the Tribunal To Decide Constitutional Questions: A Case

In the *Martin* case, Mr. Martin suffered from chronic pain caused by work-related injuries. He received benefits and rehabilitation from the Workers' Compensation Board of Nova Scotia. However, regulations prevented him from getting these benefits for more than four weeks. Martin appealed the board's decision to end his benefits to the Appeals Tribunal, on the grounds that the regulations infringed his right to equality under s. 15 of the *Canadian Charter of Rights and Freedoms*.

The Workers' Compensation Board argued that the tribunal had no authority to hear a Charter argument, under a complex test that the Supreme Court had established to determine which tribunals have the power to hear Charter arguments. The Supreme Court clarified and simplified its test. It ruled that if administrative tribunals implicitly or explicitly have jurisdiction to decide other questions of law, they are presumed to have the power to decide constitutional questions unless the context requires the opposite conclusion.

An example of a context that would rebut the presumption that a particular tribunal can decide constitutional questions is where a statute provides for a tribunal to determine questions of law and does not expressly exclude constitutional questions, but the same statute or another one expressly confers the right to decide this kind of constitutional question on a different administrative body and establishes a straightforward procedure for redirecting this kind of issue to the other body.

If the tribunal does not have explicit authority to decide constitutional questions and has not previously ruled on its authority, it may take one of two approaches when asked to hear an argument about constitutional validity:

1. the tribunal may ask the parties to address whether such authority exists and, if so, what is the scope of that authority, before deciding whether to hear the constitutional question; or
2. the tribunal may assume that it has jurisdiction to decide constitutional questions and proceed to do so, unless one of the parties questions its authority.

The tribunal may develop internal or published guidelines as to which approach its members should take.

When Constitutional Questions Should Be Decided

It is often convenient for a tribunal to decide constitutional questions before a hearing. However, the stage at which a constitutional question should be addressed depends on the nature of the question and the kind of information needed for the decision.

If the question is purely a question of law, the tribunal may choose to decide it before hearing evidence. If the question is more complex, involving an analysis of facts and evidence, the tribunal may either

---

5 *Nova Scotia (Workers' Compensation Board) v. Martin; Nova Scotia (Workers' Compensation Board) v. Laseur*, [2003] 2 SCR 504; 2003 SCC 54.

- hear the constitutional arguments before hearing evidence, but reserve its decision until the end of the case; or
- hear the constitutional arguments at the end of the hearing, along with the final arguments on the other issues raised, and make its decision at that time.

Procedure for Bringing a Motion

The requirements for bringing a motion on a constitutional question vary widely among federal and provincial tribunals.

In some cases, any person who intends to raise a constitutional question before a tribunal is required by statute to give notice to the attorney general of Canada or the attorney general of the province, or both, before arguing the issue. For example, the *Federal Courts Act*[6] requires notice to both attorneys general before a constitutional question is presented to a federal tribunal. Similarly, Ontario's *Courts of Justice Act*[7] (CJA) prohibits Ontario tribunals from considering constitutional questions without prior notice to the two attorneys general. In some provinces, such as Saskatchewan and New Brunswick, the statutes apply only to arguments before courts; in others, such as Newfoundland, it is unclear whether the statutory requirements apply only to courts or also to tribunals.

The notice to an attorney general should set out the facts relating to the constitutional question and the issues that will be raised. In Ontario, the form that the notice must take is specified in the CJA. Once notice has been served on the attorneys general, they have the right to participate in the argument, although usually they do not.

The tribunal should ensure that notice has been served before hearing the arguments of the parties. If notice has not been given, a party may object to the hearing of the arguments. Moreover, the tribunal may not grant any remedy requested unless proper notice has been served.

CHAPTER SUMMARY

One of the key reasons for establishing tribunals is that they can settle disputes in less time and at less cost than courts. In earlier years, they achieved these savings, in part, by holding hearings without the preliminary procedures used in the courts. However, this approach also meant that tribunals often sacrificed fairness and thoroughness to speed and convenience. In recent years, the trend has been toward increased use of pre-hearing procedures as a means of improving both efficiency and fairness.

Some procedures are basic and may be required by statute—for example, identifying participants in the proceeding and notifying them of the hearing. Many tribunals also require parties to disclose at least some of their evidence before the hearing.

Tribunals may encourage the parties to engage in pre-hearing negotiations aimed at resolving issues or settling the case, and some tribunals assist the process through mediation. In addition, procedural matters may be addressed at pre-hearing conferences and through preliminary motions brought by parties to the proceeding.

---

6 RSC 1985, c. F-7.

7 RSO 1990, c. C.43.

Ideally, through disclosure, mediation, and rulings on motions, the issues can be resolved without a hearing or the hearing can be shortened. These mechanisms, along with pre-hearing conferences, also increase the transparency—and therefore the fairness—of the tribunal's proceedings.

KEY TERMS

affidavit   a statement sworn before an authorized person such as a lawyer in which the person signing the statement sets out facts that he or she affirms to be true

alternative dispute resolution   a procedure that makes use of mechanisms such as mediation, conciliation, and arbitration to facilitate the resolution of issues in a dispute without recourse to a hearing before a tribunal

disclosure   a pre-hearing procedure in which parties are required to present evidence relevant to the proceeding

evidence   information that a party seeks to use in a legal proceeding to prove or disprove a contention or allegation

examination for discovery   a form of disclosure in which one party orally questions another party under oath or affirmation

interrogatory   a form of disclosure in which one party submits written questions to another party, which that party is required to answer in writing

intervenor   a person who is granted the right to participate in a proceeding, but without the full range of rights granted to a party, because he or she may be adversely affected by the outcome or can provide assistance to the tribunal in deciding the dispute

intervenor status   the right of a person to participate in a proceeding without the full range of rights usually granted to a party; may be authorized by statute or provided for in a tribunal's procedural rules

mediation   a method of alternative dispute resolution in which an impartial person who has no decision-making authority intervenes in a dispute in order to assist the parties in settling the issues

motion   an oral or written application to a court or tribunal to rule on an issue in a proceeding

moving party   a party who brings a motion; *see also* responding party

notice   a document that informs a person of a legal proceeding that may affect the person's interests or in which the person may have a right to participate

particulars   details that explain or clarify matters related to evidence, arguments, or remedies disclosed before or in the course of a proceeding

party   a person who has a right to participate in a legal proceeding

party status   usually, the right of a person to participate fully in a proceeding; may be granted by statute or at the discretion of the tribunal

pre-hearing conference   an informal meeting or formal hearing in advance of the main hearing in a proceeding, held for the purpose of making procedural decisions or resolving issues

proof of service   a written statement affirming that a notion of motion has been served on all parties to a proceeding and indicating how and when the notice was served

responding party the party who is required to respond to a motion brought by another party; *see also* moving party

***sine die* adjournment** adjournment for an indefinite period

witness statement a written statement provided by a party to other parties or to a court or tribunal, or both, setting out the expected evidence of a person the party expects to call as a witness; also known informally as a "will say"

KEY CASES

Intervention Before Courts and Tribunals

Peel (Regional Municipality) v. Great Atlantic & Pacific Co. of Canada Ltd.
(1990), 74 OR (2d) 164 (CA)

FACTS: The People for Sunday Association of Canada, a non-profit group with members from religious groups, trade unions, and small retail businesses, applied to intervene in the appeal of a decision that held that the *Retail Business Holidays Act*, RSO 1980, c. 453, which limited Sunday shopping, was unconstitutional and contrary to the *Canadian Charter of Rights and Freedoms.*

ISSUE: What was the test for intervenor status?

DECISION: When determining whether to grant intervenor status, the court had to consider the following: the nature of the case; the issues in the case; and whether the People for Sunday Association as intervenor would likely make a useful contribution without causing injustice to the principal parties. Allowing intervenor status in a Charter case is often particularly desirable, because Charter decisions tend to have a greater effect on people other than the litigants. In this case, the People for Sunday Association represented a large number of people with a direct interest in the outcome of the appeal, it had special knowledge and expertise of the subject matter, and it had a different perspective from the attorney general, who would be making similar arguments in support of the Act.

Jurisdiction To Hear Charter Arguments

Nova Scotia (Workers' Compensation Board) v. Martin; Nova Scotia (Workers' Compensation Board) v. Laseur, [2003] 2 SCR 504; 2003 SCC 54

FACTS: Two workers suffered from the disability of chronic pain caused by work-related injuries. They received temporary disability benefits and rehabilitation from the Workers' Compensation Board of Nova Scotia. However, the regulations excluded chronic pain from the regular workers' compensation system, and ended their benefits after four weeks. The workers argued before the Workers' Compensation Appeals Tribunal that this infringed their right to equality under s. 15(1) of the *Canadian Charter of Rights and Freedoms.*

ISSUE: Did the Appeals Tribunal have jurisdiction to hear the Charter argument?

DECISION: The Appeals Tribunal had jurisdiction to consider the constitutionality of the challenged provisions of the Act and the regulations. Administrative tribunals that have jurisdiction to decide questions of law arising under a legislative provision are presumed to also have jurisdiction to decide the constitutional validity of that provision. In this case the provisions violated the Charter, and the Nova Scotia government was directed to amend them.

REVIEW QUESTIONS

1. Why do tribunals use pre-hearing procedures?

2. What is "disclosure," and what forms does it take?

3. What is a "pre-hearing conference," and what kinds of issues may be addressed at a PHC?

4. Explain the difference between a "party" and an "intervenor."

5. Explain the difference between "evidence" and "particulars."

6. If some of the parties reach a settlement, what is the effect on the rights of other parties who do not wish to accept the settlement?

7. What is "mediation," and what are its advantages and disadvantages compared with adjudication of a dispute?

8. What is a "motion," and how do procedures for preliminary motions differ from those for motions at the main hearing?

9. Name four types of issues that may be resolved through preliminary motions.

EXERCISES

1. Your client, a landlord, wants to make an application to the Ontario Rental Housing Tribunal to evict a tenant for not paying rent. Please draft this application. What form would you use to make the application? What information would you include in the application? How would you serve the notice of your application, and to whom? Within what time are you required to serve the application? How will you satisfy the tribunal that you have properly served the notice on everyone entitled to it?

    When the tribunal establishes a date for the hearing of your client's application, who is entitled to receive notice of the hearing? Draft the notice of hearing. What information should be contained in the notice? Who is responsible for serving this notice? How will the person responsible for serving the notice satisfy the tribunal that it has been properly served?

2. Describe and compare the rules of practice for three tribunals dealing with the following subjects:

    a. How to raise a constitutional question before the tribunal

    b. The conduct of a pre-hearing conference

    c. How to bring a motion in advance of a hearing

    d. Disclosure of evidence by parties to each other and/or to the tribunal before a hearing

    e. The use of mediation, conciliation, or other forms of alternative dispute resolution.

3. Name three Ontario statutes that provide that documents that will be used as evidence at a hearing must be provided to a party before the hearing begins. In each case, describe the subject matter of the proceeding, the type of body holding the hearing, who is required to produce the documents, and who is entitled to receive them.

FURTHER READING

Andromache Karakatsanis, "Problem-Solving with ADR: The Tribunal Perspective" (1995-96) vol. 9 *Canadian Journal of Administrative Law and Practice* 125.

Robert Macaulay and James Sprague, *Practice and Procedure Before Administrative Tribunals* (Toronto: Carswell) (looseleaf), chapters 11 and 12.

CHAPTER 8

Tribunal Procedures During Hearings

LEARNING OBJECTIVES

After reading this chapter, you will understand

- the differences between an oral hearing, an electronic hearing, and a written hearing;
- the advantages and disadvantages of each of these hearing formats;
- the roles of various participants in a hearing; and
- the stages of a hearing and the procedures usually followed at each stage.

[I]t is of fundamental importance that justice should not only be done, but should manifestly and undoubtedly be seen to be done.

Lord Hewart in *R v. Sussex Justices*, [1924] 1 KB 256, at 259

INTRODUCTION

Like pre-hearing procedures, the conduct of hearings varies greatly between tribunals. Some of these differences flow from statutes governing particular tribunals. Some reflect the tribunal's preference for more formal or less formal procedures, or the complexity of the cases brought before the tribunal. The following examples illustrate the range of differences in hearing procedures:

- Most tribunals hold their hearings in public; a few hold them in private.
- Some tribunals follow the strict rules of evidence established by the courts; others provide much greater latitude in the kind of information that the parties may present.
- Some tribunals require witnesses to give testimony under oath; others do not.
- Some tribunals permit intervenors; others do not.

Even within a tribunal, the conduct of hearings may vary, depending on the nature of the issues and the number and sophistication of the participants.

HEARING FORMATS

There are three possible formats for a hearing: oral, electronic, and written. The advantages and disadvantages of each are described below.

Oral Hearings

In an oral hearing, all the participants are physically present in the same place, receiving the same information at the same time. This format offers several advantages, in particular the following:

- Oral presentation of arguments and testimony reduces the need for documentation and therefore saves preparation time and costs.
- Communication is direct and efficient.
- Physical presence of participants allows for assessment of the credibility of parties, witnesses, and representatives, as well as observation of the tribunal's responses.
- Procedures such as cross-examination, presentation of arguments, and responses can be carried out efficiently.
- The tribunal has direct control of the hearing process and can intervene as necessary.
- The transparency of the oral format promotes procedural fairness.

The main disadvantages of an oral hearing are the cost of the hearing space and, in some cases, the time and cost involved in travel to and from the hearing location.

Electronic Hearings

An electronic hearing is generally held through a telephone conference call (a teleconference) or a video conference. These formats offer the following advantages:

- Particularly in the case of a teleconference, and sometimes for a video conference, there are savings in time and costs if tribunal members and participants do not have to travel to the hearing location.
- As in the case of an oral hearing, there is reduced reliance on written documents and therefore a saving in preparation time and costs.
- A video conference allows for observation of participants and tribunal members, as well as direct responses.
- A video conference is transparent and often procedurally efficient, and it gives the tribunal reasonably good control of the hearing process.

Disadvantages of electronic hearings include the following:

- For a video conference, there may be costs for facilities as well as travel time and costs for at least some participants.
- Documents must be transmitted in advance of the hearing, and delays may occur in any necessary updating of evidence.
- A teleconference does not allow for observation and may be procedurally inefficient (for example, if participants talk for too long or talk over each other).
- In a teleconference, the tribunal may have difficulty identifying the speakers and controlling the hearing process.
- A teleconference provides less assurance of transparency and procedural fairness than is possible with an oral hearing or a video conference.
- For both teleconferences and video conferences, the quality of communication may not be either predictable or reliable.

Written Hearings

In a written hearing, all the information—evidence, arguments, and responses—must be prepared in written form and exchanged between the tribunal members and other participants. This format offers two possible advantages:

- It eliminates the travel time and costs that may be incurred for an oral hearing or a video conference.
- It eliminates the cost of providing hearing facilities.

Against these advantages are a number of disadvantages. As one former tribunal chair has noted, "written hearings are not necessarily faster, cheaper or simpler."[1] The main disadvantages are as follows:

- The parties, representatives, and tribunal all incur significant costs for the preparation of documents.
- Further costs, in time and/or money, are incurred for the distribution of documents. E-mail and fax are the cheapest and fastest forms of delivery, but neither is secure. In addition, some participants may lack the technology for transmitting material electronically. Mail is relatively inexpensive but may be slow and also not secure. Couriers are fast and secure, but expensive.

Distribution of Documents by Fax: Security Concerns

"Good evening. We begin with a CTV News exclusive that goes to the heart of one of those worst nightmare scenarios. Private banking information that you thought was safe and secure is instead out there floating around. In a stunning breach by the Canadian Imperial Bank of Commerce, financial information from customers at hundreds of CIBC branches that was supposed to have gone to bank offices was being faxed mistakenly to a scrap yard in Ridgley, West Virginia. Despite pleas from a frustrated scrap yard owner, the faxes kept coming right up to this week."

— Lloyd Robertson, *CTV News and Current Affairs*,
broadcast November 25, 2004

- There is also a heavy cost in time for the preparation and processing of documents. Evidence and arguments must be distributed in advance of the hearing; then the parties must prepare and distribute their questions and counterarguments; the tribunal panel must prepare and distribute its own questions; and finally, the tribunal must write and deliver its decision. In addition to the time spent preparing written materials, delays may occur at all these stages. As a result, the hearing may take much longer than it would in an alternative format.
- The quality of the documentation may vary. Further delays will occur if many points need to be clarified.

---

1 Margot Priest, "Amendments to the Statutory Powers Procedure Act (Ontario): Analysis and Comments," in Philip Anisman and Robert F. Reid, eds., *Administrative Law Issues and Practice* (Scarborough, ON: Carswell, 1995), 85-108, at 93.

- Communication is indirect, and there is no opportunity for observation. This is a concern if credibility is an issue.

- Updating of evidence takes additional time.

- The tribunal's control of the hearing process relies on the drafting and distribution of clear procedures for document preparation and distribution. Time limits may be set out in the notice of hearing or in separate procedural rules. The enforcement of deadlines for various stages of the process may further complicate the conduct of the hearing.

- Since a written hearing provides no opportunity for oral cross-examination, the tribunal may use interrogatories to obtain clarification and reach a decision. These too can extend the hearing process.

- A written hearing lacks transparency and may provide little assurance of procedural fairness.

Comparison of Hearing Formats*

Factors to be considered	Oral hearing		Electronic hearing		Written hearing	
	Adv.	Dis.	Adv.	Dis.	Adv.	Dis.
Time						
Travel		X	X (TC)	X (VC)	X	
Documents	X			X		X
Procedures	X		X			X
Cost						
Travel		X	X (TC)	X (VC)	X	
Facilities		X	X (TC)	X (VC)	X	
Documents	X		X			X
Communication						
Quality	X			X		X
Directness	X		X			X
Observation	X		X (VC)	X (TC)		X
Efficiency (immediacy/updating)	X		X			X
Conduct of hearing process						
Control	X			X		X
Efficiency	X		X (VC)	X (TC)		X
Fairness/transparency	X		X (VC)	X (TC)		X

* Adv. = Advantage.   Dis. = Disadvantage.   TC = Teleconference.   VC = Video conference.

Choice of Hearing Format

ORAL VERSUS ELECTRONIC OR WRITTEN HEARING

Oral hearings have traditionally been the most common form of hearing. For many years, the enabling statutes or common law fairness rules did not permit the use of an alternative format. In Ontario, for example, the *Statutory Powers Procedure Act*[2] (SPPA) did not allow written or electronic hearings until 1994.

Oral hearings are still often preferred because they encourage fairness. However, tribunals that are not constrained by legislation may hold a hearing in any format that facilitates a fair process.

ELECTRONIC VERSUS ORAL HEARING

Section 5.2 of Ontario's SPPA permits a tribunal to hold an electronic hearing unless a party satisfies the tribunal that holding an electronic hearing rather than an oral one is likely to cause significant prejudice to that party. The notice of the hearing must state that where the tribunal is satisfied that such risk of prejudice exists, it will hold an oral hearing instead.[3]

In choosing between an electronic and an oral hearing, the tribunal may consider which format is better suited to the public interest. For example, many members of the public may be affected by the outcome of the hearing and may wish to attend, either as participants or as observers. In such cases, a hearing by teleconference may not be as appropriate as an oral hearing. However, it may be possible to satisfy the public interest through a video conference if a facility can be made available where members of the public can view the proceedings on a screen.

For an electronic hearing, documents must generally be in the hands of all participants and the tribunal panel before the hearing begins. It is usually difficult to transmit documents to the parties and the panel once the proceedings are under way. It is also inefficient to interrupt the hearing while other parties read a document for the first time or listen to a party read it to them. The tribunal may therefore specify in the notice of the hearing the dates by which the parties must exchange and file all documentary evidence.

A tribunal may conduct an electronic hearing largely as it would an oral hearing. However, teleconference hearings, in particular, involve some variations in procedure. For example, before the hearing, the tribunal should provide directions on the participants who will speak and the order of speakers. During the hearing, it should require each speaker to identify himself or herself before speaking and discourage interruptions.

Witnesses may be examined and cross-examined in the usual manner. However, if the witness will be questioned about the contents of numerous or lengthy documents, the pace will have to be adjusted to ensure that all participants and the panel can follow the documentary references. In these circumstances, an oral hearing may be more appropriate than an electronic hearing.

WRITTEN VERSUS ORAL HEARING

Some tribunals are authorized by statute to hold written hearings. Except where prohibited by statute or common law fairness requirements, tribunals may hold

---

2 RSO 1990, c. S.22.

3 Section 6(5)(c) of the SPPA.

written hearings in certain circumstances even without express statutory authority. The courts have held that written hearings do not necessarily violate the rules of natural justice or procedural fairness. They have allowed federal tribunals to hold written hearings despite objections where the proceedings would not infringe common law fairness principles.[4]

In Ontario, s. 5.1 of the SPPA allows a tribunal to hold a written hearing unless a party satisfies the tribunal that there is good reason not to do so. The notice of the hearing must state that where a party objects on this ground and satisfies the tribunal that the objection is justified, the tribunal will hold an electronic or oral hearing instead.[5] Since the tribunal must then choose between these alternatives, the notice may also invite the objecting party to identify a preference. If an oral hearing is preferred, the party should indicate how an electronic hearing would likely cause him or her significant prejudice.

Instead of notifying parties of the intention to hold a written hearing, and then receiving and considering objections, a tribunal may find it more practical to determine in advance whether the parties consent to a written hearing. If all parties consent, it is likely that a tribunal can hold a written hearing even without explicit statutory authority. For example, Ontario's Workplace Safety and Insurance Appeals Tribunal holds written hearings on consent and without any express statutory authority other than a general power to control its own procedure.

COMBINING ORAL, ELECTRONIC, AND WRITTEN HEARINGS

Sometimes the most efficient process is to hold part of a hearing orally, part electronically, and part in writing. For example, in an oral hearing, if an expert witness lives in another jurisdiction and the witness's schedule makes personal attendance difficult, or if the cost of travel and accommodation is too high, the witness might testify electronically or in writing, particularly where credibility is not an issue.

In Ontario, s. 5.2.1 of the SPPA permits a tribunal to hold "any combination of written, electronic and oral hearings" in one proceeding. As long as the appropriate notice is given and there is no prejudice to any party, it is unlikely that a court would rule against the use of a combined format.

Procedures in an Oral or Electronic Hearing

The conduct of an oral or electronic hearing usually consists of the following sequence of procedures (discussed in more detail below):

- The tribunal presents introductory comments.
- The tribunal addresses preliminary matters, such as motions on jurisdictional issues, disclosure, or procedural issues.
- The parties present opening statements.
- The parties present their evidence.
- The parties present closing arguments.

---

4 *Hoffman-La Roche Ltd. v. Delmar Chemicals Ltd.*, [1965] SCR 575; *National Aviation Consultants Ltd. v. Starline Aviation Ltd.*, [1973] FC 571 (CA).

5 Section 6(4)(b) of the SPPA.

The hearing ends with the closing arguments. After the proceeding is concluded, the tribunal either gives ("renders") its decision or postpones ("reserves") the decision to a later date.

Procedures in a Written Hearing

Quite different procedures apply to the conduct of a written hearing, usually consisting of the following:

- The tribunal sends a notice to the parties setting out the issues to be addressed and specifying the next step and the deadline for its completion.
- The party who is required to prove the issue in dispute sends documentation of the evidence and arguments to the other parties and the tribunal.
- The tribunal requests written responses, including both evidence and arguments, from the other parties by a specified date.
- The responding parties send their responses to the tribunal and to the other parties.
- If the responses raise questions or request further clarification, the tribunal may grant the first party to present evidence an opportunity to respond in writing.
- The tribunal arranges for members of the public to obtain access to all documents in the written hearing.
- The tribunal notifies the parties that the hearing has been completed.
- The tribunal begins writing a decision.
- When the decision is complete, the tribunal sends it to the parties.

PARTICIPANTS IN THE HEARING AND THEIR ROLES

The principal participants in the hearing are the **adjudicator** (the presiding tribunal member or a panel of members) and the parties. The hearing may also include intervenors, representatives, witnesses, tribunal staff, agency and tribunal counsel, and a court reporter. The respective roles of these participants are briefly described below.

The Parties

The parties include the person who initiated the proceeding and any other person specified by statute, entitled by common law to respond to the initiator, or recognized as a party by the tribunal. In Ontario, ss. 10 and 10.1 of the SPPA set out the rights of parties to a tribunal proceeding. Parties may

- be represented by counsel or an agent,
- call and examine witnesses,
- present evidence and arguments, and
- cross-examine witnesses

In Quebec, ss. 13(4) and 134 of the *Administrative Justice Act*[6] give parties the right to be represented before all adjudicative bodies and the right to examine and

---

6 RSQ, c. J-3.

cross-examine witnesses to the extent necessary to ensure fair proceedings before the Administrative Justice Tribunal.

Sections 4 and 5 of Alberta's APA give parties the right to furnish evidence and make representations and to contradict or explain allegations made against them by an authority; but the right to contradict or explain includes a right to cross-examine only where cross-examination is the only way to provide a fair opportunity to do this. The APA does not provide a right to counsel.

Under British Columbia's ATA, parties have the right to summon and examine witnesses and to cross-examine other parties' witnesses; to be represented by counsel or an agent; and to make submissions (ss. 32 and 38).

Under common law principles, the parties have additional rights, such as the right to be present throughout the hearing and the right to an unbiased tribunal.

APPLICANT OR APPELLANT

The person who has set the proceeding in motion is known as the **applicant**. If the proceeding is an appeal of a decision of a government official or agency or of another tribunal, this person may be known as the **appellant**.

The applicant may be a private individual, a group, or an organization. In disciplinary or regulatory proceedings, the applicant may be the agency staff. (See "Agency Staff as Parties.")

Agency Staff as Parties

Agency staff may be the applicant in a proceeding. For example, if the governing body of a self-regulating profession receives a complaint about the conduct of a member, the staff of the agency may investigate the complaint. If they find supporting evidence, the staff may lay charges against the individual. They will then be responsible for proving the charges before the governing body's tribunal.

Agency staff may also be respondents in a proceeding. For example, in the case described above, if the professional involved has had his licence to practise suspended or revoked, he may apply to the governing body to be reinstated. The respondents may then be the agency staff if there are grounds for opposing the application.

In some proceedings, such as an application by a regulated business for approval of an increase in rates, agency staff may play a neutral role, providing unbiased expertise to the hearing panel. Often, however, when agency staff are parties to a proceeding, their role is to represent one side in the case.

Since the tribunal is required to be unbiased, it must treat the evidence provided by staff with the same impartiality that it brings to consideration of the evidence of the other parties. Similarly, the tribunal should not give agency staff preferential treatment or communicate privately with them about any aspect of the case.

RESPONDENT

The **respondent** is the party who is required to reply to the application, allegation, or appeal brought forward by the applicant. Usually, the respondent opposes the remedy sought by the applicant.

Respondents, like applicants, may be private individuals, groups, or organizations. For example, when a developer seeks approval for an official plan amendment or applies for a building permit or a septic system permit, the respondents may include neighbours, ratepayer groups, the municipal council, and provincial or federal government departments. When a regulated business such as a telephone company or cable provider asks a regulatory agency to grant an increase in rates or access to a new market, the respondents may include competitors, subscribers, and other consumer groups, as well as agency staff. (See "Agency Staff as Parties.")

Intervenors

As compared with parties, intervenors play a more limited, supporting role in the proceeding. They have an interest in the outcome sufficient to warrant their participation, but not sufficient to merit party status. When intervenors are allowed to participate, any restrictions that may apply are usually set out in the tribunal's procedural rules. For example, the tribunal may accept written evidence of an intervenor but not oral evidence, or it may permit an intervenor to provide testimony on some but not all of the issues in the case.

Representatives

Parties and intervenors are generally represented in a proceeding by a lawyer (also known as **counsel**) or by a paralegal, law clerk, or other **agent**. The role of a representative, or advocate, is to assist his or her client in preparing and presenting the case and to take any further action after the tribunal has rendered its decision.

Preparing the case usually consists of the following functions:

- researching the law;
- obtaining information about the tribunal's practices and procedures;
- explaining the hearing process to the client;
- locating and interviewing witnesses;
- setting a hearing date convenient to the client and the witnesses;
- preparing, serving, and filing documents required by the tribunal;
- advising on strategy;
- deciding what evidence to present; and
- deciding the order in which the client's witnesses will be called.

Presenting the case involves some or all of the following functions:

- making preliminary motions;
- making opening statements;
- questioning the client and his or her witnesses;
- cross-examining the witnesses of other parties;
- raising reasonable objections to questions asked of the client or witnesses;
- making motions;
- presenting arguments; and
- making closing arguments.

The role of a lawyer differs in some respects from that of an agent. Generally, under rules of professional conduct established by provincial law societies, a lawyer is not permitted to testify at a hearing in which he or she is representing a client. An agent, on the other hand, may sometimes be a witness. For example, a real estate appraiser may argue the case for a property tax reduction on behalf of a client while also giving evidence about his or her own research into the value of the client's property.

Differences in the status of lawyers and agents in a proceeding are also recognized by some statutes and regulatory bodies. For example, in the event of abuse of a tribunal's process, s. 23(3) of Ontario's SPPA gives the tribunal authority to bar an agent, but not a lawyer, from the proceeding. However, a lawyer who abuses the tribunal's process may be subject to disciplinary action by the provincial law society. Agents, on the other hand, are unregulated in most provinces. (See "Respect for the Tribunal's Rules of Process.")

Respect for the Tribunal's Rules of Process

- Both lawyers and agents have a duty of courtesy and honesty to the tribunal. While they are expected to defend their client's interests vigorously, they may not mislead the tribunal or disrupt its proceedings.
- A lawyer or an agent may not intervene in a proceeding with the sole intention of creating a delay.
- A lawyer or an agent may not give evidence under the pretense of questioning witnesses or making submissions to the tribunal.

Violation of any of these rules may be considered an abuse of process.

Witnesses

Witnesses provide the factual information, and in some cases the expert opinions, that the tribunal considers in arriving at its decision. The evidence of witnesses is obtained through questioning by the parties or their representatives, and sometimes by the hearing panel.

Witnesses may be called upon by representatives of the parties to give evidence at the proceeding. In addition, some statutes, such as s. 12 of Ontario's SPPA, give the tribunal authority to require witnesses to attend an oral or written hearing. The summons issued by the tribunal lists any documents or other things that the witness must bring to the hearing.

Section 11 of the SPPA gives any witness the right to be represented by counsel or an agent, but only for the purpose of advising the witness of his or her rights, such as the right to refuse to disclose privileged information. Quebec's AJA, Alberta's APA, and British Columbia's ATA do not give witnesses a right to their own representative.

Section 49 of British Columbia's ATA states that if a witness refuses to attend, answer questions, or produce documents, a court may punish him or her for contempt of the tribunal. Under s. 13(1) of Ontario's SPPA, witnesses are required to answer any question put to them unless a party objects and the tribunal excuses the witness from answering the question. Section 133 of Quebec's AJA states that witnesses before the Administrative Justice Tribunal may not refuse to answer questions put to them by the parties or by the administrative tribunal. Section 13 of the *Canadian Charter of Rights and Freedoms*[7] gives witnesses broad protection from having their testimony used against them in any other proceeding. In Ontario, similar protection is provided under s. 14 of the SPPA against the use of evidence in a civil proceeding.

---

7 Part I of the *Constitution Act, 1982*, RSC 1985, app. II, no. 44.

Tribunal Staff Providing Administrative Support

Although courts always have their own staff (registrars or clerks) present in the courtroom to assist the judge, many tribunals do not provide this support to their adjudicators. However, at some tribunals, agency staff will assist the adjudicator with tasks such as handling exhibits and swearing in witnesses.

Agency Counsel and Tribunal Counsel

Counsel for a tribunal may play one of two distinct roles:

1. presenting a case to the tribunal on behalf of a party such as the tribunal staff or the staff of a related agency that acts as a prosecutor or as an advocate; or

2. giving legal advice and assistance to the adjudicator.

Lawyers performing the first role are referred to as "agency counsel" and those performing the second are called "tribunal counsel."

The reason for making this distinction is that when agency lawyers represent the agency as a party, the interests of the agency are not the same as the interests of the tribunal. The interests of the agency are to prove its case; the interests of the tribunal are to make an impartial and independent decision. Usually, when an agency is a party, the tribunal and the agency are separate bodies, or the tribunal members are separated structurally from other functions of the agency. Recognition of this separation in the conduct of the proceeding reduces the possibility of bias and conflict of interest by distinguishing the tribunal in its role as adjudicator from the agency acting as a party in the case. The role of agency counsel is therefore restricted to representation of the agency as a whole or some part of the agency other than the tribunal.

On the other hand, the tribunal members often require their own legal adviser to assist them in making an impartial decision. This function is clearly different from that of agency counsel. Some of these differences are summarized below.

Agency counsel may play an adversarial role—that is, opposing the positions of other parties. They should have no communication with the adjudicator outside the hearing room, and the tribunal should give them no access to information in its possession unless other parties have the same access.

In contrast, tribunal counsel provide direct assistance to the tribunal on matters of procedure and legal interpretation. In an inquisitorial hearing in which the tribunal itself calls witnesses, tribunal counsel will choose the witnesses to be called, prepare them for testifying, and conduct the examination of them in the proceeding. If the parties (including agency counsel) also call witnesses, tribunal counsel may question those witnesses, but usually only to clarify rather than challenge their testimony.

Unlike agency counsel, tribunal counsel are permitted to assist the panel behind the scenes. Unless a statute requires that legal advice given to an adjudicator must be shared with the parties,[8] the advice given by tribunal counsel to the panel

---

8 For example, s. 39(6) of the Ontario *Human Rights Code*, RSO 1990, c. H.19, states, "[T]he Tribunal may seek legal advice from an adviser independent of the parties and in such case the nature of the advice shall be made known to the parties in order that they may make submissions as to the law."

may be treated as privileged; that is, it may not be revealed to the parties. However, this question is open to some debate.

In giving legal advice, tribunal counsel must be careful not to infringe on the adjudicator's decision-making role or to favour one side in the dispute over the other. The kind of assistance that an adjudicator may expect from tribunal counsel is discussed further in a later section of this chapter (see "Consultation with Tribunal Counsel").

Court Reporter

A court reporter (sometimes referred to as a "verbatim reporter") may be present at the hearing to record all the testimony, and sometimes the arguments, in the exact words of the speaker. The reporter may create the record either by simultaneously repeating the spoken proceedings on audiotape or by typing them in shorthand on a word processor. The reporter may later transcribe the recorded information into document form.

Some tribunals are required by statute to record their proceedings. Where recording is optional, because of the high cost of court reporters, tribunals may choose not to record their proceedings, or they may use direct transfer to audiotape. However, it is difficult for a person who was not present to produce an accurate transcript from a tape recording. Using a trained, certified court reporter provides some assurance that the transcription will be accurate.

In some cases, the tribunal will not pay for a court reporter but will permit parties to provide one at their own expense. Some tribunals also permit parties to tape-record the proceedings for their own benefit. However, a transcription of a tape made by a party will not be accepted by a tribunal or a court as a complete and accurate record of the proceedings in a subsequent appeal or judicial review of the decision.

The Adjudicator

The role of the adjudicator involves the following responsibilities:

- establishing procedures for the conduct of the hearing;
- implementing those procedures in a fair and flexible, but efficient and effective, manner;
- listening attentively and making detailed notes of evidence and arguments;
- maintaining control over the hearing process; and
- making a fair and reasoned decision that reflects the evidence, the law, and the merits of the case.

Adjudicators usually act as passive umpires, calling the plays but not significantly helping any party to make its case. However, some tribunals play a more active role in investigating, presenting witnesses, and questioning witnesses.

Parties, intervenors, representatives, and witnesses are entitled to punctuality, attentiveness, patience, courtesy, and respect from tribunal members. At the same time, tribunal members are entitled to the same from the other participants. Participants who are late, long-winded, repetitive, or rude invite a negative response from adjudicators.

HEARING PROCEDURES

Introductory Remarks

Tribunals often open their proceedings with introductory comments about the purpose of the hearing and the process. The information presented generally depends on the nature of the hearing and the experience of the participants. A shorter briefing will be required for counsel who are familiar with the hearing process than for unrepresented parties, who are unlikely to have an in-depth understanding of how tribunals in general, and this one in particular, work.

At the beginning of the hearing, the panel chair will often

1. introduce herself and any other members of the panel;

2. state the names of the parties and briefly describe the purpose of the hearing;

3. confirm that all parties or their representatives are present, and verify the representatives' names and qualifications (that is, whether they are lawyers or agents);

4. ask whether there is any other person present who wishes to participate in the proceedings, and if so, give all parties an opportunity to make submissions as to whether the person or persons should be given standing to participate as a party or intervenor;

5. describe the hearing process—for example,

   a. whether the parties will be invited to make opening statements,

   b. whether evidence is to be presented under oath or unsworn, and whether orally or in writing,

   c. the order in which the parties will present their case,

   d. the right of parties to cross-examine and re-examine witnesses,

   e. whether the parties will have an opportunity to submit reply evidence, and

   f. whether the parties will be entitled to present closing arguments;

6. ask whether anyone has any questions about the tribunal's procedure; and

7. ask whether any of the parties wish to raise preliminary matters before the hearing begins (for example, requests for adjournment, clarification of procedures, or jurisdictional issues).

The panel chair may also

- inform the parties of any past tribunal or court decisions that may be relevant to the issues in the hearing;

- explain the limits of the tribunal's jurisdiction (its authority to hold the hearing and the kinds of remedies that it can and cannot provide);

- explain whether the parties might expect an oral decision at the end of the hearing or a subsequent written decision, and advise the parties of any tribunal guidelines as to how soon after a hearing decisions should be released; and

- inform the parties of procedures for appealing the tribunal's decision.

Appendix D at the end of this book is a sample opening statement provided by one Ontario tribunal as a guide for its members.

Preliminary Matters

Some tribunals encourage parties to bring motions well in advance of the hearing for the tribunal's decision on any preliminary matters, such as requests for adjournment, requests for additional disclosure of evidence, recognition of additional parties or intervenors, challenges to the tribunal's jurisdiction, and procedural issues. Nevertheless, at the commencement of the hearing, parties may ask the adjudicator to make rulings on one or more preliminary matters before hearing opening statements and evidence.

The adjudicator's first task is to determine whether these matters should be decided before the hearing proceeds or whether they should be dealt with during or after the hearing. If the adjudicator cannot decide the issue without first hearing extensive evidence, it may be more appropriate to address it at the end of the proceeding.

If there are several preliminary motions, the adjudicator's second task is to determine the order in which they should be heard. For example, if a party brings a motion to adjourn and another person brings a motion to be recognized as a party, it may be appropriate to decide the party status motion first. If the person is made a party, he or she will be entitled to support or oppose the request for adjournment.

JURISDICTION

The parties may ask the adjudicator to determine whether the tribunal has jurisdiction to hold a hearing or to grant the remedy requested. If the adjudicator decides that the tribunal has no jurisdiction, the hearing should not proceed unless a party obtains a court ruling that the tribunal does have jurisdiction. If the adjudicator decides that the tribunal does have jurisdiction, the hearing may proceed even if a party subsequently challenges this ruling in a court or before another tribunal.

It is within the adjudicator's discretion whether to adjourn the hearing until the issue has been decided or to continue the proceeding. In exercising that discretion, the adjudicator may consider a variety of factors, including the possible consequences of delaying the hearing and the seriousness of the challenge to jurisdiction.[9]

ABSENCE OF A PARTY OR REPRESENTATIVE

If a party or a party's representative is not present at the start of the hearing, the adjudicator may proceed, provided that he or she is satisfied that the person was properly notified of the date, time, and place of the hearing. The tribunal's procedural rules may state the appropriate means of notifying a party and the method of establishing that notice has been served.

In many cases, the person responsible for giving notice proves that notice was given by providing the tribunal with proof of service—that is, a copy of the notice and a signed or sworn statement setting out how and when the notice was given.

---

9 For a discussion of the factors that may be relevant in deciding whether to proceed, see *Prassad v. Minister of Employment and Immigration* (1989), 57 DLR (4th) 663, at 687 (SCC).

The parties and the adjudicator should check the notice to ensure that it correctly states the date, time, and location of the hearing. They should also check the proof of service to verify how and when the person was served. In addition, if the person who served the notice is present, she may testify to having served the document.

If the adjudicator is not satisfied that the absent person received proper notice, he should adjourn the hearing, and either ensure that the person is served with notice or make further inquiries to determine the reason for the person's absence.

Even if the adjudicator is satisfied that the absent person was properly notified, it is still advisable for the tribunal to inquire into the reason for the person's absence before proceeding. The adjudicator may ask the tribunal staff or one of the parties to phone the person to determine whether he is on the way or has forgotten to appear. The adjudicator should avoid making such telephone calls himself.

If the adjudicator is still unable to determine why the person is absent but has sufficient evidence that the person was properly notified, the hearing may proceed. If this case is the only one on the adjudicator's docket for the day, it is appropriate to wait a reasonable time (often 30 minutes is considered reasonable) before proceeding. The adjudicator should state for the record how he established that the person was notified, what steps he took to find out the reason for the person's absence, and how long he waited before beginning the hearing.

If there are several cases on the docket, the adjudicator may decide to proceed with other cases and defer the hearing until later in the day. By the time the adjudicator deals with some of the other cases, the person may have arrived or may have sent an explanation of his absence that will help the adjudicator to decide whether to proceed or adjourn.

REQUEST FOR ADJOURNMENT

Adjournments raise the cost of proceedings, create more work for tribunal staff, and sometimes seriously inconvenience the tribunal members and other participants, particularly if the adjournment occurs at the last minute. Many people have busy schedules, and some may have to travel long distances to attend the hearing. If the case is one in which the community has an interest, observers also may be inconvenienced.

For these reasons, tribunals do not like unnecessary requests for adjournment, and representatives who make such requests do not endear themselves to adjudicators.

Generally, if a hearing date has been set well in advance and with the consent of the parties, a party should request an adjournment only because of matters beyond his control, such as the sudden illness of the party or his representative or a key witness. Representatives should avoid double booking and should ensure that they, their client, and their client's witnesses are available before agreeing to a hearing date.

If an adjournment is requested, the adjudicator must grant it if a failure to do so would deprive a party, through no fault of his own, of the right to a full and fair hearing. However, if a party has brought problems on himself—for example, by retaining a representative who is not available on the scheduled date, by retaining a representative at the last minute, or by leaving insufficient time for preparation of the case—the adjudicator may be justified in refusing an adjournment.

Adjournments have been granted so liberally in the past that many lawyers and agents have come to expect that the first request for adjournment will be approved almost automatically. However, government demands for tribunals to work more efficiently have resulted in closer scrutiny of adjournment requests. If a tribunal considers that it can no longer afford the luxury of frequently adjourning and rescheduling hearings, it may issue rules of procedure or practice directions setting out the tribunal's policies and expectations. Both the adjudicator and the parties can use such rules or guidelines to assist in determining when fairness requires an adjournment and when it does not.

REQUEST FOR A STAY OF PROCEEDINGS

Before the main part of the hearing begins, a party may request a **stay of proceedings**. This term has two meanings. First, a stay of proceedings may refer to permanent suspension of a hearing because holding the hearing would result in serious wrongdoing or harm to a party. In effect, the case is dismissed or "quashed," or decided in the party's favour without a hearing. Second, a stay of proceedings may refer to temporary suspension of the hearing until other proceedings have been completed. It is this second use of the term that is addressed here.

There are two situations in which a temporary stay of proceedings may be requested:

1. where a party is subject to civil or criminal proceedings arising out of the same conduct that is the subject of the tribunal's proceeding; and

2. where the party is seeking judicial review of some aspect of the tribunal's proceeding—for example, a procedural ruling or interim order issued by the tribunal.

There is no requirement that tribunals must grant a temporary adjournment in either of these situations. One of the purposes of setting up specialized tribunals is to provide for the expeditious resolution of disputes. This purpose would be defeated if tribunals were required to stay their proceedings for an indefinite period while a criminal or civil court dealt with a matter, particularly when court proceedings might take several years.

In deciding whether to grant a stay, a tribunal may consider the same factors that it would apply to an adjournment under a jurisdictional challenge, discussed above.[10] One important factor is whether the court dates have been set and the trial or judicial review is likely to proceed in the near future. Otherwise, the tribunal's proceeding may be suspended indefinitely.

If a party requests a stay of proceedings because the issues to be determined by the tribunal are identical to those that the court will decide, this may be a good reason to grant the stay. However, the issues are seldom the same, and the standard of proof in court is often higher. If the issues are the same but the standard of proof is different, the outcome of the court proceedings may not determine the tribunal's decision.

Another reason for requesting a stay is to reduce the risk that evidence given during the tribunal's proceeding will be used against a party in court. As discussed earlier, both s. 13 of the Charter and, in Ontario, s. 14 of the SPPA provide protection against such use. However, there is a danger that even though the evidence itself cannot be used in future court proceedings, it may lead to other incriminat-

---

10 Ibid.

ing evidence against the party in those proceedings. In general, this is not a sufficient reason to suspend the tribunal's hearing, since courts often have the power to exclude such evidence. However, there may be circumstances where the potential prejudice to a party from permitting disclosure is so great that it justifies a stay of proceedings.

Hearing of the Case on the Merits

Once the preliminaries are complete, the adjudicator will call on the parties to present their case. Depending on the length and complexity of the hearing and the sophistication of the parties, the adjudicator may invite the parties to give opening statements, or he may skip this procedure and move directly to the presentation of evidence.

OPENING STATEMENTS

Opening statements can help to focus the hearing. In short hearings involving simple issues, asking the parties to give opening statements may not be an efficient use of time. However, opening statements can be useful in some circumstances, particularly where the tribunal has required little advance disclosure of evidence and the parties are hearing the details of each other's case for the first time.

Opening statements may deal with such matters as the witnesses who will be called, the number and order of witnesses, the nature of their evidence, the probable duration of the hearing, and, most important, the issues to be addressed. Identification of the issues can help the adjudicator, other parties, and intervenors to concentrate on the evidence that is most relevant to the resolution of the dispute. Stating the issues and describing the evidence can also help the parties to streamline their case. Sometimes, opening statements reveal to the parties that they agree on matters that they thought were in dispute, or that the matters in issue are different from those they had assumed. Occasionally, the revelation of each party's case to the other party will lead to the withdrawal of all or part of an application or appeal, or an early settlement.

Opening statements are usually optional, and one or more of the parties may wish to waive the right to "open." In the courts, a responding party often has the right to defer its opening statement until it begins its case. Unless the tribunal has a rule to the contrary, it will usually respect the wishes of parties who prefer to waive or defer their opening statements.

EVIDENCE

After any preliminary issues have been dealt with and any opening statements have been made, the parties present their evidence. Unless the tribunal sets other requirements, the usual order of presentation is as follows:

1. evidence of the party who initiated the proceeding, followed by
2. evidence of any other parties with a similar interest in the outcome, followed by
3. evidence of the opposing parties.

This stage of the hearing includes the questioning of witnesses by the parties or their representatives. The procedures for the examination of witnesses and the presentation of other evidence are discussed in detail in chapter 9, Presenting Evidence at a Hearing.

Burden of Proof and Standard of Proof

The burden of proof and the standard of proof (both discussed briefly in chapter 6, Advocacy Before Administrative Agencies and Tribunals) are central to the adjudicator's assessment of the evidence and the arguments, and the ultimate decision in the case, as well as some procedural decisions.

The burden, or onus, of proof is the obligation to establish a particular fact or present a particular kind of evidence. Often the party who initiated the proceeding has the overall burden of persuading the adjudicator of the correctness or merit of her position. However, where evidence is in the hands of a different party, that party may have the obligation to produce the evidence.

The standard of proof is the degree of certainty of a fact that a party must establish in satisfying the burden of proof. In a criminal case, the standard of proof is proof beyond a reasonable doubt. That is, the person who has the onus of proving a fact must establish it as a near certainty. In tribunals, unless a statute or tribunal ruling provides for a higher or lower standard, a fact may be proven on a balance of probabilities. That is, a fact is considered established if it is shown to be more likely true than false.

Sometimes the statute governing the tribunal specifies the burden and standard of proof. In many cases, however, the statute is silent and the tribunal will be required to decide these matters on the basis of what is fair and reasonable. There may be several burdens and standards of proof relating to different issues that may arise. In addition, the manner in which these requirements are met will depend on whether the tribunal follows an adversarial or an inquisitorial process in arriving at the truth.

If the tribunal relies on an adversarial process, it is the party who bears the burden of proving a fact who must provide evidence establishing that fact to the degree of probability required by the applicable standard of proof. In contrast, if a governing statute authorizes the tribunal to follow an inquisitorial process, the tribunal itself may have the onus of collecting sufficient evidence to resolve the issue. For example, in a hearing dealing with a request for release from custody, the tribunal may be required to determine whether the release of the person will pose a threat to public safety. If there is insufficient evidence for the tribunal to answer the question to the required level of certainty, the statute will indicate, explicitly or implicitly, what course of action the tribunal must take.

Questioning of Witnesses by the Adjudicator

The authority of an adjudicator to question witnesses may depend on the provisions of the statute governing the tribunal and the nature of the hearing process (for example, whether it is adversarial or inquisitorial). Some statutes permit the adjudicator, implicitly or explicitly, to ask most of the questions, either directly or through tribunal counsel. However, many tribunals, including those governed by Ontario's SPPA, are expected to follow the adversarial approach to questioning.

In an adversarial hearing, the parties are responsible for bringing out the relevant information through examination of their own witnesses and cross-examination of the witnesses of other parties. The adjudicator usually asks questions for the purpose of clarifying evidence rather than helping a party to fill in gaps in its case. Nevertheless, adjudicators generally may question witnesses directly, provided that they do not intervene to an excessive extent—that is, to an extent that interferes with the conduct of a party's case or suggests a bias for or against one or more of the parties.

When adjudicators question a witness, they should give all parties an opportunity to ask further questions arising from the witness's responses.

Appropriate Time for Tribunal Questions

Sometimes it is appropriate for adjudicators to ask a question as soon as it comes to mind, especially if it is a minor point of clarification. However, some adjudicators believe that it is better to hold back their questions until both the examination-in-chief and the cross-examination are complete. Delaying questions reduces the possibility that the adjudicator will inadvertently interfere with a party's presentation of its case, and it may also reduce the need for intervention. Adjudicators often find, if they wait, that one of the parties will ask the question that the adjudicator had in mind.

One commentator on the proper conduct of judges has noted:

"Do not too soon assume that you know more about the case than counsel—he may have planned all along to ask the very question that springs to your lips but to defer it to a later time in his examination or cross-examination."

J.O. Wilson, *A Book for Judges* (Ottawa: Supply and Services, 1980), 48

CLOSING ARGUMENTS

After all the evidence has been heard, each party is usually entitled to an opportunity to present closing **arguments** or **submissions** (also called "summing up"). With one exception, failure to provide this opportunity is a breach of procedural fairness that may provide grounds for striking down the tribunal's decision. The exception is that if the person who has the burden of proof has given her final arguments and has not convinced the adjudicator, the adjudicator may decide the case in favour of the opposing party without having to hear that party's arguments. In other words, the adjudicator must always hear a party's arguments before finding against that party, but if those arguments are unconvincing, the adjudicator need not hear the arguments of the party in whose favour he will decide.

The purpose of final arguments is to permit each party

1. to summarize its case in the manner most favourable to it, without distorting the evidence, referring to facts that were not part of the evidence, or misleading the tribunal as to the law; and

2. to attempt to persuade the adjudicator to find in its favour.

Arguments usually summarize the significant evidence as the party sees it, set out the inferences that the party would like the tribunal to draw from the evidence, provide that party's view of the law, and describe the remedy or order that the party would like from the tribunal.

Arguments will usually be given orally, but sometimes may be presented in writing. It is not clear whether, in Ontario, tribunals have authority under the SPPA to require parties to give their closing arguments solely in writing. Although adjudicators sometimes prefer to receive arguments in writing because it may make their work easier, representatives may object to this because of the added cost to their client, because of delay while written arguments are exchanged between parties, or because representatives feel that they are more persuasive when they can state their arguments face-to-face with the ultimate decision maker.

In most cases, adjudicators specify the order in which arguments are to be presented. Usually, the parties present arguments in the same order in which they presented evidence, and each party may be permitted a brief reply to the opponent's arguments.

When the adjudicator has heard the closing arguments and replies, the hearing ends. The adjudicator then reviews all the evidence and arguments, and arrives at, or reserves, the tribunal's decision. The procedures followed at that final stage of the case are discussed in chapter 12, Tribunal Decision-Making Procedures.

Consultation with Tribunal Counsel

As discussed earlier, tribunals may have their own in-house counsel, or retain outside counsel, to provide legal advice and assistance with respect to a particular case.

There are two stages at which a tribunal must determine what help it can get from its own counsel: during the hearing and after the hearing. At each stage, the kind of help will depend to some extent on whether counsel is neutral or is taking the side of one of the parties against the other. This section focuses on the role that tribunal counsel may play up to the close of the hearing—that is, until all parties have made their final submissions. The role that tribunal counsel may play once the hearing is over is discussed in chapter 12, Tribunal Decision-Making Procedures.

Where a tribunal exercises a disciplinary function over a profession or licensed business, tribunal counsel may act as prosecutor. In this situation, counsel is in an adversarial role in relation to one of the parties to the hearing.

In such cases, counsel typically does not represent the tribunal itself but rather the tribunal's staff who have prepared the case against the person alleged to have violated standards. The process is generally structured in a way that ensures that neither the counsel presenting the case nor the tribunal staff have any communication with the adjudicator outside the presence of the opposing party and that the staff receive no preferential treatment from the adjudicator. Moreover, it is improper for tribunal counsel who has acted as prosecutor to advise the tribunal privately after the hearing with respect to the case, or to take part in the drafting of the tribunal's decision.

In other cases, there may be two or more adversaries with no connection to the tribunal or its staff. In these circumstances, tribunals generally rely on the evidence and arguments presented by the parties and do not obtain any assistance from their own counsel. However, from time to time, an adjudicator may require independent legal advice; or, where permitted by statute and not prohibited by the rules of natural justice, the tribunal may want to call its own witnesses. In these cases, legal assistance may be provided by in-house tribunal counsel or outside counsel.

When the tribunal seeks such assistance, it is important that tribunal counsel not be perceived to be allied with any of the parties to the dispute. As the adjudicator must be seen to be impartial, so too must its legal representative. The adjudicator must maintain an open mind until all the evidence and arguments have been presented, regardless of the participation of counsel. Even if the adjudicator requests the assistance of independent counsel because he is dissatisfied with the quality of legal argument or evidence provided by the parties, he must not slavishly accept or appear to accept the legal arguments of tribunal counsel or the evidence of witnesses called by tribunal counsel.

In instructing counsel, a tribunal should emphasize that counsel's conduct should not be overly aggressive or interventionist, or appear to infringe on the adjudicator's control of the proceedings and decision-making responsibility. Any time the conduct of counsel leaves an impression that counsel has undue influence over the hearing panel, the adjudicator should take whatever steps are necessary to dispel this impression, assert the panel's independence, and demonstrate its impartiality.

A question that arises is whether a tribunal should reveal to the parties the legal opinions given to it by tribunal counsel. Sometimes the answer is provided by the tribunal's governing statute; otherwise, it is left to the tribunal to decide. One school of thought is that such information is subject to solicitor-client privilege and need not be disclosed. Another is that it is inappropriate for the tribunal to rely on private legal advice unless it is given at the hearing, where all parties have an opportunity to respond. The decision of the Supreme Court of Canada in *Pritchard*[11] has confirmed the tribunal's right not to share legal advice with the parties.

The obligation to disclose legal advice may depend to some extent on whether the advice is given during or after the hearing. Legal advice on procedural, evidentiary, and jurisdictional issues might best be given in the open hearing, if only because frequent private contact between the adjudicator and tribunal counsel while a hearing is in progress raises concerns about counsel's influence on the adjudicator's assessment of the evidence and ultimate decision.

On the other hand, in the case of advice of tribunal counsel provided after the hearing on the ultimate issues of law and policy to be decided, private consultation may be acceptable. In that situation, whether the parties should be informed of counsel's advice may depend on the extent to which this advice raises new concerns or legal issues not addressed during the hearing. The courts have stated that if a new legal or policy issue is raised during any consultation between a hearing panel and others such as other tribunal members, tribunal staff, or tribunal counsel, it should be disclosed to the parties and they should be given an opportunity to address it.[12]

CHAPTER SUMMARY

The formality and the format of hearings vary between tribunals, and within a tribunal, they may vary from case to case, depending on the complexity of the issues and the sophistication of the parties. A hearing may take place in person, with everyone present receiving the same information at the same time; electronically, by teleconference or video conference; or in writing. Each format has its

---

11 *Pritchard v. Ontario (Human Rights Commission)*, [2004] 1 SCR 809.

12 *Consolidated Bathurst Packaging Ltd. v. International Wood Workers of America, Local 2-69* (1986), 56 OR (2d) 513, at 517 (CA); aff'd. 68 DLR (4th) 524, at 565 (SCC). *Ellis-Don Ltd. v. Ontario (Labour Relations Board)* (1994), 16 OR (3d) 698 (Div. Ct.); leave to appeal denied by CA and SCC.

strengths and weaknesses, and a tribunal, in consultation with the parties, should choose the format most conducive to fairness, efficiency, and effectiveness.

Usually, the panel chair begins the proceeding by introducing the panel and explaining the purpose and process of the hearing. Next, the panel addresses any preliminary issues and invites the parties to present opening statements. The parties then call witnesses, who give evidence and may be cross-examined. When all witnesses have been heard, the parties are given an opportunity to make final submissions, and the hearing ends. The tribunal renders its decision after the hearing.

KEY TERMS

adjudicator   the tribunal member or panel of tribunal members responsible for conducting a hearing and deciding the matter in dispute

agent   a person appointed by a participant in a proceeding to represent him or her; usually distinguished from counsel; also called a "representative" or "advocate"

appellant   a person who appeals a decision of a government official, a tribunal, or a court

applicant   a person who applies for a hearing before a tribunal to obtain a decision on a matter in dispute; *see also* appellant

arguments   presentation to a court or tribunal of reasons to accept a party's point of view, including a summary of the evidence and the law that support this point of view; also called "submissions"

counsel   a lawyer who represents and advises a participant in a proceeding; usually distinguished from an agent; also called a "representative" or "advocate"

electronic hearing   a hearing held through a teleconference or video conference

oral hearing   a hearing in which all the participants are physically present in the same place, receiving the same information at the same time

respondent   the party against whom a claim is brought or who is required to respond to an application, allegation, or appeal by another party

stay of proceedings   the temporary or permanent suspension of proceedings before a court or tribunal by order of that court or tribunal or of a higher court

submissions   *see* arguments

written hearing   a hearing conducted through the exchange of written evidence and arguments

KEY CASES

Questioning of Witnesses by Adjudicator

Majcenic v. Natale, [1968] 1 OR 189 (CA)

FACTS: Majcenic was hit by a car while crossing a street. She was seriously injured and sued the driver of the car. At trial, the judge questioned several of the witnesses, especially the doctors, frequently interrupting the lawyers in their questioning.

ISSUE: Was the judge allowed to question witnesses?

DECISION: A trial judge may ask the witnesses questions, but the questioning should be kept to a minimum. The purpose of such questioning should primarily be to clarify something that the judge does not understand. The judge should not interrupt the flow of the lawyer's examination or cross-examination or take over the examination of the witness. Lawyers often plan their examinations carefully, and when the trial judge interrupts too frequently or asks too many questions, the lawyer's strategy with that witness may be destroyed. Also, when a trial judge questions a witness in a manner that appears to be a cross-examination, the jury, if there is one, may think that the judge is challenging the credibility of that witness. As well, the parties may feel that the judge is no longer impartial. A new trial was ordered.

Standard of Proof

Coates v. Ontario (Registrar of Motor Vehicle Dealers and Salesmen)
(1988), 65 OR (2d) 526 (Div. Ct.)

FACTS: A used car company controlled by Coates, and employing about 60 employees, pleaded guilty to criminal fraud and to tampering with vehicle odometers under the *Weights and Measures Act*, SC 1970-71-72, c. 36. Charges against Coates personally were dropped. As a result of these events, there was a hearing before the Commercial Registration Appeals Tribunal. The tribunal ordered the Registrar of Motor Vehicle Dealers and Salesmen to revoke the licences of Coates, and the companies he controlled, to buy and sell cars. The tribunal's reason was that the convictions of the company raised a presumption that Coates was personally involved.

FACTS: What is the appropriate burden of proof?

DECISION: Clear and convincing proof based on cogent evidence that Coates was personally involved was necessary to support the revocation of his licence. It was not enough that a company controlled by him was convicted. There were many employees of the company, and it was not reasonable to presume that Coates had knowledge of what all these employees were doing.

REVIEW QUESTIONS

1. What are the three main formats for a hearing before a tribunal?
2. What are the considerations in choosing one format over another?
3. Can a tribunal combine different formats in the same hearing?
4. What are the usual stages of a hearing? How do the procedures for these stages differ depending on whether the hearing is oral, electronic, or in writing?
5. Who may participate in a hearing?
6. What are the rights and responsibilities of each of these participants?
7. What is meant by the "onus" or "burden of proof"? Who usually has the burden of proof before a tribunal?
8. What is meant by the "standard of proof"? What is the usual standard of proof in a proceeding before a tribunal? How does it differ from the standard of proof in a criminal case?
9. What are "agency counsel" and "tribunal counsel," and how do their roles differ?
10. What kinds of help may tribunals receive from tribunal counsel, and what limits should be placed on that help to ensure fairness to the parties?
11. What kinds of issues may best be raised or decided before the tribunal proceeds with the hearing on the merits?

12. What considerations may lead a party to request an adjournment of a hearing?

13. What is a "stay of proceedings"? Why might a tribunal grant a request for a stay of proceedings?

14. In what circumstances is it appropriate for the tribunal panel to question witnesses? If the panel does ask questions, what is an appropriate way of doing this?

15. What is the purpose of closing arguments, and what are the main components of those arguments?

16. What remedies are typically available from tribunals? What remedies are typically not available?

EXERCISE

Ontario's Environmental Review Tribunal (http://www.ert.gov.on.ca) holds hearings under the *Environmental Protection Act*, the Ontario *Water Resources Act*, the *Environmental Bill of Rights*, and the *Environmental Assessment Act*. In what documents will you find the procedures that the tribunal will follow during its hearings?

What do these documents tell you about each of the following?

- The role of parties at hearings

- The role of intervenors at hearings

- The use of court reporters at hearings

- The role of tribunal counsel at hearings

- The role of expert witnesses at hearings

- Opening statements by parties

- The use of documents as evidence at oral hearings

- The procedures for filing evidence in written hearings under the *Environmental Bill of Rights*

- What factors the tribunal will consider in determining whether to hold oral, written, or electronic hearings

- When the tribunal will combine two or more oral, written, or electronic hearings

- The purpose of making site visits or inspections and the procedure for doing this.

FURTHER READING

Robert Macaulay and James Sprague, *Practice and Procedure Before Administrative Tribunals* (Toronto: Carswell) (looseleaf), chapters 12-16, 21, 21A.

Murray Rankin and Leah Greathead, "Advising the Board: The Scope of Counsel's Role in Advising Administrative Tribunals" (1993-94) vol. 7 *Canadian Journal of Administrative Law and Practice* 29.

Graham Steele, "Tribunal Counsel" (1997-98) vol. 11 *Canadian Journal of Administrative Law and Practice* 57.

CHAPTER 9

Presenting Evidence at a Hearing

LEARNING OBJECTIVES

After reading this chapter, you will understand

- what kinds of information a tribunal will and will not receive from parties in a dispute;
- how a tribunal determines whether information is admissible as evidence at the hearing;
- what makes evidence relevant, reliable, necessary, and fair;
- what elements are considered in assessing the reliability of evidence;
- what the difference is between direct evidence and circumstantial evidence, between fact and opinion, and between direct observation and hearsay;
- how the credibility of witnesses is assessed;
- what the order is of presentation of evidence;
- what procedures are followed in examining witnesses; and
- in what circumstances a tribunal may collect its own evidence, by calling its own expert witnesses or by visiting the site that is the subject of the dispute.

Administrative tribunals exist to administer the social, economic, environmental and public policies of elected politicians. Achieving the goals of these policies must not be impeded by technical evidentiary rules pressed by lawyers who argue from common law precedent rather than from logic or public policy.

There is a good reason why tribunals should not be bound by the common law rules of evidence: most of these rules are troublesome and no source of pride for lawyers.

Ian Blue, "Common Evidentiary Issues Before Administrative Tribunals and Suggested Approaches" (January 1993) vol. 4, no. 4 *Advocates' Quarterly* 385

DIFFERENCES IN THE USE OF INFORMATION BY AGENCIES AND TRIBUNALS

When a person applies for a government benefit, tax relief, a licence, or approval, or seeks a decision on some other matter that affects his interests, the decision maker will refer to the law setting out the circumstances in which the application will succeed or fail. However, before applying the law, the decision maker must determine the facts of the case. The form in which the necessary information will be received and the manner in which it will be assessed will depend on whether the decision maker is an official of a government agency or a member of a tribunal.

Agencies

Unless there is a law or a rule of practice specific to the agency restricting the information that a public official may consider, the official may receive any information in any form. In general, there is no difference between the information that the official may consider and the information that he may rely on in making the decision. However, the official must decide which parts of the information received are both relevant to the decision and reliable. In an agency, the task of weighing information and discarding what is irrelevant or unreliable is carried out at the back end of the decision-making process rather than at the front end. In contrast, in some tribunals, information is screened at the outset to determine whether it should be received.

While there is no legal requirement for advance screening of the information that an agency official may consider, the concept of jurisdiction provides safeguards against the use of inappropriate information. If it can be shown that an official refused to consider relevant information, or that he based his decision on irrelevant or unreliable information, a court may find that the official acted outside his jurisdiction and may strike down the decision.

Tribunals

Some tribunals have the same latitude as officials to receive and consider any information in any form, while others are required by law to restrict the information that they will receive. All tribunals must ultimately base their decisions on information that is both relevant and reliable.

Although there may be no statutory limitations on the kind of information that a tribunal may receive, common law principles of procedural fairness require most tribunals to place some restrictions on the kind of information they will consider, the form the information should take, and the manner in which the information is presented to them. The information put before tribunals is called "evidence."

WHAT IS EVIDENCE?

Evidence is information that a party seeks to use in a legal proceeding to prove or disprove a contention or allegation. Evidence is considered **relevant** if it is helpful in determining the answer to a question that a tribunal must address in making a decision. That is, evidence is relevant if it tends to prove or disprove the matter in issue, or if it can reasonably and fairly influence the tribunal's belief about that matter.

Evidence is "admissible"—that is, the tribunal will consider it (though not necessarily accept it as true)—if it meets this test of relevance as well as three other tests:

1. it appears to be reliable;
2. it is necessary to prove a point; and
3. receiving it appears to be fair to other parties.

These considerations are described in more detail below.

Evidence presented in an oral or electronic hearing may consist of oral or written statements, photographs, maps, charts, drawings, or physical objects, or a combination of these. Evidence used in a written hearing is necessarily restricted to information that can be presented in writing or in readily reproducible form (such as photocopies of charts and documents).

DETERMINING ADMISSIBILITY

What Is Admissibility?

The information that a court or a tribunal is permitted to consider is called **admissible evidence. Admissibility** is determined in the courts by a set of **rules of evidence**, made up of a combination of common law principles, statutory provisions, and constitutional principles. The rules that determine what will be considered evidence, and therefore can be put before the court, are complicated. Even lawyers have difficulty understanding them, and the courts spend much of their time listening to arguments about whether various pieces of information are admissible evidence.

For purposes of this discussion, the important point about court rules of evidence is that they are based on four fundamental principles. In order to be admissible, evidence must be

1. relevant,

2. reliable,

3. necessary, and

4. fair.

Courts and legal scholars have often stated that tribunals are not required to follow the complex rules of evidence used in court. This is true in the sense that tribunals have greater latitude than courts (but less latitude than government officials) to consider information that may not comply with court rules of evidence. However, tribunals are required to respect principles of procedural fairness. In the treatment of evidence, essentially a tribunal has two choices:

1. unlike a court, it can listen to a wide range of information without preliminary screening and then base its decision on selected parts of that information; or

2. like a court, it can place limits on the information it will hear.

In practice, many tribunals use both approaches.

Tribunals that do not follow a set of rules to screen out potentially inadmissible evidence must still ensure that they do not rely, or appear to rely, on information that is irrelevant, unreliable, unnecessary, or unfair. Where a tribunal has wide latitude to receive information, in presenting its decision at the conclusion of the hearing, the tribunal should state what evidence it relied on and what evidence it excluded in reaching the decision. For example, if the tribunal received unreliable information, it should demonstrate to the parties that it did not use that information.

Again, in accordance with principles of procedural fairness, tribunals should follow a consistent approach in deciding what evidence may be presented to them and what weight that evidence should be given. It is neither practical nor necessary for tribunal members to learn the complex rules of evidence used in the courts. An alternative approach is to apply the four principles underlying the rules to the available information in a particular case, in order to decide which parts of the information are admissible as evidence and which are not.[1] This process of review and selection involves four steps:

- *Step 1: Determine whether the information is relevant*   Evidence is relevant if it helps to answer a question that the tribunal must address in making its decision.

- *Step 2: Determine whether the information is reliable*   Court rules of evidence are designed to weed out any information that might mislead the court because it is unreliable. Information presented to a tribunal may be relevant to the issues to be decided, but it may be unreliable because it is unlikely to be true or because no reliable method of testing its truth or accuracy is available to the tribunal. The reliability of evidence depends largely on its source and on the form in which it is communicated. Two of the most important considerations in determining reliability are (1) whether the evidence is first-hand observation or "hearsay," and (2) whether the evidence is fact or opinion. First-hand observation is inherently more reliable than hearsay and opinion. Since hearsay evidence and opinion evidence are often unreliable, special rules apply to them. These rules are discussed below under the heading "Reliability of Evidence."

- *Step 3: Determine whether the information is necessary*   A tribunal may decide not to receive information that is relevant and reliable if, for example, it duplicates earlier evidence that is not in dispute. Alternatively, if the information is relevant but there are questions about its reliability, a tribunal may nevertheless be inclined to accept it if it is the only evidence available to a party. For example, hearsay evidence may be admissible where a party cannot refer to first-hand observation or factual evidence to prove her case.

- *Step 4: Determine whether it would be fair to hear the evidence*   Public policy or the public interest may rule out the use of information that would otherwise be admissible as evidence. If the information appears to be relevant, reliable, and necessary, the tribunal should consider whether there is any reason why it would be unfair to receive the information—that is, whether some social or personal harm is likely to arise from admitting the information, which outweighs the value of the information in proving a party's case. Applying this test, evidence may be excluded because, even though it may be true, it was obtained in an improper manner. For example, when a confession has been coerced or tricked out of a person charged with an offence, in a manner that contravenes the person's constitutional right to remain silent, the confession may be unreliable, but more important, it would be unfair for the tribunal to use it in deciding the case.

---

1   For a more detailed discussion of this approach, see Ed Ratushny, "Rules of Evidence and Procedural Problems Before Administrative Tribunals" (1988-89) vol. 2 *Canadian Journal of Administrative Law and Practice* 157; and James Sprague, "Evidence Before Administrative Agencies: Let's All Forget the 'Rules' and Just Concentrate on What We're Doing" (1994-95) vol. 8 *Canadian Journal of Administrative Law and Practice* 263.

Other instances in which evidence is inadmissible for public policy reasons, even though it may be relevant, reliable, and necessary, are situations where the prejudicial effect of the information outweighs its usefulness in proving a point in dispute (its **probative value**), or where the information is subject to some form of **privilege**, or protection from disclosure (discussed later under the heading "Privileged Information").

Our labour relations statutes generally contain a provision which astonishes many newcomers to the field, such as: "The Board may receive and accept such evidence and information on oath, affidavit or otherwise as in its discretion it considers proper, *whether or not the evidence is admissible in a court of law*." (My emphasis.)

Conceptually, this type of legislative provision has always astonished me. The implications are that the statutory and common law rules of admissibility, weight and probative value that have been hammered out on the anvil of over 500 years of experience can be disregarded on an ad hoc basis. Visions of the Star Chamber can spring into your mind, while echoes of the saying in the days of the Star Chamber that "The quality of justice is measured by the length of the Chancellor's foot" can start ringing in your ears. While such legislative provisions contain the seeds of an enormous potential for both intellectual and procedural abuse by Labour Board decision-makers, I am happy to say that in over twenty years of labour relations practice, my encounters with such abuse have been rare. In only a handful of cases can I say, mustering as much objectivity as possible, that the decision turned on evidence which was improperly admitted.

Benjamin B. Trevino, "Advocacy Before Labour Relations Boards and in Labour Negotiations," in Franklin R. Moskoff, *Administrative Tribunals: A Practice Handbook for Legal Counsel* (Aurora, ON: Canada Law Book, 1989), 7-8

Although a tribunal may be permitted to hear evidence that would not be admissible under court rules of evidence, representatives of parties also should apply the four-step process outlined above before they ask the tribunal to admit information as evidence. That is, the representative should ask himself whether the information is relevant to the issues the tribunal must decide, whether the information is inherently reliable, and whether it is likely to be necessary for the tribunal to receive the information. If the information is not inherently reliable, the representative should ask himself whether the degree of reliability can be established during the hearing, using procedures such as cross-examination or corroboration through the testimony of other witnesses. Finally, if the information appears to be relevant, reliable, and necessary, the representative should ask himself whether it meets the test of fairness.

By asking these questions, a representative can make logical and fair decisions about whether to submit particular pieces of evidence or to attempt to prove the case by some other means.

Tribunals do not always rule correctly on the admissibility of evidence. For example, a tribunal may refuse evidence that should have been admitted, or it may admit and base its decision on evidence that should have been excluded. In this situation, the representative of the party who is negatively affected by the exclusion or use of the evidence may request a remedy from the tribunal, or ultimately from the courts, to ensure a fair outcome in the case. (See "Challenging a Tribunal's Ruling on Admissibility.")

Challenging a Tribunal's Ruling on Admissibility

If the tribunal has ruled against the admission of a piece of evidence that you submitted because it did not appear at the time to be relevant, and its relevance later becomes apparent, you may ask the tribunal to reconsider its ruling and hear the evidence. The tribunal may reverse its ruling, provided that it gives all parties an opportunity to challenge this new evidence, through cross-examination or possibly by calling further evidence.

Conversely, if the tribunal admits evidence harmful to your client, and this evidence is later shown to be irrelevant or unreliable, you should ask the tribunal to disregard it. When the tribunal issues its decision, it should state in its reasons that it did not rely on the evidence, and why. If the tribunal does not do this, and there is doubt about whether it excluded the evidence in reaching its decision, you may appeal to a court to overturn the decision.

Reliability of Evidence

The reliability of the evidence on which a tribunal bases its decision is critical to the determination of a fair outcome for the parties to the proceeding. Generally, the reliability of evidence is measured along five dimensions:

- The first dimension is the means by which the information was obtained. Direct personal knowledge obtained by a witness through observation, physical examination, or testing is at the most reliable end of the spectrum, while information that a witness received from others falls at the other end.

- The second dimension relates to a witness's motivation. Where a witness has a strong incentive to be truthful, the evidence is more likely to be inherently reliable. At the other end of the spectrum, where a witness has strong reasons to fabricate evidence (as in the case of an accomplice in the matter in dispute, who expects to receive lenient treatment in return for testifying against the respondent), the information is more likely to be unreliable.

- The third dimension is the extent to which specialized knowledge or training is necessary to correctly interpret information. There is a fine line between what a person has observed and her interpretation of the observations. The observations themselves are facts; the interpretation of those observations is opinion. Opinions are less reliable than facts, because they are subjective. Evidence of a witness whose opinion is informed is more reliable than evidence of an uninformed witness.

- The fourth dimension is the extent to which the evidence points directly to the fact to be proved, or does not support the fact directly but invites the drawing of an inference about that fact.

- The fifth dimension is the degree of **corroboration**. The more strongly evidence is corroborated (confirmed or supported) by other evidence, the more likely it is to be reliable.

The degree of reliability of a particular piece of evidence along each of these dimensions will determine the **weight** that the tribunal gives the evidence in arriving at its decision. Specific aspects of evidence that tribunals may consider in establishing reliability and assigning weight are discussed in more detail below.

DIRECT EVIDENCE AND CIRCUMSTANTIAL EVIDENCE

Direct evidence is evidence given by a person who actually observed the occurrence of the event in question. **Circumstantial evidence** is evidence of circumstances that suggest the manner in which the event occurred. If a person is accused of murder, the fact that a witness saw the accused person pull the trigger is direct evidence of the identity of the killer. If the witness saw the accused running away from the building a few minutes after the time of death, this is circumstantial evidence of identity.

Direct evidence carries the greatest weight in the assessment of evidence presented in a proceeding. Circumstantial evidence is not as inherently reliable as direct evidence, but it is often the only kind of evidence available. Circumstantial evidence may be enough to prove a case if it is of sufficient quality and quantity.

OPINION EVIDENCE

One of the basic rules of evidence applied by courts is that a witness may testify only to facts within his or her own knowledge. In general, "facts within his or her own knowledge" means acts that the witness has performed himself or herself and things that the witness has observed through his or her primary senses of sight, hearing, touch, smell, and taste.

Other evidence is often excluded either because it is inherently unreliable or because its reliability cannot be determined through methods available to the court, such as cross-examination or the testimony of other witnesses. Testimony based on a witness's opinion is one example of this kind of evidence. Another is hearsay evidence, discussed below.

Tribunals have greater leeway than courts to listen to opinion evidence, but if they do, they should be aware of its limitations. Some parties will argue that the adjudicator should not allow a witness to give this kind of evidence because it would be inadmissible in court. Other parties will argue that because a tribunal has the power to hear opinion evidence, it is obliged to do so. Neither is correct. The tribunal has discretion whether to hear this evidence, and it should exercise that discretion according to the principles discussed below. It can be appropriate for tribunals to admit most evidence that courts would not listen to provided that the adjudicators state clearly in their final decision what weight they gave such evidence. However, sometimes the degree of unreliability or unfairness of evidence is so great that even hearing the evidence would be a legal error, because it would offend the principles of procedural fairness.[2]

---

2 *Re B and Catholic Children's Aid Society of Metropolitan Toronto* (1987), 59 OR (2d) 417 (HCJ); and *Re Girvin and Consumers' Gas Co.* (1973), 1 OR 421.

HEARSAY EVIDENCE

When a witness provides information to a court that he did not receive directly through personal observation, but was told by someone else, the testimony is generally not admissible as evidence. Since the witness has no first-hand knowledge of the truth of the information, the court is unable, through examination of the witness, to test whether the information is correct.

If Joe says he saw something happen, whether this is true can be tested by asking Joe questions designed to test his powers of observation, his opportunity to make accurate observations, and his memory. However, if Joe says that Susan told him something, it is impossible to test the truth and accuracy of Susan's statement by questioning Joe.

Similarly, statements in documents generally are inadmissible in a court because the accuracy of the statements cannot be tested, unless the person who wrote them down is present to testify to the truth of the contents of the document.

Statements made by someone who is not available for cross-examination are known as **hearsay evidence**, whether they are found in documents or passed on by a witness to whom they were told.

Tribunals generally may accept hearsay evidence, but in considering whether to do so, or in weighing the value of such evidence if it is admitted, adjudicators should consider the following questions:

- Is it likely that this information is reliable?
- To what extent may it be unfair and prejudicial to admit the information if its reliability cannot be tested?
- Would it be easy or difficult for the party who wishes to rely on the evidence to produce the person who can give first-hand evidence or provide the same evidence in a form more likely to be reliable?

Some documents are safer to admit than others, because the circumstances in which the statements were written down make it likely that the statements are true—for example, where the person who wrote down the information had an incentive to be truthful and is unlikely to have had a motive to lie, where the documents are of a routine nature, and where the information recorded is inherently likely to be accurate. Examples of inherently reliable documents are government documents such as deeds to land, articles of incorporation, weather records, and birth certificates, as well as many routine business records such as invoices, purchase orders, and receipts.

[T]he approach to hearsay evidence generally has been the subject of change in recent years. Nowadays, rather than being the subject of a rule of prohibition with a variety of exceptions, it is said that the admissibility of hearsay should be determined in each instance through a principled approach. . . .

In my view, the concern ought to be less about the admissibility of hearsay evidence per se and more about the quality of the hearsay evidence that is offered and received. . . .

[E]ven if hearsay is admitted, it does not obviate the need to ensure that the hearsay evidence is as reliable and trustworthy as it can be.

Nordheimer J in *R v. Allan* (2003), 64 OR (3d) 611, at 616-17

EXPERT EVIDENCE

When Should a Tribunal Hear Expert Evidence?

As discussed above, generally witnesses in court may only testify to what they have observed. They are not allowed to offer their opinions except with regard to matters within their own knowledge. The reason for this is that if the witness has no special knowledge or expertise to bring to bear in interpreting facts or observations, the judge is in as good a position as the witness to form opinions as to the meaning or significance of the evidence; therefore, the witness's opinions are of no value to the court. In a tribunal proceeding, opinion evidence is often harmless, because an experienced adjudicator will appreciate its limitations and exclude the evidence from the final decision. However, as a precaution the representative of the opposing party will likely object if an ordinary witness is allowed to offer an opinion.

Under court rules of evidence, an exception may be made for opinions provided by an **expert witness**. An expert witness is a person who, because of education or experience in a field, has an understanding of the subject on which he or she is testifying beyond that of the general public. Whether the person's knowledge and understanding are sufficient to justify admissibility of the opinion depends on the circumstances of each case. Therefore, courts generally hold a **qualification hearing** before deciding whether to permit an expert to give her opinion. Although not required to do so, many tribunals also use qualification hearings in deciding whether to listen to expert opinions. (See "Qualification Hearing Procedures.")

Qualification Hearing Procedures

In a qualification hearing, the representative of the party who has called the expert witness informs the tribunal of the nature of the opinions that will be offered and the issues to which they relate. The representative then questions the witness about his education and experience in order to demonstrate that he has the necessary knowledge on which to base his opinion. The opposing party may accept the qualifications and agree that the witness may give his opinion on the specified issues, or she may argue that the representative has not established that the witness is qualified to give an expert opinion. If the opposing party intends to argue that the witness is not qualified, the party or her representative may cross-examine the witness to bring out weaknesses in his qualifications before making this argument.

After examination and cross-examination, both parties submit their arguments. The adjudicator then rules either that the witness is qualified to give his opinion on the issues in question or that the witness lacks the necessary knowledge or experience to provide a reliable opinion and may not give this evidence.

Since tribunals are free to accept evidence that would be inadmissible in court, adjudicators may listen to opinions of witnesses who are not qualified, or they may modify or dispense with a qualification hearing. However, they must make it clear in their decisions that they have accepted only evidence that is reliable and have rejected opinions based on insufficient knowledge.

What Are the Obligations of an Expert Witness?

Tribunals allow experts to testify on scientific or technical issues because such evidence assists them in understanding complex matters. Two obligations follow from this reason for hearing expert opinions:

1. Expert witnesses should be called to testify only in areas where their evidence is needed. Representatives increasingly attempt to lend weight to their cases by finding "experts" on issues that require no special expertise. For example, where an expert is called to explain English grammar and syntax in supporting the interpretation of a clause in a legal document, the evidence may be rejected as superfluous because the average person has a sufficient understanding of grammar and syntax to form his or her own opinion.

2. If the expert is to assist, he must participate as an independent professional rather than as an advocate for the client.

Even though the expert may have specialized knowledge beyond that of an ordinary person, and his testimony may meet the "necessity" test, the fact that he is paid by one of the parties or is defending his own work for a party will affect the reliability of his evidence.

To be a helpful, neutral professional whose primary purpose is to assist the tribunal in finding the truth, rather than act as a hired gun, the expert should disclose all the facts and assumptions underlying the opinion, acknowledge any limitations and qualifications in the opinion, and fully disclose his relationship to the party on whose behalf he is testifying.

Expert witnesses should also provide the tribunal with written reports or witness statements, give oral evidence in plain English, and avoid using technical jargon except as necessary to properly explain a concept. Increasingly, tribunals, as well as courts, are demanding this kind of candour and clarity from expert witnesses, and they are criticizing in their decisions those who do not meet these requirements. Some tribunals and courts have gone so far as to enunciate standards of conduct for expert witnesses. The guidelines promulgated by one Ontario tribunal are found in appendix E.

How Can a Tribunal Evaluate the Reliability of Expert Evidence?

Expert evidence consists of opinions that are needed by an adjudicator because he or she lacks the specialized knowledge, training, or experience to resolve an issue without such assistance. How, then, is a court or tribunal supposed to decide which evidence to accept when expert witnesses give conflicting opinions?

The answer lies partly in the application of the standard of proof. Often the opinions of expert witnesses differ because the facts are uncertain. Therefore, the adjudicator may be unable to determine with certainty which opinion is correct. The problem can be resolved by clearly identifying the causes of uncertainty, the nature of the uncertainty, and the degree of uncertainty, and then applying the standard of proof to the witnesses' testimony. Remember that the party that has the burden of proof must establish the facts to the standard, or the degree of certainty, required by law. If that party's expert evidence is not sufficiently convincing—that is, if the opinions of the opposing expert are sufficiently persuasive to cast the requisite level of doubt on the evidence of the party who has the burden of proof—the standard of proof will not be met. It is not necessary for the adjudicator to determine which expert is correct, but only to determine which of the conflicting opinions achieves the higher degree of certainty.

Adjudicators can use a variety of approaches in determining the sources, kinds, and degrees of uncertainty inherent in a scientific issue and evaluating the reliability of scientific evidence. One judge has listed 14 factors that should be considered,[3] including

- the potential rate of error,
- the existence and maintenance of standards,
- the care with which the scientific technique has been employed and whether it is susceptible to abuse,
- the presence of fail-safe characteristics,
- whether the technique has generally been accepted by experts in the field,
- the clarity with which the technique may be explained,
- the nature and breadth of the inference drawn from the data, and
- the expert's qualifications and stature.

May a Tribunal Obtain Its Own Expert Evidence?

Some tribunal members find it frustrating to listen to opposing experts, each of whom claims a high degree of certainty for his own opinion and neither of whom explains the basis of that opinion clearly. Some tribunals are given the authority by their statutes to obtain their own expert evidence. For example, the Workplace Safety and Insurance Appeals Tribunal may appoint a roster of "medical assessors" to assist hearing panels by providing expert evidence. The advantage of such evidence is that it may be more impartial than evidence provided at the request of a party.

Tribunals that can retain their own experts often have rules to ensure that they do not unfairly favour these experts over the witnesses called by the parties. For example, the parties may be invited to participate in choosing the tribunal's expert; the expert's report may be made available to the parties; and the parties may be given an opportunity to cross-examine the tribunal's expert and to call their own evidence to contradict the expert's testimony.

PHYSICAL EVIDENCE

Physical evidence includes test results, documents, photographs, videotapes, motion pictures, and other objects. The key to establishing the reliability of physical evidence is to demonstrate that the object in question is authentic and has not been altered or tampered with. The most effective way to do this is to ask the person who collected or created the object to appear as a witness and verify that the object has not been changed from the time of collection or creation to the time it is presented to the tribunal. Alternatively, a witness may be called who is familiar with the object and can testify that it has not been changed since the events in question. Where a substance such as a sample of a liquid has been handled by several people or subjected to testing procedures, the integrity of the process is demonstrated by establishing a "chain of custody" (see below).

Documents

The best way to prove the reliability of documents is to have the person who prepared the document identify it and testify to its authenticity. However, this is often impractical. Other indications of reliability, discussed earlier, are whether the

---

3 *R v. Johnston* (1992), 12 CR (4th) 99; 69 CCC (3d) 395 (Ont. Ct. (Gen. Div.)).

documents were routinely created in the course of business and whether they were created by a person who had no motive to falsify them. In addition, an original is more reliable than a copy. However, if copies have been given to more than one person, comparing two copies can reveal whether one of them has been altered.

Test Results

The results of tests and analyses (of substances, for example) are used as evidence in many proceedings. They may include analyses of blood or urine samples, or of water or air quality; tests of the structural integrity of objects; assessment of the source of harm or damage; or measurement of the extent of harm or damage to individuals or objects. The integrity of test results is usually proved by verifying that accepted testing methods were used and by establishing the **chain of custody**, or continuity of possession, of the object tested. Protection of the chain of custody requires each person who handles a test sample to prevent others from having unsupervised access to the sample and to document from whom the sample was received, how it was maintained, who had access to it, and to whom it was transferred.

Photographs, Videotapes, and Motion Pictures

Photographs are generally admissible as evidence if the person who took the photograph or a person who was present at that time describes when and how the photograph was taken, and testifies that it accurately depicts the scene or event in question.

The same conditions apply to videotapes and motion pictures; however, the photographer must also be prepared to state whether the tape or film has been edited and to be cross-examined about any material that has been deleted. While the images may be admissible, admissibility of the sound portion of the tape or film is subject to further conditions. If people shown are heard speaking or if there is voice-over narration of what is shown, the speakers must be prepared to testify to the truth of the statements that were recorded, as well as the authenticity of the recording, and to be cross-examined on those statements. If this testimony cannot be provided, the tribunal may choose to exclude the entire sound recording. In this situation, it may be possible to use the visual portion of the evidence by playing the tape or film with the sound turned off.

WEIGHING EVIDENCE AND ASSESSING CREDIBILITY

While a tribunal may refuse to admit some evidence because it is inherently unreliable, it must still assess the reliability of the evidence that is admitted. Representatives can assist the tribunal in making this assessment through cross-examination, which is designed to reveal any aspects of the evidence that may raise questions about its reliability. Ultimately, however, it is the adjudicator's task to determine the reliability of each piece of evidence. This procedure is called "weighing the evidence." The assessment of the evidence of a particular witness is often referred to as "assessing credibility."

When witnesses give conflicting evidence, the adjudicator must determine which evidence is more likely to be accurate. However, accuracy is not a simple matter of truthfulness. Assessment of the credibility of a witness involves many factors, including the opportunities of different witnesses to observe the same events, the prior knowledge and understanding the witness has brought to her observations of the events, her intelligence, her powers of observation, and her exposure and susceptibility to suggestions about the interpretation of the events. (See also "Demeanour.")

Demeanour

Adjudicators often consider the "demeanour," or outward behaviour, of a witness in deciding whether she is telling the truth. They must be cautious, however, in using demeanour as a measure of credibility, since the witness's manner in presenting her testimony may reflect considerations unrelated to truthfulness. An adjudicator might, for example, ask himself, "Is this witness hesitant in answering because she is fabricating evidence, or because she is thoughtful and wants to provide the most complete factual information? Or might the hesitancy be due to cultural factors?"

Another important factor in assessing credibility is the consistency of a witness's statements, both with each other and with other evidence that is clearly true. However, inconsistency in itself is not necessarily an indication that the witness is not credible. A degree of forgetfulness and inconsistency is normal and can even enhance a witness's credibility. In fact, testimony that is excessively polished or glib may be a warning sign. Refusal of a witness to acknowledge obvious facts is also a sign of resistance to the truth.

In cross-examination, the prosecutor challenged the evidence given by the accused:

> "Do you understand that you are on trial for murder?" she asked.
>
> "Yes," replied the accused.
>
> "Do you understand the penalty for perjury?"
>
> "I certainly do," said the accused, "and it's a lot less than the penalty for murder."

When witnesses give conflicting versions of events and both appear plausible, it can be very difficult to decide which evidence to accept. There is no magic formula for assessing credibility. The adjudicator may compare both scenarios with all the available evidence in order to determine which one is more compatible with the evidence as a whole. However, in the end, the adjudicator must rely on his own knowledge and observations in determining which of the two scenarios is more inherently plausible. In doing this, the adjudicator must be willing to recognize his own limitations, including his personal biases and preconceptions, and must do his best to set them aside.

While it is desirable to determine which version of events is correct, it is not always necessary. If, in the end, the adjudicator does not have sufficient information to establish the facts, the case may be decided on the burden and standard of proof. In a tribunal that relies on an adversarial process, the party who has the onus of proving the facts in dispute will lose the case if the evidence he presents does not establish those facts to the degree of probability required by the applicable standard of proof. In a tribunal that follows an inquisitorial process, the situation may be different. The tribunal itself may have the onus of collecting sufficient evidence to answer the question before it. If the evidence is not sufficient to answer the question to the required level of certainty, the tribunal's governing statute will determine the outcome of the case.

Privileged Information

Some information is not admissible in evidence, even though it may be relevant and reliable, because it is **privileged**, or because it is protected by statute. Two important types of privileged information are the contents of communications between a lawyer (solicitor) and his client and statements made during settlement discussions. Other information that is protected from disclosure as a matter of public policy includes discussions between a doctor and her patient about the patient's health and the identity of informants when offences are alleged to have been committed.

A detailed description of the law of privilege is beyond the scope of this book. However, it is useful to know that the privilege for solicitor-client communications belongs to the client, rather than the lawyer. A lawyer may not disclose the information without the client's consent; however, the client can "waive" his privilege by disclosing or authorizing the lawyer to disclose the information. If the client discloses the information or otherwise acts in a manner that is inconsistent with its confidentiality, in some circumstances the client will be deemed to have waived the privilege, even without intending to authorize disclosure.

Impact of Information Access and Privacy Laws

The federal *Access to Information Act*[4] and *Privacy Act*[5] and the various provincial freedom-of-information and protection-of-privacy acts have two fundamental purposes:

1. to require governments, and in some provinces, hospitals and universities, to provide the public with information that need not be kept confidential; and

2. to ensure that governments do not give out information about a person that would invade his or her privacy, without first obtaining that person's consent.

How do these statutes affect tribunal proceedings? The main issue is whether witnesses who are government employees have a right to withhold from the tribunal relevant documents in their custody because of the confidentiality requirements of freedom-of-information and protection-of-privacy statutes. Under some statutes, it is an offence for a government employee to deliberately disclose information that violates a person's privacy without obtaining that person's prior consent. Consequently, some witnesses or representatives will object to the witness's answering questions at a hearing when her knowledge comes from government

---

4 RSC 1985, c. A-1, s. 2.

5 RSC 1985, c. P-21, s. 2.

documents. Witnesses also may object to providing the documents themselves, on the grounds that doing so would violate their duties of confidentiality under access and privacy laws.

In some cases, it is not clear whether these objections are valid. However, in several provinces (for example, Alberta, British Columbia, Ontario, and Saskatchewan), the access and privacy statutes specifically state that their confidentiality provisions do not prevent parties from presenting evidence to a court or tribunal and do not affect the power of a court or tribunal to compel (require) a witness to testify or compel the production of a document.[6]

In order to decide whether documentary evidence must be provided when questions of confidentiality are raised, the tribunal should review the document to determine whether it contains information that justifies its exclusion from the proceeding. If it does, the solution is not to allow the witness to withhold testimony, but to arrange for the evidence to be given in a closed hearing, provided that this procedure is permitted under the tribunal's governing statute.[7]

PRESENTING EVIDENCE

Order of Presentation

The order in which the parties will present their case is usually set out in the tribunal's rules or guidelines. Otherwise, it is determined on a case-by-case basis by a procedural ruling made at a pre-hearing conference or at the start of the hearing.

In a hearing with only two parties, usually the party who initiated the proceeding or who has the burden of proof calls his witnesses first. After the opposing party (the respondent) has called her witnesses, the first party may be given the opportunity to present further evidence in response. This is called **rebuttal** or **reply evidence**.

In most cases, no further evidence may be called after rebuttal. However, on rare occasions the rebuttal will raise an issue that is so significant that the tribunal will allow the other party to refute that evidence. This is known as **surrebuttal**, and it should be permitted only in exceptional circumstances.

In a hearing with several parties and intervenors, the order of presentation is similar but more complex. The party who initiated the process or who has the burden of proof usually calls his witnesses first. Then any other parties whose interest or position is similar call their evidence.

Next, the opposing party calls her witnesses, followed by any other parties whose interest or position is similar.

Intervenors usually present evidence after the evidence of the parties whose position they support.

Again, the leading parties (and sometimes intervenors as well) have the opportunity to present reply evidence in response to the evidence of the opposing party's witnesses.

---

6 See, for example, *Freedom of Information and Protection of Privacy Act*, RSA 2000, c. F-25, s. 38(1).

7 In Ontario, the circumstances in which a tribunal may hold a closed hearing are set out in s. 9 of the *Statutory Powers Procedure Act*, RSO 1990, c. S.22. Similar criteria are set out in s. 41 of British Columbia's *Administrative Tribunals Act*, SBC 2004, c. 45, and s. 131 of Quebec's *Administrative Justice Act*, RSQ, c. J-3.

Some tribunals may follow a different order of presentation, depending on the nature of the case. If a tribunal often begins with the evidence of a party other than the one who initiated the proceeding, or who has the burden of proof, the tribunal may explain the rationale for this practice in its procedural rules or practice directions. Alternatively, the rationale may be set out in an earlier decision of the tribunal.

Swearing In the Witness

In Ontario, tribunals may accept evidence without requiring witnesses to affirm or swear to its truth. If the tribunal "swears in" witnesses, it will be the job of the adjudicator, the court reporter, or a tribunal staff member to carry out this procedure. In recognition of Canada's religious and cultural diversity, the tribunal should offer the witness the opportunity to choose the form of oath or affirmation that will bind her conscience, such as solemnly promising to tell the truth or referring to a religious text or sacred artifact.

Usually, the person administering the oath or affirmation begins by asking the witness to state her name. If there is no written witness list, the person may ask the witness to spell her name as well. The witness is then asked whether she wishes to swear an oath or to make a solemn affirmation that she will tell only the truth.

If the witness wishes to swear an oath, she is asked to put her right hand on the religious text or sacred object she has chosen and to swear to the truth of her testimony. When the Bible is used for the oath, the witness is usually asked, "Do you solemnly swear that the evidence you will give will be the truth, the whole truth, and nothing but the truth, so help you God?" If the witness chooses instead to make a solemn affirmation, she is usually asked, "Do you solemnly affirm that the evidence you will give will be the truth, the whole truth, and nothing but the truth?"

In some tribunals, the person swearing in the witness will also ask whether she understands that it is an offence to deliberately fail to tell the truth.

Witness Examination

Each witness is first examined—that is, asked questions—by the party or representative who called him to give evidence. This is called **examination-in-chief** or **direct examination**. Then the witness may be questioned by other parties whose interest or position is similar.

Next, the main opposing party questions the witness, followed by other parties whose interest or position is similar. This stage of questioning is called **cross-examination**. (Some tribunals, such as the Workplace Safety and Insurance Appeals Tribunal, use the term **cross-questioning**.) Cross-examination is one of the primary methods of determining the reliability of evidence provided by a witness. A skilled cross-examiner will ask questions that reveal inconsistencies or inaccuracies in the witness's testimony and also bring out additional evidence helpful to her own case.

After the witness has been cross-examined, the party who called the witness may ask him further questions to clarify answers he provided or to address new issues that arose during the cross-examination. Other parties who have already questioned the witness may also ask further questions arising out of his examination by other parties. This procedure is called **re-examination**.

Finally, after the witnesses of all the parties have been questioned, parties are sometimes given an opportunity to recall witnesses or call additional witnesses for the purpose of rebutting testimony given in subsequent questioning by the opposing party. This is the reply or rebuttal stage of the proceeding, described above.

Many tribunals require parties questioning witnesses to follow, to a greater or lesser degree, certain rules used by the courts governing the form in which questions may be asked. Parties are generally more restricted in the kinds of questions they may ask when questioning their own witnesses, whether during examination-in-chief or in reply, than when they are cross-examining another party's witnesses.

In examination-in-chief, parties are expected to ask "open" rather than "closed" questions on any matters of substance. In legal jargon, **closed questions** are called **leading questions**. An **open question** invites the witness to provide an independent response. It does not suggest the answer that the questioner is looking for or contains crucial facts or conclusions that the questioner wants the witness to confirm. In other words, it does not put words in the witness's mouth. A leading question does suggest the expected answer and contain crucial information. It merely asks the witness to agree or disagree. In examination-in-chief, parties are expected to ask leading questions only on matters that are not controversial, such as undisputed background facts, or on points that the witness clearly has not understood and that need clarification. (See the examples "Open Questions and Leading Questions.")

Open Questions and Leading Questions

One way to tell a leading question from an open question is that if it can be answered "yes" or "no," it is likely to be a leading question. The following question is one that is leading on uncontroversial matters but open on matters that may be in dispute:

> Mr. Noseworthy, you are a constable with the Toronto Police Service and were on duty on March 15, 1997. In that capacity, you attended at 15 Marchmount Road in response to information that had been provided to you. Is that correct? Please tell the tribunal at what time you arrived there, and what you observed.

Typical open questions to elicit further information would be, "And what happened next?" or "What was the next thing you did?"

A leading question such as the following would likely cause the opposing party's representative to object:

> Mr. Noseworthy, I understand that in your capacity as a constable with the Toronto Police Service, you attended at 15 Marchmount Road on March 15, 1997, and at that time you observed the accused leaving the house through a broken window. You read him his rights and asked him what he was doing, and he admitted that he had broken into the house. Is that correct?

There are good reasons to place some limits on the use of leading questions, particularly in examination-in-chief. The problem with leading questions is that the person questioning the witness provides the answers, rather than the witness himself. As a result, neither the opposing parties nor the adjudicator can form a fair assessment of the witness's evidence. If instead the witness volunteered the information in his own words, his answer might convey a very different impression from the prepackaged response offered by the examining party, who naturally wants to present the information in the light most favourable to her case.

A sequence of open-ended questions, taken from an actual court record:

Crown attorney:	Then what did you do?
Police officer:	I began kicking the door.
Crown attorney:	What kind of footwear did you have on?
Police officer:	Size 12 boots.
Crown attorney:	How many times did you kick the door?
Police officer:	About ten.
Crown attorney:	What was Sergeant Harp doing while you were kicking the door?
Police officer:	Laughing at me.

In cross-examination, the examining parties are not restricted to asking open questions on points of substance. They may attempt to put words in the witness's mouth, and often do so. However, they may not browbeat the witness or distort the facts. The party who originally called the witness may object if another party asks the witness to contradict the evidence given by the principal witness in the case or by other witnesses.

Cross-examination is beyond any doubt the greatest legal engine ever invented for the discovery of truth.

John H. Wigmore, *Evidence*, rev. ed. (Chadbourn, 1974), vol. 5, paragraph 1367

In hearings involving several parties, it may not be clear whether all parties are entitled to cross-examine witnesses other than their own, particularly when either the witness or the party who called him has an interest or position that is favourable to the party seeking to cross-examine. In such situations, questioning of the witness may not be aimed at attacking his evidence or credibility, as is the usual purpose of cross-examination, but rather at strengthening them. Some adjudicators therefore limit the "friendly" cross-examination that may occur or ask the examining party to carry out an examination-in-chief, so that the adjudicator can better assess the credibility of the witness and the weight to be given to his answers.

Witness Panels

Usually, each witness is fully examined and cross-examined before the next begins his testimony. However, it is sometimes more efficient for a party to present the testimony of two or more witnesses and then make them available simultaneously for cross-examination, especially where their testimony covers similar or overlapping subjects. This format is called a **witness panel**. Some governing statutes specifically allow tribunals to use this procedure under certain conditions.[8]

When a panel of witnesses gives evidence, the person cross-examining is often given the option of addressing his questions either to the panel as a whole, in which case any of the witnesses can choose to answer, or to a specific witness on the panel. The adjudicator has a duty to allow the questioner to cross-examine on a topic as thoroughly as if each witness testified separately. However, adjudicators also have the right to prevent unnecessary repetition of questions and answers, since one of the purposes of using a witness panel is to avoid overlap and duplication of evidence.

Sometimes in separate testimony, a witness may avoid answering a question by suggesting that another witness is better qualified to provide the answer. This risk can also arise with a witness panel, where a more knowledgeable witness may defer to a less qualified or less credible witness. Another risk with witness panels is that witnesses may collude in providing consistent answers to questions, so as to avoid revealing weaknesses in their testimony.

Objecting to Questions

Representatives at a hearing are entitled to object to questions that other representatives ask witnesses, whether these are directed to their own witnesses or to other witnesses in cross-examination. The method of objecting is to stand up quickly before the witness has an opportunity to answer and state loudly and clearly that you object to the question.

Common grounds for objection are that

- the information sought does not meet one of the criteria for admissibility—that is, it is irrelevant, unreliable, unnecessary, or unfair;
- the question is repetitive or put in a bullying manner;
- the answer is unreliable (for example, based on hearsay or speculation);
- the answer is outside the witness's knowledge (as when a question asks an ordinary witness to provide an expert opinion);
- an expert witness is being asked to give opinions on a matter outside his area of expertise; or
- the examiner is asking leading questions (putting words into the witness's mouth).

It is good practice not to object except when necessary. Frequent objections waste time and annoy adjudicators. A representative should trust the adjudicator to decide when a question is unacceptable—up to a point. If the information sought offends a rule of evidence but is relatively harmless, it is better to allow the witness to answer the question. However, if the questioning will seriously mislead the tribunal or unduly lengthen the proceeding, the representative should interject.

---

8 For example, s. 15.2 of Ontario's SPPA permits a tribunal to hear evidence from witness panels, as long as the parties have first been given an opportunity to make submissions as to whether this procedure is appropriate.

From actual court records:

> Defence counsel: I object to the prosecutor objecting to my
> objecting to standard legal objections.

Keeping Track of Documentary and Physical Evidence

In many hearings, much of the evidence submitted consists of documents. Occasionally, the evidence will also include an object, such as a sample of blood, a machine part, or a videotape. Although documents may not be admitted as evidence without proof of their authenticity, they are generally accepted once a person who is sufficiently knowledgeable about their contents identifies them and testifies to their accuracy. Similarly, objects are admitted as evidence once they have been identified. These documents and objects are made part of the formal hearing record by **marking** them as **exhibits**.

Typically, once a party feels that he has laid sufficient groundwork for the document or thing to be admitted as evidence, he will tender (offer or submit) the document as an exhibit. If there is no objection, or if the tribunal accepts the document or object despite objections, the adjudicator gives the document or object a number. It is advisable to mark on each exhibit, in addition to its number, the name or file number of the case. The adjudicator or tribunal staff may write this on the document or on a tag to attach to the object, but usually they will use a stamp bearing the tribunal's name and providing space for other identifying information.

The adjudicator and each representative (or party) should keep a list of the exhibits and record on it the party who provided the exhibit, as well as the title or description of the document or thing. This list will assist the representatives and the adjudicator in keeping track of the exhibits when they are referred to later in the hearing. It will also be helpful to tribunal staff after the hearing, when the exhibits will be returned to the parties or forwarded to a court for reference in an appeal or a judicial review of the tribunal's decision.

A pre-printed form such as the one found in appendix F can be useful for keeping a record of exhibits.

Site Visits

If objects are readily movable, a party who wants to present them as evidence usually brings them to the hearing. If they are not movable, a photograph or videotape may suffice. However, in some circumstances, it may be necessary for the tribunal to examine a large and cumbersome object or to visit a site that is central to the matter in dispute, as in cases involving land use planning, environmental issues, or the cause of a traffic accident. A site visit is usually called **taking a view**.

It is not clear whether tribunals have an inherent power to take a view or can do so only if expressly permitted by statute. Assuming that a tribunal has this power and wishes to exercise it during a hearing, all parties and their representatives must be given the opportunity to participate in the site visit. If taking a view is a common practice of the tribunal, there may be rules or practice directions governing the procedure. In the absence of such rules, the adjudicator should invite submissions from the parties as to whether the tribunal should take a view and, if so, what procedures should be followed.

During the site visit, the parties and their representatives should remain within sight and earshot of each other and of the tribunal members at all times. If the hearings are being recorded, it is advisable to have the reporter attend and record all discussion that takes place during the visit.

Following the site visit, the adjudicator should request further submissions from the parties as to whether information received during the visit should be treated as evidence and what weight it should be given. The adjudicator may also hear evidence from the persons who attended, describing what they observed and their view of its significance. If the adjudicator observed something that she considers significant, she should tell the parties and invite them to make submissions or call evidence regarding the interpretation of these observations.

The difficulty with determining what is usable as evidence after a site visit is that the participants, including the tribunal members, may observe different things or have different interpretations of the meaning or significance of what they observed. For this reason, Ontario courts have ruled that the observations of a hearing panel during a site visit do not constitute evidence from which inferences may be drawn but can be used only to clarify (that is, to confirm or contradict) evidence given in the hearing room by witnesses.[9]

CHAPTER SUMMARY

While decision makers in most government agencies can receive any information provided to them and decide, within the limits of their jurisdiction, what use to make of it, tribunals are more restricted in the information they can receive and how they can use it. Information provided to a tribunal is known as evidence. Evidence may take a variety of forms, including oral statements, documents, sound or visual recordings, and objects.

The courts have developed strict and complex rules to determine the kind of evidence they will receive. Tribunals are not required to follow these rules, but they must still ensure that the evidence they accept is relevant, reliable, necessary, and fair. Tribunals and courts place the greatest weight on first-hand evidence—that is, information obtained by direct observation. Information received from another source is called hearsay, and tribunals accept it with caution. Hearsay is inherently unreliable, since the witness who reports it has no personal knowledge of whether it is true. For a similar reason, tribunals usually allow witnesses only to present facts, and not opinions. An exception is sometimes made for expert witnesses, who may be permitted to offer opinions on scientific or technical matters about which they have specialized knowledge or experience.

Tribunals generally follow a standard procedure for receiving the evidence of witnesses. Typically, the party who initiated the proceeding or who has the burden of proof is the first to call witnesses, followed by other parties with a similar interest, then the main opposing party and other parties with a similar interest, and

---

9 Note, however, that these cases deal with courts rather than tribunals and that the use that can be made of a "view" is different in other provinces: see John Sopinka, Sidney Lederman, and Alan Bryant, *The Law of Evidence in Canada* (Toronto: Butterworths, 1992), 18. In the context of administrative law, Blake states that the purpose of a site visit by a tribunal is to better appreciate the evidence and not to gather evidence: Sara Blake, *Administrative Law in Canada*, 2d ed. (Toronto: Butterworths, 1997), 54.

finally any intervenors. Sometimes witnesses give evidence in panels, rather than individually.

The first stage of witness examination is questioning by the party who called the witness, known as examination-in-chief or direct examination. In examination-in-chief, information is brought forward by open questions; leading questions, which contain or suggest the desired answers, are discouraged.

The second stage of questioning is cross-examination, in which the other party tests the reliability of the witness's evidence by asking questions designed to reveal any weaknesses in his testimony. In cross-examination, leading questions are acceptable. Once a witness has been cross-examined, the party who called the witness may be allowed to ask further questions designed to clarify any answers given in cross-examination. This stage of questioning is called re-examination.

In most proceedings, the final stage of questioning is rebuttal or reply, in which the party who first led evidence may respond to the evidence presented by the opposing party.

The overall purpose of the procedures described in this chapter is to ensure that the tribunal's decision is based on information that is relevant, reliable, necessary, and fair, and to assure all parties of fairness and consistency in their presentation of evidence at the hearing.

KEY TERMS

admissibility   the qualification of information to be received as evidence in a proceeding as determined by the tests of relevance, reliability, necessity, and fairness; *see also* admissible evidence

admissible evidence   information that a court or tribunal will receive as evidence in a proceeding because it meets the tests of relevance, reliability, necessity, and fairness

chain of custody   documented proof that physical evidence has not been tampered with, by showing "continuity of possession"; involves keeping the object under lock and key or otherwise secure, and ensuring that a record is kept of each person who handled or transported the object from the time it was received until the date of the proceeding

circumstantial evidence   evidence that tends to show that something is likely to be a fact even though no witness directly observed the event in question; evidence from which inferences about other facts can be drawn; *see also* direct evidence

closed question   *see* leading question

corroboration   confirmation or support of evidence in a case provided by other evidence

cross-examination   questioning of a witness by an opposing party or representative for the purpose of casting doubt on the reliability of the witness's testimony or bringing out additional evidence supporting the position of the opposing party; *see also* examination-in-chief

cross-questioning   *see* cross-examination

direct evidence   evidence relating to an event that is given by a witness who directly observed the occurrence of the event; *see also* circumstantial evidence

direct examination   *see* examination-in-chief

examination-in-chief initial evidence given by a witness in response to questions asked by the party or representative who called the witness to testify; *see also* cross-examination

exhibit document or other form of physical evidence accepted by a tribunal

expert evidence opinions provided by an expert witness, which are required by an adjudicator who lacks the specialized knowledge, training, or experience to resolve an issue without such assistance; *see also* expert witness

expert witness a witness who is permitted, as a result of a competence acquired through study or experience in a specialized field, to give opinions on matters related to that field as evidence before a court or tribunal; *see also* expert evidence

hearsay evidence information provided by a witness who did not obtain the information through direct observation, but heard it from another person or read it in a document written by another person

leading question a question put to a witness that contains the crucial facts or conclusions that the questioner wants the witness to confirm and merely requires the witness to agree or disagree with those facts or conclusions; generally, a question that can be answered simply "yes" or "no"; also called a "closed question"; *see also* open question

marking exhibits the procedure by which documents and other forms of physical evidence are entered into the hearing record; involves assigning an exhibit number and usually stamping or otherwise marking on the item the name or file number of the case

open question a question put to a witness that invites an independent response; a question that does not suggest the answer that is sought or contain crucial information that the questioner wants the witness to confirm; a question that does not put words in the witness's mouth; *see also* leading question

privilege the right or duty of a person to withhold otherwise admissible evidence from a court or tribunal

privileged information information that a court or tribunal cannot compel a person to disclose even though it may otherwise be admissible; *see also* privilege

probative value the usefulness of information in proving a point in dispute

qualification hearing a hearing held by a court or tribunal for the purpose of deciding whether to admit opinion evidence of an expert witness

rebuttal evidence *see* reply evidence

re-examination further questioning of a witness by the party or representative who called him or her for the purpose of clarifying any answers given during cross-examination

relevant evidence evidence that helps to answer a question that a court or tribunal must address in making a decision

reply evidence evidence called to rebut or refute the evidence presented by an opposing party; *see also* surrebuttal

rules of evidence rules used by the courts to determine the admissibility of evidence, made up of a combination of common law principles, statutory provisions, and constitutional principles, and requiring that evidence presented in court be relevant, reliable, necessary, and fair

surrebuttal   presentation of further evidence in response to an issue raised in rebuttal; *see* reply evidence

taking a view   a site visit by the adjudicator and other participants in a proceeding for the purpose of examining immovable evidence that is central to the matter in dispute

weight   the extent or degree to which evidence is reliable in deciding the issues before a court or tribunal

witness panel   a format used in a proceeding to permit simultaneous examination of two or more witnesses

REVIEW QUESTIONS

1. What is "evidence"?

2. What forms may evidence take?

3. What are the four tests that a court or tribunal applies when determining whether to receive evidence?

4. What is the term to describe information that meets these four tests?

5. Why are courts and tribunals reluctant to listen to the opinions of most witnesses?

6. What is an "expert witness," and why are expert witnesses permitted to express opinions when other witnesses are not?

7. What are the obligations of an expert witness to the party who called him or her and to the tribunal?

8. If the opinions of two expert witnesses conflict, how can a tribunal determine which opinion to accept?

9. What is "privileged information," and why are tribunals not permitted to receive it as evidence? Give three examples of information that is privileged.

10. Describe the order in which parties call their witnesses.

11. What is the difference between examination-in-chief, cross-examination, and reply?

12. What is a witness panel, and what are the advantages and disadvantages of this format for presenting evidence?

13. Explain what an exhibit is and how and why tribunals "mark" exhibits.

14. What is a "site visit"? What is the purpose of "taking a view" and what steps can a tribunal take to ensure that the information it receives during a site visit is reliable and is shared with all the parties?

FACT SCENARIOS

Scenario 1

The Hogtown Licensing Commission is an agency of the city of Hogtown. Under the municipal business licensing bylaw, it regulates the taxicab industry by issuing licences to own and drive taxis, setting standards, and holding hearings regarding the suspension or revocation of the licences of taxi owners and drivers.

Arnold W. owns and drives a taxi. Two months ago, he drove a woman from her home to her doctor's office. The following day, she complained to the commission that Mr. W. made sexual advances toward her. After investigating, the commission staff proposed to revoke Mr. W.'s licence to drive a taxi.

At the hearing subsequently held by the commissioner, the commission staff attempt to introduce evidence of three previous infractions of standards in support of their request to revoke the licence. Mr. W.'s representative challenges the admissibility of this evidence.

The evidence that the commission staff want to introduce is as follows:

- Seven years ago, a passenger complained that Mr. W. used profane language while driving her to a hairdressing appointment. The evidence consists of an inspector's report in Mr. W.'s file, stating that the inspector interviewed both the passenger and Mr. W., and that Mr. W. denied the allegations. The file also contains a letter from the passenger setting out her complaint. The commission staff intend to call the inspector as a witness, but not the complainant.

- Five years ago, a taxi owned and driven by Mr. W. had a broken trunk door, causing discomfort and inconvenience to a group of passengers. The evidence consists of an inspector's report found in Mr. W.'s file. According to the report, the inspector received a complaint from a passenger stating that because the trunk would not open, the passenger could not put his luggage in the trunk and had to put it in the back seat, crowding himself and another passenger. There is no written or signed statement from the passenger, and no evidence that anyone from the commission inspected the vehicle, notified Mr. W. of the complaint, or took any disciplinary action. The commission staff do not intend to call the inspector or the complainant to testify.

- Three years ago, Mr. W. allowed another driver to drive a taxi he owned when the brakes were worn and needed replacing. The evidence consists of a report prepared and signed by a mechanic employed by the commission to carry out safety checks on taxis, stating that she inspected the vehicle and found that the brakes were worn to the point that it was dangerous to operate the vehicle.

    1. Is any of this evidence admissible? Why or why not?
    2. If the evidence is admissible, what considerations should the commission take into account in deciding what weight it should be given?

Scenario 2

A valve was left open at the Hideous Chemical Company plant, and a clear, colourless, odourless chemical flowed into the roadside ditch. It ran down the ditch toward a pond in which a neighbour was raising trout for sale to fancy restaurants. Shortly after this incident, all the fish in the pond died.

Al B., an inspector for the Ministry of the Environment, investigated. Mr. B. is a technician who is trained to investigate pollution incidents, including the taking of samples for toxicity analysis. As a result of the investigation, the ministry gave Hideous notice that

- it would suspend the company's licence to produce chemicals at the location for three months, and
- it would issue an order for the company to replace the fish in the farmer's pond and compensate the neighbour for lost profits.

Hideous appealed the licence revocation and the order to replace the fish. The company argued that the amount of chemical spilled was insufficient to reach the pond, and moreover, the chemical in question is not toxic to fish.

At the hearing, the lawyer for the ministry asks Mr. B. how he knows that the toxic chemical entered the water and killed the fish. Mr. B. testifies that he did not take any samples of the water in the pond and have them analyzed for the presence of the chemical, but he saw the fish rising to the surface and "gulping for air, which is a sign that they are being affected by a chemical."

1. Is this evidence admissible? Why or why not?

2. If you are representing Hideous, do you raise an objection, and if so, on what basis?

3. If you are the adjudicator, how do you respond to the objection?

FURTHER READING

Ian Blue, "Common Evidentiary Issues Before Administrative Tribunals and Suggested Approaches" (January 1993) vol. 4, no. 4 *Advocates' Quarterly* 385.

P. Brad Limpert, "Beyond the Rule in Mohan: A New Model for Assessing the Reliability of Scientific Evidence" (1996) vol. 54 *University of Toronto Faculty of Law Review* 65.

Robert Macaulay and James Sprague, *Practice and Procedure Before Administrative Tribunals* (Toronto: Carswell) (looseleaf), chapters 17, 18, and 20.

Ed Ratushny, "Rules of Evidence and Procedural Problems Before Administrative Tribunals" (1988-89) vol. 2 *Canadian Journal of Administrative Law and Practice* 157.

James Sprague, "Evidence Before Administrative Agencies: Let's All Forget the 'Rules' and Just Concentrate on What We're Doing" (1994-95) vol. 8 *Canadian Journal of Administrative Law and Practice* 263.

John Swaigen and Alan Levy, "The Expert's Duty to the Tribunal" (1998) vol. 11 *Canadian Journal of Administrative Law and Practice* 277.

CHAPTER 10

Management and Control of the Hearing Process

LEARNING OBJECTIVES

After reading this chapter, you will understand

- the source and scope of a tribunal's authority to manage and control the conduct of hearings;
- the kinds of conduct at a hearing that are considered unusual or unacceptable;
- the steps that a tribunal can take to deal with unusual or unacceptable conduct;
- why a tribunal may consider it necessary to exclude members of the public from a hearing;
- why a tribunal may choose to exclude parties, and perhaps their representatives as well, from a hearing; and
- to what extent a tribunal can restrict the presence and conduct of the media at a hearing.

Most agencies are intended to be oriented towards a single purpose and to operate informally, openly and expeditiously. Their members are intended to be specialists in particular fields, one of which is not necessarily the law, and to be masters of special skills, one of which is not necessarily procedure. At the same time, the technical drafting of statutes and regulations makes it more difficult for those who are not lawyers to serve as agency members.

One might expect that, where a task is to be performed by individuals not trained in any procedural process, some care would be taken in assisting them in the conduct of this task by a detailed delineation of expected procedure in a way that will be comprehensible to them. This is not the rule, however, in our current federal administrative system. ... A statutory statement that a decision-maker has all the powers of a superior court of record is not of much assistance to a decision-maker who is unaware that some courts are "of record" while others are not (let alone that some are "superior"). ... Today's administrative system commonly expects non-legally trained individuals not only to conduct themselves in accordance with all of the complex and subtle principles of administrative law but to instruct those who appear before them in these principles as well.

Martin Freeman and James Sprague, "The Case for a Federal Administrative Powers and Procedures Act," in Philip Anisman and Robert F. Reid, eds., *Administrative Law Issues and Practice* (Scarborough, ON: Carswell, 1995), 127-46, at 135

AUTHORITY TO MANAGE THE HEARING PROCESS

The principle of procedural fairness, combined with the objective of efficiency in the conduct of hearings, requires that tribunals have both the authority and the tools to manage and control the hearing process. A tribunal's authority to manage hearings may be set out in a statute of general application or in the tribunal's own enabling statute, in the form of provisions allowing the tribunal to make its own procedural rules.[1] Therefore, the first step in the management of a hearing is for the tribunal to develop a set of procedures that contribute to a fair and smooth hearing process. The tribunal should make sure that these procedures are explained clearly and made available to tribunal members, parties, other participants, and the general public.

In developing and applying hearing procedures, a tribunal should aim for a balance between certainty, consistency, and sufficient flexibility to allow the adjudicator to depart from usual practice in unusual situations. The adjudicator should also have the flexibility, within the requirements of correct procedure, to take into account the concerns and motives of participants. For example, an aggressive representative who seems to be disregarding the rules of the tribunal may sincerely believe that she is simply defending the interests of her client; or a party whose manner is abrasive may feel that "the system" is stacked against him and may see the tribunal as a component of that system. In such cases, the adjudicator may be given discretion to respond as the circumstances seem to require, instead of automatically imposing procedural restrictions or penalties.

AUTHORITY TO CONTROL THE CONDUCT OF HEARINGS

All tribunals have an inherent right under common law to take any steps necessary to control their process. This right may be codified in a statute of general application[2] or a specific enabling statute. Statutes may also set out certain specific powers of tribunals relating to the conduct of hearings. For example, some statutes give tribunals the power

---

1 See, for example, British Columbia's *Administrative Tribunals Act* (ATA), SBC 2004, c. 45, ss. 11-13; Quebec's *Administrative Justice Act* (AJA), RSQ c. J-3, s. 11; and Ontario's *Statutory Powers Procedure Act* (SPPA), RSO 1990, c. S.22, s. 25.1.

2 See, for example, s. 11(1) of the ATA and s. 25.0.1 of the SPPA.

- to ask a court to inquire into and, if necessary, punish conduct amounting to "contempt" of the tribunal (SPPA, s. 13; ATA, s. 49);

- to bar an incompetent representative, other than a lawyer, from a hearing (SPPA, s. 23; ATA, s. 48);

- to ask a judge to issue a warrant to order requiring the attendance and testimony of a witness (SPPA, s. 12(4); ATA, s. 49);

- to issue orders or directions to prevent abuse of the tribunal's processes (SPPA, s. 23(1));

- to issue orders or directions for the maintenance of order at the hearing and, if necessary, to call on a police officer for assistance in maintaining order (SPPA, s. 9(2); ATA, s. 48);

- to award costs to a party where the conduct of another party has been unreasonable, frivolous, or vexatious, or the party has acted in bad faith (SPPA, s. 17.1; ATA, s. 47); and

- to require a party whose conduct has been improper to pay part of the tribunal's expenses in connection with the hearing (ATA, s. 47).

These powers are discussed in more detail below.

Power To Deal With Contempt

Tribunals have limited powers to deal directly with behaviour that shows disrespect for the tribunal's authority or that tends to interfere with (obstruct) the administration of justice. Examples include

- disruption of the proceeding by a participant or by a member of the public attending the hearing;

- failure of a participant to carry out a promise (an **undertaking**) made to the tribunal;

- failure of a witness to obey a summons to attend and give evidence;

- failure of a party or representative to comply with a valid order of the tribunal; and

- provision of statements to the media intended to influence the outcome of the hearing.

Such conduct may constitute **contempt** of the tribunal, equivalent to the offence of contempt of a court. Since contempt is considered a criminal offence in some circumstances, a tribunal does not have the authority to impose formal sanctions (or punishment) on the person behaving in such a manner. However, under some statutes, including the SPPA and the ATA, it has the power to refer the matter to a court for review and a decision on punishment.

Before taking this step, the adjudicator may halt the proceeding, point out the offensive behaviour, and provide the person with an opportunity to show why the tribunal should not refer the matter to a court. At this "show cause" hearing, the person may attempt to explain and justify the behaviour, or may admit that it was inappropriate and apologize, in the hope that this will be acceptable to the adjudicator. However, if the person does not wish to provide an explanation, the tribunal may not have the authority to require him to do so.

If no explanation or apology is given, or if it is given but is not satisfactory, the adjudicator may ask a court to commence formal contempt proceedings. However, this remedy should be sought only in the most serious cases. Courts will exercise their contempt powers only when the rule of law is challenged. Moreover, deciding a case of contempt is a cumbersome and time-consuming process. The tribunal must prepare a written statement of facts for the court, witnesses may be called, and the person charged may present a defence. Therefore, tribunals rarely ask courts to impose punishment for conduct amounting to contempt.

If the person responsible for the objectionable behaviour is a lawyer, an alternative remedy available to the tribunal is to report the conduct to the provincial law society. The law society requires all practising lawyers in the province to comply with strict rules of professional conduct, and it has the authority to discipline any member who breaches those rules. One of the rules is that lawyers must show appropriate respect to courts and tribunals.

It is trite observation that certain litigation can bring out the worst in legal counsel. This was one such matter in which the behaviour of counsel was so disruptive to the proper conduct of the hearing that the [Ontario Labour Relations] Board feels compelled to make several comments regarding the behaviour of counsel. … It should be stressed that none of the comments which follow are directed towards Mr. Stout, who represented his client before the Board in an entirely professional manner throughout the course of his participation in this proceeding.

Mr. Tarasuk and Mr. Abbass were, on numerous occasions, rude, interruptive, and disrespectful of other counsel appearing at the hearing, of me, as the Vice-Chair of the Board assigned to hear this matter, and of the Ontario Labour Relations Board, as an institution. Mr. Abbass, in particular, seemed to take pleasure in continually disrupting the course of this proceeding. Both Mr. Abbass and Mr. Tarasuk appear to hold the view that each has the unqualified right to interject personal opinions or snide commentary at will during opposing counsel's argument. On innumerable occasions I directed each of Mr. Abbass and Mr. Tarasuk to refrain from such conduct. Each was advised that he would have an opportunity, at the appropriate time, to respond to opposing counsel's argument. However, my directions were regularly ignored or challenged by counsel and more often than not caused Mr. Abbass and Mr. Tarasuk to more vigorously interject, resulting, on occasion, in the need for me to raise my voice above theirs in order to maintain some semblance of order in the hearing room.

UFCWIU Local 175 v. Vic Murai Holdings Ltd.,
[1996] OLRB Rep. 106, at 148 (Shouldice)

Unless there is no other way to maintain control of the proceeding or to ensure that a party has responsible representation, the adjudicator may decide to wait until the hearing is finished and a decision has been rendered before instituting formal contempt proceedings or making a complaint to the law society. If this action is taken while the hearing is in progress, the person concerned will likely request an adjournment until the proceedings before the court or the law society are complete, thereby delaying the hearing indefinitely. If the adjudicator continues the hearing in these circumstances, she risks allegations that her decision cannot be impartial.

Even if the adjudicator delays any action until after the decision has been rendered, and does not forewarn the person concerned of her intention to do this, the offending person may argue that the adjudicator was biased throughout the hearing and that the decision should be struck down (assuming that the person lost the case). On the other hand, if the adjudicator tells a lawyer or other representative that the tribunal may take future action, with this possibility hanging over his head, the representative may be unable to pursue his client's case as vigorously as he might otherwise have done.

These concerns make it difficult for an adjudicator to decide whether to take action and, if so, when it should be taken.

Power To Bar a Representative

As suggested above, one aspect of fairness of a proceeding is that the parties have responsible representatives. The SPPA reinforces this requirement by giving a tribunal the power to bar a representative (other than a lawyer) from participating in the hearing if he is incompetent or does not understand and carry out his duties and responsibilities as his client's advocate. In the event that the representative is a lawyer, the tribunal can make a complaint to the law society, as in the case of conduct constituting contempt. The ATA permits a tribunal to eject any person (including a lawyer) from a hearing if he or she disobeys an order or direction of the tribunal (s. 48).

Power To Compel Witnesses

Under the SPPA, if a witness has been served with a summons and either has failed to attend or refuses to provide the evidence required by the summons, the tribunal can ask a judge to issue a warrant to arrest the witness and, if necessary, detain her until she testifies. There are similar powers in the ATA.

In general, witnesses are required to answer all questions put to them by the party who calls them. If an objection is to be made, it should be made by the party or the representative who called the witness, not by the witness. A witness may not object to a question or refuse to answer it unless an objection has been raised by the party or representative who called the witness, and the objection has been upheld by the tribunal.

However, there may be exceptions. In some cases, the party who has called a witness may not be prepared to protect legitimate interests in confidentiality raised by the witness, either because the party and the witness have competing interests, or because the party's representative does not have access to information needed to determine whether an objection should be made. In such cases, it may be appropriate for the witness to raise the objection and to request an adjournment, so that he can arrange to have his own counsel attend and assist him. Section 11 of the SPPA provides for a limited right of witnesses to be advised of their rights by their own counsel or agent. The witness's representative can take no other part in the proceeding unless the tribunal gives permission.

Power To Prevent Abuse of Process

The inherent common law right of tribunals to control their process gives rise to the power to act to prevent an abuse of that process, even without specific statutory authority. **Abuse of process** is a term used by courts and tribunals to refer to conduct by a participant in a proceeding involving a flagrant and serious violation of the rules of procedure or other reasonable expectations of the court or tribunal. As mentioned earlier, the SPPA permits tribunals to make orders to prevent abuse of process. The ATA (s. 31) authorizes BC tribunals to dismiss without a hearing cases that give rise to an abuse of process.

Power To Maintain Order

Occasionally, a tribunal may be confronted with disorderly conduct or behaviour that seriously disrupts the proceeding. In Ontario, under the SPPA, and in British Columbia, under the ATA, a tribunal has a broad power to deal with such conduct, first by ordering or directing the offending person(s) to obey the tribunal's rules of procedure, and second, if the conduct continues, by calling on the police to maintain order.

Generally, police intervention should be a last resort. However, sometimes disorderly conduct may be a sign of possible violence. If a tribunal member feels that a person's behaviour is threatening or potentially dangerous, he should take preventive action, such as halting the proceeding and calling the police, in order to remove the risk of harm to others present at the hearing.

Power To Award Costs

Generally, tribunals do not have the power to award costs at a hearing. However, some individual enabling statutes authorize individual tribunals to award costs. In addition, a trend appears to be developing to provide for costs, at least under limited circumstances, in statutes of general application. Ontario's SPPA was amended in 1999 to permit a tribunal to award costs to a party where another party has behaved unreasonably or in other ways considered improper, or has acted in bad faith. This power can serve to deter parties from engaging in disruptive or obstructive conduct at a hearing. Tribunals subject to British Columbia's ATA have a general power to award costs in accordance with regulations that may be made. In addition, as mentioned above, this statute contains an unusual provision permitting the tribunal to demand reimbursement for its own expenses incurred as a result of a party's improper conduct.

REPRESENTED VERSUS UNREPRESENTED PARTIES

In responding to an unruly or uncooperative party, an adjudicator must often consider whether the party is represented at the hearing or acting for himself. If the party is represented, the adjudicator is entitled to hold the representative responsible for his client's conduct. Representatives, particularly those who are lawyers, are expected to have a basic understanding of the hearing process and the tribunal's rules of procedure, and to follow those rules, as well as to keep the behaviour of their client and witnesses under reasonable control. If, on the other hand, the party is unrepresented, it is sometimes better for the adjudicator to give him an opportunity to express his anger or frustration, rather than deal with him strictly according to the tribunal's standards of practice and procedure. The individual may simply need to let off steam for a moment and will then settle down for the remainder of the hearing.

It is important to keep in mind that parties to a dispute are often upset and distrustful, particularly if they have no representative. An adjudicator can earn the respect and cooperation of the parties, as well as other participants, by treating them also with respect.

PROTESTERS

Occasionally, a hearing that deals with issues of concern to the broader community will attract protesters. They may demonstrate outside or even bring signs and banners into the hearing room. If they are present while the hearing is under way, they may cheer statements that support their position and boo or laugh at statements for which they have contempt. Their behaviour may make it difficult for the adjudicator to keep control of the hearing, maintain decorum, and preserve the integrity of the tribunal. In dealing with the situation, the adjudicator and other members of the tribunal must try to achieve a balance between respect for the protesters' constitutional right to freedom of expression and the need to protect the rule of law.

ABUSIVE PARTICIPANTS

There is a fine line between venting or letting off steam and being abusive. As stated above, it is often reasonable for an adjudicator to permit a party to vent, provided that this behaviour does not seriously interfere with the progress of the hearing. Abuse is a different matter. If a participant behaves abusively toward the tribunal or other participants, this conduct should be quickly stopped. Threats, unfounded or irrelevant accusations of wrongdoing, and discriminatory remarks of any kind are unacceptable. (See "Dealing with Abusive Behaviour.")

Dealing with Abusive Behaviour

Laurel Copley, a former immigration adjudicator with the federal government, suggests a "three strikes and you're out" rule for abusive behaviour:

- Stop the individual who is speaking, remind him that this is a formal administrative hearing, and tell him that his behaviour is unacceptable and will not be tolerated.

- If the behaviour continues, warn the individual that unless it ceases, he will be asked to leave and the tribunal will reach its decision without his input.

- Follow through. If the individual ignores the warning, ask him to leave the hearing. If he refuses to leave, it may be necessary to adjourn the hearing. If a party is asked to leave, arrangements may be made for her to participate from a distance—for example, by sending her transcripts of evidence and allowing her to make submissions in writing.

CLOSED ("IN CAMERA") HEARINGS

Section 2(b) of the *Canadian Charter of Rights and Freedoms*[3] has been interpreted to require that court proceedings be held in public except in unusual circumstances.[4] It is not clear whether this ruling applies to tribunals as well. However, the integrity and credibility of the administrative justice system are founded on the principle that generally hearings should be held in public. This principle has been codified in two statutes of general application governing tribunals.

Section 9 of Ontario's SPPA requires tribunals to hold hearings that are open to the public unless the requirement of confidentiality for matters involving public security or information of an intimate personal or financial nature outweighs the public interest in an open hearing. Even an electronic hearing must be open to the public (except in these circumstances) unless it is impractical. In a written hearing, this openness is achieved by providing the public with access to the documents submitted. Section 41 of British Columbia's ATA requires that oral hearings be open except under circumstances similar to those in s. 9 of the SPPA. It is silent as to whether electronic or written hearings must be open, except to state in s. 41(3) that in all hearings the documents submitted must be accessible to the public except where private or public interests in confidentiality override the public interest in open hearings. Section 10 of Quebec's AJA requires that generally hearings must be held in public but permits a private or "closed" hearing where this is necessary to maintain public order.

Generally, a **closed hearing** (or a hearing held *in camera*, to use the Latin phrase) is attended by all parties, their representatives, and any other individuals whose presence is necessary to assist them, such as expert witnesses. Apart from tribunal members, staff, and a court reporter (if required), no one else is permitted to be present. In some cases (discussed below), it is necessary to close only part of the hearing. To ensure procedural fairness, tribunal members should hear the submissions of all parties before deciding whether and to what extent the hearing should be closed.

When all or part of a hearing is closed, arrangements must be made to protect the confidentiality of information disclosed during the private proceeding. For a fully closed hearing, the record of the proceeding will be sealed and unavailable to the public. For a partially closed hearing, only those portions of the documented record that relate to that part of the proceeding will be sealed. In addition, the tribunal should apply procedural rules requiring the persons who attend the hearing to maintain the privacy of information disclosed in their presence. (Samples of such rules are set out in the "Model Rules of Procedure" produced by the Society of Ontario Adjudicators and Regulators.) (See "Protecting the Confidentiality of a Closed Hearing.")

EXCLUSION OF MEDIA FROM A HEARING

Hearings that are open to the public are also open to the media. Hearings that are closed to the public may or may not be closed to the media, depending on the governing statute that applies to the tribunal.

---

3 Part I of the *Constitution Act, 1982*, RSC 1985, app. II, no. 44.

4 See *R v. Southam Inc. (No. 1)* (1983), 41 OR (2d) 113.

Protecting the Confidentiality of a Closed Hearing

To ensure that a closed proceeding remains confidential, the parties and their representatives and witnesses are often required to sign an undertaking, before the closed session begins, that they will not reveal the oral evidence given or show anyone the documentary evidence received. They may also be required

- to keep confidential any notes they may take,
- not to make copies of documents or notes, and
- to return all documents to the party who tendered them or to the tribunal when the hearing is over.

An example of such an undertaking is included in appendix G of this book.

A tribunal may also order that documentary evidence provided by the participants and any transcript of oral evidence be sealed and kept separate from the public hearing record. Tribunal staff may be instructed to return these documents to the party whose privacy is to be protected after the hearing is over and the deadline for any appeal has passed.

As it may not be necessary to keep confidential all the evidence heard during the closed hearing, after consulting the parties, the tribunal may order the release of any portions of the documentary evidence or of the transcript of oral evidence that are not sensitive. This information will then be available to the public.

For example, in Ontario, tribunals subject to the SPPA may exclude the media from a hearing only by closing the hearing to the public. The limited conditions under which a hearing may be closed have been described in the preceding section.

By contrast, in Quebec, s. 130 of the AJA provides the authority for the Administrative Tribunal of Quebec (ATQ) to allow journalists to attend a closed hearing unless the tribunal considers that their presence may prejudice a person whose interests may be affected by the proceeding. However, a journalist who is granted access to a closed hearing is prohibited from publishing anything that would identify "a person concerned" unless otherwise authorized to do so by the law or by the tribunal. ("Publishing" in this context is given its broad meaning of making information available to the public, whether by radio or television broadcasting or by publication in a newspaper, magazine, book, or other form.)

An order of a tribunal (or a court) prohibiting the publication of information disclosed in a proceeding is called a **publication ban**. It appears that as a general rule, if the media are allowed to attend a hearing, a tribunal cannot forbid the publication of information disclosed in the proceeding unless specifically authorized to do so by statute. For example, as described above, the AJA provides for a partial publication ban in the case of a journalist attending a closed hearing. Section 131 of the AJA also gives the ATQ a broader authority to ban the publication of information where necessary either to maintain public order or, in the case of confidential information, "to ensure the proper administration of justice." At this time, the SPPA provides no specific authority for a tribunal to issue a publication ban.

The inherent authority of tribunals to control their proceedings allows them to impose reasonable conditions on the conduct of representatives of the media (including reporters, camera operators, and sound recorders) during the hearing. For example, the tribunal may require camera technicians or photographers to station their equipment in a part of the hearing room that is out of the line of vision of participants and other observers; prohibit movement of equipment except during breaks in the hearing; and prohibit the use of noisy equipment and distracting lighting. For certainty and consistency, it is helpful for a tribunal to set out these conditions in its rules of procedure; however, some tribunals may prefer to issue orders governing the conduct of media representatives on a case-by-case basis.

EXCLUSION OF PARTIES FROM A HEARING

One of the fundamental principles of fairness is the right of a party to be present throughout a hearing. However, in the rare case where it is necessary to keep information confidential even from a party, a tribunal may deny the party access to that information. For example, a party may refuse on principle to sign a confidentiality undertaking, or the party's past behaviour may provide evidence that the party cannot be trusted to comply with such an undertaking. The party, and in some circumstances the party's representative (as well as witnesses), may be required to leave the hearing room while testimony is being given and may be refused the opportunity to examine documents or other evidence. British Columbia's ATA explicitly permits exclusion of parties and intervenors where necessary to ensure the proper administration of justice (s. 42).

If a valid reason exists for refusing to disclose information to a party, counsel representing the party may be permitted to peruse the information on an undertaking not to disclose any information to the client and to use the information only for the purpose of the proceeding. However, in some cases, the information is so sensitive that disclosure even to counsel is not permitted.

Sara Blake, *Administrative Law in Canada*, 2d ed. (Toronto: Butterworths, 1997), 38

CHAPTER SUMMARY

Tribunals have the authority under common law to control their process. This authority may be codified in statutes granting tribunals specific powers for managing and controlling their hearings. Some tribunals have more powers than others. These powers may include the power to make rules of procedure, to ask a court to punish for contempt, to expel or refuse to hear obstructive or incompetent agents, to require witnesses to testify, to call for the assistance of police, and to award costs for improper conduct.

Generally, tribunals must hold public hearings; however, most tribunals have a limited power to hold closed hearings, excluding the public from attending and from having access to a record of the proceeding, and often excluding the media as well. A closed hearing may be held in order to protect confidential information, or to preserve public security or public order. In rare cases, a party may be excluded from part of a hearing or denied access to evidence.

Bearing in mind that conduct that appears unreasonable to tribunal members or to another party may be reasonable from the point of view of other participants, the tribunal should exercise its powers of control with restraint. The adjudicator should aim to balance the need to keep order and maintain respect for the process against the experience and motivation of the participant whose behaviour does not conform to the tribunal's rules.

KEY TERMS

abuse of process   conduct by a participant in a proceeding involving a flagrant and serious violation of the rules of procedure or of other reasonable expectations of the court or tribunal

closed hearing   a hearing held "*in camera*" or behind closed doors (in private), in which the only persons permitted to attend are those directly involved in the case, such as parties, their representatives, and necessary witnesses

contempt   conduct that shows disrespect for the authority of a court or tribunal or that tends to interfere with (obstruct) the administration of justice; examples include disruption of the proceeding by a participant or by a member of the public; failure of a participant to carry out a promise (an undertaking) made to the court or tribunal; failure of a witness to obey a summons to attend and give evidence; failure of a party or representative to comply with a valid order of the court or tribunal; and provision of statements to the media intended to influence the outcome of the proceeding

in camera hearing   *see* closed hearing

publication ban   an order issued by a court or tribunal prohibiting the publication of evidence and other information disclosed in a proceeding

undertaking   a promise made to a court or tribunal to fulfill a specific obligation, such as producing a document or other evidence relevant to a proceeding

KEY CASES

Contempt

West End Development Corp., Re (1994), 29 Admin. LR (2d) 71 (Ont. EAB)

FACTS: Counsel failed to appear at a pre-hearing conference before the Environmental Appeal Board, on a date and time that had been confirmed in writing by the counsel's office. Her failure to appear was due to a misunderstanding at her office as to which person in the office was responsible for the file.

ISSUE: Was there a case for contempt under s. 23(1) of the *Statutory Powers Procedure Act*, RSO 1990, c. S.22?

DECISION: An order under s. 23(1) of the *Statutory Powers Procedure Act* was not appropriate. There was an innocent explanation that was reasonable and acceptable. This was not a case of contempt.

The Tribunal's Contempt Powers

Canadian Broadcasting Corporation v. Cordeau (1979), 101 DLR (3d) 24 (SCC)

FACTS: The Canadian Broadcasting Corporation (CBC) allegedly broadcast a picture of a witness at an inquiry into organized crime, contrary to an order by the police commission that the photograph not be published. The CBC was summoned to appear before the police commission on charges of contempt.

ISSUE: Did the provincial legislature have jurisdiction to confer on an administrative tribunal the power to punish for contempt *ex facie* (not in the face of the tribunal)?

DECISION: Administrative tribunals such as the police commission do not have an inherent power to punish for contempt, therefore such power must be conferred by statute, or it does not exist. The authority of the provincial legislature to confer this power in a statute is also limited. The legislature may not give the police commission the power to investigate or punish contempt committed *ex facie*. The legislation should be interpreted narrowly on the assumption that the legislature did not intend to exceed its authority. Interpreting the relevant legislation strictly, there was no intention to confer broad *ex facie* contempt powers to the police commission. The allegation against the CBC was for contempt *ex facie*, and the police commission had no jurisdiction to inquire into it.

The Tribunal's Power To Manage and Control the Hearing Process

Chrysler Canada Ltd. v. Canada (Competition Tribunal), [1992] 2 SCR 394

FACTS: The Competition Tribunal issued an order against Chrysler Canada Ltd. under part VIII of the *Competition Act*, RSC 1985, c. C-34, requiring Chrysler to resume supplying car parts to a customer. The director of investigation and research, having reason to believe that Chrysler failed to comply, filed a motion with the tribunal initiating contempt proceedings. Chrysler argued that the tribunal lacked jurisdiction to hear contempt proceedings.

ISSUE: Did the Competition Tribunal have jurisdiction over civil contempt for breaches of its orders under part VIII of the *Competition Act*?

DECISION: At common law only superior courts have the power to punish for contempt. However, clear statutory language can override the common law and confer contempt powers on an inferior tribunal. In this case, s. 8(1) of the *Competition Tribunal Act*, RSC 1985, c. 19 (2d Supp.) is the basis of the tribunal's jurisdiction. It provides that the tribunal has jurisdiction "to hear and determine all applications made under Part VIII of the *Competition Act* and any matters related thereto."

Section 8(2) of the *Competition Tribunal Act* confirms the tribunal's jurisdiction. It expressly confers powers on the tribunal, with respect to enforcement of the tribunal's orders, including contempt for breach of its orders.

REVIEW QUESTIONS

1. What rules of procedure or practice directions can a tribunal make under British Columbia's *Administrative Tribunals Act* that will help its members to maintain control of a proceeding and prevent unnecessary delay or disruption of the hearing?

2. Apart from rule-making powers, list the powers given to Ontario tribunals under the *Statutory Powers Procedure Act* and to the tribunal under the *Administrative Justice Act* that can assist them in maintaining order and avoiding unnecessary delay.

3. What steps can a tribunal take if a lawyer or other representative is incompetent? What if the problem is not incompetence but disrespect for the tribunal or for other parties or their representatives or witnesses?

4. In what circumstances can a tribunal close its hearings to

   a. the public and

   b. the media?

5. When can a tribunal

   a. exclude a party from a hearing or

   b. prevent a party from examining evidence?

FACT SCENARIOS

Scenario 1

You are representing a party at a hearing that will last several weeks. The lawyer representing one of the other parties frequently arrives half an hour to an hour late. The tribunal has criticized this conduct, but it continues.

Your client suggests that you should ask the tribunal to impose a penalty on the lawyer for being late.

1. What action do you ask the tribunal to take?

2. What arguments do you make in support of your request?

3. What is the statutory or common law basis for your arguments?

Scenario 2

You are representing a neighbourhood association at a hearing to determine whether to approve a waste disposal site in the area. The residents are worried that the facility will result in heavy traffic, air pollution, water pollution, noise, odours, and dust. The tribunal panel has made comments that lead your client to believe the tribunal is not sympathetic to these concerns and is likely to approve the facility.

Your client has instructed you to announce to the tribunal that its members consider it biased and are withdrawing from the proceeding. All the members present at the hearing will then stand up and walk out of the hearing room, and you will follow them. Outside the building, the association's executive will hold a press conference and denounce the tribunal as a kangaroo court.

You tell your client that you need to consider this plan. After researching the law and reviewing your client's strategic options, what course of action do you advise?

FURTHER READING

David B. Braund and Carole A. Prest, *Ontario Rules: SOAR's Model Rules of Practice for Administrative Justice Agencies* (Courtice, ON: Society of Ontario Adjudicators and Regulators, 2000).

Paul Lordon, "Administrative Tribunals and the Control of Their Processes" (1997-98) vol. 11 *Canadian Journal of Administrative Law and Practice* 179.

Robert Macaulay and James Sprague, *Practice and Procedure Before Administrative Tribunals* (Toronto: Carswell) (looseleaf), chapter 9.

Jeffrey Miller, *The Law of Contempt in Canada* (Scarborough, ON: Carswell, 1997).

CHAPTER 11

Conduct Outside the Hearing

LEARNING OBJECTIVES

After reading this chapter, you will understand

- why participants in a hearing should not discuss any aspect of the case with the adjudicator or another member of the tribunal unless all other participants are also present;

- why tribunal members should limit their social contact with participants in a hearing and with individuals and organizations that are likely to appear before the tribunal;

- whether participants and tribunal members should talk to the media about a case that is under way;

- why tribunal members should not comment publicly on decisions of the tribunal; and

- whether tribunal members may make public statements on issues that the tribunal has ruled on in the past or may decide in the future.

In the ordinary course, decisions of this Court, as with any other court, must speak for themselves without further elaboration by any member of the court, except through the medium of a later decision of the Court. However, in a circumstance where misstatement of a decision is substantial and the potential consequences of the misstatement are significant, the unusual step of indicating the existence and extent of the misstatement has to be considered, lest silence be taken to be confirmation of the misstated position.

Letter from Clyde Wells, chief justice of Newfoundland, to Kirk Makin, reporter, *The Globe and Mail*, December 12, 2002 (see "Defence of a Ruling: Exceptional Circumstances?" on page 211)

INTRODUCTION

There are not only rules of conduct and procedure for the hearing of a case, but also standards of conduct to be upheld by participants and tribunal members outside the hearing room, before, during, and after the hearing. This chapter describes the standards that apply to conduct in the following contexts:

- communication outside the hearing between participants and tribunal members;
- social contact between tribunal members and individuals or organizations that may appear in future proceedings;
- contact with the media; and
- public statements by adjudicators about previous decisions of the tribunal or issues that may come before the tribunal.

A model code of conduct that addresses such matters has been prepared by the Society of Ontario Adjudicators and Regulators for consideration by tribunals. It is available online at http://soar.on.ca/soar-code.htm.

"EX PARTE" COMMUNICATION

Ex parte communication (meaning, in Latin, communication "on one side only") refers to communication between a party in a proceeding and the adjudicator or other members of the tribunal from which other parties and panel members are excluded. The principle of procedural fairness, and in particular the obligation of impartiality, prohibits *ex parte* communication in tribunal proceedings.

Accordingly, a participant in a hearing should never attempt to discuss any aspect of the case with an adjudicator—or, generally, with other members of the tribunal—unless all other members of the panel and all other participants are present. Similarly, an adjudicator should not ask for or receive written or oral communications about the proceeding from any party to a hearing that is being considered or has been scheduled or begun, unless all other parties and panel members are fully informed and involved. These restrictions mirror the standard of conduct expected of judges regarding communication with participants in a case outside the courtroom.

The tribunal's procedures should ensure that participants do not have direct access to tribunal members outside the hearing room. Telephone calls and correspondence from parties should be channelled through tribunal staff, who can accept inquiries and provide the information requested either independently or after consulting the adjudicator and perhaps other members of the tribunal. Staff are generally trained to screen information received from parties before passing it on to panel members, so as to eliminate any information that may lead to bias or create the appearance of bias. Staff can also ensure that any communication from one of the parties is made available to all panel members and other participants as well. Without the full involvement of all parties, even the most innocent inquiry from one of the participants may be viewed by the others as an improper attempt to influence the adjudicator. Similarly, if a tribunal member wants to inform the parties about a procedural matter—for example, that a hearing must be postponed because of a death in the adjudicator's family—the tribunal staff, not the tribunal member or adjudicator, should make the telephone call or sign the letter. Procedures such as these can ensure that no issue will be decided, or appear to have been decided, without all parties being given an opportunity to contribute to the decision.

No judge should talk with one counsel about any case in the absence of other counsel. Discussions with all counsel involved in a case out of a courtroom and in the absence of a court reporter, ought, in general, to be avoided. All proceedings in a trial are matters of record and it is improper that agreements or rulings should be made and not recorded. There also exists the danger that such agreements or rulings may be misunderstood, or, in rare cases, deliberately misrepresented in a courtroom before a jury. Litigants must have a natural and proper distrust of any proceedings in the case which are not open to their hearing.

J.O. Wilson, *A Book for Judges* (written for the Canadian Judicial Council) (Ottawa: Supply and Services, 1980), 52

During hearings, even casual conversations outside the hearing room raise concerns among the parties. In the case of long hearings or hearings in small communities with a limited range of facilities for accommodation and meals, it may not be practical for adjudicators and participants to avoid any contact outside the hearing. In addition, in brief encounters near the hearing room, a failure to engage in everyday exchanges—such as discussing last night's hockey game or tomorrow's weather—may be interpreted as arrogance. However, participants and adjudicators must realize that even the most harmless conversation from which some parties are excluded can raise the possibility of bias. At the very least, adjudicators should attempt to have any conversation with a participant in full view of the other participants, and they should ensure that any casual remarks exchanged with one party are balanced by similar treatment of other parties over the course of the hearing. (See "The Dangers of Fraternization.")

CONTACT WITH THE MEDIA

A party's strategy for obtaining a favourable decision may include creating public interest in the case through publicity in newspapers, on radio and television, or over the Internet. The party's representative should be prepared to provide advice on the advantages and disadvantages of such publicity and, if the party decides to proceed, to suggest how to go about making these arrangements. The representative may also be called upon to act as a spokesperson in interviews with the media.

The guarantee of freedom of expression in the *Canadian Charter of Rights and Freedoms* (s. 2(b))[1] gives parties and their representatives wide latitude to publicize their views. However, it is important not to argue the case in the media. Statements made outside the hearing room that are intended to influence the outcome of the hearing may constitute contempt of the tribunal. It is also important to ensure that information provided to the media is consistent with evidence given at the hearing. Remember that tribunal members also read and listen to the news. If they see in the newspaper, or hear on the radio or television, details about the case that do not appear in the evidence in the hearing, other parties will be concerned that the tribunal has been influenced by information that is incorrect or at least not subject to challenge through cross-examination.

1 Part I of the *Constitution Act, 1982*, RSC 1985, app. II, no. 44.

The Dangers of Fraternization

It is clearly inappropriate for an adjudicator or tribunal member to have social contact with participants in a hearing that is under way. But how should an adjudicator or member handle social situations involving individuals or organizations that are likely to appear at future hearings? This is a difficult question. Even in such cases, **fraternization** (friendly social interaction) can be a problem.

One of the most useful discussions of fraternization is found in a book written by an American administrative law judge. In the United States, these judges play a similar role to adjudicators in many Canadian tribunals.

> Public attitudes about judicial conduct have become stricter in recent years, and judges should be sensitive to this change. A Judge should limit social activities with friends or colleagues if there is any likelihood of their being involved in matters coming before the Judge. It is not enough merely to avoid discussing pending matters; a Judge should shun situations that might lead anxious litigants or worried lawyers to think that the Judge might favour or accept the views of friends more readily than those of unknown parties.

> One approach is for Judges to maintain their personal ties but disqualify themselves in any case in which a friend appears. If the bar is small this may be unfair to counsel and their clients, and impractical as well. An alternative course is to describe publicly the relationships whenever a friend or associate is involved and offer to disqualify oneself if so requested. This puts an unfair burden on objecting counsel by requiring him to imply publicly that the Judge may be biased; also, if done frequently, it may seem to be avoidance of the Judge's own responsibility. In any event, a Judge must avoid the appearance of impropriety. Thus the Judge should not regularly play bridge or golf or dine with lawyers whose firms may appear before him, nor should he actively participate in politics or political meetings.

> Judges must accept a certain amount of loneliness. They needn't become recluses, but they should realize they are no longer "one of the boys," and that they live in a critical and suspicious world.

— Merritt Ruhlen, *Manual for Administrative Law Judges* (Washington, DC: Administrative Conference of the United States, 1982)

Tribunal members should not discuss with the media any case that is in progress or is expected to come before them. Even a casual comment may be interpreted as showing bias toward or against a party or prejudging the issue. As discussed in the next section, even after a case has been decided, it is only in exceptional circumstances that an adjudicator or other member of the tribunal should issue public statements on a decision.

COMMENTS ON THE TRIBUNAL'S DECISIONS

As a general rule, adjudicators should not defend, explain, or comment on decisions of the tribunal in the media or in other public forums. Again, a similar constraint applies to judges with respect to decisions of the courts.

A tribunal's rulings will not be immune from criticism—by the media, by politicians, by the academic community, or by unsuccessful parties. However, adjudicators must generally not respond to such criticism, even if they feel it is unfair. The risk with public comments is that they create uncertainty about the tribunal's reasons for the decision. For the parties in the case and as a matter of public record, it will not be clear whether the reasons to be relied on are the ones provided when the decision was rendered at the conclusion of the hearing, or the further explanations reported in the media.

The decisions of a tribunal should speak for themselves. To ensure that they do, the adjudicator in a case should make every effort to state the reasons for the decision as clearly and as fully as possible. Only in exceptional circumstances should an adjudicator respond to requests by the media or persons other than the parties in a hearing to explain or defend a decision. Even then, any statements on the case should generally be provided by the tribunal chair, registrar, or counsel.

Defence of a Ruling: Exceptional Circumstances?

In 2003, *The Globe and Mail* reported that a unanimous ruling of the Newfoundland Court of Appeal appeared to criticize the Supreme Court of Canada by saying that judicial activism had gone too far. This ruling caused quite a stir, because in the legal community it is not considered proper for the lower courts to criticize the rulings of the Supreme Court. In fact, although all three judges agreed on the outcome of the case, only one of the judges made the comments about activism.

Clyde Wells, the chief justice of Newfoundland, wrote a letter to the reporter who wrote the *Globe* story, with the consent of the other two judges, to point this out.

Was it appropriate for the chief justice to comment in public about the judgment?

John Crosbie, the former federal minister of justice, didn't think so. He made a formal complaint against the chief justice to the Canadian Judicial Council. The council is responsible for investigating complaints about the conduct of judges and making rulings about whether their conduct is proper.

On March 12, 2003, the Judicial Conduct Committee exonerated the chief justice. The chair of the committee said that Wells was right to write the letter because "a Council policy endorses a role for chief justices in correcting errors in public reports of judicial decisions."

Who was right: former justice minister Crosbie or the Canadian Judicial Council?

Would the result be the same if one of the judges on the panel that made the ruling wrote to the *Globe* to explain the comments about judicial activism?

The constraints outlined above do not apply where it is found that there are errors or ambiguities in a decision. In this situation, the adjudicator, on his own initiative or at the request of a party, may issue a written statement correcting the errors or clarifying the reasons, provided that all parties are first consulted if there is any doubt about whether a change should be made.[2] (See "Criticism of Decisions by Representatives.")

PUBLIC STATEMENTS BY ADJUDICATORS

The last question addressed here is whether adjudicators may speak in public or write about issues that may come before them. In general, the fact that before appointment to a tribunal, an adjudicator has expressed his views on issues that may be the subject of subsequent hearings does not prevent him from serving on the tribunal, although it may disqualify him from deciding cases involving those

---

2 *Chandler v. Alberta (Association of Architects)* (1989), 62 DLR (4th) 577 (SCC). See also SPPA, s. 21.1; ATA, s. 53; and AJA, ss. 153, 154. The *Human Rights Code*, RSO 1990, c. H.19, s. 39, states: "A member of the Tribunal hearing a complaint … shall not communicate directly or indirectly in relation to the subject-matter of the inquiry with any person or with any party or any party's representative except upon notice to and opportunity for all parties to participate."

Criticism of Decisions by Representatives

If you represent the losing party in a case, there is nothing to prevent you from criticizing the tribunal's decision in the media or some other public forum. You are entitled to say that you believe the decision is wrong and to explain why. However, your criticisms should be restrained and well-founded. Avoid targeting individual tribunal members, who, like judges, are prohibited from speaking out in their own defence.

If a tribunal's processes and decisions are frequently unfair, representatives can seek a remedy by, for example, documenting trends, lobbying the tribunal to improve its attitude and practices, and lobbying the government to appoint better-qualified or more empathetic tribunal members.

issues. However, once appointed, the adjudicator must avoid taking any position in public that may lead parties to believe that he will not approach the issues before him with an open mind.

CHAPTER SUMMARY

In addition to rules of conduct for adjudicators and participants at the hearing itself, there are standards of conduct that apply outside the hearing room, before, during, and after the hearing. Generally, participants must avoid actions that may be seen as attempts to influence the tribunal panel. Similarly, adjudicators and other tribunal members must avoid any conduct that may suggest that they are open to influence or that they are biased for or against any party.

In particular, during the hearing, there should be no communication regarding any aspect of the case between a participant and a tribunal member unless all other participants and members are also present or otherwise fully informed and involved. Outside the hearing room, even brief and casual exchanges between participants and tribunal members should be limited, and any suggestion of favouritism should be avoided. Similar constraints apply to social relations between tribunal members and individuals or organizations that may appear at future hearings.

Parties should exercise caution in making public statements about the case while the hearing is in progress. After the tribunal has issued its ruling, the losing party may criticize the decision in public, within reasonable limits. There are tighter restrictions on public statements by tribunal members, particularly with respect to cases currently under consideration, but also regarding previous decisions of the tribunal and positions on issues that may be the subject of future hearings. These constraints reinforce the principle of procedural fairness and the tribunal's obligation to remain impartial in arriving at its decisions.

KEY TERMS

ex parte   Latin term meaning "on one side only"; refers to a statement or application made to an adjudicator or panel member by a party to a proceeding in the absence of other parties or panel members

fraternization   friendly social interaction; refers to social relations between tribunal members and actual or potential participants in a proceeding

KEY CASES

Ex Parte Communications

Kane v. Board of Governors of University of British Columbia, [1980] 1 SCR 1105

FACTS: Kane, a university professor, was found to have been making unauthorized personal use of university computers. The university suspended him for three months without pay and ordered him to pay restitution to the university. Kane appealed the suspension to the board of governors. The BC *Universities Act* provided that the university president was a member of the board "and shall attend its regular meetings." Therefore, the president attended Kane's hearing before the board of governors. The president responded to questions from the board, but did not pose any questions to Kane. At the end of the hearing, Kane was asked to leave so that the board could deliberate. The president, however, remained throughout the deliberations, and although he did not participate in the discussions or vote on the final decision, he did answer questions directed to him by board members. The board approved the three-month suspension without pay and the order for restitution. Kane sought judicial review of the board's decision.

ISSUE: Were the board's *ex parte* discussions with the president improper?

DECISION: The principles of natural justice were breached, because the president had answered questions after the hearing and in Kane's absence. A tribunal must listen fairly to both sides, giving the parties a fair opportunity to correct or contradict any relevant statement prejudicial to their position. The tribunal must also refrain from holding private interviews with witnesses or hearing evidence in the absence of a party subject to discipline. It did not matter whether the evidence given in Kane's absence actually influenced the board's decision, as long as it was capable of doing so. If the board required further information, it should have waited until Kane was present and asked the questions in his presence. Or, at the very least, the board should have informed Kane of the additional information it had received from the president and given him an opportunity to respond.

Reasonable Apprehension of Bias: Multiple Roles of Participants

Bailey v. Registered Nurses' Association (Saskatchewan), [1996] 3 WWR 497 (Sask. QB)

FACTS: Three registered nurses were dismissed by their director of nursing after a hearing before a disciplinary panel of the Saskatchewan Registered Nurses' Association. Their director was also the president-elect of the nurses' association at the time of the investigation and hearing. The prosecutor at the discipline hearing had been counsel for the investigation committee, when the nurses were investigated. His firm was general counsel for the nurses' association, and was responsible for training discipline committee members. In fact, the prosecutor had personally trained the chair of the discipline committee. In addition, the prosecutor's law firm regularly advertised in the nurses' association magazine and had contributed $5,000 to the association's building fund prior to the hearing. During the hearing, there was a noticeable degree of familiarity between the panel and the prosecutor.

ISSUE: Was there a reasonable apprehension of bias, particularly with respect to the prosecutor's familiarity with the panel?

DECISION: The process was flawed from the beginning of the investigation to the conclusion by the discipline committee. The discipline committee did not appear to have understood that issues of fairness and bias were involved. The nurses would understandably have perceived bias when they tried to raise a defence challenging the management practices of their director, who also happened to be president-elect of the nurses' association. Ordinarily it was not objectionable for counsel to hold multiple roles, especially in administrative practice. In this case, however, the relationship between the committee and the prosecutor raised a reasonable apprehension of bias because of its degree and because of all of the surrounding factors that raised concerns of unfairness and bias. These factors included the familiarity between the prosecutor and members of the discipline committee; that the committee chair had been trained by the prosecutor; that the prosecutor's law firm had provided training for the committee; that the law firm regularly advertised in the nurses' association magazine; and that the law firm had contributed $5,000 to the building fund of the nurses' association. Together, these factors created a relationship between the discipline committee and the prosecutor sufficient to raise a reasonable apprehension of bias.

Social Contact Between Adjudicators and Parties

United Enterprises Ltd. v. Saskatchewan (Liquor and Gaming Licensing Commission), [1997] 3 WWR 497 (Sask. QB)

FACTS: United Enterprises operated a tavern. Its liquor licence was suspended by the licensing authority, and it appealed the suspension to the licensing commission. At the hearing, lawyers for the licensing authority and members of the commission referred to each other by their first names. They walked to and from the hearing room together, and the licensing authority lawyer was invited to a barbecue by the commission chair on the evening after the hearing. In contrast, the lawyer for United Enterprises was referred to by his last name and had no contact with commission members outside the hearing. The commission ultimately upheld the suspension. United Enterprises appealed the decision, arguing that the friendly relations between counsel for the licensing authority and members of the commission raised a reasonable apprehension of bias. United sought reinstatement of its licence on the ground that it was no longer possible to have a fair hearing.

ISSUE: Did the familiarity between the authority's lawyer and members of the commission create a reasonable apprehension of bias?

DECISION: The familiarity between the licensing authority's lawyer and members of the commission raised a reasonable apprehension of bias. However, the court could not substitute its own decision for the decision of the licensing authority to suspend the liquor licence. A new hearing before a differently constituted commission was ordered.

REVIEW QUESTIONS

1. Should a party's representative call a tribunal member to find out when the hearing of his or her case is likely to be held? Explain.

2. Should a tribunal member call a party's representative to inform him that another party has asked for an adjournment and ask whether the adjournment is acceptable to the representative's client? Explain.

3. How should a tribunal handle social relations between tribunal members and individuals or groups that frequently appear before the tribunal?

4. To what extent are tribunal members free to write or speak about issues that the tribunal has decided in the past or may decide in the future?

5. What factors should a party consider in deciding whether to comment publicly on the tribunal's decision?

FACT SCENARIOS

Scenario 1

You represent a party in a hearing. During a recess, a reporter comes up to you and comments that some of the panel's questions suggest that the tribunal is biased against your party's case. How do you reply?

Scenario 2

You are a representative for a party at a hearing held out of town. You enter the hotel dining room and see the adjudicator eating breakfast alone. Do you join her? What if she invites you to join her? What if the lawyers representing two of the three other parties are already at the table?

Scenario 3

You appear frequently before a tribunal that hears appeals from decisions of the government when it refuses applications for social assistance. This tribunal often decides in favour of the government and against applicants. You have just received a decision that does not take into account much of the evidence that you put before the tribunal. A reporter asks you to comment on the decision. What do you do? What if the reporter asks you to comment on the overall conduct of the tribunal as well as the specific decision?

Scenario 4

You are at a hearing before the Ontario Rental Housing Tribunal. The party you represent faces eviction for having a noisy dog. During a recess, when you are in the washroom cubicle, you hear two people enter the washroom. One of them says to the other that he hates dogs. You peek and see that it is the adjudicator talking to the court reporter.

1. Do you take any action, and if so, what and when?

2. Suppose you are the adjudicator who made this comment and the appellant's representative questions your conduct in the hearing room later that day. What do you do?

3. Suppose the hearing panel in this case consists of three adjudicators. The person in the cubicle who overhears this conversation is not the appellant's representative but one of the other panel members. What, if anything, should that panel member do?

FURTHER READING

John Swaigen, *A Manual for Ontario Adjudicators*, 1st ed. rev. (Courtice, ON: Society of Ontario Adjudicators and Regulators, 1999), chapter 14.

CHAPTER 12

Tribunal Decision-Making Procedures

LEARNING OBJECTIVES

After reading this chapter, you will understand

- the degree of consensus (agreement) among adjudicators that is required for a tribunal's decision in a case;

- the kind of information that a decision must be based on;

- sources of assistance to a tribunal in making its decision and drafting its reasons;

- a tribunal's obligation to consult parties when relying on legal authorities not included in evidence at the hearing;

- the kinds of remedies that may be granted in tribunal decisions;

- why tribunals must give reasons for their decisions;

- what should be included in the reasons for a decision;

- solutions to the problem of delay in the release of a decision;

- who are the first persons to be informed of the tribunal's decision; and

- how the requirement of procedural fairness affects the way the decision is communicated.

The mischief of penetrating the decision process of a tribunal member is exactly the same as the mischief of penetrating the decision process of a judge.

Apart from the practical consideration that tribunal members and judges would spend more time testifying about their decisions than making them, their compellability would be inconsistent with any system of finality of decisions. No decision ... would be really final until the judge or tribunal member had been cross-examined about his decision. Instead of appeal or extraordinary remedy [judicial review], a system would grow up of review by cross-examination. In the case of a specialized tribunal representing different interests the mischief would be even greater because the process of discussion and compromise among different points of view would not work if stripped of its confidentiality.

Agnew v. Association of Architects (Ontario)
(1987), 64 OR (2d) 8, at 14 (Div. Ct.)

OVERVIEW OF THE DECISION-MAKING PROCESS

The decision-making process of a tribunal is more rigorous than that of other government agencies. To reach a decision, decision makers in administrative agencies

- identify the issue(s) to be settled;
- obtain relevant information from the person who will be directly affected by the decision;
- apply the agency's policies, guidelines, or criteria to the facts; and
- consult other persons whose interests may be affected by the decision.

Usually, the agency issues its decision in a letter, often using a standard form. As a general rule, there is no statutory requirement for an agency to give reasons for its decision.

The adjudicator of a tribunal makes the decision in a case on the basis of information provided at a formal hearing. Following the hearing, the adjudicator

- identifies the issue or issues raised by the parties in the course of the hearing;
- reviews and weighs the evidence related to the issue(s) that the parties presented at the hearing;
- reviews the arguments of the parties in support of their respective positions on the issue(s);
- makes findings of fact based on the evidence;
- determines the law and any administrative policies or guidelines that apply to the facts;
- applies the law, policies, and guidelines in order to reach a decision; and
- writes the decision and the reasons for the decision.

Where a panel of adjudicators conducts the hearing, an additional stage may be the negotiation of a consensus, or agreement, on the decision among the members of the panel.

Often a tribunal reaches its decision not long after the hearing. It then issues the decision to the parties, either orally or in writing. In more complex cases, the tribunal may conclude that it needs more time to consider the issues, and it will inform the parties that it is **reserving the decision**. It will then continue its review of the case and release a written decision at some future date. When a tribunal issues a written decision, it may be required to issue written reasons as well.

Several important elements of the decision-making process are discussed in more detail in the sections that follow.

RULES OF CONSENSUS AND DISSENT

Where a case is decided by a panel rather than a single adjudicator, there must be a minimum level of consensus, or agreement, on the decision among the panel members. If the panel has an odd number of members, the general rule is that the decision of the majority is the decision of the tribunal. This rule is sometimes explicitly stated in a statute.[1]

If the panel has an even number of members and there is a tie, there are three possible solutions:

1. In the case of a two-member panel, the governing statute may require a unanimous decision.[2]

2. The governing statute may provide for a tie-breaking vote.[3]

3. Otherwise, and in most cases, the hearing must be held again.

If one or more members disagree with the majority decision, most tribunals permit the minority to write their reasons for disagreeing, called a **dissent**. Generally, governing statutes do not state whether a tribunal must issue a dissent with its decision,[4] and the right of parties to be provided with dissenting reasons has not been clearly established as an aspect of procedural fairness. However, in most cases, a dissent is included with the tribunal's decision and reasons.

BASIS FOR THE DECISION

Tribunals differ from administrative agencies with respect to the kind of information they may rely on in making a decision. Decision makers in government agencies may receive information from many sources and in many forms. They may rely on any of this information that is relevant to the decision; however, procedural fairness may require them to disclose the basis for the decision and to give the persons affected an opportunity to challenge it.

As a general rule, tribunal adjudicators may base their decisions only on information obtained during the hearing in the form of evidence presented by the parties. There are two exceptions to this rule that are recognized in common law and in some statutes. These exceptions are explained below.

Facts That May Be Accepted Without Proof

The first exception relates to two categories of facts that a tribunal may accept without proof—in legal language, facts of which it may **take notice**. Both Ontario's

---

1 See, for example, s. 4.2(3) of Ontario's *Statutory Powers Procedure Act* (SPPA), RSO 1990, c. S.22, and s. 145 of Quebec's *Administrative Justice Act* (AJA), RSQ, c. J-3.

2 Ibid.

3 For example, s. 145 of Quebec's AJA states that where opinions are equally divided, the president or vice-president of the Administrative Tribunal of Quebec, or his delegate, has the right to make the decision. Ontario's SPPA does not contain a tie-breaking provision.

4 An exception is s. 145 of Quebec's AJA, which specifies that if a member of a panel dissents, the grounds for dissent must be recorded in the decision.

Statutory Powers Procedure Act and Quebec's *Administrative Justice Act* refer specifically to these two categories of facts.

The first category consists of facts that are so commonly known that they are not disputed by reasonable people. Such facts are referred to in s. 16(a) of the SPPA as "facts that may be judicially noticed" and in s. 140 of the AJA as "facts so well-known as to not reasonably be questionable." Obvious examples are the statement that a horse is a mammal or that the normal length of a human pregnancy is about nine months. In the context of a hearing, an adjudicator who is familiar with local geography, for example, may take notice of the location of a street within a municipality, even if no evidence has been presented as proof of this fact.

Mr. Justice Cartwright ... was a member of a panel of the Supreme Court of Canada sitting on an appeal from an expropriation assessment of a garden nursery. One of the comparable properties used in evidence was the Sheridan Nursery on Yonge Street in Toronto which was located within a few blocks of the house in which Mr. Justice Cartwright lived before moving to Ottawa. He asked whether it could be usefully used as a comparable property since it was as he well knew a corner property and had two frontages. Counsel answered that there was no evidence that the property was a corner property. "Well then," he replied, "I shall wipe it from my mind." Counsel all knew that he would.

The Law Society Gazette

The second category of facts that may be accepted without proof consists of facts that can be immediately and accurately demonstrated by reference to readily accessible and reliable sources. Section 16(b) of the SPPA refers to facts in this category as "any generally recognized scientific or technical facts, information or opinions within [the tribunal's] scientific or specialized knowledge." Section 141 of the AJA refers to "facts that are generally recognized and ... opinions and information which fall within [the adjudicator's] area of specialization or that of the division [of the tribunal] to which he is assigned."

Tribunal members sometimes find it frustrating that they are appointed to a tribunal because of their specialized knowledge of the subject matter of its hearings, yet they are limited in the extent to which they can apply that knowledge or verify evidence by conducting their own research. The second exception to the general rule allows adjudicators to apply their knowledge in their own field, but only to matters that are inherently uncontroversial.

Canada's leading text on evidence states that judges are not required to inform the parties in a case that they intend to take notice of a fact, because if it is the kind of fact of which the judge is entitled to take notice, it cannot be successfully contradicted by any evidence the parties may produce.[5] Nevertheless, if the adjudicator of a hearing intends to take notice of a fact, it is advisable for her to inform the parties of her intention and to give them an opportunity to make submissions on this

---

5 John Sopinka, Sidney Lederman, and Alan Bryant, *The Law of Evidence in Canada* (Toronto: Butterworths, 1992), 988.

point, even if she believes that the facts are so obvious that there is no need of proof. In this way, fairness and the appearance of fairness will be upheld.

Reliance on Legal Authority

While it is clear that adjudicators have a limited ability to rely on facts for which there is no need of proof, it is less clear whether they may consider legal authorities not included in the evidence presented at the hearing.

The general rule is that if in the course of writing the decision, the adjudicator finds a judgment of a court or a statutory provision that is relevant to an issue raised at the hearing but was not referred to by the parties, he may rely on that authority without informing the parties of his intention to do so. However, an adjudicator should not rely on a legal authority that addresses an issue that was not raised at the hearing without first giving the parties an opportunity to make submissions and, where appropriate, lead evidence. This common law rule[6] is spelled out in s. 142 of Quebec's AJA: "The Tribunal may not base its decision on grounds of law … if it has not first given the parties, other than parties who have waived their right to state their allegations, an opportunity to present their observations."

ORDERS AND REMEDIES

A tribunal's decision often includes **orders** for specific measures to be taken to redress or compensate for the wrong at issue in the case, or to relieve or prevent recurrence of the situation giving rise to the dispute. These orders are sometimes referred to as **remedies**.

Generally, the remedies that a tribunal may grant are limited to those specifically authorized by a governing statute. If a remedy is not provided by statute, the tribunal probably cannot grant it. For example, in the absence of a statutory power, a tribunal may not award costs. (See "Examples of Remedies That May Be Granted by a Tribunal.")

Tribunal decisions are usually forward-looking; that is, they result in orders to carry out or cease some activity in the future, rather than punish past conduct or require compensation or restitution for harm caused. Even remedies such as suspension or revocation of a licence are intended primarily to protect the public and improve future conduct rather than punish past wrongdoing. However, when a hearing involves charges of professional misconduct, the tribunal's governing statute usually provides that if the individual involved is found guilty, she may also be required to contribute to the cost of the investigation and prosecution.

ASSISTANCE IN MAKING THE DECISION OR DRAFTING THE REASONS

As a general rule, "He who hears must decide." In other words, only the tribunal members who heard a case may make the decision. In some instances, a statute

---

6 *Consolidated Bathurst Packaging Ltd. v. International Wood Workers of America, Local 2-69* (1986), 56 OR (2d) 513, at 517 (CA); aff'd. 68 DLR (4th) 524, at 565 (SCC); and *Ellis-Don Ltd. v. Ontario (Labour Relations Board)* (1994), 16 OR (3d) 698 (Div. Ct.); leave to appeal denied by CA and SCC.

Examples of Remedies That May Be Granted by a Tribunal

Remedies reflect the purpose of the proceeding.

In regulatory proceedings involving an application for approval of an activity, the remedy is usually to grant approval with or without terms or conditions, or to refuse approval.

In regulatory proceedings involving noncompliance with standards of service or performance, remedies may include

- a reduction of rates for services provided to the complainant,
- an order to upgrade the service to certain classes of consumers,
- an order to provide service in ways that are less intrusive on rights such as privacy or are more user-friendly, or

- an order to provide service in ways that conserve energy or protect the environment.

Some regulatory tribunals have authority to order payment of compensation to victims of incompetent or dishonest work, although usually this requires a separate proceeding in court.

In disciplinary proceedings, the remedies may include

- a reprimand,
- a fine,
- suspension or revocation of a licence,
- the imposition of conditions or limits on the right to practise, or
- the imposition of requirements to upgrade qualifications.

may provide authority for the tribunal as a whole to substitute its decision for that of the hearing panel. However, tribunals rarely make use of such provisions.[7]

The general rule does not prevent individuals associated with the tribunal from providing the adjudicator with limited assistance in reaching the decision or drafting the reasons for it. However, in providing such assistance, no one may put pressure on the adjudicator or hearing panel to decide for or against a particular party.

Adjudicators may ask for suggestions or advice, or obtain clerical assistance, from other tribunal members and tribunal staff. In addition, when tribunal counsel or outside counsel engaged by the tribunal has acted as a neutral adviser during the hearing, the adjudicator may also consult counsel at the decision-making stage. Again, it must be emphasized that the ultimate decision remains the adjudicator's alone; adjudicators may not delegate their decision-making authority to counsel.

When an adjudicator obtains legal advice about a case in progress, the question arises whether this advice must be shared with the parties. Some statutes specifically include this requirement.[8] Where the statute is silent, it is now clear that the parties have no right to be informed. In the *Pritchard* case,[9] the Supreme Court of Canada ruled that unless a statute specifies that a tribunal must share the advice received from counsel with the parties, it has no duty to do so.

---

7   For example, Ontario's *Human Rights Code*, RSO 1990, c. H.19, s. 39.

8   Ibid.

9   *Pritchard v. Ontario (Human Rights Commission)* (2003), 63 OR (3d) 97 (CA); aff'd. 2004 SCC 31; (2004), 238 DLR (4th) 1.

REQUIREMENT TO GIVE REASONS

Until 1999, when the Supreme Court of Canada issued its decision in *Baker v. Canada*,[10] it was not clear whether tribunals had a duty to give written reasons for their decisions. The ruling in *Baker* established that, in cases where the outcome will seriously affect the rights or privileges of an individual, procedural fairness requires not just tribunals, but also other statutory decision makers, to give reasons for the decision.

The giving of reasons is required by the ordinary man's sense of justice. It is also a healthy discipline for all who exercise power over others.

H.W.R. Wade, *Administrative Law*, 6th ed. (London: Oxford University Press, 1988)

Section 13 of Quebec's AJA, s. 51 of British Columbia's *Administrative Tribunals Act*,[11] and s. 7 of Alberta's *Administrative Procedures Act*[12] require that where an authority exercises a statutory power in a way that adversely affects a person's rights, the authority must provide written decisions with reasons. Under s. 17(1) of Ontario's SPPA, a tribunal must give its final decision or order in writing, but it is required to provide written reasons only if a party requests them. This rule does not apply to other statutory decision makers.

In my opinion, it is now appropriate to recognize that, in certain circumstances, the duty of procedural fairness will require the provision of a written explanation for a decision. The strong arguments demonstrating the advantages of written reasons suggest that, in cases such as this here the decision has important significance for the individual, when there is a statutory right of appeal, or in other circumstances, some form of reasons should be required. This requirement has been developing in the common law elsewhere.

L'Heureux-Dubé J in *Baker v. Canada (Minister of Citizenship and Immigration)*, [1999] 2 SCR 817, at 848

Writing the Reasons

While the Supreme Court in *Baker* established a requirement that statutory decision makers must give reasons for certain decisions, it did not specify what must be included in those reasons. Because the decision-making process is more rigorous for tribunals than for administrative agencies, it is likely that the reasons of tribunals should also be more detailed.

---

10 *Baker v. Canada (Minister of Citizenship and Immigration)*, [1999] 2 SCR 817.

11 SBC 2004, c. 45.

12 RSA 1980, c. A-2.

The sequence of stages in a tribunal's decision-making process was outlined at the beginning of this chapter. The logic and analytical detail of that sequence should be reflected in the reasons.

The reasons should set out

- the issue(s) addressed in the case;

- a summary of the evidence, indicating not only the evidence that the adjudicator has relied on, but also evidence that he rejected, with reasons;

- findings of fact based on the related evidence; and

- a statement of the law and any applicable policies and guidelines that determined the adjudicator's decision.

If a panel heard the case and the decision was not unanimous, the reasons may also include a statement of dissent, with related reasons.

The reasons—and, of course, the decision itself—should be written in clear, concise plain language. There should be no confusion or uncertainty about either the ruling in the case or the facts and analysis on which it is based.

Tribunal members and officials should consider the audience for their decisions and write them in a way that will meet the needs of that audience. The main audience is the parties to the proceeding—most important, the person who has been denied what he or she is seeking. The decision should explain to that person, as clearly, persuasively, and diplomatically as possible, why he or she was unsuccessful. There are often other audiences to keep in mind: the legal community, who look for guidance on how to prepare and present future cases; the decision makers' colleagues and superiors; the media, if the situation is newsworthy; and politicians, academics, and the general public.

RELEASE OF THE DECISION

Dealing with Delay

Parties often complain about delays in the release of tribunal decisions. However, there is little that a party can do to speed resolution of the case. Most representatives are reluctant to make repeated inquiries, since these may only annoy the adjudicator. If the delay becomes unreasonable, a party can apply for judicial review, asking a court to order the tribunal to produce a decision or order a new hearing before a different panel. However, this is a costly way to obtain a remedy.

Some legislators have attempted to solve the problem by including provisions in statutes that require a tribunal to produce a decision within a specified time after the conclusion of the hearing. Ontario's SPPA leaves the setting of deadlines to the individual tribunal, requiring only that tribunals establish guidelines for completing their proceedings (s. 16.2). Quebec's AJA goes further. Section 146 requires the tribunal to render its decision within three months unless the president of the tribunal has granted an extension to the hearing panel. If there is excessive delay, the president of the tribunal can withdraw the decision from a member of the panel. The decision of the other members will then be binding, as long as there is a quorum. If there is no quorum after one member is disqualified, the case must be heard again—presumably by a different panel.

Communication of the Decision

All parties in a proceeding have a right to receive the tribunal's decision. As discussed earlier, in many cases, they also have a right to receive written reasons. Fairness requires that all parties receive the decision at the same time, or as close to the same time as methods of communication permit. Fairness also requires that the parties be informed of the final decision before it is made available to any other person (excluding tribunal members, staff, or counsel involved in preparation of the decision).

In the simplest situation, the adjudicator may deliver an oral decision at the end of the hearing, with all parties or their representatives present. In the case of a written decision, including a reserved decision, the procedure may be more complicated. For example, it may be necessary to fax the decision or to deliver it by courier, particularly if one or more parties live out-of-town. If a party does not have access to a fax machine, the tribunal may deliver the decision to that party orally, by telephone, at the same time as other parties are receiving it by fax.

If a reserved decision involves a matter of public interest, subject to cost considerations, the tribunal may choose to announce it at a public meeting. The tribunal will notify the parties and the public of the location, date, and time of the announcement. At the meeting, the adjudicators or other tribunal members, or their representatives, will deliver the decision, perhaps reading it aloud along with the reasons for it. Copies of the decision will be made available to those attending.

CHAPTER SUMMARY

Both tribunals and other agencies have a duty, when an application or request is made to them to grant a right or benefit or confer a privilege, to make a decision in a timely manner, to provide reasons for the decision, and to communicate the decision and reasons to the relevant parties.

For agencies other than tribunals, the process of making a decision may be fairly informal. A wide variety of information may be used and a variety of officials may be involved in making the decision. Although reasons must be provided, they need not describe in detail the considerations that went into making the decision.

In contrast, tribunals are restricted in the kinds of information they can take into account, and they must follow more restrictive procedures than other agencies follow in reaching their decision. Often their reasons must be more detailed and must be communicated to all the parties, preferably at the same time.

Where a tribunal consists of more than one member, the majority's decision is usually the tribunal's decision. Where a tribunal has an even number of members, the statute governing the tribunal dictates what happens in the event of a tie. However, tribunal members generally work together to achieve consensus and try to avoid ties or dissenting decisions.

Tribunals generally must base their decisions on facts proven by the parties, but there are exceptions for information so obvious or well known that it needs no proof. Tribunals should not base their decisions on legal grounds or policy considerations that were not advanced by the parties without first advising the parties and hearing their views.

Only the adjudicators who heard the case, and only if they were present throughout the entire proceedings, are entitled to participate in a tribunal's decision.

However, adjudicators can obtain limited assistance from tribunal staff in reaching their decision and writing the reasons, provided that they make the decision themselves and do not delegate the decision making to others or allow others to pressure them.

A good decision is one that sets out the issues, evidence, facts, law, and applicable policies and guidelines, and that explains the reasons in clear, concise language. It should also clearly state what remedy it is providing and what, if anything, a person is ordered to do.

An agency or tribunal can only provide remedies or make orders that are permitted by statute. The remedies available to tribunals are generally forward-looking; that is, they can require someone to do or refrain from doing something in the future. Generally, tribunals cannot punish someone for past behaviour, and in most cases they cannot order compensation, although there are exceptions.

When the decision is released, all parties should receive the decision at the same time, or as close to the same time as possible, to avoid any appearance of bias.

KEY TERMS

dissent   a written statement of an adjudicator's disagreement with the decision of the majority of adjudicators on a court or tribunal panel, usually setting out the reasons why the adjudicator would have reached a different decision

order   a legally enforceable remedial measure issued by a government official, tribunal, or court; term sometimes used for the decision of a tribunal; *see also* remedy

remedy   a measure that an authority such as a government official, court, or tribunal can take to prevent, redress, punish, or compensate for a wrong, or to relieve, cure, or correct a condition

reserve a decision   hold back a decision following a proceeding for further consideration and release by the court or tribunal at a later time

take notice   accept certain facts without proof as valid information that a court or tribunal may take into consideration in reaching a decision in a proceeding; usually applies to matters that are so well known that they are not open to question and to generally recognized scientific, technical, or other specialized knowledge

KEY CASES

Delay in Making a Decision

Ramsay v. Toronto (City) Commissioners of Police (1988), 66 OR (2d) 99 (Div. Ct.)

FACTS: Ramsay was allegedly beaten by three police officers. He made a complaint, which led to an internal investigation. Ramsay then sued the police officers and named the chief of police as a defendant. The report of the public complaints officer was completed and forwarded to the chief of police. According to the governing legislation, the chief of police was required to review the report and decide whether any further action should be taken. The chief refused to review the report until the civil action concluded, arguing that the review would place him in a conflict of interest with his officers. Ramsay applied for judicial review seeking an order requiring the chief of police to review the final report and refer it to the complaints commission for a hearing.

ISSUE: Could the police chief refuse to review the report until the conclusion of the civil suit?

DECISION: The purpose of the complaints procedure was to provide inexpensive, quick, and effective action in dealing with complaints against police. The police chief's refusal to review the final report of the complaint until the conclusion of the civil suit would frustrate the purposes of the complaints process. The court ordered the chief to review the final report and make a decision. However, since the chief ultimately had discretion as to whether he would act on the report by referring it to the commission, the court could not order him to refer the complaint or to carry out any other action.

Scope of Tribunals' Right To Consult Before Deciding

Ellis-Don Ltd. v. Ontario (Labour Relations Board) (2001), 194 DLR (4th) 385 (SCC)

FACTS: A union filed a grievance with the Ontario Labour Relations Board alleging that the employer, Ellis-Don, had subcontracted work to non-union subcontractors contrary to the collective agreement. The first draft of the panel's decision dismissed the grievance. However, when the decision was reviewed by the full board in accordance with its standard practice, the board determined that although the panel's reasoning was not incorrect, the reason for dismissing the grievance was not necessarily sufficient or determinative. The panel decided to change its ruling and uphold the grievance. Ellis-Don sought judicial review of the decision.

ISSUE: Are adjudicators allowed to change their decisions after consultation?

DECISION: Adjudicators may alter their draft decisions if certain rules are respected. The consultation must be restricted to questions of policy and law, and not touch on questions of fact. The decision makers must arrive at their own conclusions. The change in the panel's decision in this case concerned a matter of law and policy. The panel did not appear to have changed its understanding or assessment of the facts, and therefore the change in decision did not breach any rules of natural justice.

Scope of Tribunals' Right To Consult Before Deciding

International Woodworkers of America, Local 2-69 v. Consolidated-Bathurst Packaging Ltd., [1990] 1 SCR 282

FACTS: A three-member panel of the Ontario Labour Relations Board ruled that Consolidated Bathurst had failed to bargain in good faith by not disclosing its plans to close a plant during negotiations for a collective agreement. During the panel's deliberations, the full board met to discuss the policy implications of the panel's draft decision. The findings of fact made by the three-member panel were accepted by the full board. Consolidated Bathurst sought judicial review of the panel's decision.

ISSUE: Were the discussions by the full board appropriate?

DECISION: Full board meetings are a practical means of calling upon the experience of all board members when deciding important matters of policy. This helps to achieve consistency and coherence by avoiding the possibility that different panels will decide similar issues in a different way. The board must be allowed to consider the broader policy implications of its decisions. Factual matters concerning the actual parties may only be examined and discussed by the panel members who heard the evidence, and the parties must be given a fair opportunity to present their case before the panel. The participation by other board members at the full board meeting did not amount to "participation" in the final decision. Discussions between panel members and other members who did not hear the evidence was not necessarily a problem, because it did not prevent the panel members from making an independent decision. The full board meeting was an important element of a legitimate process and not "participation" by members who had not heard the parties. The discussions were limited to policy matters, and the panel members ultimately come to their own decision based on the evidence they heard and the law and policy as discussed in the meeting of the full board.

Scope of Tribunals' Right To Consult Before Deciding

Tremblay v. Quebec (Commission des affaires sociales), [1992] 1 SCR 952

FACTS: Quebec refused to reimburse the cost of bandages to Tremblay, a social assistance recipient. Tremblay appealed this decision to the Commission des affaires sociales. The appeal was heard by two commissioners, and a draft decision favourable to Tremblay was signed by the commissioners and sent to the commission's lawyer for verification and consultation, according to the established practice at the commission. Since the lawyer was on vacation, the president of the commission reviewed the draft. He then sent the two commissioners a memo in which he disagreed with their decision on a point of law. At the request of one commissioner, issue was submitted to a "consensus table" for consideration. At that meeting, a majority of members disagreed with the draft decision and one of the commissioners changed her mind and wrote an opinion unfavourable to Tremblay. The commissioners were then divided on the question and the matter was submitted to the president of the commission for resolution. He decided the matter as he had indicated in his earlier memo.

ISSUE: Did the process used by the commission contravene the rules of natural justice?

DECISION: The consultative process adopted by the commission was not consistent with the rules of natural justice. A consultative process that includes a meeting by the whole board, designed to promote consistency in decision-making, is generally acceptable. However, that process must not limit the freedom of the panel to decide according to its own conscience, and it must not create an appearance of bias in the minds of the parties. The "consensus tables" held by the commission, although optional in theory, were in practice compulsory when legal counsel determined that the draft decision was contrary to previous decisions. The fact that the president of the commission expressed his contrary opinion to the commissioners, and then became the "tie-breaker" was also a breach of the rules of natural justice.

REVIEW QUESTIONS

1. If a panel of three adjudicators holds a hearing and one of them disagrees with the decision of the other two, how does the tribunal deal with this situation?

2. In making a decision, may an adjudicator take into account information other than evidence presented during the hearing?

3. If an adjudicator is considering reliance on facts not presented at the hearing, what procedures should he follow?

4. May adjudicators consult others when making a decision? If so, what kinds of assistance may they seek, and what are the limits on the participation of others?

5. Are tribunals and other agencies required to give reasons for decisions? If so, in what circumstances are reasons required?

6. What are the characteristics of a well-reasoned decision?

7. Do adjudicators have a duty to reach a decision within a reasonable time? What can parties do if there is excessive delay in the release of a decision?

8. How should a tribunal's decision be communicated to the parties?

EXERCISES

1. Who is the "audience" for a tribunal decision? That is, with whom should the adjudicator try to communicate when writing the decision?

2. List the reasons why a tribunal adjudicator or other statutory decision maker should give clear and understandable reasons for the decision that he or she has reached.

3. Should an adjudicator take the time to draft detailed reasons for her decision if this means that the decision will not be released for several months after the hearing, or should she issue the decision soon after the hearing with the bare minimum of reasons? Explain.

FURTHER READING

Lisa Braverman, *Administrative Tribunals: A Legal Handbook* (Aurora, ON: Canada Law Book, 2001), chapter 4.

S.R. Ellis, Carole Trethewey, and Frederika Rotter, "Tribunals—Reasons, and Reasons for Reasons" (1990-91) vol. 4 *Canadian Journal of Administrative Law and Practice* 105.

Robert Macaulay and James Sprague, *Practice and Procedure Before Administrative Tribunals* (Toronto: Carswell) (looseleaf), chapter 22.

R.A. Macdonald and David Lametti, "Reasons for Decision in Administrative Law" (1989-90) vol. 3 *Canadian Journal of Administrative Law and Practice* 123.

Michael H. Morris, "Administrative Decision-Makers and the Duty To Give Reasons: An Emerging Debate" (1997-98) vol. 11 *Canadian Journal of Administrative Law and Practice* 155.

CHAPTER 13

Challenging Decisions of Tribunals and Administrative Agencies

LEARNING OBJECTIVES

After reading this chapter, you will understand

- the most common reasons for challenging decisions of tribunals and administrative agencies;
- the methods, or review mechanisms, available for challenging decisions;
- who is entitled to make use of these review mechanisms;
- in what circumstances these review mechanisms are available;
- the time limits for raising a challenge;
- the effect of a challenge on a party's duty to comply with the decision;
- the standards that the courts apply in reviewing a decision; and
- the remedies available in the case of a successful challenge.

Given the courts' constant demands that [the system of administrative justice] remake itself, it is questionable if it is a system at all. Dr. Johnson might have said that, as with "a dog walking on its hinder legs," the wonder is not that the "system" works badly, it is that it works at all. Judicial review is a poor way to run a railroad. ...

[T]he courts have shown only a dim perception of the lives and times of the tribunals. I am quick to add that this is not the fault of the judges. They do their best. But lacking, as most do, hands-on experience in the administrative law system, they can hardly be expected to display greater understanding of it.

This raises the question whether supervision by the courts is not the cause, rather than the solution, of the problems. I read most of the administrative law decisions of Canadian courts, or summaries of them, and they are all over the lot. They are lamentably inconsistent, contradictory, and inscrutable. The system is sick, but are we going to the right doctor?

Justice Robert F. Reid, "Judicial Review: A Poor Way To Run a Railroad," in Law Society of Upper Canada, *Administrative Law: Principles, Practice and Pluralism* (Scarborough, ON: Carswell, 1993), 455-60, at 458-59

In an article on advocacy before administrative tribunals, Willard Estey, a former justice of the Supreme Court of Canada, perhaps with tongue planted firmly in cheek, gave the following general rule for effective advocacy: "Never seek to quash an administrative board to which you must one day inevitably return."[1]

Good advice, no doubt, but sometimes there is no choice but to challenge the procedures and rulings of agencies. Moreover, it need not be a career-ending move. Agencies will often understand that challenges are sometimes in their interests. Appeals, petitions, and other forms of review of agency decisions provide opportunities to clarify the law and to achieve consistency where agency members have different interpretations of law or policy. Since panels of a tribunal cannot bind each other, external reviews provide an opportunity for final and binding rulings on issues about which panels disagree. A well-founded challenge can be viewed as an opportunity to validate sound practices and decisions and to strengthen the agency's performance by indicating areas for improvement.

COMMON GROUNDS FOR CHALLENGING DECISIONS

The decision of an administrative agency or a tribunal (collectively, "an agency") may be challenged by a person affected by the decision—usually the person or party directly involved, but in some cases a third party, such as a person or group in the community. The purpose of the challenge is to have the decision reviewed and overturned by the agency itself or by an external authority such as a court.

For a request for review to be accepted, there must be valid grounds for objecting to the decision. The following are among the most common grounds for challenging the decisions of agencies:

- The agency acted outside its jurisdiction. For example, a tribunal applied a law that it has no authority to apply, or it granted a remedy that it has no statutory authority to grant.

- The agency failed to take action that it was under a legal obligation to take.

- The agency improperly delegated a decision that it was obliged to make itself. For example, a tribunal allowed counsel or tribunal members not present at the hearing to determine the decision in a case.

- In exercising its discretion, the agency failed to consider options or factors that it was obliged to take into account, or it took into account irrelevant factors. For example, a tribunal based its decision on evidence that had no bearing on the issues in the case.

---

1   Philip Anisman and Robert F. Reid, *Administrative Law: Issues and Practice* (Scarborough, ON: Carswell, 1995), 190.

- The agency misinterpreted the applicable law.

- The agency acted in bad faith. For example, an adjudicator heard and decided a case in which he had a conflict of interest.

- The agency failed to follow fair procedures. For example, a tribunal failed to give adequate notice of a hearing to a party; an adjudicator failed to grant a necessary adjournment; or a panel of adjudicators exhibited bias in favour of one of the parties.

AVENUES FOR REVIEW OF DECISIONS

Administrative Agencies

Most government decisions that directly affect the rights, interests, and privileges of citizens are subject to some form of review by a higher authority. Decisions made by officials of a department or an administrative agency are often initially reviewed by superiors within the department or agency. In addition, several mechanisms may be available to persons affected by the decision to initiate a review by an independent authority.

In some cases, the agency's enabling statute provides a right to appeal to an independent tribunal. Alternatively, unless the decision deals strictly with matters of legislation or policy, the complainant may be able to apply for a judicial review—that is, a review by a court (a procedure discussed in a later section of this chapter). However, the courts have discretion whether to accept applications for judicial review. If the agency's legislation provides for a review by a tribunal, a court will usually insist that the individual first seek a remedy through this route before asking a court to review the decision. If the decision of the tribunal is also incorrect, generally a court appeal or judicial review is available.

An internal or external review by a monitoring official or agency may also be available. Most governments also have officials who monitor the operations and programs of departments and agencies to ensure that they are operating effectively, efficiently, and fairly; spending public funds prudently; and accounting properly for these expenditures. Some of these watchdogs are quasi-independent officials within a department or agency, while others are independent officers of the legislature, reporting to the legislature as a whole rather than to the government.

The best-known independent watchdogs are the **ombudsmen**, who have authority to investigate complaints from citizens about almost any form of unfair treatment by government officials. An ombudsman cannot overturn a decision but can recommend a different result in the individual case and fairer practices generally.

There are various other officials who conduct reviews of government programs and in some cases investigate individual complaints. They include

- provincial auditors and the federal auditor general, who review the effectiveness and efficiency of government programs and spending;

- environmental commissioners, who comment on the fairness and effectiveness of environmental programs;

- ethics or integrity commissioners, who ensure that politicians do not engage in activities that constitute a conflict of interest;

- provincial and federal information and privacy commissioners; and

- federal government officials who monitor the implementation of official languages legislation, the treatment of prisoners in federal penitentiaries, and matters related to air travel.

While these officials fulfill an important role in ensuring that government officials act responsibly and within their jurisdiction, this chapter focuses on the principal authorities to which a challenge of an agency's decision may be addressed—tribunals, courts, and ombudsmen.

Tribunals

Most tribunal decisions are open to review by the tribunal itself (often called "reconsideration," "reopening," or "rehearing") or by a court, or both. When a complainant wishes to challenge a decision, it is often quicker and cheaper to ask the tribunal to conduct an internal review where this option is available, before seeking a remedy from the courts. If that solution fails or is unavailable, the complainant may apply to a court by way of either appeal, if this is authorized by the tribunal's governing statute, or judicial review. Generally, a court will not undertake judicial review if there is a statutory right to an appeal and the complainant has not exercised that right.

In some cases, a tribunal's decisions may be reviewed by another tribunal, but this is unusual. In addition, ombudsmen may have a limited power to review the decisions of tribunals and recommend remedies.

Time Limits for Raising a Challenge

Complainants and their representatives need to be aware that there may be a deadline for raising a challenge to an agency's decision.

Generally, in the case of reconsideration of a decision by a tribunal, the tribunal itself will specify any time limit in its rules of procedure for the conduct of the review. However, the timing of the review may also be subject to a requirement under the tribunal's governing statute. For example, s. 21.2(2) of Ontario's *Statutory Powers Procedure Act*[2] (SPPA) states that the review must take place "within a reasonable time" after the decision was made. British Columbia's *Administrative Tribunals Act*[3] (ATA) requires parties to apply for clarification of tribunal decisions within 30 days.

For an appeal of a tribunal's decision to a court, there is usually a statutory time limit requiring the complainant to file the appeal within a relatively short time (often 30 days) after receiving the tribunal's decision.[4]

The time limits for applying for judicial review may vary from province to province. Some provinces, including Ontario, British Columbia, and Prince Edward Island, have legislation governing judicial review procedures. In Ontario, there are no specified time limits; however, as a matter of practice, if the court considers that there is excessive delay, it may deny the application.

---

2 RSO 1990, c. S.22.

3 SBC 2000, c. 45.

4 For example, Ontario's *Environmental Protection Act*, RSO 1990, c. E.19, s. 144(2).

EFFECT OF A CHALLENGE ON COMPLIANCE WITH THE DECISION

Application To "Stay" the Decision

A person challenging a tribunal's decision or order does not want to comply with the order before its validity has been decided. The procedure for stopping a decision from taking effect is called an application to **stay** the decision. A stay is an order issued by a tribunal or court suspending the decision that is being challenged, usually until the challenge has been either decided or abandoned. However, in some circumstances, the tribunal or court that is hearing the challenge may lift the stay before it has completed its review—for example, if it finds that the complainant is deliberately delaying proceedings.

Normally, a request to the tribunal to reconsider its decision does not automatically stay the operation of the order, unless the tribunal's rules of practice state otherwise. In most cases, a request for reconsideration must be accompanied by a separate application for a stay until the tribunal has completed its review of the decision.

In the case of review by a court, in Ontario an appeal generally operates as a stay of the tribunal's decision.[5] In contrast, an application for judicial review in Ontario does not itself stay the decision; however, a party may apply separately for a stay.[6] Depending on the governing statute, in an appeal or judicial review application the stay request must be made to the tribunal, or it must be made to the court conducting the review, or it may be made to either.

Test for Granting a Stay

The accepted test for granting a stay is set out in *RJR-MacDonald v. Canada*.[7] The party seeking the stay must convince the decision maker that

1. there is a substantial issue to be determined,

2. the party seeking the stay will suffer irreparable harm if a stay is not granted, and

3. the balance of convenience favours the granting of a stay.

Generally, the threshold for meeting the first requirement is low, unless granting the stay would nullify the tribunal's order. The more important question is whether failing to grant a stay would cause the party irreparable harm.

SPECIFIC REVIEW MECHANISMS

Reconsideration by the Tribunal Itself

Tribunals have a limited power to review and change their own decisions even without any statutory authority to conduct such a review, and a much broader

---

5 Section 25(1) of the SPPA.

6 *Courts of Justice Act*, RSO 1990, c. C.43, s. 106.

7 *RJR-MacDonald v. Canada (Attorney General)*, [1994] 1 SCR 311.

authority to do so where the statute establishing the tribunal or some other statute authorizes this practice. As stated earlier, this review procedure is known as **reconsideration, reopening,** or **rehearing**.

In Ontario, s. 21.2(1) authorizes tribunals to review their decisions if they consider it "advisable" to do so and if they have made rules governing the conduct of such reviews. The same provision also gives tribunals wide discretion in determining the consequences of a review. Specifically, they may "confirm, vary, suspend or cancel" the decision.

In Quebec, s. 154 of the *Administrative Justice Act*[8] (AJA) authorizes the Administrative Tribunal of Quebec to review its decisions where a new fact is discovered that could have changed the decision, where a party who should have been heard was not heard, or where a defect in the procedure or decision is sufficiently serious that it could render the decision invalid. The procedure for conducting a review is set out in the statute.

These provisions reflect an important change in the law. Traditionally in common law, when a tribunal rendered a decision, the rule known as *functus officio* applied. This Latin term means "having discharged its duty." It implies that once the decision is made, the tribunal has exhausted its authority. Unless a statute expressly provides otherwise, the tribunal cannot change the decision, except to correct minor errors such as clerical errors and errors of calculation, or to clarify ambiguities.

In the 1989 decision in *Chandler v. Alberta*,[9] the Supreme Court of Canada determined that tribunals have a broader power to amend their decisions. The court said that even without explicit statutory authority, "if the tribunal has failed to dispose of an issue which is fairly raised by the proceedings and of which the tribunal is empowered by its enabling statute to dispose, it ought to be allowed to complete its statutory task."[10] Othe court decisions have permitted—and even required—tribunals to reconsider their decisions in cases where it is clear that a factual error influenced the decision of an adjudicator[11] and where a tribunal's order inaccurately reflected a settlement made by the parties.[12]

In Ontario, under the SPPA, a tribunal may have even greater power to reopen and reconsider as long as it makes rules governing the exercise of this power. Usually, the rules define a two-stage process. The first stage consists of evaluating requests for review against specific criteria to determine whether the tribunal should undertake such a review. If the answer is "yes," the rules then specify who should conduct the review and how it should be conducted. The Society of Ontario Adjudicators and Regulators has prepared model rules that can be adopted or modified for this purpose.[13]

---

8 RSQ, c. J-3.

9 *Chandler v. Alberta (Association of Architects)* (1989), 62 DLR (4th) 577 (SCC).

10 Ibid., at 597.

11 *Ontario (Employment Standards Officer) v. Metro International Trucks Ltd.*, [1996] OJ no. 538 (QL) (Gen. Div.).

12 *Kingston (City) v. Ontario (Mining and Lands Commissioner)* (1977), 18 OR (2d) 166 (Div. Ct.).

13 Available online at http://soar.on.ca/soar-rules_prac.htm.

Appeals and Applications for Judicial Review

APPEALS

A person may **appeal** a decision of an official or a tribunal to a court or other independent authority only where this alternative is set out in the agency's governing statute. The statute may provide for an appeal on questions of law alone, on questions of law and jurisdiction, or on questions of fact or law. In some cases, the statute will provide for an appeal on questions of law to a court and on questions of fact, policy, or the public interest to a government official, Cabinet minister, or Cabinet.[14]

Where the appeal is to a court, usually the only evidence that can be put before the court is the evidence that was before the tribunal. The parties cannot present additional evidence. Sometimes the appeal is "as of right"; in other words, no permission is needed. However, some statutes provide for an appeal only "with leave"; that is, the party who wants to appeal must persuade the court to grant permission. The criteria for obtaining leave are either set out in a statute or the court's rules of procedure, or are part of the common law. These criteria often involve convincing the court that the appeal raises an important legal issue and has reasonable prospects for success.

Usually, only the tribunal's final decision can be appealed. A party who wants to challenge a procedural ruling of the tribunal, or argue that the tribunal does not have jurisdiction, must seek judicial review before the final decision. However, courts are reluctant to permit judicial review applications partway through a proceeding. They will often refuse to permit parties to interrupt proceedings.

In addition to providing a right to appeal, governing statutes generally specify the procedures to be followed in hearing the appeal and the remedies available to the court.

Where an appeal is available, the complainant is usually required to seek a remedy through this mechanism before applying for judicial review. Where there is no statutory right to appeal, application for judicial review is the only means of bringing a challenge of a decision before the courts. (See "Petitions to Cabinet.")

JUDICIAL REVIEW

While some statutes provide for a right to apply for appeal of an agency's decision, the availability of a remedy through judicial review is usually more limited. **Judicial review** refers to a review of an agency's decision by a court that has an inherent authority to ensure that the agency has not acted outside its jurisdiction. The person seeking a remedy must apply to the court for judicial review, and acceptance of the application is granted at the discretion of the court. This limit on access to judicial review contrasts with the right to appeal provided by the authority of a statute.

---

14 For example, s. 144 of Ontario's *Environmental Protection Act*, supra note 4, provides for an appeal from the Environmental Review Tribunal to the Divisional Court on questions of law, and to the minister of the environment on any matter other than a question of law (for example, questions of fact or interpretation or application of policies). Section 95 of the *Ontario Municipal Board Act*, RSO 1990, c. O.28 provides for a petition to Cabinet from decisions of the Ontario Municipal Board.

Petitions to Cabinet

The governing statutes of a few agencies provide a right to challenge an agency's decision by submission of a petition to Cabinet, instead of providing a right to appeal. There are some important differences.

- In reviewing a petition, Cabinet has greater power to take political considerations into account than is the case for an authority hearing an appeal.

- Cabinet's decision on the petition may not be appealed to a court or other authority.

- Cabinet's decision also may not be the subject of an application for judicial review.

- Cabinet is not bound to follow rules of natural justice or procedural fairness. It can obtain any information and advice from government staff, including information not put before the agency, and need not reveal what information it considered.

- Cabinet is not required to make a decision, and if it does make a decision, it need not give reasons.

- Because there are often no fixed rules of procedure, it is possible that individuals or organizations who did not participate in the tribunal proceedings may be allowed to make representations to the Cabinet.

- Cabinet may consider issues or base its decision on grounds not raised before the tribunal.

A party to a tribunal proceeding or a person directly affected by the decision of a government official can seek judicial review of a decision on the grounds that the tribunal or official exceeded the agency's jurisdiction. Exceeding jurisdiction can consist of acting outside the powers provided by statute, failing to follow the requirements of a statute, or following an unfair procedure. However, the courts have ruled that a decision that is clearly not supported by the evidence is also a jurisdictional error and subject to judicial review. Since this is the kind of error that would normally be addressed in an appeal, by treating this as a matter of jurisdiction, the courts have given themselves a power of review almost as broad as if an appeal were available.

Where the legislature does not want to provide an appeal mechanism and is concerned that a court may conduct a review of a matter that is properly the subject of an appeal, it will insert a **privative clause** into the agency's governing statute. A privative clause attempts to restrict or prevent review by a court of certain actions or decisions of the agency. (See "Privative Clauses.")

In practice, however, privative clauses have had little success in preventing judicial review, because the courts have ruled that they are inapplicable to matters

Privative Clauses

Here is an example of a privative clause from the Ontario *Labour Relations Act, 1995* (SO 1995, c. 1, sched. A, s. 116):

> No decision, order, direction, declaration or ruling of the Board shall be questioned or reviewed in any court, and no order shall be made or process entered, or proceedings taken in any court, whether by way of injunction, declaratory judgment, certiorari, mandamus, prohibition, quo warranto, or otherwise, to question, review, prohibit or restrain the Board or any of its proceedings.

of jurisdiction. With respect to privative clauses in provincial statutes, the Supreme Court of Canada has ruled that any provincial law that prohibits the courts from considering whether a tribunal has exceeded its jurisdiction is unconstitutional.[15] In addition, the courts generally have interpreted errors of jurisdiction to include almost any substantial error of fact or law. This leaves little room for privative clauses to insulate agency decisions from judicial review.

Privative clauses have had some effect, however, in influencing how critically a court will scrutinize an agency's decision. This point is discussed further below in the section dealing with the standard of review applied by the courts ("Deciding Which Standard Applies").

Like an appeal, a judicial review hearing is generally limited to the tribunal's record. Parties may supplement the evidence before the tribunal with affidavits containing additional evidence only in exceptional circumstances—for example, to demonstrate that there was a complete absence of evidence before the tribunal on an essential point, or where the evidence was unavailable during the original proceeding and is practically conclusive of the issue before the court.[16]

WHO MAY APPEAL OR SEEK JUDICIAL REVIEW

Since appeals are available only when provided for in a statute, the only persons who have the right to appeal an agency's decision are those specifically authorized by the section of the statute establishing that right. In most cases, the relevant legislation is the enabling statute governing the particular agency. Neither Alberta's *Administrative Procedures Act*[17] nor Ontario's SPPA contains a right of appeal, although the SPPA does recognize that a decision of a tribunal may be appealed to a court or other authority.[18] Quebec's AJA provides for appeals in certain cases but

---

15   *Crevier v. Attorney-General of Quebec* (1981), 127 DLR (3d) 1 (SCC).

16   *Keeprite Workers' Independent Union v. Keeprite Products Ltd.* (1980), 114 DLR (3d) 162, at 170 (Ont. CA); and *Canadiana Towers v. Fawcett* (1978), 90 DLR (3d) 758, at 763 (Ont. CA).

17   RSA 1980, c. A-2.

18   As discussed earlier, s. 25(1) of the SPPA provides that an appeal effectively stays a decision of a tribunal.

not in others.[19] Usually, statutes give only a party or a person directly affected a right to appeal. However, if the appeal is to a superior court, the court may have authority under its rules of practice to permit intervenors to participate.

For judicial review applications, the common law determines who may initiate proceedings. Provincial statutes governing judicial review procedures do not address this question.

The parties in a tribunal hearing generally have a right, also known as **standing** (or, in Latin, ***locus standi***), to apply for judicial review of the tribunal's decision. Intervenors do not automatically have standing, but they may be permitted to apply at the discretion of the court.

In the case of decisions of officials and agencies other than tribunals, usually the applicant for judicial review must have a direct and substantial interest in the decision. Generally, this means a property right or financial interest.

Traditionally, the courts have refused to accept applications for judicial review where a public right or interest is involved except in the following circumstances:

- the attorney general consents to the applicant being granted standing; or
- the person will suffer some special damage peculiar to himself or herself as a result of interference with a public right; or
- the person will suffer no greater damage or harm than the rest of the public, but the person qualifies for public interest standing.

To decide whether a person qualifies for public interest standing, the courts apply a four-point test:

1. The issue that the person wants to raise is serious or important.
2. The issue is **justiciable**—that is, one that a court can decide.
3. The applicant has a genuine interest in the issue.
4. There is no other reasonable and effective way to bring the issue before the court.

With respect to the third point, the kind of interest required for public interest standing need not be a financial or property interest. For example, a demonstrated history of educating the public about an issue or promoting the values involved may be sufficient.

STANDARD OF REVIEW

In the past, the courts would sometimes give an agency more latitude for error on a decision brought for judicial review than one brought on appeal.

In order to pass on appeal, the decision had to be correct. If the decision contained a legal or factual error that affected the outcome of the case, it was usually overturned. The requirement of correctness was strictly applied. The courts did not recognize that in some cases there may be no single "correct" interpretation of the law or the facts—rather, there may be more than one reasonable interpretation, which could provide an equally valid basis for the decision.

---

19 See s. 159 of the AJA.

In judicial review proceedings, sometimes the courts did not require the agency to be correct, but only reasonable. The courts recognized that if the decision was reasonable, they should not second-guess the agency's reasoning and conclusions.

The uncertainty created by these inconsistencies in treatment was addressed by the Supreme Court of Canada in a series of judgments. Initially, the court set out three **standards of review** that the courts should apply in reviewing agency decisions: **correctness**, **reasonableness** *simpliciter* (simple reasonableness), and **patent unreasonableness**. In this context, "standard of review" refers to the degree of error or the level of uncertainty about the reasonableness or correctness of an agency's decision that a court will tolerate in deciding whether to accept or overturn the decision.

Although the lower courts tried to follow the Supreme Court's direction in applying these standards, they remained unclear as to which standard applied in a particular case. As a result, they continued to deal differently with cases heard on appeal and those examined through judicial review.

In 2003, the Supreme Court made a further attempt to create greater consistency in treatment. In *Dr. Q. v. College of Physicians and Surgeons of British Columbia*[20] and *Law Society of New Brunswick v. Ryan*,[21] the court declared that the courts should apply the same standards of review to all court decisions reviewing the decisions of agencies, whether the challenges were brought on appeal or by application for judicial review. The court went to some effort to clarify the differences between the three standards of review. It also set out guidelines for the courts to follow in deciding which standard was the most appropriate in a particular case.

An important element of the standard of review is the idea of **deference** to the judgment of an agency. In some circumstances, the courts should accept the agency's decision even if they disagree with it. Generally, when the agency is making a decision that is clearly within its jurisdiction, such as weighing evidence and making findings of fact, the court should not substitute its own views even if it disagrees with the decision, as long as the decision is not completely irrational. However, if the agency is determining the limits of its own jurisdiction—a purely legal question—the courts should be more willing to substitute their own views for those of the agency.

[handwritten note: ★THE COURT SHOULD GIVE MORE RESPECT TO THE BOARD'S DECISION MORE HANDS OFF]

The Supreme Court's explanation of the differences between the three standards of review is summarized below, along with the court's guidelines for deciding which standard applies in a particular case.

Correctness

A decision is correct when there is only one right answer and the agency gave that answer. It is incorrect if the agency came to the wrong conclusion. For example, if the issue is one on which a tribunal has less expertise than the court, such as a question of interpretation of a statute that the tribunal is not usually called upon to apply, and the court disagrees with the tribunal's conclusion, the court will generally overturn the decision. In such cases, the court is said to "owe no deference" to the tribunal.

---

20 *Dr. Q. v. College of Physicians and Surgeons of British Columbia*, [2003] 1 SCR 226.

21 *Law Society of New Brunswick v. Ryan*, [2003] 1 SCR 247.

"Reasonableness *Simpliciter*"

"Reasonableness *simpliciter*" (translating the Latin) means simple reasonableness. As the expression implies, this standard allows a court to accept an agency's decision that is based on a reasonable interpretation of the facts or the law, as opposed to a single correct answer. The test for determining simple reasonableness is whether the agency has given reasons for its decision and, if so, whether the reasons show a logical connection between the evidence and the agency's conclusions. A court may find a decision to be reasonable even if a relevant issue is not dealt with in the reasons, as long as there is recorded evidence on the issue that is consistent with the agency's overall findings. Where the standard is simple reasonableness, the courts are required to give the agency's decision considerable deference.

A decision will be unreasonable only if there is no line of analysis within the given reasons that could reasonably lead the tribunal from the evidence before it to the conclusion at which it arrived. If any of the reasons that are sufficient to support the conclusion are tenable in the sense that they can stand up to a somewhat probing examination, then the decision will not be unreasonable and a reviewing court must not interfere. ... This means that a decision may satisfy the reasonableness standard if it is supported by a tenable explanation even if this explanation is not one that the reviewing court finds compelling. ...

Iacobucci J in *Law Society of New Brunswick v. Ryan*, [2003] 1 SCR 247, at paragraph 55

Patent Unreasonableness

In *Ryan*, the Supreme Court described a patently unreasonable decision as one containing a defect so obvious that there can be no doubt that the decision itself is defective. The decision is "clearly irrational" or "evidently not in accordance with reason," and so flawed that "no amount of curial deference can justify letting it stand."[22] Unless a decision can be characterized as irrational, the courts must defer to the agency even if they do not agree with its decision.

Of the three standards, patent unreasonableness implies the highest degree of deference to the agency. Even if the court finds that the agency's conclusions are incomplete or poorly reasoned, it will overturn the decision only if no other court could possibly agree with it.

When asked to explain "standard of review" to non-lawyers, I say that it is the degree of rigour that a court applies in reviewing the decision of an administrative tribunal. This sometimes prompts the question, "Well, wouldn't the court want to do its best every time?"

At the risk of causing administrative law scholars to throw up when they read this, here is a summary of my usual explanation. The

---

22   Ibid., at paragraph 52.

court applies a complex legal analysis (the functional and pragmatic approach—another wondrously mind-numbing phrase) to determine how much deference or respect it will give the tribunal's decision.

At one end is correctness, where the court applies the test: Do I agree with you? ("You" being the tribunal.) In the middle is reasonableness simpliciter, or I don't agree with you, but I can see where you're coming from. Finally, at the other end of the scale is patently unreasonable, which means You're crazy.

Douglas Mah, "Think Latin Is Hard To Learn? Try Administrative Law,"
The National, June-July 2003

Deciding Which Standard Applies

The Supreme Court has provided direction to the courts to assist them in deciding which standard applies in a particular case. Even before the decisions in *Dr. Q.* and *Ryan*, the Supreme Court directed the courts to use a "pragmatic and functional approach"[23] in reviewing agency decisions. The court demonstrated how that approach would apply in the case before it. First, the court asked, Is the issue before the tribunal one that was intended by the legislators to be left to the exclusive jurisdiction of the tribunal? If the answer is "yes," the court will not substitute its view of what is right for the tribunal's view unless the tribunal's decision is not just unreasonable, but patently unreasonable.

The Supreme Court elaborated on what constitutes a pragmatic and functional approach in *Dr. Q.* and *Ryan*. The overall aim is to discern the intent of the legislators in enacting the particular statute, keeping in mind the constitutional role of the courts in maintaining the rule of law. The courts are not to view this process of discerning the legislative intent as "an empty ritual"[24] or to apply the process mechanically. More specifically, discerning intent requires the courts to consider the following four factors in every case:

1. the presence or absence of a statutory right of appeal or a privative clause;

2. the expertise of the agency relative to that of the court reviewing the issue in question;

3. the purpose of the legislation and, in particular, of the provision; and

4. the nature of the question—for example, whether it is one of fact, law, or mixed fact and law.

The Supreme Court has stressed that none of these factors is conclusive, and the four factors may overlap. Therefore, they must be considered together. In addition, different factors may be given different weight in different circumstances.

The court went on to provide more specific guidance on how the four factors are to be used in determining the appropriate standard of review. These suggestions are summarized below.

---

23 *Pushpanathan v. Canada (Minister of Citizenship and Immigration)*, [1998] 1 SCR 982; (1998), 160 DLR (4th) 193, at 209.

24 *Dr. Q.*, supra note 20, at 238.

Right To Appeal Versus Privative Clause

A statute that provides for a right of appeal is an indication that the legislature welcomes close scrutiny of the agency's decisions, and therefore invites the courts to give less deference to those decisions. A court's approach in this case will lean toward the correctness standard. On the other hand, a statute that contains a privative clause is an indication that the legislature does not want the courts to interfere with the agency's decisions, and supports a more deferential standard of review. Where there is a privative clause, a court's approach will therefore lean toward the standard of reasonableness *simpliciter* or patent unreasonableness. If the statute contains neither a privative clause nor a right of appeal, the legislature's position is neutral and does not suggest any particular standard of review.

The Agency's Expertise

The expertise of the agency relative to that of the court is often the most important of the four factors. The court should look at the issue that the agency addressed in the decision and ask itself, Who is better able to address this particular issue, the agency or the court? In the case of a tribunal, the court may then consider questions such as the following:

- Does the work of the tribunal involve specialized knowledge?
- Do tribunal members have experience and expertise in the area of activity regulated through the tribunal?
- Are individual tribunal members assigned to cases that draw upon their particular area of knowledge?

Generally, the court will have more expertise in answering legal questions. However, the degree to which the court will defer to the agency will depend to some extent on the kind of legal question addressed in the decision. For example:

- A tribunal will generally be given more deference on a question of law that arises within its jurisdiction than on one that limits its jurisdiction.
- A tribunal will often be given more deference in interpreting the statute that governs its area of activity than in interpreting some other statute.
- A tribunal's interpretation of the constitution will be given no deference.

Thus, even though the standard of review applicable to a legal interpretation will frequently be correctness, in some cases the court will accept that reasonableness *simpliciter* is the more appropriate standard.

Apart from matters of legal interpretation, an agency may be considered to have greater expertise than the court when its governing statute requires decision makers to have expert qualifications or experience in a particular area, or to play a particular role in policy development. If an agency is frequently called upon to make findings of fact in a distinctive legislative context—for example, determining the appropriate standards of conduct or rules of practice for lawyers, doctors, or plumbers—the court may defer to the agency's judgment in those areas, applying the reasonableness *simpliciter* or patent unreasonableness standard rather than the standard of correctness.

Purpose of the Statute and Provision

Since the primary aim of the pragmatic and functional approach is to reveal the intent of the legislature, the purpose of the applicable statute is relevant in deciding how much deference a court should give an agency. For example, if one of the purposes of the statute in question is to give the public a right to an independent review of a government department's decisions, this will suggest that the court should give deference to an agency set up specifically to provide such a review when it is considering the issues delegated to it by the legislature. If the statute deals with complex issues that require an agency to balance competing considerations (such as deciding between the government's need to keep certain information confidential and the public's right of access to government information), the court should be reluctant to substitute its view of the appropriate balance for that of the agency.

A statutory purpose that requires a tribunal to select from a range of remedial choices or administrative responses, is concerned with the protection of the public, engages policy issues, or involves the balancing of multiple sets of interests or considerations will demand greater deference from a reviewing court.

McLachlin CJ in *Dr. Q. v. College of Physicians and Surgeons of British Columbia*, [2003] 1 SCR 226, at 240

Nature of the Question

Finally, the court must consider the nature of the question under review: is it a question of fact, law, or mixed fact and law? In deciding on the appropriate standard of review, the court should determine whether the question involves, for example, the application or interpretation of government policies or guidelines; the interpretation of standards or practices in an industry, trade, or profession regulated by the tribunal; or a determination of the public interest. These considerations will generally indicate questions of fact or mixed law and fact. On the other hand, a question involving the interpretation of a statute will clearly be a question of law.

The determination of the standard of review and the degree of deference on a particular decision may be particularly difficult for this factor. Questions of law are the simplest to deal with, since the standard of correctness will often apply (as discussed above under "The Agency's Expertise"). For questions of fact, the court will generally give the agency more deference, but may be less inclined to accept an agency's decision where the facts do not relate to the agency's area of expertise. Some questions of fact—for example, those relating to matters of interpretation or subjects on which the facts are far from clear—may involve a greater degree of subjectivity in arriving at a decision. In these cases, the appropriate degree of deference is more uncertain. In the case of questions of mixed fact and law, the court may apply all three standards in combination, depending on the balance of these elements in the question addressed in the agency's decision. (See "How Much Progress Have We Made?")

How Much Progress Have We Made?

Several years before the Supreme Court's decisions in *Dr. Q.* and *Ryan*, Justice Barry described the frustration experienced by many judges who were asked to review agency decisions:

> [i]n attempting to follow the court's distinctions between "patently unreasonable," "reasonable," and "correct," one feels at times as though one is watching a juggler juggle three transparent objects. Depending on which way the light falls, sometimes one thinks one can see the objects. Other times one cannot and, indeed, wonders whether there are really three distinct objects there at all.
>
> *Miller v. Workers' Compensation Commission (Nfld.)* (1997), 154 Nfld. & PEIR 52, at 57-58 (Nfld. SCTD).

The Supreme Court's judgments in *Dr. Q.* and *Ryan* attempted to clear up the confusion and uncertainty surrounding court reviews of agency decisions. In defining the three standards of review and setting out specific directions on how they should be applied, the court hoped for more consistent results from appeal and judicial review proceedings. Despite the Supreme Court's best efforts, lower courts have found it difficult to distinguish clearly between the three standards and to know which is the correct one to apply in a particular case. Not surprisingly, the decisions in appeal and judicial review proceedings still reflect a great deal of subjectivity—and, as a result, continuing inconsistencies in the treatment of agency decisions.

It may seem as if we haven't made much progress. However, this area of the law is complex, and it is still evolving. Perhaps future decisions of the courts will eventually create the certainty that we hope for in proceedings guided by the fairness principle.

When the finding being reviewed is one of pure fact, this factor will militate in favour of showing more deference towards the tribunal's decision. Conversely, an issue of pure law counsels in favour of a more searching review. This is particularly so where the decision will be one of general importance or great precedential value.

McLachlin CJ in *Dr. Q. v. College of Physicians and Surgeons of British Columbia*, [2003] 1 SCR 226, at 241

WHO MAY REPRESENT THE PARTY IN AN APPEAL OR JUDICIAL REVIEW

In an appeal to a tribunal, government official, minister, or Cabinet, a party may represent himself or herself or be represented by a lawyer or an agent.

In a court proceeding, representation is determined by the rules of the court in the particular jurisdiction. In Ontario, most appeals to courts and all applications for judicial review are heard by the Divisional Court, a branch of the Superior Court of Ontario. The level of court will vary from province to province. In proceedings of the Divisional Court or other courts at this level (known as "superior courts" or "courts of inherent jurisdiction"), an individual who was a party to a tribunal decision may represent himself or have a lawyer, but cannot have a representative who is not a lawyer. A corporation must either hire a lawyer or obtain permission from the court for one of its officers or directors to represent it.

CAN THE AGENCY DEFEND ITS DECISION?

Although the agency's decision will be defended in a court proceeding by the party or person favoured by the decision, the agency may not want to rely entirely on that defence, particularly if the party or person represents himself instead of retaining a legal adviser. Members or officials of the agency may have a better understanding of the issues on both sides of the case, and they can usually offer a more complete explanation of the reasons for their decision. However, agencies do not have an inherent right to appear in a court proceeding. Practice varies for different agencies and in different jurisdictions.

In the case of tribunals, some governing statutes explicitly permit the tribunal to participate in a court proceeding. In the absence of a statutory right, the tribunal may apply to the court for permission to participate. Some courts provide a limited right to participate where the issue concerns the tribunal's jurisdiction. Other courts grant a tribunal the right to defend the merits of its decision as well. Some tribunals routinely ask the court for permission to intervene for that purpose, while others generally leave it to one of the parties to defend the decision.

REMEDIES AVAILABLE FROM THE COURT

Generally, in an appeal or judicial review proceeding, when the court decides to overturn the decision of an agency, the court may choose to substitute its own decision, or it may inform the agency of its error and send the case back to the agency, asking it to make the decision again. If the original proceeding of a tribunal did not provide sufficient evidence to support a correct or reasonable decision, the court may order the tribunal to hold further hearings and make a new ruling based on that evidence.

In an appeal, the court may rule that the agency made an error of law, or sometimes an error of fact. In a judicial review, the court may rule that the agency acted unfairly or outside its jurisdiction. Depending on the ruling, the court may order the agency to do anything that it was required, and failed, to do; prohibit it from doing anything that it was not authorized to do; or declare that what it did was not in accordance with the law.

More specifically, the court may

- order the agency to make the decision it should have made;

- substitute the decision the agency should have made;

- declare that an action taken or a decision made by the agency is invalid and has no effect;

- order the agency to take some action that is a step on the road to making its decision;

- order the agency not to take some action it intended to take; or

- exercise the discretion that the agency should have exercised and grant the applicant the relief she was seeking from the agency.

Unlike the civil courts, the court reviewing a tribunal's decision cannot usually award damages to a party harmed by the decision. However, in some cases—for example, where an agency has been negligent or has acted in bad faith—a party may claim damages in a separate civil suit.

Stated Case

The **stated case** is a procedure available to some tribunals, but not generally to other agencies, to help them to avoid making an error in a decision. A tribunal's entitlement to use the procedure must be expressly provided for in the tribunal's governing statute. Many tribunals do not have access to this preventive mechanism.

A tribunal "states a case" by asking a court to clarify or resolve an important point of law that is being raised before the tribunal. In contrast to most judicial proceedings, which seek to correct an error after it has been made and usually after the tribunal has issued its decision, the right to state a case permits a tribunal, on its own initiative or at the request of a party, to formulate a legal question and ask the court for its opinion at any time during the hearing process.

Generally, it is the tribunal, rather than the parties, that has the right to decide whether to refer a question to the court. The tribunal also usually decides the content of the question as well, although tribunals often confer with the parties before submitting the question to the court.

Since the stated case procedure is a privilege, tribunals should exercise discretion in making use of it. Courts will not look favourably on tribunals that submit non-essential questions or questions on which a court's opinion is not required.

A tribunal should not state a case unless the opinion is essential to the board's ability to deal with the matter before it.

Robert Macaulay and James Sprague, *Practice and Procedure Before Administrative Tribunals* (Toronto: Carswell) (looseleaf), 24.2

Review by the Ombudsman

In some cases, a person or a party affected by an agency's decision may submit a complaint to the federal or provincial ombudsman regarding the decision itself or a procedure that the agency followed in making the decision. The ombudsman may respond by conducting a review and making a recommendation; however, he may be more constrained in reviewing the decisions of tribunals than in scrutinizing those of other agencies and government officials.

If a tribunal has held a hearing following the requirements of procedural fairness and has issued a decision based on the evidence presented, it may be inappropriate for someone who has not heard the evidence to substitute his own views on the merits of the decision. (Remember the rule "He who hears must decide.") Although the Ontario Ombudsman's Fairness Standards provide assurance that "[a]ppropriate respect for the independence and expertise of decision-makers is shown to agencies, boards, commissions and tribunals,"[25] some tribunals have questioned whether the ombudsman may properly evaluate the merits of a tribunal decision, as distinguished from the fairness of the procedures used to reach that decision.

---

25 Ombudsman Ontario, *Ombudsman Fairness Standards*, available online at www.ombudsman.on.ca. These are standards that the ombudsman uses in reviewing the fairness of actions by government.

CHAPTER SUMMARY

Occasional reviews of an agency's decisions, whether internally or by external authorities such as the courts or the ombudsman, should be welcomed by the agency's decision makers. Reviews provide an opportunity to validate sound decisions and to strengthen the agency's performance by indicating areas for improvement.

In addition, since panels of a tribunal cannot bind each other, external reviews provide a forum where final and binding rulings can be made on issues about which panels may not agree.

Agency decisions are usually open to review on the basis of a serious error of law or fact, an unfair procedure, an improper exercise of discretion, or an action that is outside the agency's jurisdiction. Reviews are often initiated by the parties or persons directly affected by the decision, through the submission of a formal complaint about the decision itself or the procedures followed in reaching the decision.

There are several mechanisms for conducting reviews of agency decisions. Some are available for decisions of any agency and some are tailored specifically to decisions of a tribunal. These mechanisms include reconsideration of a decision by the tribunal itself, statutory appeal, application for judicial review, the "stated case" procedure, and review by a watchdog agency such as an ombudsman.

In many cases, the reviewing authority has the power to overturn a decision and substitute or order a different one. Some authorities, such as senior officials, Cabinet ministers, or the ombudsman, may only make a recommendation.

KEY TERMS

appeal   request for a review of an agency's decision by a higher authority such as a court or a senior government official or body; a right that is available only when provided by statute; distinguished from judicial review

correctness   standard applied by a court to an agency's decision where there is only one correct answer to the question addressed; one of three standards of review to be applied by the courts in an appeal or judicial review proceeding; *see also* patent unreasonableness, reasonableness *simpliciter*

deference   a court's willingness to accept a decision of an agency rather than substitute a different decision of its own; referred to in the context of standards of review in appeal or judicial review proceedings, often implying a duty or obligation of the court to the agency ("owe deference")

functus officio   Latin term meaning "having discharged its duty"; having made its decision, the tribunal has exhausted its authority and cannot change the decision, except to correct minor errors such as clerical errors and errors of calculation, or to clarify ambiguities, unless a statute expressly provides otherwise

judicial review   review of a decision of an agency by a court with inherent authority to ensure that the agency has not acted outside its jurisdiction; distinguished from appeal

justiciable   falling into the category of subjects that are appropriate for examination by a court of justice

locus standi   Latin term meaning "a place to stand"; *see* standing

ombudsman   an independent official reporting to the legislature with authority to investigate complaints of unfair treatment and to recommend a different decision in an individual case, and fairer practices generally

patent unreasonableness   defect or error in an agency's decision of such significance that a court is left in no doubt that the decision must be overturned; one of three standards of review to be applied by the courts in an appeal or judicial review proceeding; *see also* correctness, reasonableness *simpliciter*

privative clause   provision included in an agency's governing statute for the purpose of restricting or preventing judicial review of specified actions or decisions of the agency; intended to preserve the distinction between matters that are the subject of an appeal and matters that may be addressed by judicial review

reasonableness *simpliciter*   simple reasonableness; an alternative to correctness as a standard for accepting an agency's decision, based on a determination that the agency's interpretation of the law or the facts, or both, is reasonable; one of three standards of review to be applied by the courts in an appeal or judicial review proceeding; *see also* correctness, patent unreasonableness

reconsideration   the procedure established by a tribunal to review its decision when a party provides evidence or argument that the decision may be wrong or unreasonable; also called rehearing or reopening

rehearing   *see* reconsideration

reopening   *see* reconsideration

standard of review   the degree of error or the level of uncertainty about the reasonableness or correctness of an agency's decision that a court will tolerate in deciding whether to accept or overturn the decision

standing   the right to be heard or to appear during a proceeding before a court or tribunal; *see also locus standi*

stated case   a request by a tribunal to a court to give its opinion on a question of law formulated by the tribunal, together with any facts that the tribunal considers necessary for answering the question

stay   an order issued by a tribunal or court suspending the decision that is being challenged until the challenge has been decided or abandoned

KEY CASES

The Scope of Judicial Review

Ottawa (City of) v. Ontario (Attorney General) (2002), 64 OR (3d) 703 (CA)

FACTS: Hydro One applied to the Ontario Energy Board for approval to build a transmission line. The board heard the case on the merits, and at the same time, pursuant to s. 32 of the *Ontario Energy Board Act*, SO 1998, c. 15, stated a case on a question of law for the opinion of the Divisional Court. The board approved the transmission line, and the Divisional Court quashed the stated case without considering it on the merits. Since the board had been able to render its decision in the original application, the court concluded that the board was *functus officio* and unable to state the case.

ISSUE: Was the board *functus officio* after the application was decided on the merits, or could the board still state a case on a question of law for the opinion of the Divisional Court?

DECISION: The board could state a case under the Act and was not limited to stating a case based only on an issue in a particular application. The question stated had general application. The opinion of the Divisional Court would be useful to the board in fulfilling its statutory mandate.

Scope of Judicial Review

Service Employees' International Union, Local 333 v. Nipawin District Staff Nurses Assn., [1975] 1 SCR 382; 41 DLR (3d) 6

FACTS: The Nipawin District Staff Nurses Association applied to the Labour Relations Board to determine that the nurses association was an appropriate bargaining unit for collective bargaining with the employer. The Service Employees' International Union opposed the application, arguing that the nurses association was not a "trade union," but was a "company-dominated organization." The Labour Relations Board agreed that the nurses association was a "company-dominated organization" within the meaning of s. 2(e) of the *Trade Union Act*, RSS 1972, c. 137, and was therefore not a trade union. However, it failed to make a specific finding that the nurses association was an "employer or employer's agent," an element of the definition of "company-dominated organization."

ISSUE: Did the Labour Relations Board make a proper inquiry under the *Trade Union Act*? Did it act beyond its powers as conferred to it under the legislation?

DECISION: The question was whether or not the nurses association was a trade union, and the Labour Relations Board found that it was not. It was not required to make an explicit finding on each element of the definition. It acted in good faith and its decision could be rationally supported by a reasonable interpretation of the statute.

Standard of Review

Dr. Q. v. College of Physicians and Surgeons of British Columbia, [2003] 1 SCR 226; 2003 SCC 19

FACTS: An inquiry committee of the College of Physicians and Surgeons found that Dr. Q. was guilty of infamous conduct. A patient, who had sought help for depression, alleged a sexual relationship with Dr. Q. , who denied the allegations. The committee accepted the patient's evidence over that of Dr. Q., and the Council of the College suspended Dr. Q. from practising medicine. On an appeal under the *Medical Practitioners Act*, RSBC 1996, c. 285, the reviewing judge set aside the inquiry committee's decision, disagreeing with its findings as to credibility. The Court of Appeal dismissed the college's appeal because it could not conclude that the reviewing judge was "clearly wrong."

ISSUE: Did the judge apply too strict a standard of review by reconsidering the committee's findings on credibility? Did the Court of Appeal apply an inappropriate test in assessing the decision of the reviewing judge?

DECISION: The reviewing judge applied too strict a standard of review and wrongly substituted her own view of the evidence for that of the committee. The standard of "clear and cogent evidence" did not permit the reviewing judge to re-evaluate the evidence. The reviewing judge failed to determine the appropriate standard of review, and inappropriately applied a correctness standard where the standard should have been reasonableness. She failed to address the need for deference to the committee that actually heard the evidence, especially with respect to determinations of credibility.

The Court of Appeal applied an inappropriate test. It wrongly determined that the standard for assessing the reviewing judge's decision was whether, in her re-evaluation of the evidence, she was clearly wrong. This was not a judicial review of an administrative decision, but an appellate review of a subordinate court. Therefore, the question of the right standard was a question of law and was to be answered correctly. The Court of Appeal should have corrected the reviewing judge's error. It should have assessed the committee's decision based on the appropriate standard of reasonableness.

Standard of Review

Law Society of New Brunswick v. Ryan, [2003] 1 SCR 247; 2003 SCC 20

FACTS: A complaint was filed against a lawyer practising in New Brunswick by two of his clients. The clients had hired the lawyer to represent them in a wrongful dismissal claim. For over five years, the lawyer did nothing with the file, and lied repeatedly about it. At one point he gave the clients a forged court decision dealing with their case. Eventually, he admitted that the "whole thing was a lie," and the clients filed a complaint with the Law Society. The Law Society's Discipline Committee decided that the lawyer should be disbarred. The lawyer appealed, arguing he was under a mental disability. After considering medical and psychiatric evidence, the Discipline Committee confirmed that disbarment was appropriate. The New Brunswick Court of Appeal disagreed, and substituted a penalty of indefinite suspension, with the possibility of being able to practise law again.

ISSUE: Was reasonableness *simpliciter* the appropriate standard of review and was it properly applied by the New Brunswick Court of Appeal?

DECISION: The Supreme Court of Canada overturned the decision of the Court of Appeal, and restored the order for disbarment of the Discipline Committee. There are only three standards for judicial review of administrative decisions: correctness, reasonableness *simpliciter*, and patent unreasonableness. Although the statute permitted an appeal from decisions of the Discipline Committee, the expertise of the committee, the purpose of its enabling statute, and the nature of the question in dispute all suggested a more deferential standard of review than correctness. The appropriate standard was reasonableness *simpliciter*.

Where the appropriate standard is reasonableness *simpliciter*, a court must not interfere unless the decision, taken as a whole, was unreasonable. The decision need not be supported by a compelling explanation—a tenable explanation is sufficient. There was nothing unreasonable about the Discipline Committee's decision to disbar a member when his repeated conduct was so egregious. The Discipline Committee provided reasons for disbarment that were tenable and grounded in the evidence.

Standing in Applications for Judicial Review

Finlay v. Canada (Minister of Finance), [1986] 2 SCR 607

FACTS: Finlay was a "person in need" within the meaning of the Canada Assistance Plan, and sought a declaration that cost-sharing payments by Canada to Manitoba pursuant to the plan were illegal. In accordance with the cost-sharing arrangement, an amount was deducted from his monthly social allowance for a period of 46 months. This had the effect of reducing the amount of a social allowance payment below the cost of his basic requirements. He also sought an injunction to stop the deductions because of provincial non-compliance with the conditions and undertakings imposed by the plan. He claimed to be prejudiced by the provincial non-compliance.

ISSUE: Did Finlay have standing to seek the declaratory and injunctive relief?

DECISION: While Finlay did not have a sufficiently direct and personal interest in the legality of the federal cost-sharing payments to bring him within the general requirement for standing, he should be recognized, as a matter of judicial discretion, as having public interest standing to bring his action. Finlay met the criteria for public interest standing. His action raised justiciable issues, which were serious issues, and he had a genuine interest in them. If Finlay were denied standing, there would be no other way to bring these issues before a court.

REVIEW QUESTIONS

1. List as many grounds as you can for challenging the decisions of bureaucrats and tribunals in the courts.

2. List five methods of challenging the procedures or decision of a tribunal or government official.

3. If a party has challenged the decision of a tribunal, how can she stop the decision from taking effect while it is under review? What factors will a court or tribunal consider when deciding whether to temporarily suspend the effect of a tribunal decision?

4. When does a party have the right to appeal a decision and when is it necessary instead to make an application for judicial review?

5. Does a person who was not a party at a tribunal hearing have a right to appeal or seek judicial review of the tribunal's decision?

6. What are the three standards of review used by the courts in deciding whether to defer to an agency's decision? Explain how these standards differ from each other.

7. In what circumstances will the court apply each of the three standards of review?

8. List the remedies a court can grant in an appeal or judicial review of an agency's decision.

EXERCISE

Using a computer database of provincial statutes, list the tribunals in your province that fall into the following categories and the related statutory provisions:

1. The tribunal is

   a. not subject to any statutory appeal,

   b. subject to an appeal only on questions of law,

   c. subject to an appeal on questions of fact or law, or

   d. subject to an appeal on policy or public interest grounds.

2. The parties in a hearing of the tribunal

   a. always have a right to appeal,

   b. have a right to appeal only with the permission of a court,

   c. have a right to appeal only with the permission of the tribunal or some other body that is not a court.

3. Where there is a right to appeal, the appeal is

   a. to a court or

   b. to some other person or body.

4. Where the appeal is to a court, the appeal is

   a. to a court of inferior (statutory) jurisdiction, or

   b. to a superior court.

5. Decisions of the tribunal are subject to a privative clause.

6. The tribunal's governing statute authorizes the tribunal to reconsider its own decision.

FURTHER READING

Lisa Braverman, *Administrative Tribunals: A Legal Handbook* (Aurora, ON: Canada Law Book, 2001), chapter 5.

Michael Bryant and Lorne Sossin, *Public Law* (Toronto: Carswell, 2002), chapter 4.

Robert Macaulay and James Sprague, *Practice and Procedure Before Administrative Tribunals* (Toronto: Carswell) (looseleaf), chapters 24, 27A, and 28.

CHAPTER 14

Enforcement of Tribunal Orders

LEARNING OBJECTIVES

After reading this chapter, you will understand

- the source of the authority to enforce decisions or orders of a tribunal;
- who may apply for enforcement of a tribunal's order;
- the various methods of enforcing tribunal orders and the circumstances in which a particular enforcement mechanism may be used; and
- the remedies that are available from a court once it has been established that an order of a tribunal has not been followed.

In some instances, enforcement of an order is up to the parties themselves and the tribunal has no role to play. ... The notion that the intervention of the court is necessary to enforce agency orders is offensive to some public regulators because it undercuts the principle that each agency is the master of its own proceedings. This tug of war between agencies and courts has crystallized over the exercise of the power to commit for contempt.

John I. Laskin, "Enforcement Powers of Administrative Agencies," in *Law Society of Upper Canada Special Lectures: Administrative Law* (Scarborough, ON: Carswell, 1992), 223

AUTHORITY TO ENFORCE A TRIBUNAL ORDER

Tribunals rarely enforce their own decisions (referred to here as "orders"). Unless a statute specifically provides for the tribunal to enforce its orders, it is unlikely that the tribunal has this authority.

For most tribunals, the authority for compelling enforcement of an order and the procedures to be followed are set out in the tribunal's governing statute. In Ontario, s. 19 of the *Statutory Powers Procedure Act*[1] (SPPA) and s. 54 of British

---

1 RSO 1990, c. S.22.

Columbia's *Administrative Tribunals Act*[2] (ATA) contain such enforcement provisions for tribunals governed by the Act. In the absence of a statutory right, the common law determines enforcement authority. Section 156 of Quebec's *Administrative Justice Act*[3] (AJA) makes decisions of the Administrative Tribunal of Quebec enforceable when deposited with a court.

WHO MAY APPLY FOR ENFORCEMENT OF AN ORDER

If a party in a tribunal proceeding fails to comply with an order issued by the tribunal in its final decision, it is usually up to the party who will benefit from the decision to take action to enforce the order. In some cases (discussed below under "Enforcement Mechanisms and Remedies"), other persons who were not parties in the proceeding also may be entitled to take action.

ENFORCEMENT MECHANISMS AND REMEDIES

Statutes and common law provide three main mechanisms for enforcement of tribunal orders:

1. treating the order as an order of a civil court and using civil court procedures to obtain compliance;

2. treating the violation of the order as an offence and prosecuting the violator in a criminal court proceeding; and

3. treating the violation as contempt and initiating contempt proceedings in a superior court.

In some cases, it may also be possible to seek enforcement through judicial review by a superior court.

The circumstances in which each of these mechanisms is available are discussed below.

Civil Court Order

In Ontario, the most common enforcement mechanism is to give the tribunal's order the status of an order issued by a civil court. In some cases, a statute deems the tribunal's order to be a court order,[4] and it is not necessary to apply for such treatment. Otherwise, the injured party or the tribunal must apply to register the tribunal's order with a civil court. An order that is deemed to be an order of the court or registered as a court order can be enforced in the same way as an order issued by that court. Giving the order the status of a civil court order also permits the court to find the violator in contempt (as discussed below).

---

2 SBC 2004, c. 45.

3 RSQ, c. J-3.

4 For example, s. 19(1) of the SPPA provides that where a certified copy of the decision or order is filed with the court, the order is deemed to be an order of the court at the time it is filed.

If the order requires a person ("the debtor") to pay money to another person ("the creditor"), the creditor will request a court official to seize the bank account, wages, or other property of the debtor and to pay the creditor the amount specified in the order. If the order requires a person to take or refrain from taking some action other than paying money, it is usually necessary to obtain an order from a judge compelling compliance.

Prosecution as an Offence

If a statute provides that failure to obey a tribunal's order is an **offence**, the party who will benefit from the order, the government, and often others (such as public interest groups concerned with an issue) who may not be directly affected by the violation may prosecute the violator. **Prosecution** involves laying a charge and proving the violation in a criminal court. An advantage of prosecution is that the right to prosecute is usually not limited to parties in the tribunal's proceeding. However, some statutes restrict the right to prosecute to the attorney general or a government department or agency.[5]

Most statutes provide that the penalty on conviction is a fine. Where this is the case, the court may not have the power to order compliance. However, some statutes provide for other remedies, such as probation, remedial orders, or even imprisonment.[6]

Contempt Proceedings

The availability of contempt proceedings in a particular case may arise in one of three ways:

1. through treating the violation of the order as a breach of a civil court order (as described above);

2. through a statutory provision stating that contempt is an available remedy; or

3. through the inherent common law right of superior courts to protect the integrity of tribunal decisions.

A tribunal's governing statute may explicitly provide that failure to comply with an order of the tribunal constitutes contempt of the tribunal or of court. Tribunals usually do not have the authority to punish a person for contempt. Statutes generally permit the injured party either to ask the tribunal to apply to a court, or to apply directly himself to a court, to find the violator in contempt.

---

5 Section 61(1) of the *Freedom of Information and Protection of Privacy Act*, RSO 1990, c. F.31 makes it an offence to wilfully disobey an order of the information and privacy commissioner. Section 61(3) prohibits prosecution of this offence without the consent of the attorney general.

6 Fine only: *Truck Transportation Act* (TTA), RSO 1990, c. T.22, s. 33(1); fine and imprisonment: TTA, s. 33(2); other remedies: *Environmental Protection Act*, RSO 1990, c. E.19, ss. 183(2), 190, and 190.1.

In the absence of a statutory provision, a superior court has the inherent authority to find the violator in contempt. The court will automatically grant the injured party standing to seek this remedy. The court also has discretion to grant standing to others who are affected by the violation or by an order that the court may make to remedy the violation. It is doubtful that the tribunal itself would have standing to launch such an application without explicit statutory authority to do so. Tribunal powers are limited to those provided by statute, and courts are reluctant to interpret those powers to imply this kind of power.

Courts have broad powers to punish for contempt. They can order a wide range of remedies, including a reprimand, a fine, an order to carry out the tribunal's order, or imprisonment of the violator until he agrees to comply with the tribunal's order.

Mandamus and Injunction

It is possible that an injured party could also launch a civil action or apply to a superior court for judicial review, resulting in an order requiring the violator to comply with the tribunal's order (known in Latin as *mandamus*) or an order requiring the violator to cease disobeying the tribunal's order (known as an **injunction**). However, as there do not appear to be any court decisions in which this mechanism has been used successfully, it is not clear whether it is generally available.

CHAPTER SUMMARY

Tribunals generally do not have the authority to enforce their own decisions or orders. If a party fails to comply with an order, it is usually the responsibility of the injured party to take legal action to obtain enforcement of the order.

The authority to compel enforcement of a tribunal's order is often set out in the tribunal's governing statute. The most common mechanisms for enforcing orders are to treat the order as equivalent to an order of a civil court and provide for enforcement in the same manner as for an order of that court; to treat the violation of the order as an offence for which the violator can be prosecuted in a criminal court; or to treat the violation as equivalent to contempt of court and to seek a ruling of contempt from a superior court. The remedies available under these mechanisms include an order to comply, a fine, seizure of assets, and even imprisonment, depending on the method of enforcement applied.

In addition to the three main mechanisms, there is some possibility that an injured party could apply to a superior court for judicial review, resulting in an order of *mandamus* or an injunction compelling compliance. However, it is not clear whether a court would accept and act on such an application.

KEY TERMS

injunction   an order issued by a court requiring a person (usually a party to a civil action) to perform some act or refrain from some conduct harmful to the party who seeks relief

mandamus   Latin term referring to an order of a court to a governmental official, department, or agency compelling the performance of a public duty

offence   violation of a prohibition or failure to meet a standard or to comply with a duty specified by law

prosecution   the laying of a charge and proving of an offence against an alleged offender

KEY CASES

The Courts' Power To Punish for Contempt

MacMillan Bloedel Ltd. v. Simpson, [1995] 4 SCR 725

FACTS: A logging company, MacMillan Bloedel, had obtained an injunction from the British Columbia Supreme Court prohibiting protest activities interfering with its operations in Clayoquot Sound. Seventeen-year-old J.P. was charged with contempt of court after he ignored the injunction and continued his protest activities. Under the *Young Offenders Act*, RSC 1985, c. Y-1, in force at the time, J.P. should have been tried in youth court, but his application to have his case heard there was denied. Instead, he was tried in the British Columbia Supreme Court, since the order he breached had originated in that court. J.P. was convicted of contempt and sentenced to 45 days' imprisonment and a fine.

ISSUE: Was the provision of the *Young Offenders Act* that required charges of contempt against youth to be heard by the youth court unconstitutional?

DECISION: The section of the *Young Offenders Act* granting exclusive jurisdiction over contempt proceedings to the youth court was unconstitutional. Criminal contempt of court differs from most other offences in that it is a dispute between an individual and the court itself. Although transfer to the youth court of the power to try youth for contempt is permissible, transfer of exclusive jurisdiction to the youth court is not, because it deprives the superior court of an inherent power. In other words, it attempts to remove a power that cannot be removed except by constitutional amendment. The rule of law requires that courts be able to enforce their orders and ensure that their processes are respected. Removing the power to punish contempt by youths would affect the court's ability to enforce its own orders. Given the youth court's expertise in dealing with young people, it will, in most instances, be preferable for the youth court to try and punish a youth for contempt of a superior court order, but the superior court must still retain its jurisdiction.

The Courts' Power To Punish for Contempt

United Nurses of Alberta v. Alberta (Attorney General), [1992] 1 SCR 901

FACTS: The Alberta Labour Relations Board filed directives with the court of Queen's Bench forbidding strike action by the province's nurses. In violation of these directives, the nurses went on strike anyway. The nurses' union was found to be in contempt of the directives and fined.

ISSUE: Can a union be found in contempt?

DECISION: A union can be held liable for contempt. Board orders filed with the court have the same force as orders of the court. Therefore, the directive filed by the board could provide the basis for the union's contempt conviction even though the directive did not originate with the court. As long as an accused breached a directive in a manner that amounted to public defiance of the court's authority, the court could find the accused in contempt. If an accused convicted of contempt wished to challenge the validity of the directive, it could do so by challenging the board's jurisdiction to make the order. Finally, even though the directive could provide the basis for a contempt conviction, the board was not enacting criminal law when it issued the directive. The directive was not criminal in nature; the union's actions in breaching the directive were criminal.

REVIEW QUESTIONS

1. Can a tribunal enforce its own orders or must a party take action to require enforcement?

2. What are the three main methods for enforcing a tribunal's order?

3. Are other methods of enforcement available?

4. How can a party find out what methods of enforcement are available for orders of a particular tribunal?

5. What are the sources of the authority to punish a person for violating a tribunal's order?

6. If the injured party is successful in proving that another party has violated a tribunal's order and that the order should be enforced, what remedies may the court or the tribunal provide?

FACT SCENARIO

A journalist makes a request to the Ontario Ministry of the Environment for records relating to inspections of a waste disposal site. The ministry refuses to disclose these records and the journalist appeals this refusal to the Ontario information and privacy commissioner. The commissioner orders the ministry to disclose the records within 15 days.

One month later, the journalist still does not have the records. She writes to the minister asking him to comply with the commissioner's order. There is no answer. She writes again two weeks later and again receives no answer. Finally, the journalist writes to the commissioner, asking him to enforce her order.

1. What remedies are available
   a. to the journalist and
   b. to the commissioner?

2. What are the remedies if the order that is violated was issued by one of the following:
   a. the Canadian Human Rights Commission,
   b. the Saskatchewan Labour Relations Board,
   c. the Quebec Police Commission,
   d. the Canadian Dairy Commission,
   e. Ontario's Licence Appeals Tribunal, or
   f. Ontario's Environmental Review Tribunal
      i.   in a hearing under the Environmental Protection Act,
      ii. in a hearing under the Environmental Assessment Act, or
      iii. in a hearing under the Environmental Bill of Rights?

FURTHER READING

Robert Macaulay and James Sprague, *Practice and Procedure Before Administrative Tribunals* (Toronto: Carswell) (looseleaf), chapters 29, 29A, and 42.

John I. Laskin, "Enforcement Powers of Administrative Agencies," in *Law Society of Upper Canada Special Lectures: Administrative Law* (Scarborough, ON: Carswell, 1992), 191-234.

Appendixes

Interpreting Statutes, Regulations, and Bylaws

LEARNING OBJECTIVES

After reading this appendix, you will understand

- why it is necessary to interpret statutes, regulations, and bylaws;
- the difference between traditional and modern approaches to statutory interpretation;
- the meaning of purposive and contextual analysis of statutes;
- the difference between a strict and a liberal interpretation of a statute; and
- the tools available for interpreting statutes.

There is no better way to exercise the imagination than the study of law. No artist ever interpreted nature as freely as a lawyer interprets the truth.

Jean Giradoux

Whether the law entitles a person to some right, benefit, or privilege, imposes a duty, restricts that person's freedom, or requires that a particular procedure be followed sometimes depends on how the law is interpreted. For example, if a law says a pension benefit is available to the "spouse" of a deceased person, does the law include only a partner in a traditional, state-sanctioned marriage between a man and a woman, or does it also include a partner in a common law marriage (often referred to as a "common law spouse") or a partner in a same-sex marriage? The answer depends on how one interprets the word "spouse."

THE ROLE OF STATUTORY INTERPRETATION IN EFFECTIVE ADVOCACY AND DECISION MAKING

Those who represent individuals or groups in dealing with the government start with a set of facts. They must find out what law applies to these facts. They may be called upon to persuade a decision maker that a law should be interpreted in a way that advances the interests of the client.

If a law can be interpreted in more than one way, the decision maker has to determine which interpretation is correct. If a person and the government agency disagree about whether the law permits him or her to have a benefit or privilege or imposes on him or her some obligation, a tribunal will often be authorized to resolve the question. Then, both the person (or his or her representative) and the decision-making agency will try to persuade the tribunal to adopt their interpretation of the law. The representative may argue that his client, a woman in a same-sex relationship, is a "spouse" within the meaning of the statute, while the agency may argue that only members of heterosexual unions are "spouses."

A court or tribunal always applies law to the facts of the case. However, if the opposing parties argue for different meanings for a word, phrase, or provision, the court or tribunal must decide which interpretation of the law is correct before it can apply the law. Even where the legislation gives government officials or tribunal members broad discretion in deciding what course of action to take, the exercise of this discretion may involve the interpretation of laws in accordance with the spirit and intent of the law that governs the process or proceeding.

The interpretation of laws passed by elected assemblies—whether those laws are statutes, regulations, or municipal bylaws—is known as "statutory interpretation," and the principles used in interpreting laws are known as "rules of statutory interpretation." These are not really rules, but a set of principles or guidelines that flow from the rules of grammar and syntax, logic, and common sense. These rules have been developed by the courts as part of the common law, and some remain only within the common law. However, many of them are now codified in statutes. Each province, as well as the government of Canada, has passed a statute called the *Interpretation Act*, which sets out some of the rules to be used for interpreting the statutes of that jurisdiction.

THE TRADITIONAL APPROACH TO STATUTORY INTERPRETATION

A number of different approaches to statutory interpretation were developed by the courts: the plain meaning rule, the golden rule, and the mischief rule.

The Plain Meaning Rule

The plain meaning rule was often used as a starting point in the interpretation of a law. A court or tribunal looked only at the words of the statute to be interpreted; if they were clear, the court or tribunal had to give effect to them, regardless of the consequences. However, this approach often did not provide a definitive answer, because if the meaning of a law were perfectly clear, there would be no need to interpret it. Interpretation is necessary only when a statute has more than one potential meaning.

An example of the plain meaning approach is the rule that every word in a statute must be deemed to have a meaning. A word cannot be ignored even if it appears to be redundant, inconsistent with other language in the statute, or inserted by mistake.

The Golden Rule

The golden rule was a variation on the plain meaning rule. A court or tribunal was permitted to ignore the plain or literal meaning of the words of a statute only if adherence to the plain or literal meaning would lead to an absurd result. An absurd result is one that the legislature could not possibly have intended because it is clearly inconsistent with the spirit and intent of the law. For example, if a statute deals with a specialized field and a word in that specialized field has a different meaning from its ordinary meaning, and it is apparent from the context that the specialized meaning is intended, the court or tribunal may interpret the word as having the specialized meaning.

The plain meaning and golden rule approaches to statutory interpretation were based on the premise that the legislators meant exactly what they said, and that this original intent should guide one's interpretation unless it would lead to an absurd result or a result that was contrary to the obvious spirit and intent of the law. If the legislation said something you didn't think it should, or if it failed to say something you thought it should, you couldn't change the meaning or supply the missing pieces. You were to assume—even though this assumption may have been wrong—that the legislators, in the words of Horton the elephant, said what they meant and meant what they said. (See "An Example of the Plain Meaning Approach?")

Since these approaches assumed that the words in question have a plain or literal meaning, they disallowed or discouraged the use of external aids to interpretation. For example, a plain meaning approach would not consider the headings within a statute or the preamble to the statute, since these are technically not part of the provisions that impose legally binding requirements. Similarly, it was generally considered improper to look at earlier drafts of a statute, discussion papers produced by government before introduction of a bill, or statements made by politicians during debates on the bill.

> **An Example of the Plain Meaning Approach?**
>
> One day at the law office one lawyer said to the other, "You really look terrible this morning." The other lawyer replied, "I woke up this morning with a splitting headache, and whatever I do, I can't get rid of it." The first lawyer told him, "When that happens to me, I take a few hours off work, go home, and make love to my wife. That always works for me."
>
> Later that afternoon, the first lawyer remarked that his colleague looked much better. "I took your advice," the other lawyer said, "and it worked. By the way," he added, "you've got a beautiful house."

The Mischief Rule

The mischief rule was developed in an attempt to avoid the overly strict and literal interpretation of statutes that results from using a plain meaning approach. The mischief rule required a court or tribunal to determine the "mischief" the legislature was trying to prevent by making the law. In other words, the court or tribunal sought to recognize the problem that the legislature was trying to solve or the good that it was trying to do, and then interpreted provisions in a way that achieved this goal. The mischief rule has been incorporated into most interpretation acts. For example, Ontario's *Interpretation Act* states:

> Every Act shall be deemed to be remedial, whether its immediate purport is to direct the doing of any thing that the Legislature deems to be for the public good or to prevent or punish the doing of any thing that it deems to be contrary to the public good, and shall accordingly receive such fair, large and liberal construction and interpretation as will best ensure the attainment of the object of the Act according to its true intent, meaning and spirit.[1]

---

1 RSO 1990, c. I.11, s. 10.

This approach is closer to the modern approach to interpreting statutes, but like all approaches it has its limitations. Who can be sure, for example, that all the members of a legislature had the same goal when they voted for a statute, or what problem the government really intended to address when it introduced the statute? Moreover, the problem to be solved may often be defined broadly or narrowly. For example, your province's *Highway Traffic Act*, which sets the rules for the road, contains the following definition: "Motor vehicle includes an automobile, motorcycle, and motor assisted bicycle, unless otherwise indicated in this Act." The Act was passed before snowmobiles were invented and has not been updated. The Act says that motor vehicles must be driven on the right side of the road. The police stop a driver of a snowmobile and charge her with driving on the left side of the road. She argues that her snowmobile is not a "motor vehicle" as defined in the Act, so she is guilty of no offence.

In determining the correct interpretation of "motor vehicle," the court must consider whether the intent of the legislature was

- to regulate the conduct of drivers only of cars and other existing types of vehicles;

- to regulate all motorized devices with wheels, such as cars and motorized bicycles; or

- to ensure the safety of all users of the road, and therefore to regulate any device driven on the road, whether it had wheels or tracks and whether or not it existed at the time the term "motor vehicle" was defined.

THE MODERN APPROACH TO STATUTORY INTERPRETATION

The approach to statutory interpretation currently favoured by courts and legal scholars does not focus to the same extent on the literal words of the statute or attempt to read the minds of the legislators. The "modern approach," as it is usually called, assumes that where the meaning of a provision is disputed, the words of the provision probably have no single plain meaning. If they did, the parties would not likely invest time and money trying to convince a court or tribunal of their different interpretations. The modern approach also does not assume that sufficient evidence is available to discern what the legislators had in mind when they passed the law.

The modern rule has been described as follows:

> Courts are obliged to determine the meaning of legislation in its total context, having regard to the purpose of the legislation, the consequences of proposed interpretations, the presumptions and special rules of interpretation, as well as admissible external aids. In other words, the courts must consider and take into account all relevant and admissible indicators of legislative meaning. After taking these into account, the court must then adopt an interpretation that is appropriate. An appropriate interpretation is one that can be justified in terms of (a) its plausibility, that is, its compliance with the legislative text; (b) its efficacy, that is, its promotion of the legislative purpose; and (c) its acceptability, that is, the outcome is reasonable and just.[2]

---

2 Ruth Sullivan, *Driedger on the Construction of Statutes*, 3d ed. (Toronto: Butterworths, 1994), 151.

The modern approach is often described as a "contextual and purposive" analysis.

Using this approach to interpreting a statute, one looks first at the specific words, phrases, or provisions that are to be interpreted. If they are not clear on their face, then one looks at the neighbouring parts of the statute to see whether their meaning becomes clear in this context. If there is still any ambiguity, one looks at the statute as a whole for clues. One may also look at how the statute relates to or compares with other statutes that deal with similar subject matter. This is called a "contextual analysis": one looks at the context in which the word, phrase, or provision is found for clues as to its meaning.

Contextual analysis is closely related to, and overlaps with, "purposive analysis." If the meaning of a word, phrase, or provision is not clear on its own, one looks at the statute as a whole and tries to determine what problem the statute was intended to solve and by what means. If the word, phrase, or provision has two equally possible interpretations, the purpose of the statute may indicate which of the two meanings is more consistent with the goal of the statute. The theory is that the interpretation that fulfills the purpose of the statute must be the one that the legislators intended. (See "An Example of Contextual Analysis?")

Contextual and purposive analyses are both very subjective. They can be used creatively to glean the hidden meaning of legislation, but they can also be abused, by allowing a decision maker to impose his or her own values when there is no clear meaning. It is not the adjudicator's role to fix the legislature's mistakes. If an unclear provision can be made clearer with intellectual honesty and rigour, the decision maker should do so. But if the legislature has simply not done its job, the adjudicator should not twist or torture language or logic to fix the problem, as tempting as this may be, and a good advocate should not promote this. Rather, the adjudicator should apply the law as written, even if this leads to an unpalatable result.

> ## An Example of Contextual Analysis?
>
> The judge said to the prisoner in the dock, "You look familiar. Have you ever been up before me?"
>
> "I don't know," said the prisoner. "What time do you get up?"

STRICT AND LIBERAL INTERPRETATION

An example of purposive analysis is the rule that laws that encroach upon the rights and freedoms of individuals are to be interpreted strictly (narrowly). These laws include statutes whose purpose is to prohibit conduct, punish violations, or impose taxes. Such laws should be interpreted in the manner most favourable to the person affected by them. In contrast, statutes that are intended to be preventive or remedial should be interpreted more liberally or expansively; that is, they should be interpreted in a manner that helps solve the problem the statute was intended to address, with less concern about the impact they may have on those affected by them.

TOOLS FOR INTERPRETING STATUTES

When researching the meaning of a statutory provision, use the tools provided by the Act itself before looking at external sources of information. Look for definitions of the word or phrase in question in the statute and look at how the word or phrase has been used in other parts of the statute. Is it used consistently throughout the statute or does it have different meanings in different parts of the statute? Also consider any explanations of the purpose of the statute or provision. These may be found in the preamble to the statute, in headings, or in marginal notes. Next, determine whether courts or tribunals have interpreted the provision in question.

If this does not resolve the question, move to external sources, such as dictionary definitions of the words or phrases in question, definitions of the words or phrases in other statutes, and court and tribunal decisions that have interpreted similar words, phrases, or provisions in other statutes.

Finally, you may turn to statements of general principles, such as intepretation acts, drafting conventions, maxims, and presumptions. These are rarely definitive, but they provide guidance.

Legislative History and Legislative Evolution

If one wants to look at the full context of a statute, it is sometimes necessary to go beyond the words of the statute to look at how the statute was developed (legislative history) and how it evolved over time through amendments after it was passed (legislative evolution).

Legislative history is the process of development of a statute, from the identification of a problem and proposed solutions by the legislators to the final wording passed by the elected assembly or approved by the executive branch of government. This historical context can include study papers (often referred to as white papers) or commission reports and statements made by politicians in the legislative assembly or municipal council, as well as wording changes made after a law was introduced as a bill but before it was finally passed as a law. In the past, courts frowned upon the use of legislative history as an interpretive aid, but they are more receptive toward it today.

Legislative evolution refers to amendments made after a law came into effect. Over the years, a law may be amended many times. If one wants to understand a provision in the current version of a statute, the similarities and differences between this version and past versions may shed light on whether an amendment was intended to continue an idea expressed in a previous version, or whether it was meant to modify the original concept.

Interpretation Acts

In determining the meaning of a provision, one can turn to several sources of information. As mentioned earlier, every province has an *Interpretation Act*, which addresses some questions that commonly arise in the interpretation of statutes. For example, s. 29(1) of Ontario's *Interpretation Act* defines a range of words and terms, from "Act" to "year." The Act provides that if any of these words or terms are used in any Ontario statute or bylaw, they are to be given the meaning set out in the *Interpretation Act* unless the context requires otherwise. Thus, a "person" is defined to include "a corporation and the heirs, executors, administrators or other legal representatives of a person" any time this word is found in any Ontario law, unless the context requires a broader or narrower interpretation. Another rule in the Act (s. 29(2)) states that the word "shall" is generally to be construed as imperative and "may" as permissive.

Definition Sections

Most statutes, regulations, and bylaws contain a list of definitions of terms used in the enactment. If one is attempting to determine the meaning of a word or phrase in the statute, the definition section may resolve any possible ambiguity about the meaning of the word or phrase in that statute.

If a word is not defined in the enactment itself, one may look at how it is defined in other enactments. The closer the purpose of the other enactment is to the purpose of the one in question, the more persuasive the argument will be that the word or phrase in the enactment one is interpreting should be interpreted as defined in the other enactment.

Dictionaries and Textbooks

If a word or phrase is not defined in the statute in question, one may look at the definitions in ordinary dictionaries. Dictionaries often contain several definitions for a word, some of which support the interpretation one favours and some of which don't.

Whether the ordinary dictionary definition will apply may depend on whether the word or phrase is to be given its ordinary meaning or whether it is a technical term. For example, "instrument" has several different meanings. In ordinary usage, it means a tool or implement. In the context of a law dealing with music, however, it may mean only a musical instrument. In a law dealing with health, it may mean only a medical instrument. "Instrument" also has a specialized legal meaning. In the legal context, an instrument is a document, usually one with some binding legal effect.

If a statute deals with a specialized area, it may also be useful to look at books in that field, such as textbooks or specialized dictionaries, for the meaning of a term. For example, there are medical, scientific, and engineering dictionaries.

Court and Tribunal Decisions

If a word or phrase is not defined in a statute or in an *Interpretation Act*, the most conclusive way to determine its correct interpretation is to find out how the courts have interpreted it in other parts of the statute, or in statutes intended to cover similar ground in the same jurisdiction or in other jurisdictions. The answer can be sought in case law reporters, case digests, textbooks, and, where they exist, annotated versions of the statute. (See appendix B.)

It is also useful to look for provisions in other statutes that are similarly worded to the one in question, and find out how courts have interpreted those provisions. One might then argue that the same interpretation should be given in the statute in question because the statutes are similar in structure and purpose, or that a different interpretation would be more reasonable because of differences in the purposes or subject matter of the statutes or in the wording of the provisions.

If a superior court has interpreted the provision in question in the same statute, this interpretation is binding on a tribunal in the same jurisdiction. If, however, there is no existing judicial interpretation of the provision, or if there are conflicting interpretations, it may be necessary to use a variety of tools in combination.

English and French Versions

A Canadian rule of statutory interpretation is that the English and French versions of laws have equal weight and should be interpreted in a way that, wherever possible, gives them the same meaning. One may thus compare the English and French versions of a statute to resolve ambiguity. For example, if a word in the English version has more than one meaning, the French version may offer a clue as to which meaning is most similar to the word used in French.

Preambles, Purpose Sections, Marginal Notes, and Headings

Statutes often have a preamble or "purpose section," and marginal notes or headings for each section. The preamble and headings or marginal notes are not considered part of the wording of the statute itself, but they may be used with caution to shed some light on the meaning of a provision. Purpose sections and definitions, which are considered an integral part of the statute, have greater weight.

Drafting Conventions, Maxims, and Presumptions

Courts and tribunals recognize that drafters of legislation have developed standard ways of expressing ideas. They know that if a particular construction is used, it is likely to convey a particular meaning, and they tend to give it that meaning. For example, legislative drafters generally use the word "shall" to indicate that an act is mandatory, and "may" to signify that it is discretionary. Therefore, if a provision states that "the applicant shall file a notice of appeal within 10 days," the court will interpret this to mean that the notice must be filed, and if it is not, there may be legal consequences. However, this rule is not determinative (that is, it does not conclusively decide the issue). Where the context requires a different interpretation, the court will interpret a provision containing "shall" as only directing, rather than requiring, an action.

The courts have developed a number of "maxims," usually expressed in Latin, as guidelines for interpretation based on these conventions of legislative drafting.

Two commonly cited maxims deal with the interpretation of lists. The kind of word used to begin or end a list may be a clue, for example, as to whether the list is exhaustive (complete) or whether the provision is intended to cover not only the things in the list but also anything similar.

Ejusdem generis ("of the same kind") says that a general word that follows particular and specific words of a similar nature takes its meaning from those words and is considered to be limited to the same class.

For example, if a statute provides that horses, cows, sheep, pigs, and other farm animals must be kept enclosed behind a high fence, one might interpret "other farm animals" using the *ejusdem generis* rule as meaning animals raised for sale or for use in farming operations, but as not meaning barn cats, field mice, or barn swallows, even though they are other animals found on farms.

Expressio unius est exclusio alterius ("to express one thing is to exclude another") says that the inclusion of one thing in a statute, but not other things that one would expect to find when that thing is mentioned, is the legislature's way of indicating that it intends to exclude those other things.

For example, s. 6 of the *Winnipeg General Hospital Act*[3] exempts "property used for hospital purposes" from certain kinds of tax. The section states that hospital property includes "property used … for necessary parking facilities, interns' quarters, school of nursing, nurses' residence, power house or laundry." The Manitoba court had to decide whether the term "hospital property" included two apartment buildings owned by the hospital and rented to hospital staff. Applying the *expressio unius* rule, the court held that the legislature, in making such a long and detailed list, would have included apartment buildings rented to staff if it meant to. Because the apartment buildings were not included in the list of property exempt from taxation, the buildings were subject to tax.[4] (See "An Example of Expressio Unius Est Exclusio Alterius?")

Two other commonly cited maxims are:

- *Verba ita sunt intelligenda ut res magis valeat quam pereat*   Words are to be understood to carry out the object and not to have the object fail.

- *Verba posteriora, propter certitudinem addita, ad priora, quae certitudine indigent, sunt referenda*   Later words, added for certainty, are to be referred to preceding words that need certainty.

Courts and tribunals will also apply certain presumptions when interpreting statutes. However, these presumptions are generally rebuttable. That is, if the presumption does not lead to an appropriate result, the court or tribunal need not follow it.

An Example of Expressio Unius Est Exclusio Alterius?

Two lawyers went to a restaurant and ordered drinks. When the drinks arrived, each lawyer took a sandwich from his briefcase and began to eat.

The owner rushed over to the table and exclaimed, "You can't eat your own sandwich here!"

The lawyers looked at each other, shrugged, and exchanged sandwiches.

One of the most important presumptions is the presumption against retroactive operation of statutes. In interpreting a statute, unless a statute explicitly states that it applies to events that took place before it was passed, a court or tribunal will generally find that the statute only imposes consequences on people for future action. In the words of former Chief Justice Dickson, a statute should not "reach into the past and declare that the law or the rights of parties as of an earlier date shall be taken to be something other than they were as of that earlier date."[5]

The presumption of compliance with constitutional norms requires that where legislation is open to two interpretations, one of which would render the law invalid, the court or tribunal should choose the interpretation that avoids invalidity, even though it may limit the scope or effectiveness of the provision.

The presumption of stability provides that in interpreting amendments to laws, the legislature must not be presumed to have intended to depart from the previous law any further than it expressly stated.

---

3 RSM 1968, c. 103.

4 *Medical Centre Apartments Ltd. v. Winnipeg (City)* (1969), 3 DLR (3d) 525 (Man. CA).

5 *Gustavson Drilling (1964) Ltd. v. Minister of National Revenue*, [1977] 1 SCR 271.

APPENDIX SUMMARY

Government decision making often requires the decision maker to choose between two or more possible meanings of a law or policy. The advocate's job is to persuade the decision maker to choose a reasonable interpretation that reflects his or her client's interests. Over the decades, courts have developed principles of statutory interpretation that are derived from logic, rules of grammar and syntax, and common sense. Legislatures have also helped by including definition sections in statutes and passing statutes like the *Interpretation Act* that set out principles for interpreting all laws within their jurisdiction.

The traditional approach to statutory interpretation started with a search for the plain meaning of provisions. Courts seldom looked outside the statute itself for clues. This approach was gradually eclipsed by approaches that focus more on the purpose of provisions and what they are intended to accomplish. Today, courts and tribunals attempt to give provisions a meaning that is in harmony with the legislators' intent by looking at the purpose of the statute as a whole and the context in which the disputed words appear. They are also much more willing to consider external sources of information, such as debates in the legislature, white papers, and ministerial statements.

REVIEW QUESTIONS

1. Why do laws require interpretation?

2. When will a court or tribunal depart from the plain meaning of a provision in interpreting a law?

3. When the meaning of a law is unclear, what approaches will a court or tribunal use to ascertain its meaning?

4. What is "contextual analysis"?

5. In what ways are the modern and traditional approaches to statutory interpretation different? In what ways are they similar?

6. Where would you look to find the meaning of a word if it is not defined in a statute?

7. If the meanings of the English and French versions of a provision are different, how would the correct meaning be determined?

8. Can the preamble or internal headings in a statute be used to assist in interpreting its provisions? If so, what is their value as interpretive tools compared with the value of a definition or purpose section within the statute?

9. If a provision contains a list, how would you determine whether the list is intended to be exhaustive or whether items not in the list are also covered by the provision?

EXERCISES

1. Section 18 of Ontario's *Environmental Protection Act* (RSO 1990, c. E.19) permits a director of the Ministry of the Environment under certain circumstances to make an order requiring the owner of property to "monitor"

the discharge of a contaminant into the natural environment. What does the term "monitor" mean in this context?

There are a variety of chemicals in the groundwater surrounding your client's factory and the ministry is having difficulty determining what they are and whether they are dangerous. Under s. 18, the director orders your client to pump the water out of the ground and store it in large tanks for an indefinite period and to take samples and have them analyzed by the laboratory. Using the tools described in this appendix, answer the following questions. Is pumping and storing the water "monitoring"? Is collecting and analyzing water samples "monitoring"?

The Act states:

Order by Director re preventive measures

18(1) The Director, in the circumstances mentioned in subsection (2), by a written order may require a person who owns or owned or who has or had management or control of an undertaking or property to do any one or more of the following:

1. To have available at all times, or during such periods of time as are specified in the order, the equipment, material and personnel specified in the order at the locations specified in the order.

2. To obtain, construct and install or modify the devices, equipment and facilities specified in the order at the locations and in the manner specified in the order.

3. To implement procedures specified in the order.

4. To take all steps necessary so that procedures specified in the order will be implemented in the event that a contaminant is discharged into the natural environment from the undertaking or property.

5. To monitor and record the discharge into the natural environment of a contaminant specified in the order and to report thereon to the Director.

6. To study and to report to the Director upon,

    i.   measures to control the discharge into the natural environment of a contaminant specified in the order,

    ii. the effects of the discharge into the natural environment of a contaminant specified in the order,

    iii. the natural environment into which a contaminant specified in the order is likely to be discharged.

Grounds for order

(2) The Director may make an order under this section where the Director is of the opinion, upon reasonable and probable grounds,

(a) that the nature of the undertaking or of anything on or in the property is such that if a contaminant is discharged into the natural environment from the undertaking or from or on the property, the contaminant will result or is likely to result in an effect mentioned in the definition of "contaminant" in subsection 1(1); and

(b) that the requirements specified in the order are necessary or advisable so as,

(i) to prevent or reduce the risk of the discharge of the contaminant into the natural environment from the undertaking or from or on the property, or

(ii) to prevent, decrease or eliminate an effect mentioned in the definition of "contaminant" in subsection 1(1) that will result or that is likely to result from the discharge of the contaminant into the natural environment from the undertaking or from or on the property.

2. The provincial *Land Use Planning Act* states, "Any person may appeal a municipal zoning bylaw to the Planning Review Board." The statute does not define "person."

However, the provincial *Interpretation Act* defines "person" as follows:

In every Act, unless the context otherwise requires,

"person" includes a corporation and the heirs, executors, administrators or other legal representatives of a person to whom the context can apply according to law.

The municipality has passed a zoning bylaw rezoning a tract of land to permit an oil company, Petrocon, to establish a gasoline refinery. Save Our Soil (SOS), an unincorporated association of local residents and naturalists, appeals the zoning bylaw to the planning board on the grounds that air emissions, discharges of effluent into a local watercourse, and possible spills and leaks of petroleum products and other chemicals will interfere with the use and enjoyment of their homes and will contaminate the soil and groundwater in a nearby woods and wetland.

Before the board, Petrocon argues that SOS has no standing to bring an appeal because it is not a "person." Is SOS a "person" for the purposes of this section of the *Land Use Planning Act*?

3. Section 21 of the British Columbia *Freedom of Information and Protection of Privacy Act* (RSBC 1996, c. 165) provides in part:

21(1) The head of a public body must refuse to disclose to an applicant information

(a) that would reveal ...

(ii) commercial, financial, labour relations, scientific or technical information of or about a third party,

(b) that is supplied, implicitly or explicitly, in confidence, and

(c) the disclosure of which could reasonably be expected to

(i) harm significantly the competitive position or interfere significantly with the negotiating position of the third party,

(ii) result in similar information no longer being supplied to the public body when it is in the public interest that similar information continue to be supplied,

(iii) result in undue financial loss or gain to any person or organization, or

(iv) reveal information supplied to, or the report of, an arbitrator, mediator, labour relations officer or other person or body appointed to resolve or inquire into a labour relations dispute.

Lawyers who provide legal aid to those who cannot afford it are paid for their services by the Department of the Attorney General, which is a public body subject to the *Freedom of Information and Protection of Privacy Act*. The rates at which lawyers are paid are determined by negotiations between the ministry and the British Columbia Bar Association (BCBA). In fact, a statute provides that the BCBA will act as the bargaining agent for all the lawyers in the province and the lawyers will be bound by the agreement between the Department of the Attorney General and the BCBA.

On behalf of your client, you make a request to the office of the Attorney General for memoranda and correspondence relating to the most recent negotiations between the BCBA and the department.

The department refuses access to the information on the grounds that this is "labour relations" information under s. 21(1)(a)(ii) of the *Freedom of Information and Protection of Privacy Act*.

You believe that this is a misinterpretation of the statute. You argue that the term "labour relations" refers to negotiations between an employer and a labour union representing employees, not negotiations between a government agency and an independent association representing professionals.

What light do the following shed on the proper interpretation of "labour relations" in s. 21(1)(a)(ii) of the *Freedom of Information and Protection of Privacy Act*?

a. the preamble or purpose section of the *Freedom of Information and Protection of Privacy Act*;

b. any other provisions of the *Freedom of Information and Protection of Privacy Act* that use the phrase "labour relations";

c. the definitions, if any, of the term "labour relations" in other BC statutes; and

d. the definitions, if any, or usage of the term "labour relations" in other Canadian freedom of information statutes.

FURTHER READING

Robert C. Dick, *Legal Drafting*, 2d ed. (Toronto: Carswell, 1985).

Ruth Sullivan, "Statutory Interpretation in a New Nutshell" (2003) vol. 82 *Canadian Bar Review* 51.

Ruth Sullivan, *Sullivan and Driedger on the Construction of Statutes*, 4th ed. (Toronto: Butterworths, 2002).

Research Tools and Procedures

LEARNING OBJECTIVES

After reading this appendix, you will understand

- what kinds of documents to look for when preparing to represent a client before a tribunal or other agency;

- what kinds of publications contain these documents;

- what other sources of information can be accessed;

- how to obtain pertinent information from libraries and the Internet; and

- that some sources of information cost money, while others are free.

Cases by the million! Libraries so labyrinthine as to require a guide! The leaves of the books like the leaves of the trees! Who can now read all the reports of cases dealing with the law of consideration for informal promises, stating the reasons deemed sufficient for enforcing such promises, laying down the doctrines and constructing the definitions? Certainly not the writer of this volume.

Arthur L. Corbin, *Corbin on Contracts*, vol. 1 (St. Paul, MN: West Publishing, 1963), 489

CATEGORIES OF USEFUL INFORMATION

Whether one is assisting a client to apply for a benefit, recommending to a regulatory agency what practices it should allow in an industry or profession, or appearing before a tribunal, one may need to find the following categories of records:

- Laws of general application that apply to the activities of the agency. Such laws may be statutes, regulations, or municipal bylaws. Laws of general application that may affect the jurisdiction or procedures of agencies include the *Statutes Act*, the *Regulations Act*, and the *Interpretation Act* of Canada and of various provinces. In the case of municipalities, these laws include the *Planning Act* and the *Municipal Act*. For most tribunals, the province's *Judicial Review Procedure Act* sets out procedures for challenging the decision of an official or tribunal in court. In Quebec, Ontario, and Alberta, there are general statutes that set out minimum rules of procedure for a variety of tribunals and sometimes other statutory decision makers.

- Statutes, regulations, or bylaws that establish the agency or set out its jurisdiction and procedures. For example, the Ontario Municipal Board is established by the *Ontario Municipal Board Act*, but it gets some of its powers from other statutes such as the *Planning Act*.

- Court decisions that interpret laws of general application that apply to an agency.

- Court decisions that interpret laws that govern the specific agency.

- Court decisions that interpret administrative law concepts such as jurisdiction, discretion, delegation, procedural fairness, and natural justice.

- Decisions and rulings of the agency in question.

- Decisions and rulings of agencies in other jurisdictions that carry out functions similar to the agency in question or that are governed by statutes that are similar in wording.

- Rules and regulations made by the agency itself to govern the processing of requests and applications to it or the conduct of proceedings before it.

- Guidelines and policies that the agency uses in making its decisions.

- Forms used by the agency and by the public in applying to the agency or appearing before it (for example, application forms, statutory declarations, and summonses to witnesses).

SOURCES FOR OBTAINING THIS INFORMATION

Primary Sources and Secondary Sources

Sources of information can be divided into primary sources and secondary sources.

Primary sources are publications that contain the full text of documents such as laws, cases, rules, guidelines, policies, and forms.

Secondary sources are publications that summarize, analyze, interpret, or explain the primary records. They include case digests, legal encyclopedias, dictionaries of legal words and phrases as they have been interpreted by the courts, textbooks, **law journals** that contain articles about various topics or areas of law or practice, and brochures or pamphlets published by the agency itself to assist the public in using its services.

Some publications are a combination of primary and secondary material. For example, **annotated** statutes contain the full text of the statute, but they also contain analysis of the overall purpose and operation of the statute, as well as analysis of each section of the statute and a description of court or tribunal cases that have interpreted that section. Similarly, casebooks are a kind of legal textbook that often combine court or tribunal decisions or excerpts from these decisions with commentary and explanations of the legal principles established by these cases.

General Publications and Topical Publications

Sources of information may also be described as general or topical. General publications contain all the laws of a province or all the decisions of a specific court or selected decisions of all courts on a variety of issues.

Topical publications deal with specific subject matters such as labour relations, environmental protection, occupational health and safety, torts, or administrative law.

Media in Which Legal Information Is Recorded

The publications described above can be found in several media. They include paper documents such as books, periodicals and pamphlets, Internet Web sites, Internet search engines and directories, CD-ROMS, and audiotapes. Some publications are available in just one medium (for example, only online or only on paper); however, legal publications are increasingly available both electronically and on paper.

LOCATING PRIMARY SOURCES OF ADMINISTRATIVE LAW

The full, unedited text of **bills**, statutes, regulations, and bylaws; court and tribunal decisions; and court and agency rules, guidelines, and policies can be found in the manner described below.

Bills, Statutes, and Regulations

The powers and duties of any body established by a statute can be found in the statute or in regulations made under the statute. This applies to ministries of government, government agencies, boards and commissions, universities, and the governing bodies of self-regulating trades and professions.

A bill is a version of a statute that has been introduced in Parliament or a provincial legislature, but not yet passed. The original bill may be amended by the legislature or its committees, sometimes more than once, before it is passed. The contents of a bill and its status (whether it has been given first, second, or third reading; whether it has been referred to a committee; whether it has been passed, and whether it is in effect) may be ascertained by subscribing to a bills subscription service operated by the government or by a private publisher. Some government Web sites also provide this information. The text of federal bills and the bills of several provinces are available online from LexisNexis Canada.

The contents of statutes and regulations may be found in three media: paper, CD-ROM, and Internet search engines. The federal government and the provincial governments periodically publish compilations of all the statutes and regulations that are in force in their jurisdiction. New regulations are found in the *Canada Gazette*, published by the federal government, and in the gazettes published weekly or biweekly by provincial governments. Governments also often produce bound versions of individual statutes soon after they are passed, and compile in a single volume all the statutes passed in a year.

Federal and provincial statutes and regulations are also available on CD-ROM. The *Ontario Statute Citator* and the *Canada Statute Citator*, which used to be available only on paper, can now be installed on a computer. Updates are published several times a year. These **statute citators** contain all public statutes that are in effect; the text of all regulations made under these statutes; and the history of the statutes and regulations, including the date of the law's passage and, on a section-by-section basis, the date of passage of every amendment.

The citators also list recent court decisions that have interpreted each section of each statute. For a more complete list of cases, it is necessary to look elsewhere.

All federal statutes and the statutes of most provinces are also available on the Internet through free Web sites and commercial services.

The statutes of several provinces are available on the provincial government Web site. For example, all Ontario public statutes and regulations are available on the Ontario government's Web site at www.e-laws.gov.on.ca. The government's goal is to add amendments within 14 days after each change is made. All laws on the site are searchable—for example, by word or phrase. The site also includes reference tables that allow users to check for recent changes in the law.

The statutes and regulations of Canada and several provinces and territories can also be found on the Canadian Legal Information Institute (CanLII) Web site at www.canlii.org and on LexisNexis Canada (formerly Quicklaw). Access to CanLII is free; access to LexisNexis is by paid subscription, either an hourly rate for search time or a monthly flat rate.

Bylaws, Resolutions, and Other Information of Municipal Agencies

Where a municipal body is created by a bylaw or resolution of the municipal council, at least some of its powers and responsibilities will be set out in the resolution or bylaw. (The functions might be found partly in a statute such as the *Municipal Act* and partly in bylaws or resolutions.)

Resolutions and bylaws are generally not published and must be obtained from the clerk of the municipality or a department head or other official who may have a copy. However, some of the larger Ontario municipalities post their bylaws on their Web sites. For example, Toronto's bylaws are available at www.city.toronto.on.ca.

Court and Tribunal Decisions

The text of a court or tribunal decision can be located in two ways: by reference to its name ("*Doe v. Joe*" or "*Re Wigle Estate*" or by its **citation** (or, colloquially, its "cite"). The citation for a case is a combination of the year the case was decided (or sometimes the year it was published in a **law report**), the abbreviated name of the law report, the volume and/or series of the law report, the page number where the decision is found, and the abbreviated name of the court (if the court is not already understood from the name of the law report). A typical case citation looks like this:

Re Knowles (1997), 26 CELR (NS) 71 (Ont. EAB)

In this case, "*Re Knowles*" is the name of the case (also known by lawyers as the title of proceedings or style of cause); "(1997)" is the year the case was decided; "26" is the volume number; "CELR" stands for *Canadian Environmental Law Reports*; "(NS)" means "New Series"; "71" is the page number; and "(Ont. EAB)" stands for the Ontario Environmental Appeal Board. So this citation tells you that the decision in the case of *Re Knowles* was made by the Environmental Appeal Board, released in 1997, and is published in volume 26 of the new series of the *Canadian Environmental Law Reports*, starting at page 71.

The first problem one faces with a case citation is finding out what the abbreviation of the name of the publication stands for, if one is not already familiar with it. For example, if you do not know that CELR stands for *Canadian Environmental Law Reports*, you will have difficulty finding the case even though you have its citation. Lists of abbreviations of the names of law reporters and law journals are found at the front of several publications, including the *Index to Canadian Legal Literature* and the *Canadian Law Dictionary*.

Electronic databases have their own citation system. For example, in a case citation that gives the law report as "OJ," the law report is *Ontario Judgments*, which is a computerized publication of the decision. The decision may or may not also be available in a print publication such as the CELR.

There are three main ways to find decisions of courts and tribunals: look in law reports (also called **law reporters** or law reporting services); look at the Web site of the court or tribunal in question; or look at a database or electronic directory in which decisions are collected.

Law reports are collections of court and tribunal decisions deemed by experts in the field to be significant because they shed new light on the interpretation of the law. Most law reports periodically publish a cumulative index of cases, in which a case can be located either by name or by subject matter.

Some electronic databases include only cases selected for their significance from the vast number of court and tribunal decisions rendered each year. Other databases contain all the decisions of a particular court or tribunal, regardless of their legal importance.

Law reports and databases of cases may be regional (the *Maritime Law Reports*, the *Alberta Law Reports*), topical (the *Canadian Environmental Law Reports*, the *Canadian Human Rights Reporter*), or by court (the *Supreme Court Reports*, the *Federal Court Reporter*).

DECISIONS OF COURTS THAT INTERPRET STATUTES GOVERNING AGENCIES

On paper, there are several general-purpose law reporting services that publish court decisions considered to be significant because they shed new light on the interpretation of the law. They include the *Ontario Reports*, which publishes decisions of all levels of the Ontario courts, and the *Dominion Law Reports*, which publishes decisions of courts across Canada. Some of these decisions interpret the statutes that govern administrative bodies.

There are also law reports that are restricted to the decisions of a particular court. For example, the *Federal Trial Reports* carries decisions of the Trial Division of the Federal Court of Canada. This court interprets statutes passed by the government of Canada, including ones under which federal government agencies operate. There are two law reporters that carry only the decisions of the Supreme Court of Canada: the *Supreme Court Reports* and the *National Reporter*.

ADMINISTRATIVE LAW COURT DECISIONS

Decisions of courts that have interpreted the application of common law principles of administrative law, such as natural justice, procedural fairness, and the rule against subdelegation, in relation to specific administrative bodies can be found in the general law reporters and annotation services listed above.

PROCEDURAL LAW COURT AND TRIBUNAL DECISIONS

Specific Tribunals or Categories of Tribunals

There are several commercially published law reporters devoted to specific tribunals or categories of tribunals. These law reporters usually publish decisions of the tribunal that the editors deem to be significant, as well as court decisions that interpret the powers of the tribunal or its procedures. For example, the *Canadian Human Rights Reporter* includes court decisions interpreting federal and provincial human rights statutes as well as significant decisions of the Canadian Human Rights Commission and provincial human rights commissions. The *Canadian Environmental Law Reports* compiles decisions of courts across Canada that interpret environmental laws, but it also includes significant decisions by environmental tribunals such as the Alberta and British Columbia Environmental Appeal Boards and the Ontario Environmental Review Tribunal. Occasionally, CELR will also include a summary of the report of a royal commission on an environmental concern.

Law reporters on paper that are devoted to the decisions of an individual tribunal and court decisions interpreting the powers of that tribunal include the *Ontario Municipal Board Reports*, produced by a commercial publisher, and the *Ontario Labour Relations Board Reports*, published by the board itself.

Administrative Law Case Reporting Services

There is one commercial law reporter devoted solely to administrative law decisions from across Canada that is available both on paper and through a commercial Internet search engine. The *Administrative Law Reports* includes significant decisions of individual tribunals as well as administrative law decisions of all levels of courts throughout Canada.

LexisNexis Canada offers three databases of administrative law cases: *Administrative Law Topical* (ADMT) and *Administrative Law Cases from Quicklaw* (ADMQ), both of which contain court decisions since 1968; and *Décisions en droit administratif des cours québécoises* (ADQC), which has cases going back to 1986.

Although there are relatively few publications on paper that are devoted to collecting the decisions of an individual tribunal, comprehensive collections of every decision of certain individual tribunals are available on the Internet from two sources: LexisNexis and the Web sites of the tribunals themselves. For example, LexisNexis provides access to the decisions of at least 4 British Columbia tribunals, 4 Manitoba boards, 5 New Brunswick tribunals, and 19 Ontario tribunals. These boards and tribunals include the Ontario Alcohol and Gaming Commission, the BC Commercial Appeals Commission, the Ontario Employment Standards Tribunal, the disciplinary panels of the Law Society of Manitoba, the Manitoba Automobile Injury Compensation Commission, and the Ontario College of Teachers.

Also accessible on LexisNexis are the decisions of at least 15 federal boards and tribunals. They range alphabetically from the Canada Agricultural Review Tribunal to the Canadian Radio-television and Telecommunications Commission.

It is also possible on the Internet to compare how tribunals in different jurisdictions have dealt with the same problem or interpreted similar statutes. For example, LexisNexis has databases for decisions of the Labour Relations Board of Canada, Alberta, British Columbia, Manitoba, New Brunswick, Newfoundland and Labrador, Ontario, and Saskatchewan.

Tribunals that maintain Web sites with all their decisions include the federal Privacy Commissioner, the information and privacy commissioners of Alberta, British Columbia, and Ontario, and Ontario's Environmental Review Tribunal. Tribunal Web sites are often accessed through the Web site of the provincial or federal government that established the tribunal.

LOCATING SECONDARY SOURCES OF ADMINISTRATIVE LAW

Descriptions, summaries, and analyses of statutes, regulations, bylaws, court and tribunal decisions, agency rules, guidelines, and policies, and analysis and commentary about them can be found in the manner described below.

Textbooks

There are numerous Canadian, US, and British textbooks that deal with administrative law as a whole or with specific areas of administrative law such as bias. Canadian texts include Blake, *Administrative Law in Canada*; Brown and Evans, *Judicial Review of Administrative Action in Canada*; Jones and deVillars, *Principles of Administrative Law*; Macaulay and Sprague, *Practice and Procedure Before Administrative Tribunals*; and Mullan, *Administrative Law*. Most of these texts are available only on paper.

Law Journals

General law journals that deal with a variety of topics sometimes contain articles about administrative law. For example, in 2002, the *Canadian Bar Review* published an article by Laverne A. Jacobs and Thomas S. Kuttner entitled "Discovering What Tribunals Do: Tribunals Before the Courts." The article was also published on the Internet at www.ciaj-icaj.ca/English/publications/papersarticles/discoveringwhattribunalsdo.html.

A few law journals are devoted exclusively to administrative law topics. The *Canadian Journal of Administrative Law and Practice* is published by Carswell and is available on paper and through Carswell's commercial Internet search engine. From the early 1990s to 1999, Carswell also published *Reid's Administrative Law*. The American Bar Association publishes the *Administrative Law Review*, which covers more esoteric and specialized issues than those covered by Canadian publications.

Most law journals are still available only on paper, but increasingly they are becoming available on the Internet. Law journals published by a university or nonprofit association may be available on the university or association's Web site. Some law journals that are published on paper by commercial publishers are also available online through the publishers' electronic research facilities (see below).

A comprehensive *Index to Canadian Legal Literature* is available both on paper and online. It is possible to locate articles in most Canadian law journals through the *Index*. Articles are listed by author, title, and subject matter. One of the listed topics is administrative law.

Legal Encyclopedias

Legal encyclopedias are legal textbooks that cover a wide variety of areas of law, from A (abandonment, administrative law) to Y and Z (young offenders, zoning).

For each subject, they provide a summary of the law in the jurisdiction they cover, as well as case citations supporting each rule or principle described. At least one legal encyclopedia, the *Canadian Encyclopedic Digest*, is available on CD-ROM as well as through a commercial search engine on the Internet.

Case Law Digests

Case law digests are regularly updated collections of summaries of significant court or tribunal decisions arranged alphabetically by subject matter. There are case law digests for specific areas of law as well as case law digests that are encyclopedic; that is, they cover a wide variety of areas of law. The *Canadian Abridgement* is one digest that is available on paper, on CD-ROM, and through a commercial search engine on the Internet. It contains summaries of significant court decisions, grouped by subject matter. One of the subject areas is administrative law.

Case Citators

Once a case has been considered significant enough to report, it is important to determine when the courts have followed the decision and when they have rejected it, or found that it does not apply to the case before them. Publications that list significant court decisions and track how they are applied in subsequent cases are called "citators" or "citations."

These publications do not contain the text of the court decision; rather, they simply identify the law reports in which the decision is reported. *Canadian Case Citations*, which is part of the *Canadian Abridgement* series, is published by Carswell. It contains citations for cases decided by courts throughout Canada from 1867 on.

Case citations are available on paper, on CD-ROM, and through online commercial research facilities.

Legal Dictionaries

Legal dictionaries are usually general in nature, although there are a few topical legal dictionaries, such as the *Dictionary of Environmental Law and Science*, published by Emond Montgomery. There does not appear to be a legal dictionary devoted to administrative law, but general legal dictionaries such as *Black's Law Dictionary*, the *Dictionary of Canadian Law*, and the *Canadian Law Dictionary*, and *Words and Phrases Legally Defined* explain administrative law concepts such as natural justice, procedural fairness, jurisdiction, and subdelegation, as well as relevant Latin phrases such as *audi alteram partem*.

Online legal dictionaries include www.lectlaw.com and www.thelawoffice.com.

Conference Proceedings

For topics that are too specific or narrow or new to get detailed treatment in more permanent form, papers presented at topical conferences are a useful source of information. Papers are often provided to conference participants in printed form and, more and more, on CD-ROM. Conference organizers often tape the oral presentations and sell the audiotapes. A narrow topic such as a lawyer's perspective on practice before a specific tribunal, or the tribunal chair's description of recent developments, may be the subject of a conference presentation that is recorded on paper, CD-ROM, and/or audiotape.

COMBINED PRIMARY AND SECONDARY SOURCES

Annotated statutes and statute annotators, statute citators, and legal casebooks combine primary and secondary sources.

Annotated Statutes and Statute Annotators

An annotated statute is a book that contains the full text of a statute as well as section-by-section commentary on the meaning of that particular statute and citations of court or tribunal decisions that have interpreted each section of the statute. Examples are Maciura and Steinecke, *The Annotated Statutory Powers Procedure Act*; Libman, *The Annotated Contraventions Act*; Keeshan and Steeves, *The Annotated Federal and Ontario Interpretation Acts*; and Greenspan and Rosenberg, *Martin's Annual Criminal Code*.

A statute annotator, although similar in name, is a little different from an annotated statute. It contains all the statutes of a particular jurisdiction such as a province, with a list of cases that have interpreted each provision of each of the statutes.

Statute Citators

Statute citators list cases that have interpreted provisions of statutes. *Canadian Statute Citations*, part of the *Canadian Abridgement* series, lists every section of each federal statute and all provincial statutes, together with the citations of court decisions that have interpreted each of them.

Citations for recent cases that have interpreted provisions in statutes of Canada are in the *Canada Statute Citator*, and recent cases that have interpreted Ontario statutes are on the *Ontario Statute Citator* CD-ROM. For federal and Ontario decisions before 1990, it is necessary to look in earlier paper editions of the citators.

Casebooks

Casebooks contain lengthy extracts from important court decisions together with commentary on them and references to other related cases. They are generally more useful as a teaching tool than as a research tool.

WEB-BASED RESEARCH

The primary and secondary sources of legal information described above can all be found in print, and in some cases on CD-ROM, but most of the same information can now be found much faster, and sometimes at less expense, on the Internet.

Search Engines and Directories

If you know the URL of a particular Web site that contains the kind of information you are looking for, you may access the site on your computer. However, if you know the topic you want to research but don't know which Web sites contain the information, you can find relevant sites through search engines and directories. You type in the keywords or phrases you are looking for, and the search engine or directory produces links to the pages of Web sites that contain these words or phrases.

GENERAL SEARCH ENGINES

General search engines that produce good results are Google, www.google.com; Lycos, www.lycos.com; Excite, www.excite.com; Infoseek/GO, www.go.com; and Alta Vista, www.altavista.com.

LEGAL SEARCH ENGINES, DIRECTORIES, AND WEB SITES

There are two kinds of legal directories, search engines, and Web sites: commercial search facilities to which users must subscribe and pay a fee, and free search facilities.

Commercial Search Engines and Directories

Among the most comprehensive and established commercial database directories are LexisNexis/Butterworths, which incorporates Quicklaw, and eCarswell/Westlaw. Subscribers to these online legal research services pay a fee for access. In some cases subscribers can choose between a monthly flat rate or an hourly rate for actual search time. Rates vary according to the number of users in the law firm or company that subscribes.

Quicklaw/LexisNexis/Butterworths

LexisNexis Canada (formerly Quicklaw), www.lexisnexis.ca, focuses on Canadian information sources, although it also contains some foreign information, particularly from the United States and the United Kingdom. It has hundreds of legal databases containing court and tribunal decisions, statutes and regulations, newsletters, law journals, papers, articles, legal texts, and legal directories. LexisNexis, www.lexisnexis.com, is similar, but with a focus on US law, although it also contains some Canadian information.

ECarswell/Westlaw

ECarswell, www.carswell.com/ecarswell/index.html, offers topical case law databases integrated with legislation and commentary, including case citations and statute citations.

Westlaw, http://directory.westlaw.com, offers US, Australian, UK and other foreign law databases containing cases, statutes and administrative agency materials, law reviews and other periodic literature, legal forms, and legal news.

CCH Canadian

CCH Canadian, www.cch.ca, offers topical newsletters online. Its Canadian Legislative Pulse provides the current status and recent progress of bills from all Canadian jurisdictions.

Free Legal Search Engines, Directories, and Web Sites

Much of the information available on commercial Web sites is also available on free Web sites, so it is often possible to avoid paying fees for information such as court and tribunal decisions, legislation, and some law journal articles.

Some Web sites consist mainly of links to other Web sites and have very little information. Other Web sites contain a wide variety of legal information, including statutes, case law, and law journal articles.

The following search engines and directories link to a variety of legal Web sites:

- Lawrunner, which is powered by AltaVista and offered by the Internet Legal Resource Guide Web site; Bar-eX, www.bar-ex.com; FindLaw LawCrawler, http://lawcrawler.findlaw.com; Access to Justice Network (ACJNet); and Lexum (discussed below).

- ACJNet Canada, www.acjnet.org, provides access to Canadian legislative materials by jurisdiction, answers to frequently asked questions about law in Canada and links to CanLII and the Web site of the Canadian Department of Justice. It also carries news releases about law and justice.

- Australasian Legal information Institute Database, www.austlii.edu.au, provides access to primary legal materials such as decisions of Australian courts and tribunals and most Australian state and federal legislation, as well as secondary Australian legal materials. It also has links to databases containing cases and legislation from New Zealand, the United Kingdom, and Ireland (BAILII); Hong Kong (HKLII); and various Pacific islands (PacLII).

- British and Irish Legal Information Institute, www.bailii.org, is a source of British and Irish cases and legislation with links to free full-text legal journals and other journal article abstracts. It also contains links to other world collections including Australasia, Canada, Hong Kong, and Pacific Islands.

- Canadian Legal Information Institute, www.canlii.org, contains the full text of Canadian federal, provincial, and territorial statutes and regulations; and over 115,000 court decisions, tribunal decisions, and administrative agency rulings. The information is organized by jurisdiction with hyperlinks between case law and legislation.

- Canada Legal, www.canadalegal.com, is a directory of Canadian legal resources on the Internet.

- Catalaw, www.catalaw.com, provides links to a variety of Canadian, US, UK, and Australian legal Web sites and directories.

- Cornell University's Legal Information Institute, www.law.cornell.edu/uscode, provides searchable full-text access to the *United States Code*, a compilation of all federal statutes passed by Congress and signed by the president (or passed over the president's veto). This includes the *Administrative Procedures Act*, which codifies rules that federal agencies must follow for rule making and holding hearings.

- Court Web sites: Some courts also maintain Web sites containing all their decisions as well as other information such as their rules of practice and practice directions.

Supreme Court Web sites:

– The Supreme Court of Canada, www.scc-csc.gc.ca, provides access to hundreds of decisions, the progress of cases currently before the court, and instant e-mail updates as new decisions are released.

– The US Supreme Court, www.supremecourtus.gov, provides information about the court, its procedures, and recent opinions.

Provincial and territorial court Web sites:

– Alberta, www.albertacourts.ab.ca
– British Columbia, www.courts.gov.bc.ca
– Manitoba, www.manitobacourts.mb.ca
– New Brunswick, www.canlii.org/nb/cas/nbca/
– Newfoundland and Labrador, www.canlii.org/nl/cas/nlca/
– Nova Scotia, www.courts.ns.ca
– Ontario, www.ontariocourts.on.ca/appeal.htm
– Prince Edward Island, www.canlii.org/pe/index_en.html
– Quebec, www.tribunaux.qc.ca/mjq_en/c-appel/index-ca.html
– Saskatchewan, www.sasklawcourts.ca
– Nunavut, www.canlii.org/nu/cas/nuca/
– Northwest Territories, www.justice.gov.nt.ca/dbtw-wpd/nwtjqbe.htm
– Yukon, www.canlii.org/yk/cas/ykca/

• Findlaw, www.findlaw.com (see Lawcrawler, below).

• Global Legal Information Network, www.loc.gov/law/lguide/index.html, Guide to Law Online, prepared by the US Law Library of Congress, is an annotated guide to sources of information on government and law available online. The site includes links to other sites for legal information.

• Internet Legal Resource Guide, www.ilrg.com, lists legal indexes and search engines as well as law journals and publications available online.

• Jurist Canada, www.jurist.law.utoronto.ca, contains legal news, abstracts of articles from Canadian law journals, first chapters of new law books, and papers published by Canadian law professors.

• Jurist Legal Education Network, http://jurist.law.pitt.edu, contains legal news, US federal statutes, rules, codes, and case law, as well as state regulations.

• Lawcrawler, http://lawcrawler.findlaw.com, contains legal news; US federal legislation and Supreme Court decisions; US state legislation and state court decisions; and information on legal subjects such as constitutional law, patents and trademarks, criminal law, and labour law.

• LawGuru, www.lawguru.com, is a US site that provides access to more than 400 legal search engines and databases. It contains over 4,000 legal questions with answers.

• Legal Journals on the Web, www.infolibrary.yorku.ca, is part of the York University Law Library and contains a list of full-text journals that are accessible online free of charge.

• Lexum, www.lexum.umontreal.ca, contains statutes and regulations, case law from courts and tribunals, periodicals, Canada–US treaties, and other international law resources.

- World Wide Legal Information Association, www.wwlia.org, contains a legal dictionary and material from the United States, Canada, Australia, New Zealand, and the United Kingdom.

APPENDIX SUMMARY

Understanding the functions and structures of administrative bodies, and preparing to advocate a position to them, involves finding rules, policies, and guidelines the bodies have published and the decisions they have issued. It also requires finding decisions of the courts that have interpreted the powers and duties of these agencies. This information is in a variety of places, ranging from the agency offices to the Internet. Publications include both primary and secondary sources. Primary sources are publications that contain the full text of policies, guidelines, rules, regulations, statutes, agency rulings, and court decisions. Secondary sources contain commentary, analysis, and explanations of these rules and rulings. This information is often available from the government, from agencies themselves, and from commercial publishers of legal materials. The information may be found on paper, on audiotapes and videotapes, on CD-ROM, and on the Internet. Some of it is costly, but often the same material is available free of charge online.

KEY TERMS

annotation   a note or comment on a court or tribunal decision or a provision of a statute, regulation, or other rule or guideline, intended to explain its meaning

bill   in parliamentary and legislative practice, a version of a statute, or in municipal practice a version of a bylaw, introduced in the legislative assembly to be passed as a law

case citator   *see* citator

citation   information identifying where a statute, regulation, bylaw, court or tribunal decision, or article is published

cite   as a noun, colloquial for "citation" (see above); as a verb, to refer to a case or law as authority for a proposition such as a particular interpretation of a law

citator   "a research book containing lists of references or cites that serve two main functions: first and foremost, to help you assess the current validity of a case statute or other law; and secondarily, to provide you with leads to additional laws" (West's *Legal Thesaurus/Dictionary*)

law journal   a periodic publication containing scholarly articles about legal issues, often discussing the significance of laws and court and tribunal decisions

law reporter   a periodic publication containing either the full text or a summary of decisions of courts and tribunals as they are released

law reports   *see* law reporter

reporter   *see* law reporter

statute citator   *see* citator

REVIEW QUESTIONS

1. Explain the difference between a primary source and a secondary source of information about the law.

2. What information is found in the citation for a court or tribunal decision?

3. Where would you look for the full text of a statute, regulation, or court or tribunal decision other than a paper publication?

4. What is the difference between a law journal and a law reporter?

5. Name one journal and one law reporter that specialize in publishing information about administrative law.

6. What is the difference between a case citator and a statute citator?

7. What is the difference between an annotated statute and a statute annotator?

8. If you want to know how courts or tribunals have interpreted a specific word or phrase found in a statute, where would you look?

9. What kinds of legal information are available on the Internet?

10. What kinds of legal information are available on CD-ROM?

EXERCISES

1. Using any of the sources discussed in this appendix, list the statutes under which the Ontario Municipal Board operates. Describe in one paragraph for each statute the functions the board carries out under that statute.

2. Find the following cases on paper and electronically, and explain how you located them without having a citation:

   a. *Spy Hill v. Bradshaw*

   b. *Crocock v. Orion Insurance Co.*

   c. *Morisette v. The Maggie.*

3. Ontario's *Crown Agency Act* contains the following definition of "Crown agency":

   In this Act, "Crown agency" means a board, commission, railway, public utility, university, manufactory, company or agency, owned, controlled or operated by Her Majesty in right of Ontario, or by the Government of Ontario, or under the authority of the Legislature or the Lieutenant Governor in Council.

   Find three court or tribunal decisions that have considered whether a particular body falls within this definition, and list them, including their full citations. Explain where you looked for this information and where you found these cases.

4. List five law journals that have published articles dealing with administrative law in the past five years, and include the full citation of each article.

5. The word "control" is used in many legal contexts; for example, statutes provide that it is an offence to have care or control of a vehicle while impaired, and insurance policies sometimes provide that the insurance

coverage is in effect only while property or premises are under the custody or control of the insured person.

Find five cases that interpret the meaning of "control" in different legal contexts. List the cases with full citations and explain how you located them.

WORKS CITED

Sara Blake, *Administrative Law in Canada*, 3d ed. (Toronto: Butterworths, 2001).

Donald J.M. Brown and John M. Evans, *Judicial Review of Administrative Action in Canada* (Toronto: Canvasback) (looseleaf).

Daphne Dukelow, *The Dictionary of Canadian Law*, 3d ed. (Toronto: Carswell, 2004).

B.A. Garner, ed., *Black's Law Dictionary*, 7th ed. (St. Paul, MN: West Group, 1999).

Edward L. Greenspan and Marc Rosenberg, *Martin's Annual Criminal Code* (Aurora, ON: Canada Law Book) (annual).

Laverne A. Jacobs and Thomas S. Kuttner, "Discovering What Tribunals Do: Tribunals Before the Courts" (2002) vol. 81 *Canadian Bar Review* 616.

David P. Jones and Anne S. deVillars, *Principles of Administrative Law*, 4th ed. (Toronto: Carswell, 2004).

M. David Keeshan and Valerie M. Steeves, *The 1996 Annotated Federal and Ontario Interpretation Acts* (Scarborough, ON: Carswell, 1995).

Rick Libman, *The Annotated Contraventions Act* (Toronto: Carswell, 2004).

Robert Macaulay and James Sprague, *Practice and Procedure Before Administrative Tribunals* (Toronto: Carswell) (looseleaf).

Julie Maciura and Richard Steinecke, *The Annotated Statutory Powers Procedure Act* (Aurora, ON: Canada Law Book, 1998).

David Mullan, *Administrative Law*, 5th ed. (Toronto: Emond Montgomery, 2003).

John B. Saunders, *Words and Phrases Legally Defined*, 3d ed. (London: Butterworths, 1988).

William A. Tilleman, ed., *Dictionary of Environmental Law and Science* (Toronto: Emond Montgomery, 1994).

John A. Yogis, *Canadian Law Dictionary*, 5th ed. (Hauppauge, NY: Barrons, 2003).

FURTHER READING

Suzanne Gordon and Sherifa Elkhadem, *The Law Workbook: Developing Skills for Legal Research and Writing* (Toronto: Emond Montgomery, 2001).

Margaret Kerr, *Legal Research: Step by Step* (Toronto: Emond Montgomery, 1998).

McGill Law Journal, *The Canadian Guide to Uniform Legal Citation*, 5th ed. (Toronto: Carswell, 2002).

Web Sites for Legal Research Techniques and Tips

Best Guide to Canadian Legal Research, http://legalresearch.org.

Internet Legal Resource Guide, www.ilrg.com.

Doing Legal Research in Canada, www.llrx.com.

LawGuru, www.lawguru.com (contains Internet legal research tips on its legal research metasearch page).

The Great Library, www.library.lsuc.on.ca (maintained by the Great Library of the Law Society of Upper Canada; reviews legal Web sites and contains legal research suggestions).

Quebec Law, www.bibl.ulaval.ca (a guide for researching Quebec law, in English).

Selected Administrative Agencies: Their Mandates, Powers, and Procedures

THE CANADIAN HUMAN RIGHTS COMMISSION AND THE CANADIAN HUMAN RIGHTS TRIBUNAL

The *Canadian Human Rights Act*[1] implements government policy in relation to a single subject matter—the prevention of discrimination—by creating two separate agencies, a regulatory agency and a tribunal. This is an example of an attempt to separate investigatory, prosecutorial, and adjudicative functions that can conflict when carried out within a single agency.

But this is separation with a twist. Even though the bodies are designed to be relatively independent of each other, the legislators have given the Canadian Human Rights Commission, which appears as a party before the Canadian Human Right Tribunal, a limited ability to make regulations that dictate to the tribunal how it must interpret the Act.

The commission is part of a legislative scheme for identifying and remedying discrimination based on sex, race, age, and religion. The commission is responsible, among other things, for maintaining close liaison with similar bodies in the provinces, for considering recommendations from public interest groups and any other bodies, and for developing programs for public education.

The commission also has a law-making function. Parliament has delegated to it the power to make binding regulations, as long as they are consistent with the Act itself.

When establishing policies to implement the Act, the commission issues a draft, then carries out a formal consultation with interested parties. It then revises the draft policies, taking into account the feedback it has received.

---

1 RSC 1985, c. H-6.

The commission also employs investigators and investigates complaints of discrimination. The investigators report their findings to the commission. If the commission finds that there is sufficient evidence to support the allegations, it will try to negotiate a settlement between the complainant and the alleged discriminator.

If the alleged discriminator denies the allegations and refuses to provide redress, the commission requests the president of the tribunal to appoint a panel of tribunal members to hold a hearing and determine whether there has been discrimination and, if so, what sanctions should be imposed.

The tribunal is largely independent of the commission and of the government. It has a different president from the commission and different members.

The tribunal's function is adjudicative; it has no policy-making function. It conducts hearings into complaints that have been referred to it by the commission. It is empowered to find facts, to interpret and apply the law to the facts, and to award appropriate remedies, such as ordering federally regulated companies to pay women the same salaries as men for work of equal value.

The tribunal operates in a manner similar to a court. The parties present evidence, call and cross-examine witnesses, and make submissions on how the law should be applied to the facts. The commission is one of the parties to the hearing. Its staff lawyers act as prosecutors, who call the commission's investigators as witnesses to prove the allegations of discrimination.

Although the tribunal is largely independent of the commission, it is not completely independent. The Act authorizes the Commission to issue "guidelines" (which are actually binding regulations) that dictate to the tribunal how it must interpret the Act in specific classes of cases. For example, the Equal Wages Guidelines tell the tribunal how it must interpret certain provisions of the Act relating to pay equity.

THE ONTARIO WORKPLACE SAFETY AND INSURANCE BOARD AND THE WORKPLACE SAFETY AND INSURANCE APPEALS TRIBUNAL

The Ontario Workplace Safety and Insurance Board (WSIB) and the Workplace Safety and Insurance Appeals Tribunal (WSIAT) are two agencies established under one Ontario statute, the *Workplace Safety and Insurance Act, 1997*.[2] The Act creates a regime that is intended to provide a regular income to workers who have been injured in the workplace or who suffer from a work-related illness and to provide such workers with medical and other forms of treatment (known as "rehabilitation") that will help them recover from their illness or injury and return to work.

This system, better known by its former name, Workers' Compensation, operates as an insurance scheme. The WSIB is funded by premiums paid by employers. Like property insurance or car insurance premiums, these premiums vary according to the risk level in each industry and the safety record of the individual company. The WSIAT, on the other hand, is funded by the government.

The WSIB acts both as a regulatory agency, with a public education component, and as a tribunal. When a worker makes a claim for income support or rehabilitation services, WSIB staff investigate the validity of the claim and make an

---

2 SO 1990, c. 16, sched. A.

initial decision whether to allow or deny it. If assistance is denied, the worker can request a review by agency staff. Conversely, employers have the right to challenge the claim on the basis that the injury or illness is imagined or resulted from an activity or exposure outside the employer's workplace. Employers can contest claims because successful claims can raise an employer's insurance rate. The WSIB does not hold formal hearings, but collects medical information from the worker's doctors, may have its own doctors examine the worker, and receives written submissions from the worker and the employer. Once all the decision-making levels within the WSIB have been exhausted, the worker or the employer may appeal the WSIB's decision to the WSIAT.

Although the WSIAT holds court-like hearings, it is not bound by the *Statutory Powers Procedure Act*[3] (SPPA) and its hearings are inquisitorial rather than adversarial. That is, the worker and the employer are parties to the appeal and may present evidence and cross-examine witnesses, but most of the evidence is collected and presented by WSIAT staff. Another reason the process is inquisitorial rather than adversarial is that there is often only one party. When a worker claims entitlement that has been refused by the WSIB, the employer often does not participate. In some cases the employer is no longer in business. Although the WSIB made the decision that is being appealed, the WSIB is not usually a party before the WSIAT, although it has the right to appear.

The WSIAT is largely independent of the WSIB, but the statute requires the WSIAT to follow WSIB policies where applicable. For example, if the WSIB forms a policy that illnesses that arise purely from stress, and not from any physical act or exposure to some noxious substance, are compensable only under certain narrow circumstances (for example, where the worker suffered stress as a result of seeing the death of another worker in an industrial accident), the WSIAT may not broaden the circumstances in which it will compensate for stress. This is a change from the previous practice, where the WSIAT, which did not share the WSIB's interest in reducing employers' premiums, often recognized illnesses or injuries that the WSIB refused to recognize.

Workers and employers may represent themselves or retain lawyers or agents to represent them in dealing with the WSIB and the WSIAT. However, workers can get advice and assistance as well as representation from the Office of the Worker Adviser, an agency of the Ministry of Labour. Similarly, another agency of the ministry, the Office of the Employer Adviser, provides advice and representation to employers with fewer than 100 employees. Larger employers must represent themselves, hire their own representatives, or rely on the results of WSIB and WSIAT investigations and presentation of the case by agency staff before the WSIAT.

SOCIAL BENEFITS TRIBUNAL

In Ontario, financial assistance is available from the government to individuals who are unable to support themselves through two statutes. Under the *Ontario Works Act, 1997*,[4] the Ontario government provides financial assistance (known as

---

3 RSO 1990, c. S.22.

4 SO 1997, c. 25, sched. A.

"social assistance" or "welfare") to individuals who are unemployed, provided that they show they are attempting to obtain employment. The Act is administered by "service managers" designated by the Ministry of Community and Social Services. These service managers are usually local municipalities of district social services area boards, which represent several municipalities.

The *Ontario Disability Support Program Act, 1997*[5] provides income support for people with disabilities, including children with severe disabilities. It is administered by the Ministry of Community and Social Services.

An individual who is refused financial assistance or whose financial assistance has been cancelled, revoked, or put on hold, or who is not satisfied with the amount of social assistance granted, can appeal the decision to the Social Benefits Tribunal (SBT), but only after applying for an internal review. The internal review must be requested within 10 days after receiving the unfavourable decision. A different staff member in the office that made the unfavourable decision conducts this review.

Thirty days after an unfavourable internal review decision, or 40 days later if no decision has been made within 10 days after the review request, the individual may appeal the official's decision to the SBT. The appeal can be launched using an appeal form that is available at the office that made the unfavourable decision, from the SBT head office in Toronto, at community legal clinics, or online.

The SBT is separate from the Ministry of Community and Social Services and the local offices that administer these financial support programs. It is based in Toronto, but its members travel throughout the province and hold hearings in the area where the applicants live. Tribunal hearings are similar to those of a court, but less formal. The SPPA applies to its hearings.

The parties in an SBT hearing are the applicant and the office that made the unfavourable decision. Parties are entitled to be represented by lawyers or agents, but a representative may not also be a witness. Staff lawyers or community legal workers employed by community legal clinics established to provide legal assistance to the poor often represent applicants free of charge.

The applicant is required to send any documents he or she intends to rely on to both the SBT and the agency that made the unfavourable decision at least 20 days before the hearing. These documents often include medical and psychiatric reports, drug lists, prescriptions and drug receipts, doctors' letters, separation and child custody agreements, immigration papers, and job search lists. The agency that made the unfavourable decision is also a party and may send the decision maker to testify, call witnesses, and cross-examine the applicant. Most hearings last one and a half hours or less.

If an applicant notifies the SBT that he or she does not speak English, the tribunal will provide a professional translator. The tribunal will not permit friends or relatives of the applicant to translate.

Either party may request the tribunal to reconsider its decision by submitting an application for reconsideration, including reasons why the tribunal should hear the appeal again, within 30 days after the tribunal's original decision.

The statutes provide for an appeal to the Divisional Court on questions of law.

---

5 SO 1997, c. 25, sched. B.

PATENTED MEDICINE PRICES REVIEW BOARD

Having access to prescription drugs can be a matter of life and death. One way the government of Canada ensures that drugs are affordable is to limit the prices that drug manufacturers can charge.

The government has established an agency to set the price of new drugs. The Patented Medicine Prices Review Board was established under Canada's *Patent Act*.[6] The five members of the board are appointed by the federal Cabinet, but are nominated by the federal minister of health. Under the Act, the minister may appoint an advisory panel consisting of representatives of provincial health ministers, representatives of consumer groups, and representatives of the pharmaceutical industry to recommend suitable candidates for the board.

Once a new drug has been shown to be safe and effective and is approved for sale in Canada, but before the manufacturer can sell it, the person or company that holds the patent on the medicine (usually the manufacturer) must notify the board of its intention to sell the product and provide information about the intended selling price, the costs of making and marketing the drug, and its selling price in other countries. The board can also order disclosure of the company's revenues from selling other medicines in Canada and its Canadian expenditures on research and development of medicines. Negotiations then begin between the patent holder and the board over what price the manufacturer will be permitted to charge.

The board can also review whether the price of a drug already available in Canada is excessive.

The board's mandate is to determine whether the selling price of a drug is excessive. If it decides the price is excessive, it can order the manufacturer to sell the drug at a lower price, or to reduce the price of another drug to offset the higher price. The board can also order the company to pay money to the government to offset its profits.

In deciding whether the price of a drug is excessive, the board is permitted to consider the following factors:

- the prices at which the drug has been sold;
- how this price compares with the price of comparable medicines in the same market;
- the price at which the drug and comparable drugs have been sold in other countries;
- changes in the consumer price index; and
- any other factors specified by regulations.

In reviewing these factors, the board has guidelines to determine whether the price is excessive. For example, if the proposed price of a new drug is higher than the highest-priced existing drug used to treat the same disease, the board will reduce the price of the new drug to a price similar to that of the existing drug. The board also tries to set prices at the median charged for the same drug in other industrialized countries. Drug companies may apply to the board for annual price increases, but these are limited to increases in the consumer price index.

---

6   RSC 1985, c. P-4.

The board has authority to hire staff as well as to retain experts with technical or specialized knowledge. The staff monitor pricing practices and investigate whether drug companies are charging excessive prices. If they conclude that a price is excessive, they prepare a report setting out their findings. They submit this report to the chair of the board, who decides whether it is in the public interest to hold a hearing into any allegations of excessive pricing.

The board is not permitted to make an order to reduce the price of a drug or compensate the government for excessive profits, unless it first holds a hearing at which the patent holder is given the opportunity to challenge the proposed order. The hearing must be open to the public, except where disclosure of information would cause the patent holder or others "specific, direct and substantial harm" (s. 86(1) of the *Patent Act*). The board must give notice of the hearing to the federal minister of industry and provincial health ministers, all of whom are entitled to participate in the hearing.

If the chair of the board determines that a hearing is warranted, he or she convenes a panel of board members to adjudicate the matter. Under the board's rules of practice and procedure, the staff are responsible for presenting the case to the hearing panel. The staff have a lawyer to present the case, and the hearing panel has its own lawyer.

Through their lawyer, the board staff call witnesses and present documentary evidence, cross-examine witnesses for the drug company, and make arguments on procedural issues as well as on what the outcome of the hearing should be.

The Act does not provide for an appeal of the board's orders, but at common law judicial review would be available to a party who alleges that the board has exceeded its jurisdiction or followed unfair procedures.

Environmental Appeal Board Procedure for Hearing

[Note: words in italics are for direction of the chair and are not to be spoken.]

Good morning (afternoon), this is a hearing by the Environmental Appeal Board under the Environmental Protection Act (the Ontario Water Resources Act) (the Pesticides Act).

The subject matter of this hearing is an application …

(Read second paragraph of the style of cause in the Notice for Hearing.)

(Introduce Board members)

On my right is …, and on my left is …, who are members of the Board. My name is …, and I will be chairing this hearing today.

(Independence of the Board)

For those of you who have not appeared before the Board on a previous occasion, I wish to advise you that we are an independent Board which is required to hear applications under various environmental Acts. Although the members of this Board are appointed by the Government of Ontario, we are not employees of the Ministry of the Environment and Energy or any other government department. We have no knowledge of the matters in issue in this application except for the decision that is being appealed, the applicant's notice of appeal setting out the grounds for the appeal, and the notice entitled Appointment for Hearing (and)

(Read list of the other materials you have received— if any—along with the notice.)

The Board can uphold the Director's decision/order, amend it, revoke it, or substitute a different decision/order.

(Parties to the proceedings)

The Board will now address the matter of parties. The Director of the Minister of the Environment and Energy (Public Health Unit) and the applicant *(name the applicant)* are automatically parties to this proceeding. The Board has the authority to specify additional persons as parties to this hearing. Any person may give testimony under oath or affirmation that is relevant to the hearing, but this person does <u>not</u> need to be specified as a party to do so.

A person who is made a party has the additional right to cross-examine witnesses, to call other people as witnesses, and to make statements and arguments. In addition, parties have a right to appeal the Board's decision to the Minister of the Environment and Energy or to the Court.

First, may I please have the name and address of counsel or the agent representing the applicant.

(Chairman should make sure counsel or agent states on the record that he/she is representing the applicant.)

*(Where the applicant is **not represented** by a lawyer or agent, state the following)*

Madam/Sir: You do not need to have a lawyer or agent to represent you at this hearing, but I would like to know if you intend to represent yourself or if a lawyer or agent is representing you?

(If they respond that they have a lawyer (or agent)—ask why their lawyer (or agent) is not present today. If they state they wish to be represented by a lawyer (or agent)— ask why they do not have a lawyer or agent present.)

Now, who is representing the Director of the Ministry of the Environment and Energy (Public Health Unit) at this hearing? Would you please give us your name and address and the name of the Director you act for in this matter. Thank you very much.

Are there any other people here today who wish to testify or be specified as parties at this hearing? All persons who have not been called as witnesses by either the applicant or the Ministry of the Environment and Energy (Public Health Unit) and who wish to testify, or wish to file documents, or to cross-examine witnesses, or to make a statement should identify themselves now please ...

(As each person responds, ask:)

Would you please state your name and address. Do you wish to be named as a party? Why?

(When each person has given you their reason to be a party, ask the MoE and the applicant if they have any objection to this person being named a party. You should get their consent, if possible, before naming any person as a party. If either the MoE or the applicant objects, you—as the Board—have authority under Section 24 of the Environmental Protection Act to specify parties.)

The Board recognizes Ms/Miss/Mrs./Mr. … as a party to these proceedings.

The procedure for this hearing will be as follows:

All parties will be requested to make an opening statement. It would be beneficial if the parties could outline what they think will be the issues in this case and make a brief summary of the evidence they intend to call and any other matters they think will assist the Board in conducting this hearing. It may be helpful if you advise the Board of the names of the witnesses you wish to call and give some estimation of the time required to present your case.

All witnesses must give their evidence under oath or affirmation.

The Director from the Ministry of the Environment and Energy (Public Health Unit) will present its case first. The applicant and any other parties will be allowed to cross-examine any witnesses called by the Ministry (Public Health Unit). Upon completion of the cross-examination of each witness, the Ministry (Public Health Unit) shall be entitled to re-examine the witness on matters which arose for the first time during the cross-examination of the witness.

Environmental Appeal Board Guidelines for Technical and Opinion Evidence

THE PURPOSE OF THESE GUIDELINES

Technical staff, advisors, consultants and "expert" witnesses routinely give scientific and technical information and their professional opinions in reports and testimony on important issues which the Board must resolve. The opinions given usually purport to be the independent professional judgment of the advisor or witness, based on his or her considerable experience and training. The Board relies on the professional integrity and ethics of these witnesses.

The purpose of these guidelines is to assist parties, their representatives, and their witnesses who will give scientific, technical, and opinion evidence to prepare for, and present, evidence to the Environmental Appeal Board. The Board seeks to ensure the reliability of scientific and technical evidence and opinion evidence provided to the Board. Comprehensive and reliable evidence will promote efficiency and fairness in the Board's process, decrease cost and delay, and make the hearing process less adversarial.

TECHNICAL AND SCIENTIFIC EVIDENCE

Many witnesses, particularly government employees, appear before the Board to give evidence of scientific and technical observations, tests, measurements, and estimates. They are able to collect this information because of special training and experience. While these witnesses are often not considered "experts" who interpret scientific and technical evidence and provide opinions, they collect, compile, and to some extent interpret, information that is essential to the Board's understanding of the issues and often forms the basis for "expert" opinion evidence. In these guidelines, these witnesses are referred to as "technical witnesses" and the scientific and technical information they convey is referred to as "technical evidence."

OPINION EVIDENCE

Generally, lay witnesses, including technical staff of companies and government agencies, may only state facts, that is, observations made with their physical senses, or in the case of persons with appropriate training, observations made with specialized equipment, for example, taking samples and analyzing them in a laboratory and recording the results. They may not give opinions about the significance of the results of such measurements for environmental quality or human health.

To give opinion evidence, a witness must have specialized education, training or experience that qualifies him or her to reliably interpret scientific or technical information or to express opinions about matters for which untrained or inexperienced persons cannot provide reliable opinions. Such matters often include whether pollution has caused or is likely to cause significant harm to air, water, or soil. Such witnesses are often called "expert witnesses." In these guidelines, we refer to them as "opinion witnesses."

THE ROLE OF THE TECHNICAL WITNESS

The Board expects the witness giving technical or scientific evidence to remain within his or her area of competence. The witness should not attempt to interpret the meaning or significance of tests, observations and measurements unless qualified to do so. The witness should disclose in advance to other parties all measurements, tests, observations, and data relating to the issues about which he or she will give evidence, and disclose in examination-in-chief all information relevant to the issues before the Board, regardless of which party the information appears to favour. Observations, tests or measurements that do not appear to support the position of the party for whom the witness is testifying should also be stated. For example, a lab result should not be withheld because the witness considers it inaccurate or unreliable. Rather, the witness should disclose the result in pre-hearing disclosure and during evidence in chief and should explain why he or she does not rely on it.

THE ROLE OF OPINION WITNESSES

Opinion evidence from a properly qualified "expert" witness should be based on accurate facts, reliable estimates, and accepted or tested techniques or methods of investigation, measurement, and analysis.

The need for guidelines for opinion evidence and for opinion witnesses to have a proper understanding of their role was commented on in *National Justice Compania Naviera v. Prudential Assurance Co. Ltd. ("The Ikarian Reefer"),* reported at [1993] 2 Lloyd's Law Reports 68. This English court decision listed the duties and responsibilities of expert witnesses in civil cases (at pp. 81-2) after noting that despite considerable effort on the part of the judge to reduce the scope of the expert evidence and the length of the trial, a great deal of unnecessary time was nevertheless taken by this evidence. He attributed this to a misunderstanding on the part of some expert witnesses as to their proper role in the hearing process.

This decision was cited with approval by the Ontario Court (General Division) in *Perricone v. Baldassarra,* [1994] OJ 2199, action 92-CU-60340-CM, at pages 14, 17 and 18. The Ontario Court made the following observations on the role of an expert and the use of an expert's report:

When the report is overwhelmingly directed to advancing the position of the person engaging the expert's report, the report must be viewed accordingly. … [The doctor's report] does not contain the requisite indicia of evenhandedness from an expert which, to me, is crucial in the discharge of the function of an expert. … It is a role which is prescribed and, if the person rendering the evidence assumes the role of advocate, he or she can no longer be viewed as an expert in the legally correct sense; instead, he or she must be viewed as advocating the case of a party with the attendant diminishment in the credibility of the report. Expert opinions guide the court but they do not determine the matters which are to be determined by the court. I am not the first to express these concerns about the use of experts' reports.

These guidelines include several duties and responsibilities from the *Ikarian Reefer* decision, and attempt to provide direction to technical and opinion witnesses with respect to the Board's expectations of their conduct and performance. Witnesses should also be familiar with the Board's Rules of Practice relating to expert witnesses. These are available from the Board and should be provided to the witnesses by the party calling the person as a witness or the party's representative.

THE ROLE OF THE BOARD

The decisions that the Board must make involve the public interest and have serious and far-reaching environmental consequences. These decisions must be based on a balanced record, composed of nothing less than totally accurate and reliable technical information and professional opinions, presented in an expeditious hearing process. All parties and their representatives and witnesses have a responsibility to contribute to such a balanced record in an expeditious fashion to assist the Board to fulfil its duty. They are expected to make every effort to comply fully with these guidelines. The Board expects that lawyers and other representatives will provide appropriate direction to witnesses to achieve this result.

Representatives, technical witnesses, and opinion witnesses who are retained to advance the interests of their clients are expected to treat the Board with the same courtesy and respect that they would routinely demonstrate when appearing before Judges in Ontario courts.

1. PRACTICE BEFORE THE BOARD

   (a) The Board expects the opinion witnesses to provide it with assistance by way of qualified, relevant opinions and accurate information in relation to matters within his or her expertise. Objectivity and impartiality are necessary to assist the Board in making its decision.

   (b) Evidence that is influenced by the special interests of a party may be received and considered, but the Board may give this evidence little or no weight.

   (c) The witness should express an opinion to the Board only when the opinion is based on adequate knowledge and sound conviction. The witness should be reluctant to accept an assignment to provide evidence for use by the Board if the terms of reference of the assignment do not allow the witness to carry out the investigations and obtain the information necessary to provide such an opinion. A witness who accepts an assignment under these circumstances should advise the Board of the limitations that the terms of reference place on his or her ability to provide the information necessary to assist the Board in making a sound decision or to give informed opinions.

(d) Technical evidence and opinion evidence should be, and should be seen to be, the independent product of the witness uninfluenced as to form and content by the exigencies of litigation, the particular dispute before the Board, and the interests of the witness' client.

(e) The witness must never assume the role of an advocate for a party. Argument and advocacy should be left to counsel or agents presenting the party's case. This does not preclude the vigorous advancement of strongly held scientific or other professional opinions or prevent a duly qualified witness who is also a party from advancing technical and opinion evidence.

(f) The witness has a duty to change his or her opinion where circumstances, such as the receipt of new information, require it. If at any time before the Board issues its final decision, the witness changes his or her view on a material matter for any reason, particularly after having read the reports or listened to the evidence of witnesses for other parties, the change in the information and/or opinion should be communicated to the other parties and the Board without delay. Where reports or documents prepared by the witness contain errors or information which has changed, this must be promptly identified.

(g) However, the witness must not change his or her opinion or change or withhold information to suit the position taken by the party that has retained or employs him/her, or its representative. For example, the witness must not in his or her final report alter the contents or conclusions of draft reports in any way that reduces the accuracy and comprehensiveness of the report to suit a party or its counsel or other representative. Pertinent information in a draft report should not be omitted from the final report or expressed in a different manner to make it appear less or more significant than the witness considers it to be.

2. In preparing reports to be used by the witness's employer or client in determining the issues to be raised and the employer or client's position on those issues and for use as evidence, and in testifying before the Board, the witness has the following duties:

(a) It is the responsibility of the witness to make fair and full disclosure.

(b) The witness should make it clear when a particular question or issue falls outside his or her expertise.

(c) To be useful, the opinion and evidence must provide enough clear information on the assumptions, procedures used, and conclusions drawn to allow comprehension of the report as it stands, and permit fair and efficient cross-examination.

(d) When the witness is providing an opinion or giving evidence on an issue or problem area for which there are differences of professional or scientific opinion (for example, whether there is a threshold of exposure to carcinogens below which they are harmless), he or she has an obligation to make such differences clearly known to the Board and all parties. The witness should make reasonable efforts to be fully informed of those differences.

(e) The witness should state all the material facts and assumptions upon which his or her opinion is based. He or she should not omit to consider and acknowledge material facts which could detract from the opinion. Where the facts are in dispute, the Board expects that the witness will give his or her view of the facts and the proof relied upon before giving the opinion.

(f) Where the opinion and evidence are based on information contained in other documents, detailed references should be provided in any report prepared by the expert, and copies of those documents made available on request before and during the hearing. Copies of the documents should be brought to the hearing for reference on cross-examination.

(g) Parties and their representatives questioning their own witnesses are required by the Board's Rules of Practice to ask questions designed to elicit the information required by these guidelines. However, the witness is expected to disclose to the Board and to other parties all significant information and opinions, and errors, shortcomings and limiting factors even if no one has asked for them.

(h) The weight to be given to the evidence of technical and opinion witnesses will be affected by the demeanor of the witness. The witness should give direct answers to questions and should not be evasive while giving testimony, even though the answers may appear to be detrimental to the case of the witness' client or employer. Any effort to avoid answering direct questions could adversely affect the weight assigned to the witness's evidence on the issue or the evidence as a whole.

3. (a) When giving an opinion, the witness should state and explain the degree of certainty of the opinion or the level of probability that it is correct. The degree of uncertainty and the reasons for uncertainty should be candidly acknowledged. Uncertainties and assumptions inherent in measurements, estimates, projections and predictions should be clearly identified. The level of confidence or the sensitivity to error must be given.

(b) It is more helpful for a witness to base conclusions on facts and data obtained from those who possess them, rather than construct a series of possibly incorrect assumptions, hypotheses and/or models.

(c) Where there is a lack of consensus with respect to the use of a particular model or formula, the rationale for the chosen approach should be identified.

(d) If the witness' opinion is not properly researched because insufficient data are available, this shortcoming must be stated. Any limiting qualifications to the opinion should be identified. The Board expects to be told when a lack of factual information or experience will increase the probability of inaccurate conclusions or predictions. The witness should avoid speculation where data are insufficient.

(e) Where an estimate falls within a range of reasonable possibilities, based on the same data, the variance within that range should be thoroughly disclosed. Where a prediction can lead to a range of potential impacts, that range should be fully described.

4. PLAIN LANGUAGE

(a) In preparing reports and giving testimony, the witness should take into account that the hearing process is a public process in which reports and testimony must be understood by participants and observers who may not have any significant technical knowledge. Therefore, the language and writing style should be simple and direct and scientific or technical terms and concepts should be explained, where possible, in clear, simple language.

(b) Where specialized language is necessary to accurately convey information, the witness should use it rather than risk misleading or over-simplifying. However, where possible, the witness should avoid the use of scientific terms and jargon and unfamiliar acronyms, or at least fully explain those terms, so that the technical information and opinion can be easily understood. For example, measurements like 10^{-6} cm/second could be expressed (or explained) in a form more easily understood, such as .86 mm/day or 31 cm/year.

5. ISSUE RESOLUTION

(a) The Board expects that the witness will attempt to adequately address, well in advance of the hearing, the concerns raised by other parties, in an effort to resolve issues, shorten the hearing, and save time and expense.

(b) Witnesses for all parties should explore any other means of resolving areas of dispute among the parties. For example, witnesses are encouraged to meet with each other before the hearing to attempt to reach agreement on technical and scientific facts and opinions, to clarify differences of opinion and to consider whether it is feasible and advisable to reduce disagreements or uncertainty by doing additional studies or obtaining additional information. Where a site inspection may assist the witness to provide more complete and useful information, the witness should make such an inspection.

6. EFFICIENCY

(a) Reports, witness statements and information should be produced in a timely fashion to all parties.

(b) All reasonable requests for answers to written questions (often referred to as "interrogatories") must be answered promptly and thoroughly by the witness.

(c) Notwithstanding the requirements for full disclosure in guideline 2, the witness should make every effort to give succinct answers (while at the same time ensuring that they are direct and complete) to questions put to him or her in written questions and in examination-in-chief, cross-examination and re-examination, and questioning by the Board. Answers should be concise, responsive and focused on the most essential issues.

(d) During his or her testimony a witness should not be called upon to review fundamental techniques in a painstaking step-by-step fashion, and to read correspondence and other reports line-by-line and page-by-page, unless it is clear that the purpose of such elaboration warrants this expenditure of time.

7. COMPLIANCE

Failure to comply with these guidelines may result in, among other things,

(a) a decision by the Board to decline to accept the opinions or evidence of an otherwise qualified witness;

(b) the evidence may be admissible and heard, but accorded little weight;

(c) the Board may intervene to ensure that the guidelines are respected;

(d) the conduct of the witness may be noted and may be subject to adverse comment in the Board's decision;

(e) if it appears to the Board that there has been a breach of professional standards of conduct, an attempt to mislead, incompetence or negligence, extensive violation of these guidelines, or serious interference with the Board's process, the Board may report this to the professional association or licensing body responsible for compliance with standards of conduct.

Sample Exhibit Log

	Environmental Appeal Board			Exhibit Log

File Name		File No.		Page of

Members

....

....

List of exhibits put in at the hearing on the .... day of .... 20.............

Property of			No.	Description of Exhibit
Applicant	Respondent	Other		

Completed by

Environmental Appeal Board Declaration and Undertaking

FORM 4
DECLARATION AND UNDERTAKING

I _____ am _____ for
      (name)   (witness, counsel/agent, consultant, etc.)

_____

I hereby declare:

1. THAT I am ordinarily resident in Canada and am not an employee, officer, director or major shareholder of the party for which I act or of any other person known by me to be a participant in this hearing;

2. THAT I have read the Environmental Appeal Board Rules of Practice and Procedure [and the Order of the Environmental Appeal Board dated _____] that relate(s) to the release of confidential information [and I understand that this Order may be filed with the Ontario Court of Justice (General Division)]. I further understand that any breach of the terms of the Rule [and the Order] could be the subject of contempt proceedings in the Ontario Court of Justice (General Division).

I hereby undertake:

1. THAT I will maintain the confidentiality of any information or evidence that I receive pursuant to the above Rules [and the Order] and will not disclose any of this information;

2. THAT I will not reproduce in any manner, without the prior written approval of the Board, any information, notes, evidence, transcripts or written submissions dealing with the evidence taken and submissions made in relation to the information that is subject to the above Rule [and the order];

3. THAT within 35 days after the Board releases its final decision or order, I will personally deliver to [*the person submitting the confidential information*] all information provided to me pursuant to the above order, and will destroy or safeguard the confidentiality of any notes taken by me with respect to that evidence or information.

DATED AT _____, Ontario this ___ day of _____, 20__.

Signature: _____

Name: _____

Firm/Company: _____

Index